ONE YEAR DEVOTIONAL

Carried by Grace

CWR

SELWYN HUGHES

Revised and updated by Mick Brooks
Further Study: Ian Sewter

Copyright © CWR 2018

Published 2018 by CWR, Waverley Abbey House, Waverley Lane, Farnham, Surrey GU9 8EP, UK. CWR is a Registered Charity - Number 294387 and a Limited Company registered in England - Registration Number 1990308.

Issues of *Every Day with Jesus* were previously published as follows: *Prepared*, Jan/Feb 2015; *The Call*, Mar/Apr 2017; *Our True Identity*, May/Jun 2018; *Pursued by Grace*, Jul/Aug 2015; *Standing Strong*, Sep/Oct 2015; *Bringing Down Giants*, Nov/Dec 2014.

For a list of National Distributors, visit www.cwr.org.uk/distributors

Unless otherwise indicated, all Scripture references are from the Holy Bible: New International Version (NIV), copyright © 1979, 1984 by Biblica. Used by permission of Hodder & Stoughton Publishers, an Hachette company. All rights reserved.

Other versions are marked: Authorised (King James) Version (or KJV): Rights in the United Kingdom are vested in the Crown. Reproduced by permission of the Crown's patentee, Cambridge University Press. *The Message*: Scripture taken from *The Message*, copyright © 1993, 1994, 1995, 1996, 2000, 2001, 2002. Used by permission of NavPress Publishing Group. Moffatt: taken from The Moffatt Translation of the Bible. Copyright © 1987. All rights reserved. NKJV: Scripture taken from the New King James Version®. Copyright © 1982 by Thomas Nelson. Used by permission. All rights reserved. NLT: taken from the New Living Translation, Copyright © 1996, 2004, 2007, 2013, 2015 by Tyndale House Foundation. Used by permission of Tyndale House Publishers Inc., Carol Stream, Illinois 60188. All rights reserved. TLB: The Living Bible copyright © 1971 by Tyndale House Foundation. Used by permission of Tyndale House Publishers Inc., Carol Stream, Illinois 60188. All rights reserved. The Living Bible, TLB, and the The Living Bible logo are registered trademarks of Tyndale House Publishers.

Concept development, editing, design and production by CWR.

Cover image: unsplash

Printed in the UK by Linney

ISBN: 978-1-78259-062-0

Contents

Introduction

The question of who we are is one that defines us – both as people, and as Christians. We all have a part to play in the unfolding story of the Bible, and understanding our God-given identity is essential if we are to step into all that God has for us.

At whatever point in the year you begin reading these specially selected issues of *Every Day with Jesus* – and you can begin at any time – we hope you hear God speaking to you in new ways about who He is, who you are, and the adventures that you can go on together. Learning also from the life and ministry of John the Baptist and the 12 disciples, may you begin to understand your identity as a child of God, and the calling placed on you as one of His followers.

When we truly live out our identity as God's children, we are better equipped to face down whatever challenges may come our way. In *Standing Strong* and *Bringing Down Giants*, discover afresh how you can stand firm in any spiritual battle, clothed in the Armour of God and sure in the knowledge of His goodness and faithfulness.

We hope and pray these six chapters will take you on a devotional journey that redefines you as a follower of Christ, and that you will respond once again to His call to discipleship.

How to read the Bible

A question I am often asked, especially by young Christians, is this: why do I need to read the Bible?

We need to read the Bible in order to know not only God's mind for the future but how to develop a daily walk with Him. God uses His Word to change people's lives and bring those lives into a deeper relationship with Himself and a greater conformity to His will. For over four decades now I have spent hours every week reading and studying the Scriptures. God has used this book to transform my life and to give me a sense of security in a shifting and insecure world.

How do we read the Bible? Do we just start at Genesis and make our way through to the book of Revelation? There are many ways to go about reading the Scriptures; let me mention three.

One is to follow a reading plan such as CWR's *Every Day with Jesus One Year Bible* or *Cover to Cover Complete*. The great advantage of following a reading plan is that your reading is arranged for you; in a sense you are being supervised. You are not left to the vagaries of uncertainty: what shall I read today, where shall I begin, at what point shall I end?

A second approach is to thread your way through the Scriptures by following a specific theme such as *The Big Story* (also published by CWR). It is quite staggering how many themes can be found in Scripture and what great spiritual rewards can be had by acquainting yourself with them. When I started writing *Every Day with Jesus* in 1965, I decided to follow the thematic approach and I wondered how long I would be able to keep it up. Now, many years later, I am still writing and expounding on different themes of the Bible, and the truth is that I have more biblical themes and subjects than it is possible to deal with in one lifetime!

A third approach is by reading through a book of the Bible. This enables you to get into the mind of the writer and understand his message. Every book of the Bible has something unique and special to convey and, as with any book, this can only be understood when you read it from start to finish.

It is important to remember that all reading of the Bible ought to be preceded by prayer. This puts you in a spiritually receptive frame of mind to receive what God has to say to you through His Word. The Bible can be read by anyone but it can only be understood by those whose hearts are in tune with God – those who have come into a personal relationship with Him and who maintain that relationship through daily or regular prayer. This is how the Bible puts it: 'The man without the Spirit does not accept the things that come from the Spirit of God, for they are foolishness to him, and he cannot understand them, because they are spiritually discerned' (1 Cor. 2:14).

Praying before you open your Bible should not be a mere formality. It is not the *act* that will make the Bible come alive but the *attitude*. Prayer enables us to approach the Scriptures with a humble mind. The scientist who does not sit down before the facts of the universe with an open mind, is not prepared to give up every preconceived idea and is not willing to follow wherever nature will lead him, will discover little or nothing. It is the same with the reading of the Scriptures; we must come to it with a humble and receptive mind or we too will get nowhere. Prayer enables us to have the attitude that says, 'Speak, for your servant is listening' (1 Sam. 3:10).

If we are to grow in the Christian life then we must do more than just *read* the Bible – we must *study* it. This means that we must give time to poring over it, considering it, thinking about what it is saying to us and assimilating into our hearts and minds its doctrines and its ideas.

I have already pointed out that one of the ways of reading the Bible is by taking a theme and tracing it through the various books of the Bible. The pleasure this brings can be greatly enhanced by using this as a regular means of Bible study. When we study the Bible with the aid of concordances, lexicons and so on, we feed our minds, but when we study the Bible devotionally, we apply the Word of God to our hearts. Both exercises are necessary if we are to be completely rounded people but we must see that it is at the place of the devotional that we open up our hearts and expose ourselves to God's resources.

Let me encourage you also to take advantage of a reading plan as a further basis of study. Following this will enable you to cover the whole of the Bible in a set period. Those who have used this method tell of the most amazing spiritual benefits. One person who had read through the whole of the Bible in a year said to me, 'It demanded more discipline than I thought I was capable of, but the rewards have been enormous.' When I asked her what these rewards were, she said, 'I used to have a partial view of God's purposes because I dipped into my Bible just here and there as it suited me. Now, however, I feel as if I have been looking over God's shoulder as He laid out the universe, and I feel so secure in the knowledge that He found a place for me in that marvellous plan.' There can be no doubt that reading through the entire Bible in a set period enables one to gain a perspective that has tremendous positive spiritual consequences.

The third form of study – reading through a book of the Bible at a time – has the advantage of helping you understand the unity and diversity of the Bible. It is quite incredible how so many writers sharing their thoughts at different times of history combine to say similar things and give a consistent emphasis. Reading and pondering on this gives you such an appreciation of the wisdom of God in putting together this marvellous volume that it fires your soul and quickly brings praise and adoration to your lips.

I have found the best way to study a book of the Bible is to read it through once for a sense of the whole, and then to read it again, making a note of anything that strikes me, such as a principle to be applied, an insight to be stored away in my heart, or a thought to be shared with someone who is struggling.

One thing is sure, time spent with the Bible is not wasted. The more one loves God the more one will love the Bible. And the more one loves the Bible the more one will love God. Always remember that this unique volume - God's one and only published work - yields its treasures only to those who read it, study it and obey it.

Selwyn Hughes

Rev Dr Selwyn Hughes (1928–2006) was the founder of CWR and writer of *Every Day with Jesus* for over forty years.

Prepared

Time to make a difference

For reading & meditation – Luke 3:1–19

'Prepare the way for the Lord, make straight paths for him.' (v4)

At whichever point in a calendar year you begin these devotionals, the year that lies ahead is in many ways a new beginning. Whenever a new beginning is decided, preparations are made by governments, organisations, families and individuals to celebrate, say goodbye to the old and welcome in the new, with all its opportunities and challenges (and all usually with the aim of making a difference).

The theme I'd like us to consider is how we can make a spiritual difference over the next 365 days. What preparations can we make to influence the world and those around us? Consider the words in our passage today. John the Baptist's mission was 'to prepare the way'. Was there ever a greater time in history that people needed to prepare a way for the Lord than we do now?

In a world obsessed with physical wellbeing, exercise, hydration and mindfulness, has the need for spiritual health and spiritual wellbeing ever been greater? We have the same calling as John the Baptist in our fast-paced world of global change. Never before

FURTHER STUDY

Exod. 19:7-15;
Isa. 62:10-12

1. How did the Israelites prepare to meet God?

2. How can we prepare for others to meet God?

has the world been so interconnected, but it is also in flux and chaos, searching for new moorings, feeling after a new order. But without God no new order will be found. What this world needs more than anything is a people who will prepare the way. Men and women like John the Baptist, who prepared himself first, and then went out and prepared others to know God. Ask yourself: Am I spiritually fit for what lies ahead? Am I willing to be part of preparing the way and making the paths straight?

My God, help me to make a difference. Give me the strength and courage to prepare the way for You and Your kingdom. Prepare me first so that I am ready to fulfil your purposes in the days that lie ahead. In Jesus' name. Amen.

Confident in God

For reading & meditation – Luke 1:1–25

'And he will go on before the Lord, in the spirit and power of Elijah... to make ready a people prepared for the Lord.' (v17)

A s we reflect on the passage let's consider together how we might 'prepare the way'. The account tells us that John the Baptist would be confident in God and strong in faith in three areas. (1) In relation to God he would be 'great'– by knowing God and walking with Him. (2) In relation to himself he would be self-disciplined – never taking wine or other fermented drink. (3) In relation to others he would be a catalyst triggering change – turning 'the hearts of the fathers to their children and the disobedient to the wisdom of the righteous' (v17). Let's consider these further.

FURTHER STUDY

Ezra 7:1-10;
Neh. 8:1-8

1. How had
Ezra prepared
himself?

2. How did
he prepare
the people?

In God's eyes he would be great. We too need men and women who are great in the sight of the Lord and not troubled if they are not recognised by others. Regarding himself he would be self-renouncing; no wine or strong drink would pass his lips. However his life would not be entirely without intoxication; he would be filled with a more powerful spirit than alcohol – the Holy Spirit. This age needs people who can forgo things for a great cause, those who empty themselves so that they may be filled. Concerning others he would be a catalyst, coming in the spirit and power of one of the greatest of Israel's prophets – Elijah. We too need men and women who understand God's dealings in history and who will build on spiritual gains from the past.

We are also told that John would have a radical ministry – he would turn the hearts of the fathers to the children. Shouldn't it be the other way round? No, the older generation should actively try to make the world safe, just and secure for its children.

Father, I want to be strong towards You, towards myself and towards others. Meet me at the point of my need in the weeks that lie ahead. Prepare me, as You are preparing others. In Jesus' name. Amen.

A new beginning

For reading & meditation – Matthew 26:57–68

'Peter… entered and sat down with the guards
to see the outcome.' (v58)

We live, as you are aware, in a world that is caught up in great change. It is said by many that we are now living in the post-Christian era. For the first sixteen centuries after Christ, the objective truths of Scripture played a major part in shaping the world. The Bible's influence was powerful and persuasive. Then, in the eighteenth century, there arose a movement of intellectual thought in Europe that rejected external authority and enthroned personal subjective judgment. The Enlightenment, as it was called, celebrated intellectual individualism and sought to banish any idea of living by a repository of wisdom beyond one own's intellect. These past few centuries (so say some historians) have brought to an end the Christian era.

FURTHER STUDY

Ezek. 37:1-14;
Isa. 64:1-7

1. How can Christianity experience a new beginning?

2. Why may faith waste away?

Just recently I heard a television commentator say: 'Jesus Christ is now a spent force in the life of humanity.' When I heard that statement my mind went to the text that is before us today: 'Peter… sat down with the guards to see the outcome.' *The Message* version says: 'Then he slipped in and mingled with the servants, watching to see how things would turn out.' When Peter entered the courtyard of the high priest's house and sat down with the guards to see what would happen to Jesus, he thought he was witnessing the end. It certainly was the end – the end of the beginning. Although Jesus was about to have His life ended on a cross, He would come back from the dead and stamp His personality on the centuries. I predict the coming years will bring in a spiritual renaissance. And you and I must be part of it.

Father, everything within me pleads to be part of a new spiritual awakening. Nothing is impossible with You, dear Lord. Nothing. Give us a great outpouring of Your Holy Spirit. In Jesus' name I ask it. Amen.

The shrinking of God

For reading & meditation – 2 Timothy 3:1–17

'But as for you, continue in what you have learned
and have become convinced of' (v14)

Yesterday we noted how, over the past few centuries, people in general have rejected the traditional Christian view that we draw ethics, values and ideas about how to live from the Scriptures, and have established the idea that thinking people must work out the truth about life for themselves.

The idea of the post-Christian era took some time to be accepted, but now it is firmly established and appears to reign supreme. In our world secular culture takes for granted that every person works out for himself or herself all matters of basic belief (truly an i-generation!). TV more often than not portrays clergy as objects of ridicule and scorn. Our children are brought up in an educational system that is largely biblically illiterate, and has a post-Christian, sub-Christian or even anti-Christian mindset. This type of outlook controls the opinion-makers and the media. There has been a rejection of external authority for the guiding of the human life – that of God and the Bible – and instead we are seeing the enthronement of ideas whereby you work everything out for yourself.

FURTHER STUDY

Isa. 64:8-12;
Rom. 1:16-32

1. How had
God's influence
shrunk?

2. How should
we respond
to a post-
Christian era?

When I first began my Christian ministry, I could assume that the people I talked to would have a Christian paradigm directing their thoughts. But not anymore. I now feel as if I am a cross-cultural missionary talking to people whose thinking is a world apart from what was once the accepted norm. We now live in an age of a shrinking God and an outdated Bible. How is this situation to be changed? By a people who prepare themselves and prepare the way for the coming King.

**Father, I sense the urgency of the hour. Prepare me, dear Lord, so
that all I have and all I am will be available for You to use.
In Jesus' name I ask it. Amen.**

The Great Contemporary

For reading & meditation – Hebrews 13:1–8
'Jesus Christ is the same yesterday and today
and for ever.' (v8)

Two days ago I referred to a statement made by a television commentator to the effect that Jesus Christ is a spent force in the life of humanity. He went on to assert: 'The writer Carlyle was right when he stood before an Italian wayside crucifix, slowly shook his head, and said: "Poor fellow, you have had your day." There are many today who would share that view. They believe that Jesus' day is over. 'He spoke to a simple age,' they say, 'but we belong to a complicated scientific age. He was good, but not good enough for these modern times.' Yet Thomas Carlyle, in his later years, came to a different view about Jesus and made the comment that Christ's day was just beginning.

More often than not, whenever Christianity has been misunderstood it has been because it was a miserable caricature and not the real thing. If the truth were known, it is the living of Jesus' teaching by His true followers that has kept the soul of humanity alive. Jesus Christ is and has been the creator of the best and the finest in humanity. When we have hold of Him we have the key to understanding God, the meaning of the universe and our own lives. If we let go of Him then God becomes an unreal philosophy or concept. In Jesus we find, as one theologian put it, 'the near side of God'. When I listen to Jesus I hear God speaking to me in a language I can understand – a human language. Jesus is the one unspent force in humanity and stands in this age as He has stood in every age – the Great Contemporary.

FURTHER STUDY

Psa. 33:11;
90:1–4:
Rev. 11:15–17

1. How can God be relevant to both the Bronze and the computer ages?

2. What changes and what is timeless?

My Father and my God, I am so grateful for the stamp of Jesus upon the ages. But I am more grateful for His stamp upon my soul. Thank You, dear Father, for the knowledge I have of You through Your Son. May I know more. Amen.

First things first

For reading & meditation – Matthew 6:1–15

'This, then, is how you should pray:
"Our Father in heaven"' (v9)

Though I would not regard myself as a modern-day John the Baptist, I would like to help you make this year a time of spiritual preparation so that together we can meet the challenge of twenty-first-century life. But how do we begin? If, like John the Baptist, we are to be 'great' in the sight of the Lord and make the 'paths straight' it seems to me that together we need to take some steps.

The first, I think, is this: gaining a knowledge of God through spending time with Him in personal prayer. John was undoubtedly a man of prayer – he spent long hours alone with God in the desert. We do not have to retire to a desert in order to achieve spiritual 'greatness', but we do need to pray. Sometimes I wonder if Christians do not make as much impact as they did in the first century because they fail to pray. I do not think I am far off the mark when I say we cannot prepare the way if we are not willing to pray.

FURTHER STUDY

Luke 11:1-13;
Rom. 8:15-17

1. How did Jesus refer to the Creator?

2. How does receiving the Holy Spirit influence us?

Before we focus on how to sharpen up our prayer lives, however, let's first get rid of a few wrong ideas about prayer. Some view prayer as a lightning conductor to save us from the severities of God's wrath. I have been surprised at the number of Christians who have told me that they believe something bad will happen to them if they don't pray. People who hold this view tend to pray from a sense of duty rather than delight. God doesn't hold a stick over our heads and demand: 'Pray – or else'. Rather, He stands before us as a loving Father and says: 'Talk to me. I want to get close to you.' Always remember, it is to our Father we are praying, not to a tyrant or an ogre.

Loving Father, help me clear from my head all wrong ideas concerning prayer. I am so glad I can call You not just Creator, or Sustainer, or even Supreme Being, but Father. How wonderfully relational that word is. I am so thankful. Amen.

A sense of otherness

For reading & meditation – John 14:1–14

'And I will do whatever you ask in my name, so that
the Son may bring glory to the Father.' (v13)

Another unhelpful idea about prayer is that it is a reflex response – something done for one's own benefit and not for greater purposes. Many view prayer as simply providing an oasis of quiet meditation in the midst of a busy day, a way of providing calmness for the soul. A place of sanctuary.

There is no doubt that prayer does provide calmness for the soul, but that is not its primary purpose. I regard prayer as the means of bringing my whole life – spirit, soul and body – into intimate personal contact with the living God. I can commune with Him, adjust my will to His and through that relationship have a knowledge of the Creator. 'Experience shows,' says one preacher, 'that those who think of prayer only as reflex influence soon give up prayer. For it is not possible to project one's spirit continuously to that which is not responsive.'

Another misunderstanding of prayer is that it is auto-suggestion – an echo of your own voice. Those who pray relationally, however, realise it is not auto-suggestion, but Other-suggestion. Prayer would never have survived and flourished as a Christian discipline if it had been only auto-suggestion, with no voice answering our voice, no heart answering ours. I have loved these lines by F.W.H. Myers ever since I first came across them:

> *Whoso has felt the spirit of the Highest,*
> *Cannot confound nor doubt Him, nor deny,*
> *Yea, with one voice, O world, though thou deniest,*
> *Stand thou on that side, for on this am I!*

FURTHER STUDY

Psa. 138:1–8;
1 Pet. 3:12

1. What was the psalmist's experience of prayer?

2. To what does God pay attention?

Father, how can I thank You enough for the sense of otherness that I feel when I pray? Someone answers – and answers in terms of release, power, vitality, heightened accomplishment. Help me go deeper into prayer. Amen.

Forging Jesus' name

For reading & meditation – John 16:17–33

'I tell you the truth, my Father will give you whatever you ask in my name.' (v23)

W e continue clearing our minds of unhelpful concepts and ideas about prayer. Though many people regard it as such, prayer is not meant to be an attempt to bend God to our wills; it is the bending or reorientation of our wills to God. I once heard someone describe prayer like this: 'When we throw out a boat-hook and catch hold of the shore, do we pull the shore to ourselves? Rather, we pull ourselves to the shore. Prayer does not so much pull God to us as pull us to God.' The more we pray, the more our wills are aligned with God's so that He can work His will through us. Just think of it: God is willing to work through us! I love this definition of prayer: 'Prayer is not overcoming God's reluctance, but laying hold on His highest willingness.'

FURTHER STUDY

Luke 22:39–46;
Acts 19:13-20

1. How did prayer align Jesus' will to God's?

2. How did Sceva's sons forge Jesus' name?

There are certain things that are open to the contingency of humankind's will – things that will not get done unless people act. For example, we would never be able to cross the sea unless we built a boat. If God has left certain things open to the human will, is it possible that He has made certain things contingent upon prayer – things that will never be done unless we do them through the understanding and strength gained in prayer?

You will never see prayer more clearly than when you see it as your will being brought in line with the divine will. That is what praying 'in Jesus' name' is all about. It means praying the prayer Jesus would pray if He were in our shoes. When we pray for something that is clearly out of His will and add His name we are not using His name validly; essentially we are forging His name.

Father, help me this day surrender my will so that it realigns with Your will. Then I know that Your strength will be added to mine. I can be sure this prayer is in Your will. So I ask it confidently and expectantly. In Jesus' name. Amen.

Things! Things! Things!

For reading & meditation – Matthew 6:25–34

'seek first his kingdom and his righteousness, and all these
things will be given to you as well.' (v33)

A further caricature some people have of prayer is that it
consists simply of asking for things. 'Do you pray every day?'
a vicar asked one young Christian. 'No vicar,' replied the young
man, 'for there are some days when I don't want anything.' Ask
anyone who is mature in prayer and they will tell you that the
more they understand prayer and practise it, the less they find
themselves asking for things. They are more concerned about
prayer deepening their relationship with God, for they have
discovered what our text for today tells us: that
when we make God's kingdom and righteousness
our priority then all necessary things will be added.
A friend of mine sums up his attitude like this: 'In
prayer I seldom ask for things. More and more I
ask God for Himself, for the assurance that His will
and mine are not at cross-purposes, and that we are
agreed on all major and minor matters. I know, then,
that if this is so, I'll get all the things I need.'

FURTHER STUDY

Psa. 27:1-8;
84:1-12

1. What one
thing did the
psalmist desire?

2. How do we
seek God's face?

God is interested in provision, of course, and there are times
when it is right to ask for things. However, when we experience
God in loving communion, things become a side issue.

Sadly, though, for many Christians things are central. They are
like the little boy who explained: 'I love my Daddy because he gives
me pennies every day.' Penny praying, like penny loving, belongs to
childhood. An elderly saint once stood in a testimony meeting and
said: 'I wish people would love God for Himself, not for the fear of
going to hell or the hope of getting a reward in heaven.' To love God
for Himself – many of us would do well to learn from that

**Father, teach me that first and foremost prayer involves getting to
know You, and is not just a way of acquiring things. Help me to
attach more importance to knowing You than receiving things from
You. In Jesus' name I ask it. Amen.**

Two heartbeats

For reading & meditation – Mark 3:7–19

'He appointed twelve... that they might be with him
and that he might send them out to preach' (vv14-15)

We have been exploring what prayer is not; now we focus on what it is. Prayer, of course, has many elements, but fundamentally there are just two: communion and commission. Someone has described communion and commission as the two heartbeats of the prayer life. A heart has to keep beating or death sets in! All communion without commission results in death. All commission without communion also results in death. When the two beat in proper rhythm – that is life.

FURTHER STUDY

Isa. 6:1-10;
Acts 3:1-10

1. How
was Isaiah
commissioned
after
communion?

2. How does the
man's healing
link communion
and spiritual
authority?

Take the first – communion. A Christian rubber plantation owner said this: 'As I look at the rubber tree freshly tapped, with the cup nestling up against the wound and taking the sap from the heart of the tree, I am reminded of what prayer is all about. I press my empty life like a cup up against the wounds of the eternal God and take from Him life and power and redemption.'

Our text for today tells us that Jesus appointed twelve disciples for three purposes: (1) that they might be with Him, (2) that He might send them out to proclaim and (3) to have authority over evil spirits. The first thing to notice about Jesus' call to His disciples is that they were to be with Him. Relationship with Him was the priority. When that happens everything else follows. Anyone who neglects communion will find the other two elements of discipleship fading out. And it is true, also, that if we neglect commission, then communion will begin to die. Those who have communion and commission will have spiritual authority.

Lord Jesus, every day let me nestle up against Your side for I am empty without You. And every day let my cup be emptied in loving help to others and giving out to them. For Your own dear name's sake. Amen.

'Lord, teach us to pray'

For reading & meditation – Luke 11:1–4

'When he finished [praying], one of his disciples said to him,
"Lord, teach us to pray"' (v1)

Not once in my long ministry has anyone come to me and said: 'Teach me to pray'. During a pastors' conference I once asked a group of about 500 men and women to raise their hands if any person had at any time come to them with that request. Not one hand was raised. As a pastor I often asked young Christians if they would like me to help them learn the art of prayer, but never has it been the other way round.

In the passage before us today we read that when the disciples heard Jesus pray, they turned to Him and said: 'Lord, teach us to pray, just as John taught his disciples.' What was it about the prayer of Jesus that triggered in the hearts of the disciples a desire to learn to pray as He did? Familiar as most of these disciples were with the prayers of the Old Testament saints (David, Elijah, Isaiah, Jeremiah and others), they sensed there was something different about the prayer life of the Master. In answer to their request, He taught them the essence of true prayer.

The prayer can be divided into two parts: the God side, and our side. This is the God side: our Father, Your name, Your kingdom, Your will. This is our side: give us, forgive us, lead us, deliver us. Someone has called these two sides realignment and result. In the first we realign our life to the Father, to His name, to His kingdom, and in the second we gain the benefits: He gives, forgives, leads us, delivers us. The emphasis should always be on the realignment, for if we try to get results without realignment we will get nowhere.

FURTHER STUDY

1 Chron. 29:10-19;
Acts 4:24-31

1. Analyse David's prayer with realignment and result in mind.

2. Analyse the prayer of the Early Church.

My Father and my God, I echo the disciples' request: teach me to pray. If I fall down here I fall down everywhere. Give me the mind to pray, the will to pray, the heart to pray. In Jesus' name. Amen.

Everyday light

For reading & meditation – Psalm 119:129–136

'The unfolding of your words gives light; it gives understanding to the simple.' (v130)

We have been seeing that to prepare the way we need to be people of prayer. But many protest: 'I don't have much time to pray.' Consider these words of Oswald Chambers: 'We can hinder the time that should be spent with God by remembering we have other things to do. We say, "I haven't time." Of course you have time! Make time to realise that the centre of power in your life is the Lord Jesus Christ and His Atonement.'

In addition to spending time with God in prayer, we also need to spend time with the Bible. The Word of God is always central to 'preparing the way'. One of the alarming trends in today's Christian community is that many people do not read their Bible daily, or even regularly. One survey showed that 75 per cent of those researched (all committed Christians) read a newspaper every day, but only 25 per cent read their Bible every day. How sad. Are we in danger of producing a generation of Christians more interested in what newspapers say than in what God says?

FURTHER STUDY

Psa. 119:97–106;
Acts 17:1–12

1. How does God's Word prepare us?

2. Contrast the people of Thessalonica and Berea.

One of my deepest desires is to see Christians regularly read through the whole of the Bible. Can you imagine what would happen if every Christian in the world decided to take in the truths from God's Word daily? It would produce a spiritual awakening that would encircle the earth. Our text for today tells us that the unfolding (or entrance) of God's words gives light. The opposite of that is also true: the neglecting of God's words brings darkness. It may not be possible to begin every day with the Bible, but it can be our aim.

God, stir us up to see the need to begin each day with Scripture and prayer. Help me take Your light as my light. Then I shall walk with a sure and steady tread. In Jesus' name. Amen.

Thought correction

For reading & meditation – Psalm 119:17–24

'Open my eyes that I may see wonderful things in your law.' (v18)

We continue to explore how greatness in relation to God depends not only on prayer but on exposure to Scripture also. Every spiritually mature Christian I have ever known has had not only a strong prayer life but has also opened his or her mind daily (or at least regularly) to the Word of God.

Years ago I came across a man who believed that he could build his spiritual life on prayer alone, and had no time for the Bible. I asked him to tell me how he structured his prayer time, and this is what he said: 'I sit in meditation and think about the creation, the stars, the oceans and so on. Then I meditate on the Creator who made all these things, and thus I come out of my prayer time spiritually refreshed.' There was no mention of Jesus, the cross, redemption or any of the great Christian truths, and it occurred to me as we talked that he was trying to find God through the medium of his own concepts. But his ideas were just his thoughts about God.

FURTHER STUDY

Psa. 119:1-16;
2 Tim. 3:14-17

1. How does Scripture correct us?

2. How does Scripture perfect us?

I suggested as we talked that the Bible is God's revelation of Himself, and that unless our thoughts are constantly corrected by God's thoughts they can easily go off at a tangent and lead nowhere. The man was described by others in his church as 'unstable, centred on himself and subject to strange moods'. He was inner man-centred instead of Bible-centred – hence unpredictable and moody.

Our reflections on God cannot be used as the foundation for a relationship with Him. They need to be focused and brought into His framework of thought. When I look into my heart I see what I am like; when I look into the Bible I see what God is like.

Father, I see that without the Bible my thoughts can easily go off at a tangent. My soul needs Your Word as much as my body needs food. Give me a love for truth, dear Lord – Your truth as expressed in Your Word. In Jesus' name. Amen.

Why I read the Bible

For reading & meditation – Psalm 119:33–40

'Direct me in the path of your commands,
for there I find delight.' (v35)

Some time ago, when being interviewed by a reporter from a Christian magazine, I was asked: 'Have you read the Bible every day of your life since you were converted to Christ?' I said: 'No, because there have been some days when due to serious sickness or travelling across different time zones it has not been possible to do so. But there have been few days in my life when I have not turned to the Word of God – if not at the beginning of the day then certainly at some time during the day.' The next question was this:

FURTHER STUDY

Josh. 1:1-9;
Psa. 119:48-52;
John 20:3

1. What was Joshua's condition for success?

2. Why should we read the Bible?

'Why do you read the Bible?' I gave this as my reply: 'First, because within its pages I find the power and inspiration I need to live the Christian life. Second, because, in the words of Emerson, it teaches that "The lesson of life is to believe what the years and centuries say against the hours". Third, because I find in it the wisdom I need for the ordering of my inner life. Fourth, because it assures me I am supremely dear to God and that His thoughts are ever towards me. Fifth, because it unfolds for me the secrets by which men and women of the past walked the highways of hope and happiness. Sixth, because it discloses the nature of my final destiny and reminds me that my Saviour is preparing a place for me in my eternal home. Seventh, because it helps me breathe in the pure air of objective truth before I go out and face the choking dust of this post-modern generation.'

I just could not get through life without daily dipping into the Bible. It is my hope, my health, my supreme joy. There can be no spiritual greatness without daily prayer and biblical meditation.

My Father and my God, help me as far as possible to begin every day with the Bible. I read other books to get information; I read Your Book to get light. May I walk in that light. In Jesus' name. Amen.

'Quick, dust the Bible'

For reading & meditation – Psalm 19:1–14

'May the words of my mouth and the meditation of my heart be pleasing in your sight' (v14)

A woman tells of how, when she was a little girl, if her mother saw the vicar coming up the path for a pastoral visit she would shout out: 'Quick, dust the Bible'. Believe me, if there is dust on your Bible there will be dust on your soul. How best do we read the Bible? This is what I learned from one of my spiritual mentors, Dr E. Stanley Jones. He called this plan for reading the Bible 'the Seven Rs', and I use it almost every day of my life.

First, when you sit down with your Bible, relax. It is difficult to inscribe anything on a tense anxious mind. 'If you go stamping through the woods in a hurry,' said Dr Stanley Jones, 'you will see little. But sit still and the squirrels will come down the tree, the birds will draw near and nature will be alive in every twig and flower.' Second, recall. Ask questions like this as you read: Who is writing? To whom? For what purpose? What is he saying? How does it apply to me? How shall I put it into practice?

Third, rehearse. If you find something that speaks directly to your condition then turn it over and over in your mind. When Jesus was being tempted in the wilderness, He answered the devil with the precise words of Scripture. God's Word had become part of Him. Fourth, retain. When a verse of Scripture strikes you, commit it to memory. Sadly, there is little emphasis on memorising the Bible in today's Church. A young girl reading from the Bible in her church said this: 'You shall hate all men for my name's sake.' No one noticed the mistake for they had little familiarity with the words found in Luke 21:17.

FURTHER STUDY

Psa. 1:1-6;
Luke 21:17

1. What are the benefits of biblical meditation?

2. What was wrong with the young girl's reading of Scripture?

Father, help me come to Your Word relaxed and willing to let it speak to me. May my prayer always be: 'Speak, Lord, Your servant is listening.' Help me to get from it what You have put into it. In Jesus' name. Amen.

Kissing the Father's face

For reading & meditation – Psalm 119:169–176
'May my lips overflow with praise, for you teach
me your decrees.' (v171)

We continue looking at the Seven Rs – steps to help make Bible reading productive and profitable. The fifth is rejoice. Reading the Bible is a rendezvous with God. Keep in mind the written word is designed to lead you into a deeper relationship with the living Word. Enjoy your devotional time with the Scriptures. Whenever you come across truths such as salvation and redemption (they are on almost every page), rejoice that you have been chosen in Jesus and that you are destined to spend eternity with Him. When I was a young Christian I would sometimes press my lips on some text that spoke of salvation or redemption; it was so exciting, so personal. Occasionally I still do this. It feels as if I am kissing the Father's face, for His face is revealed through His words. Sometimes it seems that the words are written just for me.

FURTHER STUDY

Psa. 119:161-168;
James 1:21-25

1. How does reading the Word lead us to praise?

2. Why can we be guilty of self-deception?

Sixth, realign. As you read the Word keep realigning your life with what you read. I heard a story about a girl in Korea who enrolled in a weekly Bible class, but after attending just one session she failed to return. Someone who was also in the class saw her a few weeks later and asked: 'Why have you dropped out?' She replied: 'I haven't learned yet to fully practise what I heard.' I can't agree with her decision but I do see her point. A preacher in the Deep South of America used to pray: 'Lord, prop us up on our leaning side'. This is a good realignment prayer.

Seventh, release. When something thrills you in your Bible reading, pass it on. Share its truth with someone. The repetition will help the retention, for we will always remember what we shared.

**Father, help me see Your face in Your words I pray. May I sense in an even deeper way that when You speak in the Bible You are not just speaking generally – You are speaking to me.
In Jesus' name. Amen.**

Dialogue, not monologue

For reading & meditation – John 4:27–38

'"My food," said Jesus, "is to do the will of him who
sent me and to finish his work."' (v34)

There is one more thought we must pursue before leaving this
issue of how we can be 'great' in the eyes of God and continue
to prepare the way for Him. Many Christians, though faithful in
prayer and the reading of the Scriptures, miss out because they fail
to cultivate a listening heart. After prayer and reading, we must
learn to stop and ask: 'Father, have You anything to say to me?'

Again over the years I have asked countless Christians: How
much time do you spend listening to God?' My research reveals
it is only about 5%. If we are to benefit from our
devotionals then we should understand the need for
dialogue and not treat them as a time for monologue.
Far too many of us approach our devotional times
with the attitude, 'Listen, Lord, Your servant is
speaking,' rather than: 'Speak, Lord, Your servant is
listening.' But will God really talk to us if we listen?
Yes, if we are faithful in what He asks of us. One of
my spiritual mentors used to say: 'If we do not hear
God's voice in our lives then it is probably due to one
of two reasons: we are unwilling or we are untrained.'

Consider the first – we are unwilling. Many of us
don't want to listen to God, for we are afraid that if
God speaks to us He may say something that we don't want to hear,
or ask us to do something we don't want to do. We think God's
will is hard and too difficult to keep. This view of God's will must
be changed if we are to hear His voice. Jesus regarded the will of
God as food – something nourishing, sustaining, fortifying. Living
in harmony with God's will brings reinforcement, not restriction.

FURTHER STUDY

Gen. 18:20-33;
2 Chron.
24:17-20

1. How did
Abraham and
the Lord relate
to each other?

2. What
happened when
people would
not listen to
the Lord?

**Forgive me, Father, if I have failed to cultivate a listening heart.
Show me how to tune my heart and incline my ear to listen for Your
voice. Speak, Lord, Your servant is listening.
In Jesus' name I ask it. Amen.**

The Master's voice

For reading & meditation – John 10:1–21

'he goes on ahead of them, and his sheep follow him
because they know his voice.' (v4)

I mentioned yesterday, quoting one of my spiritual mentors, that
'If we do not hear God's voice in our lives then it is probably due
to one of two reasons: we are unwilling or we are untrained.' Many
of us talk and talk when we get into the presence of God, afraid
that if we remain quiet God may say something that we do not
wish to hear. If you want to hear God's voice then make a decision
that determines all decisions down the line – the decision that the
will of God will always come first in your life.

FURTHER STUDY

Gen. 25:21-23;
2 Sam. 5:17-25

1. How did
Rebekah resolve
her confusion?

2. How did
David combine
listening and
obedience?

Before we consider this matter of listening any
further, we must deal with the fact that there are
many (including some church attendees) who say
that it is 'pie in the sky' to believe that the Almighty
God would deign to speak to His children. But the
testimony of the Scriptures and millions of His
followers confirms the fact that God does speak to
His loved ones, and the voice they hear comes not
from within but without. I am surprised that many
Christians view the idea that God speaks directly
to us as something strange. 'God speaks to us through His Word,'
they argue, 'and that is the only way we hear His voice.' I disagree.
I have heard His voice through Scripture thousands of times, and
I have heard that voice also speaking directly to my heart. It does
not just happen any more than a radio just happens to pick up
messages. We have to be switched on and tuned in.

When the king complained to Joan of Arc that he never heard
the voice of God she replied, 'You must listen, then you will hear.'
Good advice; you will not hear unless you are willing to listen.

**Father, give me the insights and patience I require to be able to hush
all the clamorous voices in my soul that compete with Your voice.
I see the need; now help me acquire the art. In Jesus' name. Amen.**

Listening costs something

'Then Samuel said, "Speak, for your servant is listening."'
(v10)

We ended yesterday with the statement that you will not hear unless you are willing to listen. But how do we learn to listen? Let me suggest some simple steps that I hope will help you. The first we have already considered: be willing to obey whatever God says to you. We need to learn to approach God with the same attitude that Jesus displayed when He said, 'My food is to do the will of him who sent me'. Then not only will He speak but also equip.

The second is this: expect God to speak to you. It is possible to pray with no sense of expectation. Have done with all thought that God is too great and too distant to talk to you. You are His child, the object of His unceasing love and care. A sign of expectancy is to have a notebook and pen by you during your prayer time. Had I not written down the things God has said to me in my quiet time I would be a lot poorer spiritually than I am now.

FURTHER STUDY

Hab. 2:1;
Acts 9:1-19

1. How did the prophet prepare to listen to God?

2. What could listening to God cost Ananias and Saul?

Third: sit quietly in God's presence and say: 'Father, have You anything to say to me?' At first all you may hear are the voices that come from within. Gradually, though, you will learn to disentangle the voice of God from the clamour of other voices – the muffled whisperings of the subconscious, the luring voices of the flesh, the demands of personal ambition, the mutterings of self-will. To learn to keep one's ear true in so subtle a murmur of sound is a great spiritual adventure. But, as with all adventures, it may be costly in terms of time, persistence and determination. The benefits, however, are beyond all expectation.

Father, I accept that a price is involved in learning to listen, but I recognise also that the rewards are greater than the cost. Now I see the way, help me to walk in it. In Jesus' name. Amen.

Well worth the wait

For reading & meditation – 2 Corinthians 12:1–10

'But he said to me, "My grace is sufficient for you,
for my power is made perfect in weakness."' (v9)

We reflect further on the need to learn to disentangle the voice of God from the other voices we hear in our souls. Brigid E. Herman in her book *Creative Prayer*, writing in the day when Morse code was the means of communication on ships, said: 'The alert and courageous soul making its first venture upon the spiritual life is like a wireless operator on his trial trip in the Pacific. At the mercy of myriad electrical whispers, the novice at the receiver doesn't know what to think. How fascinating the ghostly pipings and mutterings, delicate scratchings and thin murmurs – and how confusing! Then suddenly there comes a remote whisper that plucks at his taut nerves – it is the call sign of his own ship. It is the expected message, and unless he had been alert he might have missed it. The soul that wants to disentangle the voice of God from the other voices must sit in silence and learn to keep one's ear true – just by listening.'

FURTHER STUDY

1 Kings 19:9-18;
Psa. 29:3-9

1. What did
Elijah hear?

2. Describe the
voice of the Lord.

What does the divine voice sound like? Different people describe it in different ways. To me it is like the voice of conscience only stronger, richer and more positive in content. Like conscience, it carries its own sense of authority with it. The trained ear recognises the divine voice, and the soul knows that its Creator has spoken. Just this morning, after I had finished my time with the Lord in prayer, I sat back and said: 'Have You anything to say to me, Father?' After a short wait – perhaps five to ten minutes – this word came: 'I love you'. That thought is found throughout Scripture, but to hear the Spirit's voice whisper it directly to my soul was worth the wait.

Father, I realise that if experience is the key then, to get experience,
I must begin – and begin as soon as possible. Forgive me if so much
of my Christian life has been taken up with talking
rather than listening. Amen.

Some necessary cautions

For reading & meditation – Acts 10:1–23

'While Peter was still thinking about the vision,
the Spirit said to him' (v19)

In the past, when I have written about cultivating the art of listening for God's voice, some have written urging me to refrain from mentioning the idea again, saying: 'Since we now have the Bible in its complete form, God does not speak directly to us. It is dangerous to teach that we can hear the voice of God speaking to us outside of Scripture.' Well, knives are dangerous. People misuse them. Yet nobody advocates the abolition of knives. Their wise use has made them an indispensable tool in every household. But there are cautions that must be considered, and it is of these I would speak now.

People have sometimes claimed that the voice of God has urged them to carry out actions that are in direct conflict with Scripture. If you hear a voice telling you to do something s not in accordance with instructions given in the Bible, then you can be sure it is not God's voice that you are hearing.

I would warn young Christians, also, against too confident an assertion that you know the voice of God, especially in the area of guidance. If you feel God has spoken to you about a change in direction, check it out with a more mature Christian, preferably a leader, mature friend or mentor. Even those with considerable experience of listening intently for God's voice confess their propensity to error. And one final comment: not every day will the voice be equally clear. The closeness of our walk with God determines that. But be assured of this: you can hear His voice. Just to think that He speaks to us is wonderful, but to hear His voice is heaven.

FURTHER STUDY

Acts 10:1-8, 44-48; 13:1-3

1. What was the result of Cornelius listening and obeying?

2. Why did the Holy Spirit speak?

My Father and my God, as I begin to see the possibilities help me not to be satisfied with the idea alone but to close in with it. From now on, in my devotional sessions may I make time for the listening side of prayer. Amen.

'Anxious indecision'

For reading & meditation – Proverbs 24:1–22

'If you falter in times of trouble, how small is your strength!' (v10)

We have been seeing that in order to prepare the way and to meet the needs of a new year we are to be a people prepared. This means having a heart that turns easily to prayer, a mind saturated in Scripture and an ear tuned in to listen to the divine voice. Now we consider the second element of making the path straight: being mature in relation to ourselves. This involves many things, of course, but one of the most significant is self-discipline. John the Baptist, we are told, drank no wine or strong drink (Luke 1:15). He was able to deny himself things – he could practise restraint.

FURTHER STUDY

Deut. 20:1-4;
Phil. 4:6-7

1. How may fear arise?

2. What is the antidote?

This is a time in history when we need men and women who can leave things behind in order to give themselves more fully to God's purposes. The concept of self-discipline does not always sit very comfortably with some of us. For example, some years ago a woman came to me with this problem. 'I get panic attacks,' she said, 'whenever anyone mentions the subject of self-discipline. Can you help me find out why?'

Some psychologists refer to this as 'anxious indecision'. Whenever she moved towards the goal of self-discipline she was plagued by a fear that she might not succeed. The more she tried to reach her goal, the stronger the fear became. But when she stopped striving, the desire to be a self-disciplined person became stronger than the fear of failure. Then, as she attempted to try again, the fear of failure became greater than her desire to be self-disciplined. She had been living like this for most of her life. But she found freedom and release from this vicious cycle.

My Father and my God, help me to be my very best for You. The business of being a Christian is serious business. I have a race to run. Help me to run it well. In Jesus' name. Amen.

Don't strive - surrender

For reading & meditation – Philippians 4:10–23

'I can do everything through him who gives me strength.'
(v13)

Yesterday we started to look at the situation of a woman who was caught up in 'anxious indecision'. Whenever she attempted to be more self-disciplined she reached the point where her fear of failure was stronger than her desire to reach her goal. When she gave up her attempt, her desire to reach her goal would return and be stronger than her fear of failure. This woman had set a good goal for herself, but the fear of failure that plagued her caused her to feel uncertain that she would reach it. In the Waverley framework we might refer to this as 'an uncertain goal'.

The resolution came for her when she discovered that self-discipline involves not only trying, but trusting too. She thought she could only achieve self-discipline through self-effort. Then she discovered that she would never find release until she was willing to admit defeat. Self-discipline is ultimately not so much our responsibility as our response to His ability. Self-discipline for a Christian is not a matter of striving; it is a matter of surrender. It all hinges on the closeness of our relationship to Jesus. The closer we are to Him, the more strength we are able to draw from Him.

FURTHER STUDY

Matt. 6:24–34;
11:28–30

1. Why may we become anxious?

2. How can we overcome anxiety?

A statement I have often made in past issues of *Every Day with Jesus* is this: when we supply the willingness, God supplies the power. Far too often we want to supply the power through self-effort. Our carnal nature likes to succeed without help from anyone else. Self-discipline is not a problem when we allow Jesus to take the heavy end of the load. Has He not promised that His yoke is easy and His burden is light (Matt. 11:30)?

**My Lord and my God, I am putting my neck into Your yoke –
uniting myself with You. But Your yoke is easy, and I am made for
it. I take Your weights on my shoulders only to find they are wings.
Amen.**

Harnessed to God

For reading & meditation – 1 Corinthians 9:1–27
'Run in such a way as to get the prize.' (v24)

A wise person wrote this in a Bible I was given as a child: 'Dependence plus discipline equals dependable disciples.' There is a great emphasis on grace in the Christian life, but grace must be permeated with discipline.

The need for this combination is illustrated by an amusing but pointed story about a woman whose arthritis had been healed after she had asked the leaders of her church to anoint her with oil and pray for her. Some months later she asked them to pray about her

FURTHER STUDY

Prov. 24:30-34;
2 Tim. 4:1-10

1. What lesson was learned?

2. What part does fighting play in the Christian life?

problem with obesity, which had arisen because of over-eating. One of the leaders said: 'I have a word for you.' Then, turning over the pages of his Bible, he read: 'This kind goeth not out but by prayer and fasting.' Where only dependence could heal, prayer was the answer. Where only self-discipline could solve the problem, that was the answer. As Christians we need to be balanced. If the forces of our life are not harnessed, they roam everywhere and

get nowhere. When they are harnessed to God, they are controlled.

Dr Charles Mayo, founder of the Mayo Clinic in the USA, walked with a limp. One day someone asked him why. He replied: 'There is a passage in the Bible that says, "They made me the keeper of the vineyards; but mine own vineyard have I not kept." I saw this coming on but I would not pay heed.' He had not disciplined himself to take the advice he gave to others, and he walked with a limp through life as a result. Many are limping lamely through life because they are not willing to be disciplined. Listen to these words again: 'Dependence plus discipline equals dependable disciples.'

My Lord and my God, help me to harness all my life in the direction of Your purposes. For I become either a servant or a master. Let nothing master me except You. In Jesus' name. Amen.

The divine order

For reading & meditation – 1 Timothy 1:1–11

'The goal of this command is love, which comes from a
pure heart and a good conscience and a sincere faith.' (v5)

Sir Winston Churchill once said: 'The future of the world is
in the hands of disciplined people.' When I first read that I
thought to myself: 'What a powerful statement.' But the more I
have reflected on it, the more I have come to see that something
needs to be added: The future of the world is in the hands of
disciplined people – those who are disciplined to achieve the
highest. If one is disciplined to achieve less than the highest then
the discipline will exhaust itself – it isn't backed by the ultimate.
And what is the ultimate? It is the moral order that
God has built into the universe.

James Moffatt's translation of verse 4 of today's
passage is helpful. Whereas the NIV translation reads,
'These promote controversies rather than God's work
– which is by faith,' Moffatt's version reads: 'such
studies bear upon speculations rather than on the
divine order which belongs to faith.' The divine order
which belongs to faith – what a powerful expression. We belong
to a divine order that was embodied in a divine Person – the Lord
Jesus Christ. When we align ourselves to Jesus we are joined to the
embodiment of an order that will outlast everything on this earth.
This is what I mean by a discipline that is backed by the ultimate.

I love the way, too, that Moffatt translates verse 5: 'Whereas
the aim of the Christian discipline is the love that springs from
a pure heart, from a good conscience, and from a sincere faith.'
Have done with the idea that discipline turns you into a rigid or an
austere person. True Christian discipline results not in repression
but freedom and spontaneity – a love that springs.

FURTHER STUDY

2 Tim.
2:1–7,14–22

1. What should
we endure?

2. What are
the results of
discipline?

**God my Father, how wrong I have been to think of discipline as
being repressive. I see that when You are in it, it brings release.
From now on I will not resign myself to the matter of discipline,
but rejoice in it. Amen.**

Artificial versus artesian

For reading & meditation – John 4:1–26

'Indeed, the water I give him will become in him a spring of
water welling up to eternal life.' (v14)

Yesterday we said that we need to be done with this idea that
discipline turns us into rigid or austere people. Discipline, when
understood and applied properly, is not repressive but resulting
in the most truly spontaneous and natural people in the world.
The law ends in liberty, for it generates (as we saw) not just a love,
but a love that springs. How sad it is that some Christians give
discipline a bad name by their rigid and gloomy approach to life. In
the early part of my Christian life I knew a man whose emphasis

FURTHER STUDY

Luke 10:21;
Heb. 12:4–17

1. How did the
Holy Spirit
affect Jesus?

2. Why does God
discipline us?

on discipline was such that he put everyone off. He
was so stern, so severe and so tense. People said
behind his back: 'If that's what Christianity does
for you then I don't want anything to do with it.' His
discipline resulted in a love that sagged.

Millions of Christians all over the world lead
disciplined lives without conveying any sense of
being harsh, grumpy or artificial. But unfortunately
there are still some who connect discipline with a sullen, miserable
countenance. A small group of people gathered at a station to
meet a minister who was coming to preach at their church. As
a man with a rather sour expression stepped off the train, one of
the group went up to him and said: 'Are you the preacher?' 'No,'
answered the man, 'I'm afraid it's my dyspepsia that makes me
look like this.'

So I say again, let's dispose of the idea that Christianity produces
rigid, unnatural people. Some Christians are like that, but it is not
Jesus that makes them that way. The disciplines that He calls us
to, when understood correctly, make us artesian, not artificial.

**My Father and my God, may I so fall in love with You that Your love
flows through everything I do – even my disciplines. If I have seen
discipline in a wrong light then help me correct my perception.
In Jesus' name. Amen.**

Free – to go nowhere

For reading & meditation – Galatians 5:1-15

'You, my brothers, were called to be free. But do not use
your freedom to indulge the sinful nature' (v13)

We continue meditating on the elements of self-discipline that
will help us 'prepare the way'. This statement, made by a
philosopher by the name of Professor Royce, struck me when I
came across it recently: 'There is only one way to be an ethical
individual and that is to choose your cause and then serve it.' He
was making the point that many philosophers make, namely that
when we have a central loyalty then this puts all other loyalties
in their place. For Christians the central cause is Jesus and His
kingdom. When we seek these first then all other
things – including self-control – are added to us.

But does it happen automatically? No, because God
doesn't just overrule us – we co-operate. We have to
be willing to receive the strength that Jesus provides
and make use of it. One writer believes that this co-
operation can be achieved by being ready to 'throw
your will on the side of being disciplined'.

There are many who throw their wills on the
side of indiscipline, which they mistakenly view
as freedom. A young girl walked to the front of a class while the
teacher was out and wrote on the blackboard: 'We want more
freedom, longer holidays, less homework, more TV and shorter
hours in school.' All the students clapped and cheered her. They
wanted to be free to do whatever they liked. Bill Gothard, an
American Bible teacher, defines freedom like this: 'Freedom is not
the power to do what we want, but the power to do what we ought.'
People who try to be free through indiscipline find that they are as
free as a ship when it loses its rudder – free to go nowhere.

FURTHER STUDY

Gen. 3:1-19;
Prov. 4:23

1. What did
freedom and
indiscipline
bring Adam
and Eve?

2. What is our
priority?

**Father, I throw myself today on the side of discipline. I want to be
free to do what I ought. In bondage to You I am free to be the person
You want me to be. I am so thankful. Amen.**

Where everything starts

For reading & meditation – Galatians 5:16–26
'But the fruit of the Spirit is love and self-control.'
(vv22-23)

It is interesting that in the passage we have read today the apostle Paul puts self-control as the last of the fruit of the Spirit whereas some religious systems would put it first. Confucianism, through self-control, would try to achieve a 'superior humanity'. Hinduism, through breath- and thought-control would aim to reach a 'realised humanity'. Stoicism, through will-control, would try to achieve a 'detached humanity'. New Age religions, through mind-control, seek to become a 'happy humanity'. Christianity, through Christ-control, results in a 'godly humanity' – people who are self-controlled because they are Christ-controlled.

FURTHER STUDY

Matt. 7:13-14;
1 Cor. 13:1-13

1. Why is the Christian life a narrow way?

2. Why does everything start with love?

We do not gain Christ through self-control; we gain self-control through Christ. We begin with love for Him and end with the strength to leave behind all things that do not contribute to His purposes for our lives. The spring of action for self-control in a Christian is not self, but the Saviour. In 2 Corinthians 5:14 we are told that the love of Christ 'compels us', or literally, 'narrows us to His way'. If we begin with self-control then we are the centre; we are controlling ourselves. This will give rise to anxiety lest we slip away from our control. But if we begin with love, then the spring of action is love for a Person, someone outside of ourselves. Thus we are released from our self-preoccupation.

One writer talks about 'the expulsive power of a new affection'. The love that flows from Jesus to us, and from us back to Jesus, breaks the tyranny of self-love and releases us to be what we can be. We begin with love and end with self-control.

Father, day by day it is becoming clearer: without Your love invading my soul self-discipline and self-control are arduous; with Your love they are adventurous. Help me start where everything Christian starts – with love. Amen.

Changing 'I' to 'U'

For reading & meditation – John 3:22–36

'He must become greater; I must become less.' (v30)

Quoting Sir Winston Churchill, we said a few days ago that 'The future of the world is in the hands of disciplined people,' but added: 'those who are disciplined to achieve the highest'. But how do we go about becoming disciplined people? The first step is this: fix it firmly in your mind that you cannot control the marginal issues of your life unless Jesus is central.

Jesus has to be the centre of our attention if we are to be spiritually self-disciplined. You see, whatever gets your attention gets you. If you give self your attention, then self will be drawn to the centre of your consciousness and everything will be arranged around the self. The word I used was 'arranged', but perhaps it would be more accurate to say 'disarranged'. To have self at the centre is to have a cancer at the centre – something invasive and destructive.

FURTHER STUDY

Gen. 29:16–20;
Luke 9:57–60;
14:25–27

1. How was Jacob's life controlled by love?

2. How does the cross change our priorities?

Decide, then, who is to get your attention – Jesus or yourself. Have one supreme controlling love at the centre of your life – love for Jesus. If you tolerate conflicting loves then sooner or later one will increase and assume control. Dr Andrew Bonar said he could always tell when a Christian was growing by listening to see how often the personal pronoun 'I' was used in conversation. 'A growing Christian,' said Dr Bonar, 'seeks to de-emphasise self and elevate the Master. He talks less and less of what he himself is doing, becomes smaller in his own sight... until like the morning star he fades before the sun.' One of the most frequently used letters on a keyboard is 'I'. If in your life the chief emphasis has been 'I' then change it. Shift to 'U'.

Lord Jesus Christ, forgive me if I have been focusing more on myself than on You. Today I make that shift. I am at Your feet, dear Lord. Help me to always look up and fix my attention on You. For Your own dear name's sake. Amen.

Commit yourself

For reading & meditation – 2 Chronicles 15:1–19

'Asa's heart was fully committed [to the LORD] all his life.'
(v17)

The first step towards self-discipline, we said yesterday, is ensuring that Jesus is central. This involves a complete surrender to Him and to all His purposes for our lives. It is no good giving up this thing and that thing unless the central self has been given up. Relinquish the central self, and that will carry everything else with it. Someone said of one man, who was a marginally surrendered person, 'He comes near to being great, but the self sticks out in everything he does.' This man surrendered the marginal but kept back the central. How sad it is when the self is so much in evidence that Jesus is not seen.

FURTHER STUDY

1 Sam. 15:2-26

1. Describe Saul's commitment to God.

2. Describe Samuel's commitment.

Discipline, then, begins at the centre. Our text for today tells us that Asa was committed to the Lord all his life. That is the basis of self-discipline; it begins in a central commitment. Professor James, from the standpoint of psychology, said this: 'When once the judgement is decided, let a man commit himself irretrievably. Let him put himself in a position where it will lay on him the necessity of doing more, the necessity of doing all.' This is sound advice, and also sound Christianity. Notice the word 'irretrievably'. Leave no door open behind you. The mind, in a fearful moment, may be tempted to take that way of escape. Don't be a person with an escape mentality.

One of the saddest verses in the Bible is this: 'As Solomon grew old, his wives turned his heart after other gods, and his heart was not fully devoted to the LORD his God' (1 Kings 11:4). Solomon was a wise man who turned into a foolish one because of a lack of discipline. He didn't guard his inner self so his outer life came down around him.

My Father and my God, I know You will not be satisfied with marginal surrender; You long for total commitment. You are asking for all of me. And I give that now – now and forever. I have You and You have me. And I am glad. Amen.

A disciplined thought life

For reading & meditation – Philippians 4:1–9

'Finally... whatever is true, whatever is noble,
whatever is right... think about such things.' (v8)

Now that we have seen the first step on the road to self-discipline
is a complete surrender to Jesus, we move on to ask: What are
some of the major areas of our lives that need self-discipline? The
first area is our thoughts. Our passage today is one of the classic
sections of the New Testament on self-discipline. We are instructed
to bring our thoughts under control by focusing on the things that
are true, noble, right, pure, lovely and so on. Notice all the things
the inspired writer tells us to focus on – not one is negative.

If you constantly think about things that are
untrue, negative, wrong or impure, then the very
disharmony of these things will invade you and
pervade you. Your peace will disappear. A man I
know and greatly respect says that sometimes he
wakes in the middle of the night feeling frightened.
This is due (so he believes) to a noise in the night
triggering something in his subconscious. When it
happens he repeats to himself these phrases: 'There
is no need for fear, no need for anxiety. Christ is here,
and from Him comes only harmony and peace.' Soon
he falls asleep again. Discipline your thoughts to focus on that
which is good, right, lovely, and the last words of the passage will
come true: 'The God of peace will be with you.'

FURTHER STUDY

Isa. 26:3;
Rom. 8:5-9;
12:1-3;
2 Cor. 10:1-5

1. How are
thoughts and
peace related?

2. How do
we renew
our minds?

If sexual thoughts are a problem then don't indulge them, for
any delay can soon develop into the doing. Don't try to dismiss
such thoughts – that doesn't work; they are best dissolved and
replaced by holy thoughts. Direct your attention to Jesus. See Him
in your imagination. To think on Him is to summon His aid.

**Father, I see that I am not so much what I think I am, but what I
think I am. Help me think always about that which is good, and
whenever wrong thoughts assail, help me outwit them by turning
my attention to You. In Jesus' name. Amen.**

Fit - not fat

For reading & meditation – Romans 14:12–23

'the kingdom of God is not a matter of eating and drinking, but of righteousness, peace and joy' (v17)

Yesterday we recognised the need to discipline our thought life. The ancestor of every action is thought. Don't harbour impure or even unworthy thoughts. As Dr George Buttrick says: 'We dramatise temptation in our secret thought, thus gathering gasoline for the devil's spark, then we wonder why we blow up.' Remember that what you take into your mind in meditation will stay there as fact.

Another area requiring discipline is that of our general health. If our bodies are the temple of the Holy Spirit then we ought to treat them with the respect God's temple deserves. Take, for example, the matter of what we eat. We must eat enough to keep us fit, but not so much it makes us fat. One church leader I knew, severely obese, used to quip: 'I am on a seafood diet – whenever I see food I eat it.' He commented: 'It was said of Jesus that He came eating and drinking. I want to be like Jesus.' People laughed at his jokes, but his obesity finally killed him. A preacher who doesn't have any control over his appetite is a preacher with little authority. His remarks from the pulpit will carry little weight – pardon the pun.

FURTHER STUDY

Gen. 25:29-34;
Phil. 3:17-21

1. How did Esau lose God's blessing?

2. What contrast did Paul make?

An interesting verse in Deuteronomy reads thus: 'From heaven he made you hear his voice to discipline you' (Deut. 4:36). This voice from heaven for discipline is turning out to be the same voice that is speaking out of the constitution of our physical make-up. The Bible and our doctors are saying the same thing: discipline yourself or perish. 'Every meal,' says a Christian physician, 'should be a sacrament offered on the altar of fitter living and finer possibilities.'

Father, I see that though the kingdom of God is not a matter of eating and drinking, yet what we eat and drink determines our fitness for the kingdom. Teach me how to master my natural desires lest they master me. In Jesus' name. Amen.

Shift your values

For reading & meditation – 1 Corinthians 6:12–20

'Do you not know that your body is a temple of the Holy Spirit… Therefore honour God with your body.' (vv19-20)

Yesterday we touched on the need to be disciplined as regards what we eat. We must be careful also about what we drink, especially alcohol. I do not believe the Bible teaches total abstinence, although I fully understand why some Christians advocate it. The Bible's emphasis is on moderation. However, I am convinced that there are some Christians who, because of their make-up, would be wise to keep away from alcohol altogether. As I meet Christians in different parts of the world I remain surprised at the number who tell me they are alcohol dependent. I encourage them to see a Christian counsellor. God wants us to draw our resources from Him, not from a bottle.

FURTHER STUDY

Psa. 104:13-15;
Eph. 5:17-18;
1 Tim. 5:23

1. Why did God give us wine?

2. What was Paul's attitude to alcohol?

What about tobacco? Shun it. Years ago (in the sixties and seventies), whenever I urged Christians to stop smoking I would get a spate of letters insisting that I was trying to interfere with people's pleasures and that smoking was not harmful. But not anymore. And why? The voice that speaks from heaven for discipline is speaking through medical science. A heart specialist said this: 'Of all the things that people take into themselves for their supposed pleasure, tobacco is one of the worst.'

We are to be at our very best for the kingdom and for the task of making Jesus known in the coming days. We were created to be dependent on Christ – and on nothing else. An undisciplined lifestyle is not an option for us. One person summed up our generation as being: 'a generation which is trying to eat and drink its way to prosperity, war its way to peace, spend its way to wealth, and enjoy its way to heaven. It can't be done.'

Father, I do not want to be in bondage to any self-imposed craving. I want to depend for comfort not on smoke but on the Saviour, not on what I get from a bottle but what I get from the Bible. Help me to shift my values. Amen.

'Refusing the good'

For reading & meditation – Ephesians 5:1–21

'Be very careful, then, how you live - not as unwise but as wise, making the most of every opportunity' (vv15-16)

The issues with which we are now wrestling may challenge our lifestyles, but they must be faced if we are to 'prepare the way'. Another matter that needs discipline is that of time. People often say to me: 'Where do you find enough time to do the things you do – writing, travelling, teaching, lecturing and so on?' I manage to find time because I have tried to follow the advice given to me by one of my spiritual mentors: 'Know the difference between ten minutes and quarter of an hour.' In photography, I gather, the quality of a picture depends not only what you include in it but what you leave out. Go over your life today and rule out those things that do not contribute. Someone asked a businessman what was the first necessity in business and he replied 'a wastebasket'.

FURTHER STUDY

2 Sam. 18:19-32;
Prov. 6:4-11

1. How did Ahimaaz's enthusiasm waste his time and David's?

2. What can we learn from the ant?

Another piece of advice given to me is this: 'Exercise the duty of refusing to do the good if it interferes with the best.' There are many things I am invited to do which are good, but if I were to do them I would not find time for the things that are best. This involves prioritising – and sticking to what we have decided. Occasionally I get it wrong, and when I do I try to get back on track.

Are you the kind of person who is always running to keep up with your tasks? Then don't be surprised if others view you as driven and demanding, the kind of person who expects others to respond to your frantic requests immediately. The man who influenced the world most – Jesus Christ – was never rushed or stressed. He simply focused on the things He knew He was called to do. Oh that we would be more like Him.

Lord Jesus Christ, not once do I read in the Gospels that You ever rushed. Yet You always seemed to have time for the things that mattered. Give me that disciplined poised life, with time for the things that need to be done. Amen.

Tame your tongue

For reading & meditation – Matthew 12:15–37

'For by your words you will be acquitted, and by your
words you will be condemned.' (v37)

One of the greatest challenges we face in our everyday living,
as we saw yesterday, is deciding what we do with our time.
The real difficulty is not so much managing our time but managing
ourselves. Far too often we allow our desires to run away with
us, succumbing to our appetites when we should be containing
them. We carry on conversations long after they have run out of
intelligence simply because we like to hear ourselves talk! And this
leads to the next item I'd like to raise: the discipline of the tongue.

One of the lessons I have learned in life is this: the
expression of a thing deepens the impression. Our
text today, which in the Revised Standard Version
reads thus, 'by your words you will be justified,
and by your words you will be condemned,' did not
mean much to me until I came to see that we become
what we say. If we continually and consistently
tell lies we become a lie. 'The deepest punishment
of telling a lie,' says one Bible teacher, 'is to be the
one who tells the lie. You have to live with a person you can't
trust.' Some Christians wouldn't dream of telling a lie, but they
may avoid telling the whole truth. Not to tell the whole truth, in
certain situations, creates a wrong impression, and that is just as
damaging as telling a lie.

FURTHER STUDY

James 3:1-12;
Eph. 4:29-32

1. Describe
the power of
the tongue.

2. What are good
and bad uses of
our tongues?

Let's prepare ourselves by learning to speak concisely and in a
straightforward manner. At one meeting, after a speaker who was
extremely verbose had finished his talk, the chairman got up and
commented: 'He couldn't have said less unless he had said more.'
Learn to say what you mean and mean what you say.

**Father, I see that if I'm not careful my words will condemn me to be
what they are. Help me discipline my tongue to speak that which is
truthful, relevant and loving. Set a watch upon my mouth, dear
Lord, and guard the door of my lips. Amen.**

A higher level

For reading & meditation – Acts 2:1–21

'Even on my servants, both men and women, I will pour out
my Spirit in those days' (v18)

We have been seeing that part of John the Baptist's
preparedness was his ability to renounce certain things;
to say 'No' to the lesser things that he might say 'Yes' to the higher
ones. And the positive outcome to his acts of saying no: he was
filled with the Holy Spirit.

It would be impossible to consider this subject of being 'a people
who will prepare the way' without reference to the Holy Spirit. If the
Holy Spirit had not indwelt him, John the Baptist would have been

FURTHER STUDY

John 1:29-34;
1 Cor. 2:9-16

1. What was
Jesus to take
and what was
He to give?

2. Why is
spiritual
discernment on
a higher level?

unable to fulfil the task given to him by God – that
of preparing people for the coming of the Messiah.
We, too, will be unprepared for making Jesus known
in this New Year unless we are filled with the Spirit.
And not just filled – but filled to overflowing.

A discerning writer has made this point: 'Generally
speaking, the Christian Church… has exhausted
itself against the problems of the present day. It will
have to be renewed on a higher level if it is to be
functionally adequate for the [future].' That 'higher
level' can be reached as we open ourselves to the

Holy Spirit. There is a river in a Californian desert, so I have been
informed, that starts out towards the sea but gets lost in the sand.
The spiritual life of many Christians is like that: it starts well but
gets lost in the sands of self-effort. We need more than our natural
talents if we are to meet the challenge of the days that lie ahead;
we need another Pentecost. These words from William Cowper say
it best: 'But oars alone can ne'er prevail, to reach the distant coast,
the breath of heaven must swell the sail, or all the toil is lost.'

**Spirit of God, fill me to overflowing I pray. Take away any coldness
that may be within me by breathing into me Your warmth. As I put
up my sails, fill them with Your breath. In Jesus' name. Amen.**

More power

For reading & meditation – Acts 1:1-11
'But you will receive power when the Holy Spirit
comes on you' (v8)

There is just no way we can meet the needs of our society without the presence and power of the Holy Spirit. In a contemporary translation of the Gospels the Holy Spirit is printed 'the holy spirit' – without capitals. Sadly this is symbolic of what is happening in some sections of the Church. The Holy Spirit is being turned into 'a holy spirit' – a vague impersonal influence.

This is not the Holy Spirit of the Acts of the Apostles. When you turn over the pages of the book of Acts you find the Holy Spirit operating not as a vague impersonal influence, but as God with His people – in them and upon them. Take another look through the whole of Acts to see just what God the Holy Spirit can do with men and women who are fully surrendered to Him. I am glad that the NIV translates a reference to Stephen like this: 'But they could not stand up against his wisdom or the Spirit by whom he spoke' (Acts 6:10). Notice the capital 'S'. The Holy Spirit indwelt Stephen's spirit, and thus the wisdom that came from him was Wisdom with a capital 'W'. You couldn't tell where Stephen's spirit ended and the Holy Spirit began.

FURTHER STUDY

Acts 6:3-8;
7:55-60;
8:5-17

1. What was noted of Stephen?

2. How did the Samaritans gain more power?

How different the Church would be if we were as reliant and as in sync with the Holy Spirit as Stephen. It would not stop us being persecuted, but it would make an unimaginable impression on the world. Jesus promised that when the Holy Spirit came at Pentecost a new power would be released in the world. That same power is available to us today. ? The Holy Spirit has not withdrawn His power or resources. Ask Him to empower you today.

God, help us we pray to rediscover Your offer to us and to live by the Holy Spirit's resources, rejoice in His presence and become effective by His power. Give us another Pentecost, dear Lord. In Jesus' name we ask it. Amen.

Turn to your resources

For reading & meditation – Colossians 1:24–29

'To this end I labour, struggling with all his energy,
which so powerfully works in me.' (v29)

Many have suggested that the problems we face in contemporary culture far outweigh the problems with which other generations had to grapple: widespread drug addiction, pornography available worldwide on the Internet, resistance to God-given authority, incivility, an independent mindset and so on.

We must be careful, however, that we do not become so taken up with the problems that we forget the resources that are available to us through the Holy Spirit. The comment has been made: 'The early Christians did not say in dismay, "Look what the world has come to," but with surprise and energy, "Look what has come to the world"'. They saw not just the ruin, but the resources to reconstruct that ruin. Though darkness increased, they saw also that grace increased all the more (Rom. 5:20). Gripped by this assurance, the committed disciples of Jesus in that first century did not allow themselves to become obsessed with the problems. Instead, they opened themselves to the Spirit to such a degree that they swung from blank despair to faith in the risen Jesus and became confident that at last sin had met its match.

FURTHER STUDY

Judg. 13:24–14:6;
16:15–21

1. What was the secret of Samson's power?

2. What did he fail to realise?

That same sense of confidence can possess you and me when we are to present the gospel to our own generation. But this confidence is not generated by hyping ourselves up with spiritual pep talks; it is based on the realisation that our lives are linked to the Holy Spirit. We make ourselves fully reliant on the resources He provides for us. The Christian life is not our responsibility but our response to His ability.

**Father, we turn to our resources. And what resources they are!
Through Your Holy Spirit we, Your people, have everything we
need to make a difference. Forgive us that we remain so weak when
You are so strong. In Jesus' name. Amen.**

They will listen

For reading & meditation – Luke 11:5–13

'how much more will your Father in heaven give the
Holy Spirit to those who ask him!' (v13)

We were meditating yesterday on the fact that the main resource we have for presenting the gospel to this generation is the Holy Spirit. A man who had had a powerful encounter with the Holy Spirit stood up in a meeting and announced: 'My life has been transformed from being a thermometer merely registering the temperature to a thermostat triggering a change.' The trouble with much of contemporary Christianity is that we register the temperature around us rather than changing it. It's too easy to forget that the Acts of the Apostles were the acts of the Holy Spirit working through the apostles.

Browsing in a second-hand bookshop, I came across a Bible, and as I opened it I caught sight of these words, which someone had written at the end of the book of Acts: 'to be continued'. What the early disciples began we are commissioned to continue.

FURTHER STUDY

John 14:12–26;
15:26–27

1. How can we do greater things than Jesus?

2. What is our responsibility?

Just before the book of Acts ends there is a fascinating verse: 'Therefore I want you to know that God's salvation has been sent to the Gentiles, and they will listen!' (Acts 28:28). Notice the phrase *and they will listen*. The Gentiles listened to Paul because the Holy Spirit worked through him. When the Holy Spirit is at work in our lives, people will listen. The reason so many do not listen is because they see and sense little of God in us. Nietzsche, the well-known German philosopher, said: 'Christians must look a little more redeemed if they are going to be taken seriously.' Drop some things from your schedule today, get alone with God and ask yourself: How powerfully does the Holy Spirit indwell me? You may have the Spirit, but does the Spirit have you?

Holy Spirit, bringer of life into death, light into darkness, plus into minus, come within me and set me on fire I pray. Pour Yourself into me. Renew me and recharge me. Help me, Father, for I am desperate. In Jesus' name. Amen.

Time to put things right

For reading & meditation – Ephesians 5:1–20
'Do not get drunk on wine, which leads to debauchery.
Instead, be filled with the Spirit.' (v18)

Perhaps nothing is more necessary if we are to meet the needs of this changing world than that we are reliant on the Holy Spirit. An author tells how he sat by a lakeside one day, making notes for a book he was writing, when a wild duck came by with her brood, foraging for something to eat. One duckling seemed to be weaker than the rest and spent so much of its time trying to keep up with the others that it had no time to feed. Many of us in the Church are like that little duckling; we tag along behind others because we are spiritually immature. We lack a plus – a margin of strength that enables us to go about our spiritual tasks with something left over.

FURTHER STUDY

Acts 19:1–7;
2 Cor. 13:5

1. What was the spiritual condition of the Ephesians?
2. Why should we examine our spiritual condition?

I have visited India on many occasions, and the Indians are among my favourite people. They are so often very polite; when you first ask them how they are they say everything is fine. Then, after a few moments, they will share the troubles they are going through. When talking to these gracious people I have learned to wait a while after asking them how they are because it is then that I will hear the real issues.

If I met you today and asked you how you are spiritually I wonder what you would say? Would you confess that you don't feel the strength of the Spirit? Then it's time to put things right. If you didn't do as I suggested yesterday – get alone with God and assess your spiritual condition – then do so today. God is preparing His people to make a difference in the days that lie ahead. And remember this: the problems ahead of us are never as great as the strength behind us. Those who prepare the way will be those full of the Spirit.

Father, help me this day to search my heart to see just how much of my life is controlled by the Holy Spirit. I don't want to enter this quest lightly. May I set my face to seek and to find You in a new way. Fill me to overflowing. Amen.

Conservative and radical

For reading & meditation – 2 Timothy 2:14–26

'If a man cleanses himself... he will be... made holy, useful to the Master and prepared to do any good work.' (v21)

We remind ourselves once more of some of the verses that this issue of *Every Day with Jesus* is based on: 'He [John the Baptist] will be great in the sight of the Lord... never to take wine or other fermented drink... be filled with the Holy Spirit... and he will... turn the hearts of the fathers to their children... to make ready a people prepared for the Lord' (Luke 1:15–17). John, we have been saying, was strong in three directions: in relation to God, himself and others. We come now to the third of these matters: sound as regards others.

John represented the best of the past because he embarked on his ministry to others in the spirit and power of Elijah. This should not be taken to mean that John was Elijah personified, but that he came with the same reformative energy and strength. He displayed Elijah's enthusiasm for a moral and spiritual renaissance. In facing the challenges of the coming year and preparing ourselves to minister to others, we need to be men and women like John, who do not lose sight of God's dealings with His people in the past, and hold to every fine gain of history.

FURTHER STUDY

2 Chron. 29:1–11,25–36

1. How was Hezekiah conservative?

2. How was he radical?

It was said of John that he would 'turn the hearts of the fathers to the children'. Similarly, this generation must turn its heart to its children – must think in terms of ensuring that the world is a safe, just and fit place to live for those who follow us. There can be no doubt that we are at an important turning-point in history. The world is changing and needs God's people to show it the way – people conservative enough to preserve the gains of the past and radical enough to trigger change.

Father, in the midst of a world in a state of flux, I see again the necessity of being spiritually prepared. I have learned how to prepare myself in relation to You and myself. Show me now what I must do as I prepare to minister to others.

A sense of history

For reading & meditation – Judges 2:1–23

'another generation grew up, who knew neither the LORD
nor what he had done for Israel.' (v10)

We said yesterday that if we are to make a difference we must
be both conservative and radical – conservative enough
to preserve the gains of the past, and radical enough to trigger
change. Think with me first about the aspect of conservatism –
holding to the best of the past. Some Christians say: 'Forget the
past… the future is what counts. Let's get to grips with what lies
ahead.' But no one can be prepared to face the future unless he
or she is willing to look back at what God has done in the past.

FURTHER STUDY

Deut. 6:10-25;
32:7;
Jer. 6:16

1. Why do
people forget
or reject the
past so easily?
2. What should
we do to have
a sense of
history?

One of the most tragic verses in the Old Testament
is the one that is our text for today. The Living Bible
words it like this: 'Finally all that generation died;
and the next generation did not worship Jehovah as
their God, and did not care about the mighty miracles
he had done for Israel.' How sad that the great things
God had done were so quickly forgotten. A theme that
has dominated my thinking throughout my life is
revival. I have never read an account of any revival
in history without finding my heart leaping to prayer
and pleading with God to act in this way again.

Many pastors tell me of their concern about what
is being read by the people of God today. Most of it focuses on
the present or the future, for instance, how to handle problems,
or will the Church go through the Tribulation? Is it wrong to
read this kind of material? Of course not. But we need to have a
retrospective look as well as a prospective one if we are to prepare
the way. Because it is vital that we have a sense of history if we
are to understand how to live effectively in the present.

**Father, help me learn more of Your great acts in the past so that they
might powerfully energise my faith for the future. As I read about
the great revivals, place in my heart a desire to pray for revival
in our land. Amen.**

Inspired – to inspire

For reading & meditation – Hebrews 11:32–12:2

'let us throw off everything that hinders and the sin that
so easily entangles' (12:1)

The matter on which we are now meditating – our tendency to
focus on the present and the future to the exclusion of the past
– is not confined to spiritual things; it is true in every area of life.

A university professor writing in a British newspaper not long
ago lamented the fact that so many of today's young people seem
disinterested in the great events of the past. 'Everyone,' he said,
'wants to know where we are going; few want to know where
we have come from.' He was generalising, of course, but he was
accurately noting a trend. It is sad when the great
men and women of the past, as well as great events,
are so quickly forgotten. There is a verse in Scripture
that says: 'Then a new king, who did not know about
Joseph, came to power in Egypt' (Exod. 1:8). How
strange that he had never heard of the exploits of
Joseph, the man who had saved the nation from
famine. Why is it that many of us are reluctant to
acquaint ourselves with the past?

FURTHER STUDY

Jer. 18:13–15;
Heb. 11:1–19

1. What horrible
thing was done?

2. How do
people of the
past inspire us?

The main cause, I think, is our preoccupation with ourselves.
We are so self-centred, so taken up with what we are doing, that
we seem to forget people lived in this world before we arrived and
made tremendous sacrifices for an important principle or liberty.
But there is another reason too: the feeling that the past cannot
help us because of the advances we have made in recent decades
– scientifically, medically and technically. Today I have invited
you to read from Hebrews 11 so that we may acknowledge the
exploits of the great men and women of the past. There is a good
reason why God inspired these verses – so they might inspire us.

**Father, I see the Bible's purpose in taking me back to the past. Help
me not to miss what You are saying to me. Give me a sense of
history – a biblical sense. In Jesus' name. Amen.**

'Put up these stones'

For reading & meditation – Joshua 4:1–24

'when your descendants ask... tell them, "Israel crossed
the Jordan on dry ground."' (vv21–22)

We continue underlining the point that it is important to
understand God's interventions and dealings with His
people in the past if we are to stay on course in the future. In the
passage before us today we see God instructing the children of
Israel to take twelve stones, and set them up at Gilgal. God had
delivered the Israelites from their enemies – the Egyptians – had
brought them through the wilderness, and now, here on the other
side of the Jordan, lay the Promised Land. "'Tell the twelve men...

FURTHER STUDY

Luke 22:14-20;
1 Cor. 11:23-30

1. What did the
Last Supper
mean to Jesus?

2. Why might
some be weak
and sick in
their faith?

to take a stone..." the Lord instructed Joshua, "and
pile them up as a monument at the place where
you camp tonight'" (vv2–3, TLB). Why this strange
command? It was given so that future generations
would be able to recall the amazing miracle of the
crossing of the Jordan on dry ground. One would
have thought that the account of such a miraculous
event would be passed down from one generation
to the next, and that succeeding generations would
not need any physical evidence to remind them of it.
God, however, knows human nature, and gave the commandment
to put up the stones to serve as a reminder because He saw that a
momentous event like that could soon be forgotten.

Dr Martyn Lloyd-Jones pointed out that since sin has dulled
our minds, we would not think about the death of Jesus so often
were it not for the ordinance of Holy Communion. When we spread
a white cloth on a table and place on it bread and wine we are
reminding ourselves by the use of these simple physical emblems
of an event in history that has changed the world.

**Father, I am so thankful for the communion table, which focuses
my thinking on Your Son's death on the cross. It's sad that
sometimes I need reminding, but I am grateful for
Your reminder nevertheless. Amen.**

Remember Him

For reading & meditation – 2 Timothy 2:1–13

'Remember Jesus Christ, raised from the dead, descended from David.' (v8)

History is replete with instances of God's great acts. They are all there for us to wonder at, but sometimes we fail to remember them. What should we recall and preserve from the past? Creation? The exodus? The exile? Yes, all these are worthy of consideration, but most of all, I believe, we must focus on the Person of the Son of God.

Yesterday we talked about the communion table and likened it to a memorial stone. Without it, we said, we might think less often about the death of Jesus. Here, in the passage before us today, Paul is making another point. Remember Jesus Christ, he says to Timothy. Not just remember what He said, or what He experienced, but remember His Person. He is the One who far surpasses in the towering greatness of His Person everything He taught or wrought. The words point us not to an historic fact but to an historic figure, not so much to the resurrection of Jesus but to the Jesus of the resurrection. Do you see the difference?

> **FURTHER STUDY**
>
> Isa. 53:1-12;
> Heb. 12:1-4
>
> 1. What does it mean to remember Jesus?
>
> 2. What does remembering Jesus do for us?

Dr James Denny, a well-known theologian, said: 'No one ever remembered Jesus.' What did he mean? He meant, I think, that Jesus is not someone to be remembered as a figure of history, for He is the Great Contemporary – He is always present. He is not behind us; He is ever at our side. So in remembering Jesus keep in mind that we are not just thinking of someone who was once with us and has gone, because He is with us still. Think often about Him, about who He is and what He has done. When we entertain Him in our thoughts we give Him deeper access to our hearts.

Father, help me to think much about Jesus, and not only recall His deeds in my mind but think about who He is, His Person, His love, His grace, His beauty. For I am what I am because He is who He is. Amen.

Can He be forgotten?

For reading & meditation – 1 Peter 1:1–12

'Though you have not seen him, you love him' (v8)

How often, I wonder, do your thoughts focus on Jesus during a working day? A friend of mine says that hardly an hour goes by without his mind engaging with Jesus. Another friend sets his phone alarm every hour, on the hour, to remind him of Jesus. Yesterday we looked at the text: 'Remember Jesus Christ'. Is it not somewhat sad that we are in danger of forgetting Him? Does the hungry man forget his food, or the thirsty man his drink, it has been asked, or the weary man his bed, or the lonely man his home? Such thoughts are inconceivable. A poet expressed this sentiment:

FURTHER STUDY

John 15:1-12;
Rev. 2:1-5

1. How do we remain in Christ?

2. How had the Ephesians forgotten Jesus?

He is a path if any be misled;
He is a robe if any naked be;
If any chance to hunger, He is bread.
Can He be forgotten? Not by me.

Of all the wonderful personalities God has sent to this world, none can compare with Jesus. So do what you can to think about Him long and often. I am not suggesting that we all should set up special memory-triggers like my friend who programs reminders on his phone hourly, but rather that we fall so head over heels in love with Jesus that He is constantly in our thoughts. Does a man or woman in the heady days of first love need a prompt to think about the one they love? Many will say the difficulty is to get the one they love out of their thoughts so that they can concentrate on their workaday tasks. No one from the past is as worthy of thought and concentration as Jesus. He is the centre of all things glorious. So determine today to think often of Him.

Lord Jesus Christ, though You have come from the past yet You are ever present. No one could ever do for me what You have done. May I never forget it. For Your own dear name's sake. Amen.

Empty covers

For reading & meditation – Psalm 119:89–96
'Your word, O LORD, is eternal; it stands firm
in the heavens.' (v89)

We continue reflecting on the thought that if we are to prepare the way we need to remind ourselves of our spiritual history and hold on to every spiritual benefit that has come to us from the past. Another thing we must protect from the past is God's Word, the Bible. Where would our world be without the sacred Scriptures? Many of the benefits we now enjoy, such as freedom, equality, law and order, care of the sick and needy, have come about as a direct result of men and women reading the Scriptures. One great social commentator said: 'It is difficult to enslave a Bible-reading people'.

FURTHER STUDY

Psa. 119:137–144;
2 Pet. 1:19–21

1. What are the characteristics of God's Word?

2. What is the origin of Scripture?

We are living in days, however, when there is a crisis of confidence in the Scriptures, even among mature Christians. Recently I read the sad story of a professor who resigned from a theological seminary because he had lost his faith in the Bible. As he gave his parting address, he held up the empty covers of a Bible and said: 'Gentlemen, this is what I bequeath to my successor.' If we do not accord the Bible its proper place, recognising it to be God's eternal Word and truth, then we will find it difficult to bring a strong spiritual influence to bear on the future.

A cartoon I saw pictured a man standing in a lending library in the year AD 2050, requesting to see a copy of the Holy Bible. 'Holy Bible,' said the assistant, 'Holy Bible. Never heard of it. Do you know the author's name?' Is that the way things will be in the future? I think not. God has preserved His Word for centuries and He will not allow it to be lost in the future.

Father, set us on fire with love for Your Word. Help us proclaim its power and preserve its integrity. Grant that this generation will not pass on to the next the empty covers of the Bible.
In Jesus' name I pray. Amen.

Take it by faith

For reading & meditation – Isaiah 40:1–8

'The grass withers and the flowers fall, but the word of our
God stands for ever.' (v8)

Yesterday we made mention of a professor from a theological
seminary who during his leaving address held up the empty
covers of a Bible and said: 'Gentlemen, this is what I bequeath to my
successor.' How different from Billy Graham. When challenged in
the early days of his ministry by critics over his use of the phrase
'The Bible says,' he went one night to his log cabin to reassure
himself of the reliability and veracity of the Scriptures. He counted
the number of times the phrase 'Thus saith the Lord' appears in
the Bible and found it is repeated over 2,000 times.
He meditated, too, on the attitude of Jesus, who said
that He had come to fulfil the law and the prophets,
and concluded that He loved the Scriptures and never
once intimated that they might be wrong.

Billy Graham went out into the forest and
wandered up and down, praying as he went: 'Lord,
what shall I do?' Kneeling down by a tree stump, he
spread his Bible on it and affirmed: 'Lord, I accept this
book by faith.' A tremendous sense of God's presence filled his heart,
and never once after that did he doubt the reliability of God's Word.

Those who have lacked confidence in the Bible will inevitably
lack confidence in their lives. If you struggle with its truths, do
what Billy Graham did: kneel down and ask God to help you
accept it by faith. Consider what would happen if every Christian,
everywhere in the world, committed himself or herself to reading
and applying the Bible to their lives and relationships every day.
There would be a spiritual renaissance such as the world has not
witnessed since Pentecost.

FURTHER STUDY

Deut. 8:1-14;
2 Pet. 3:1-9

1. Why should
people obey
the Bible?

2. Why may
people scoff
at the Bible?

**Father, help me see that it is not naive to accept the Bible by faith.
Your Word is not true because it satisfies reason, but it satisfies
reason because it is true. May I be certain of that for
the whole of my life. In Jesus' name. Amen.**

Predictions proved wrong

For reading & meditation – Matthew 16:13–20

'and on this rock I will build my church, and the gates of Hades will not overcome it.' (v18)

Almost every generation during the last 2,000 years has produced a crop of critics who have confidently predicted the downfall of the Church. Not always have those critics been from outside the Church, either. Take Bishop Joseph Butler, for instance, an eighteenth-century thinker and author of the monumental Analogy of Religion. When offered the Archbishopric of Canterbury in 1747 he declined it, declaring that it was 'too late to try to support a falling Church'. Or take Dr Arnold, the celebrated headmaster of Rugby School, who, writing in 1832, stated that no human power could save the Church as it then stood. These are just two examples of the negative predictions that have come from within the Church itself.

More often than not, of course, such negative comments concerning the Church have come from outside it. Voltaire, the famous French sceptic, stated: 'It required eleven men to build the Church, but I will prove it needs only one man to knock it down.' But he was wrong. And Arnold and Butler were wrong. For nine years before Butler issued his doleful prophecy, John Wesley had been converted in Aldersgate Street, London, and his conversion, along with that of George Whitefield two years previously, heralded the great Evangelical Revival. As for Voltaire, well he was wrong on two counts. First, it was not eleven men who built the Church – it was one Man – the Man Jesus. Second, no person will ever succeed in knocking it down. Its omnipotent Founder said: 'I will build my church.' So nothing and no one can ever prevail against it.

FURTHER STUDY

1 Cor. 3:6-11;
12:21-28

1. How is the Church built?

2. How does the Church combine diversity and unity?

My Father and my God, I am so grateful that here in time I am part of something that has an eternal existence. Church buildings can easily be knocked down, but not Your Church. It will stand throughout all eternity. Hallelujah!

Here to stay

For reading & meditation – Ephesians 3:1–21

'to him be the glory in the church and in Christ Jesus throughout all generations, for ever and ever! Amen.' (v21)

The Christian Church, as we said yesterday, is here to stay… until it is removed from earth to heaven – its final destiny. It has often been said that the Bible begins with a garden and ends with a city. That is deeply significant. Starting with a one-man paradise, it closes with a paradise packed with rejoicing people. Like a city, the Church has a history. Cities do not spring up overnight; in some cases it has taken a millennium or more to make a city. 'Rome,' says the old adage, 'was not built in a day'. So it is with the Church. It has a rich, vibrant and colourful history.

FURTHER STUDY

Eph. 5:22–32;
Col. 1:15–24

1. What is
Christ's
relationship to
the Church?

2. What
motivated Paul?

Around the turn of the sixteenth century, a Spaniard by the name of Vicente Yanez Pinzon, sailing his ship towards the sunset, entered into the mouth of the River Amazon. No European had ever done so before, and his men did not know where they were. One of the crew thought they had discovered an island. 'No,' said the captain, 'a river as great as this must drain a continent.' Contemplating the Church of Jesus, and thinking of its long procession through history, one is constrained to conclude that its source must lie somewhere in the ages past. Paul traces this Amazon back to its Andes – the hills of God in eternity.

The Church is no afterthought, no addendum, no mere incidental project of the redemptive process. The Church was in God's mind in the eternity past and will continue into the eternity to come. 'Christ made the worlds that He might build the Church,' says one theologian. 'He framed the earth that He might form the Fellowship.' Yes – the Church is here to stay. I know this for certain because the eternal God has spoken.

**Once again, dear Lord, I want to express my gratitude for the fact
that I belong to a Church that has not only a history but also a
future. And what a future! All honour and glory be to Your name.
Amen.**

Radical in loving

For reading & meditation – John 13:1–17

'Having loved his own who were in the world, he now
showed them the full extent of his love.' (v1)

DAY
51

Earlier we said that to be 'a people prepared' we need to marry
both the conservative – conserving the gains of the past – and
radical. But what does it mean to be radical? 'Radical' comes from
a Latin word meaning 'root'. A radical has the root of the past in
him yet looks for the root bear fruit now. He or she demands that
implications become applications.

Jesus was both conservative and radical. He said: 'You have heard
that it was said to the people long ago… but I tell you' (Matt. 5:21–22).
He took the best of the past and applied it in ways
that astonished those who heard Him. One person
has said: 'The past married to the future brings forth
the living present.' Conservatism or radicalism alone
bring forth nothing – nothing but controversy or
conjecture; married they can bring forth progress.

What are some of the areas in which we need to
be more radical? First, in the way we love. We talk
a good deal about love in the Church, but how effective are we at
actually demonstrating it every day? Our text tells us that Jesus,
'having loved his own… now showed them the full extent of his
love.' This demonstration of love was the greatest thing He had
done in His life, and it would be the last thing He would do in death.
There is nothing greater in life or death than to love. As Christians
we need to learn to be a lot more loving if we are to demonstrate to
people that Jesus is the One they need. It is time to show the world
the full extent of Jesus' love. 'By this all men will know that you
are my disciples,' said Jesus (John 13:35). Not 'If you fill stadiums
with a hundred thousand people,' but 'If you love one another'.

FURTHER STUDY

John 13:34-35;
1 John 3:11-18

1. What is
Jesus' new
commandment?

2. How can we
emulate Jesus?

**Father, forgive us we pray for talking about love and not showing it.
Help us to be more radical. Help us show the world the full extent of
our love – Your love. In Jesus' name. Amen.**

Putting others first

For reading & meditation – John 19:25–37

'Later, knowing that all was now completed...
Jesus said, "I am thirsty."' (v28)

We continue thinking about the need to be more radical in our loving. The one thing above all others that arrested the attention of unbelievers in the first centuries after Christ was the way Christians loved.

The Letter to Diognetus, written to explain the Christian faith to a serious enquirer, probably in the second century, says: 'These Christians know and trust God... They placate those who oppress them and make them their friends, they do good to their enemies. Their wives are absolutely pure and their daughters modest. Their men abstain from all unlawful marriage and from all impurity. If they see a stranger they take him to their dwellings and rejoice over him as a real brother. Oh how they love one another. Truly this is a new people and there is something divine in them.' This is the kind of love that will capture people's attention.

FURTHER STUDY

Rom. 5:6–8;
1 John 4:7–21

1. How and why
   did God put
   others first?

2. How do we
   prove our love
   for God?

The most effective question I have found to ascertain whether or not I am loving is to ask myself: Do I put the needs of others on the same level as my own? In the passage before us today we read that as Jesus was hanging on the cross and, 'knowing that all was now completed... [He] said, "I am thirsty."' After He had done all He could for others He thought of His own needs. We do things differently more often than not. First we quench our own thirst, then think of others. It's time for a radical rethink of our Christian commitment if we are to make an impact on the world at large. You and I need to go over our lives and consider how well we love. The times are crying out not just for love, but for a radical love.

Father, forgive us that so often our love is measured out in thimblefuls when it can be flowing from us in rivers. Stir me up, dear Lord, so that I might be more radical in my loving. In Jesus' name I pray. Amen.

Harmony-unity

For reading & meditation – John 17:20–26

'I have given them the glory that you gave me, that they
may be one as we are one' (v22)

Another area that calls for radicalism is that of Christian unity.
In a fractured world hungry for unity, Christians will have
little respect unless they can demonstrate unity. Though there are
signs that attitudes among Christians are changing, we have a long
way to go if we are to see fulfilled the prayer of Jesus that we have
read today. Contemporary Christian churches sadly at times seem
to be better at demonstrating disunity than unity.

Does this mean that we must dismantle our denominational
structures and all come together under one banner?
Not necessarily. Personally, I wish there were no
denominations, but I am not convinced that God
wants to take people out of their denomination. We
can still demonstrate unity even though we stay in our
different denominations or groups. To enjoy fellowship
in the home we do not make it a prerequisite that we
agree in everything. The home can be a place of unity
in spite of differences in temperament, style and belief.
The one thing that binds a family together, and keeps
them together when they have differences, is the fact that they
belong to each other. We need our differences as growing points.

When I was in India I learned that the music of the Hindus is
based on melody, not harmony – as is Western music. A Hindu
hearing a group singing the most marvellous close part harmony,
said: 'What a pity they can't all sing the same tune.' Had they done
so it wouldn't have been harmony. We will never achieve melody-
unity in Church unity for we cannot all sing the same part, but we
can have harmony-unity – and that will be far richer.

FURTHER STUDY

Judg. 20:1-11;
1 Cor. 1:10-17

1. What
happened when
the different
tribes came
together?

2. What was
Paul's appeal?

**Father, I see it is time for a radical shift in the way we relate to one
another. Forgive us for the way we have fragmented Your image in
this world. May Your prayer for oneness be fulfilled
in the coming days. Amen.**

Christ's 'say so'

For reading & meditation – Luke 5:1–11
'because you say so, I will let down the nets.' (v5)

We are seeing that we need to be radical in our loving, and in demonstrating Christian unity, but we also need to learn to be radical in obedience. When the disciples returned from a fruitless all-night fishing expedition on the Sea of Galilee Jesus said: 'Put out into deep water, and let down the nets for a catch.' Surprised, Peter replied: 'Master, we've worked hard all night and haven't caught anything. But because you say so, I will let down the nets.'

'Because you say so.' Could fewer words sum up a true Christian response? Down the ages men and women have put out into deep water on no other basis than Jesus' say so. Nothing has been so utterly tested in history as Jesus' rightness. He has been right in everything, and when we act on His say so then His directions are proved to be right.

FURTHER STUDY

Luke 6:46-48;
Acts 9:10-18

1. How do we know if Christ is our Lord?

2. Why did Ananias question God's instructions?

Simon Peter was half filled with doubt when Jesus told him to let down his nets once again, but he did so anyway. Notice the words 'I will'. Many times we say: 'Because You say so, I will think about it.' Or: 'Because You say so, I will keep it on hold until I feel like it.' I am convinced that there are a million projects not being launched – Christian projects, that is – that God wants done because His people do not act upon His say so. Perhaps God has been speaking to you about launching some venture for Him and, although you are sure of His say so, you have not done anything about it. Maybe He wants you to embark on something in your local community, to meet a social need, start a Bible study group in your home or work with young people. Whatever He says to you, do it.

Father, forgive me if things are not being done that You want done because I am not radical enough in my obedience. Speak to me again. Let me hear Your 'say so'. This time I promise I will obey. In Jesus' name. Amen.

Radical repentance

For reading & meditation – 2 Corinthians 5:11–6:2

'We implore you on Christ's behalf: Be reconciled to God.'
(v20)

Listen once more to the text at the top of the page: 'We implore you on Christ's behalf: Be reconciled to God.' How familiar that text sounds because of its use when speaking to non-Christians. But it is a sad fact that today's text was not addressed to the unconverted; it was written to the converted. Notice the use of the word 'we' all through the passage as Paul identifies with the people to whom he is writing. Notice also that he says: 'As God's fellow-workers we urge you not to receive God's grace in vain' (6:1). It was to fellow-workers who had received the grace of God that the plea to be reconciled to God was given. Paul was not talking about an initial reconciliation (the recipients of his letter had already experienced that), but a continuous reconciliation.

Some say: 'I was reconciled to God 20 years ago when I first became a Christian.' My question to them is this: 'But are you reconciled to God now?' How many of us can say with our hands on our hearts that self-will has not crept in and diminished our eagerness to do God's will? Or that we have never lost our first love? We need to go over our lives to see if there are any parts not reconciled to God. Always, the way back to God is through a radical repentance – repentance that goes to the roots. Here again people say: 'I repented when I first came to Christ.' But repentance must be continuous. Martin Luther once stated: 'The entire life of the believer should be one of repentance.' Scarcely anything is more essential in the Church today than that Christians be aware of the need to be continuously reconciled to God.

FURTHER STUDY

2 Sam.
11:26–12:13;
1 John 1:5–2:1

1. Why did King David need to be reconciled to God?

2. What does John explain?

Father, help me I pray to keep my accounts with You up to date. Forgive me that I am so quick to err but so slow to repent. Grant me grace not only to hear what You are saying to me now, but to act on it. In Jesus' name. Amen.

Prepared in mind

For reading & meditation – Matthew 22:34–46

'Love the Lord your God with all your heart and with all
your soul and with all your mind.' (v37)

Yet another area that needs a radical approach is that of Christian thought. We can have answers to the complex problems of our society. Jesus is being challenged from all sides – there is no need to bury our heads in the sand and criticise our opponents using the type of put-down suggested by one person: 'Scepticism is the friction of a small brain trying to absorb a great idea.' We can learn how to show that God is big enough and strong enough to meet the world's needs. Today Christians are being equipped to use their minds because our world is thinking its way to a new order. Our faith needs to function in society or it will be discarded as irrelevant.

FURTHER STUDY

Gen. 41:25–43;
Dan. 2:3–6,17

1. How did
Joseph change
his political
world?

2. How did
Daniel combine
natural and
godly wisdom?

What I am now about to suggest will not apply to all, but nevertheless it should be of concern to everyone – if only for prayer. More Christian men and women are called to become involved in science, psychology, politics and so on, so that they can stand alongside their peers and present a Christian world-view based on His Word. Although we recognise the impact that the miraculous can make through the ministry of the Holy Spirit, we also see that this is not time for ignorant piety. The world suffers as much from wrong ideas as it does from wrong wills. Christians can learn to think straight and think biblically, and bring their knowledge and understanding to bear on world situations.

Jesus spoke of loving God with the mind – He added on His own accord to the quotation from Deuteronomy (6:5). That clause might have sounded radical when He added it, but He must have seen it as important.

**My Father and my God, help us to love You not only with our hearts
and souls but also with our minds. Save our minds from stagnation.
Help us to think biblically about everything.
To the glory of Your precious name. Amen.**

Radical evangelism

For reading & meditation – Mark 16:9–20

'He said to them, "Go into all the world and preach the
good news to all creation."' (v15)

Evangelism is another area of Christian activity where we need
to be more radical. Christianity is catching, and if people don't
catch if from us then perhaps we are not sufficiently contagious.
It is a law of the personality that that which is not expressed
soon dies. If our faith is not being expressed in evangelism then
it could soon die within us.

But it is clear that as well as having a desire to share the faith
there is a need for a great radicalism in evangelism. Displaying a
poster outside a church saying 'Come in and have
your faith lifted' may be commendable, but a much
more positive declaration and demonstration will
be far more effective at meeting the needs of the
age. The majority of people can feel intimidated or
ill at ease when they step inside a church. So we
have to meet them on neutral ground: in concert
halls, theatres, sports stadiums – where they feel
comfortable. The gospel is not intended to make
people feel comfortable, some will argue. Of course it isn't, but
we must start where people are in order to lead them to where they
could be. This is how Jesus talked with the woman at the well. She
was comfortable talking about water, and when Jesus had finished
she found water that was not in the well (John 4:1–29). Evangelism
is not an imposition. A Jewish rabbi said: 'All religions are glad
to have enquirers come to them, but Christianity is different – it
seeks out the lost, it goes to the lowly, the undeserving, the sinful.'
Nothing greater could be said of Christianity, for by doing so it
is following in its founder's footsteps.

FURTHER STUDY

Luke 4:31-40;
5:1; 6:17;
1 Cor. 9:16-23

1. Where did
Jesus minister?

2. What was Paul
compelled to do?

**Father, help us be more radical in our approach to the needs of the
lost. We have delayed this issue for far too long. Give us a sense of
urgency, a sense of holy desperation to reach out and win men and
women for You. Amen.**

Saving the home

For reading & meditation – Romans 12:1–8

'Do not conform any longer to the pattern of this world,
but be transformed by the renewing of your mind.' (v2)

The final area of life we look at that cries out for a radical change is that of marriage and the Christian home. There are of course abusive situations that necessitate action; however far too many Christians follow the world's example and head for the divorce court as soon as their marriage hits trouble. There seems to be a lack of staying power when it comes to dealing with marital and family problems. We need a radical rethink if we are to maintain our integrity before the world. I love the way *The Message* translation puts today's text: 'Don't become so well-adjusted to your culture that you fit into it without even thinking. Instead, fix your attention on God. You'll be changed from the inside out... Unlike the culture around you, always dragging you down to its level of immaturity, God brings the best out of you.' It's time we Christians took those words seriously.

FURTHER STUDY

Col. 3:18–4:1;;2
Tim. 1:1–5

1. What are the
characteristics
of a Christian
home?

2. What was
Timothy's
spiritual
heritage?

And what about our homes? It is a solemn fact that children in the home catch the attitudes of their parents, rather than their words. It was prophesied of John the Baptist that he would turn the hearts of the fathers to the children. Never was such a task more necessary than today. The prodigal son came back because he had a good father. Many a young person holds steady even when doubts hit because of the strong faith of a father or mother.

The Letter to Diognetus, which we referred to earlier also states: 'The Christians hold the world together.' But we can never hold the world together unless we can hold the home together. The home is being assailed from many directions. Only radical living can save it.

**God, help us kindle in our homes a flame of pure living from which
our young ones will be able to light a torch that will never go out.
Save our homes and make them embassies of heaven.
In Jesus' name I pray. Amen.**

An unshakeable kingdom

For reading & meditation – Hebrews 12:14–29

'Therefore, since we are receiving a kingdom that cannot
be shaken, let us be thankful' (v28)

Today we end our meditations on the theme of being prepared
and preparing the way for the King. We began by asking the
question: Was there ever a time in history that needed 'a people
prepared' as much as we do now? We need to be witnesses in a
world of change, a world seeking new moorings, feeling after a new
order. We asked, too: What kind of men and women are 'a people
prepared'? John the Baptist was strong in three areas: towards God,
himself and others. Let us be strong in these three areas too, and
we likewise will be able to prepare the way.

As we mentioned yesterday, The Letter to
Diognetus commented that Christians 'hold the
world together'. This letter was written at a time
when the social order was disintegrating. It was
evident to those around them that Christians did
not belong to that decaying order; they belonged to
the indestructible order, the unshakeable kingdom.
Therefore they held the world together by their faith.
They did then, and we must do so now. We can prevent society and
individuals from falling apart by our commitment to Jesus, our
faith and ever deepening experience of God.

'The Christian,' said George Macdonald 'is the emergence of a
new type of individual as different from ordinary humanity as
ordinary humanity is different from an animal.' That is what
this world, standing as it does in the midst of change and turmoil,
needs to see – a new type of individual confident in their God and
their part in His plan. Arise, then, men and women of God. A new
day and new order awaits you. Go with confidence into the world.

FURTHER STUDY

1 Pet. 3:8-16;
2 Cor. 5:16-21

1. How can we
be a people
prepared?

2. Is a Christian
a new person or
a new creation?

**God, make us worthy of the inheritance that has been passed on to
us. And help us pass on that inheritance to others –undimmed and
untarnished. Prepare us so that we might prepare others.
In Jesus' name. Amen.**

The Call

A fan or a follower?

For reading & meditation – John 8:12–30
'Jesus… said, "I am the light of the world."' (v12)

The theme for this issue has been prompted by the concern that many Christians can settle for having their sins forgiven and the assurance of heaven when they die, rather than responding to Jesus' call to be a disciple – a people who follow in the steps of their Master, learn His ways and live His lifestyle. Church leaders attribute this trend to a failure to make clear to people what might be involved in following Jesus.

A large proportion of people new to faith, it seems, are being attracted to Jesus because of what He can do for them and they appear to have little interest in or understanding of what they might do for Him. One observer of contemporary church life says, 'Many of today's converts appear to follow Christ for the same reason they frequent their favourite restaurant: they both give them what they want. They love Jesus the same way they love the restaurant.'

Jesus came to give us life, but there is something else: He calls us on a lifelong apprenticeship as a disciple – total commitment to Him and His cause. When we try to fit Jesus around our lives rather than our lives around Him, then whatever we may choose to call ourselves we cannot truly call ourselves 'disciples'. One church leader says this: 'The Saviour is not looking for fans but followers – followers who will go with Him to death if necessary.' Those who put their own concerns before Christ may consider themselves to be His followers but in truth they could be following another gospel.

FURTHER STUDY

Acts 2:42–47;
Gal. 1:11–17;
2:15–21

1. How did the believers demonstrate their commitment to the gospel?

2. Put into your own words Paul's commitment to Christ.

**My Father and my God, my heart desires more than anything to be taken deeper into You. Help me understand all that is involved in following Your Son. Make me a true disciple.
In Jesus' name. Amen.**

Perspective matters

For reading & meditation – Luke 6:43–49

'Why do you call me, "Lord, Lord," and do not do what I say?' (v46)

Yesterday we began reflecting on the tendency to be attracted to Jesus because of what He can do for us, and the challenges in considering the implications and impact upon the lives of those He calls to follow Him. In the passage before us today, Jesus makes clear for His listeners that He anticipates more from His followers than mere lip-service. The person who says, 'Lord, Lord' but fails to do what He asks is like a man who built a house on ground without first digging foundations, says the Saviour.

FURTHER STUDY

Rom. 10:9-13;
2 Cor. 8:6-12

1. Why is it necessary to confess Jesus as Lord?

2. What perspective on giving did Paul encourage?

When I was a young man I would often hear these words: 'If you do not crown Him Lord of all, you do not crown Him Lord at all.' It is a succinct way of highlighting that unless we see our relationship to Jesus Christ as being one of commitment and trust to whatever He calls us to do and are willing to follow Him wherever He takes us, we are not really His followers at all. Our churches are filled with people who claim to be Christians yet are more concerned with pleasing themselves than pleasing the God.

A church leader reported that while he was talking to a new Christian who wanted to become a member of his church, he asked him how he was finding things in his new life. 'Fine,' said the convert, 'but I still can't come to terms with the things I have to give up.' 'Stop thinking about the things you have to give up,' said the pastor, 'and think of what Christ gave up for you.' The new Christian was stunned by this rather direct response, but it gave him a completely new perspective on the Christian life and gave him a wonderful release in his soul.

Lord God, please enable me to have the right perspective on everything. Help me to focus more on what You gave up for me and less on what I am required to give up for You. Amen.

The elements of discipleship

For reading & meditation – John 1:35–51

'Come... and you will see.' (v39)

Considering the word 'disciple' and the contexts in which Jesus used it will help us to more clearly understand what life is like for those who respond to His call. These meditations are devoted to examining day by day the many statements Jesus made concerning discipleship. To be a 'disciple' is to be a learner; a follower.

Interestingly, in today's reading all the main elements of what it means to be a learner, follower and trained one of Jesus are to be seen in concentrated form. John the Baptist says to two of his disciples, 'Look, the Lamb of God!' (v35). This was the language of spiritual insight and it caused John's disciples to move their allegiance from him to Jesus. The amazing adventure of discipleship begins when we 'look' in faith to Jesus who, like the lamb in the Old Testament sacrificial system, died as our sinless substitute. And when we truly hear that call to follow Him there is an inner response from our hearts and, like Nathanael, we recognise that Jesus is our true King (v49).

So often the discipleship lifestyle is punctuated by being stopped in our tracks by Jesus, resulting in us experiencing an inward and an outward change. Jesus, for example, foretold the change that would take place in the life of Simon, Andrew's brother, when He gave him a new name which means 'rock': 'You are Simon... You will be called Cephas (which... is Peter)' (v42). Discipleship involves trusting in Christ's redemptive sacrifice, hearing His personal call, submitting to His kingly authority and experiencing an inward change. This is the true disciple's choice.

FURTHER STUDY

1 Pet. 1:13–21;
Rev. 14:1–5

1. What does Peter say discipleship involves?

2. What vision does John have of those who follow the Lamb?

Lord Jesus Christ, words are inadequate to describe how grateful I am for the times when You stop me in my tracks and call me to follow You. Help me to keep following You no matter where You take me. Amen.

The call

For reading & meditation – Mark 1:14–20

'At once they left their nets and followed him.' (v18)

Yesterday we looked at a significant passage in which we saw Jesus calling to Him some of His first disciples. Over the next few days we shall look at similar passages, and by doing so we will profit from considering what Bible teachers describe as 'the law of first mention'. According to this principle, whenever you begin to study a topic or theme in Scripture you concentrate on the first occasion the subject is mentioned. This provides a good and reliable guide for understanding its true meaning and context.

FURTHER STUDY

Rom. 1:1–7;
1 Cor. 1:1–9

1. How does
Paul view his
own calling?

2. How were
the Corinthians
to view their
calling?

The passage before us today shows how four Galilean men became Jesus' disciples as a direct result of His call. Interestingly, in ancient times it was common for would-be disciples to seek out their own masters and teachers. Jesus, however, took the initiative in summoning people to follow Him. Over and over again in the New Testament the idea is laid down that Christ's followers are people who are called. 'Brothers,' says the apostle Paul in 1 Corinthians 1:26, 'think of what you were when you were called.' We often refer to the fact that we chose Christ, and in a sense that is perfectly true. But we ought never forget that the reason we called out to Him was because He first called out to us.

Christ's call, we note, overrides convention and custom, family obligations and business commitments. The sons of Zebedee left their father, their boats, and their business and, together with Simon and Andrew, set out to follow Jesus. His call upset their fishing careers but they went with Him to fish in larger waters and for a more important catch – people.

Lord Jesus, I realise that had You not called out to me I would never have called out to You. I think of what I was when I was called and what I am now. The difference is all because of You, Lord Jesus. And I am so grateful. Amen.

Adherents not admirers

For reading & meditation – Matthew 4:18–22

'At once they left their nets and followed him.' (v20)

This passage, a parallel to the one we looked at yesterday, brings home even more forcibly the truth that when Jesus called Peter, Andrew, James and John they left everything to follow Him. The great preacher P.T. Forsyth made the comment, slightly tongue-in-cheek no doubt, that 'Christ ruined many careers.' Yet, in reality, if we were able to speak to those whose careers Christ 'ruined' (such as Dr Martyn Lloyd Jones, who left a promising career in medicine to become a preacher), they would tell you that their careers were not so much ruined as redirected. It has to be said, of course, that Jesus does not call everyone to change his or her career. However, if He has other plans for us or if our work involves us contravening biblical principles, then He will ask us to change our job.

Jesus is not looking for admirers but adherents – not sympathisers, but men and women committed to His direction and calling. In the case of the four Galilean fishermen, it is clear that there was something so compelling about the Master that when He called them they did not hesitate to leave everything and follow Him.

Permit a personal question: would you be willing to give up everything in response to Christ's call? As I once heard it put, 'Christ does not ask everyone to give up everything for Him but He does expect them to be willing to give up everything.' Jesus has always been clear, from the very beginning, concerning the cost of discipleship. So we too as His ambassadors and representatives need also to be clear about what it means to follow Him. Jesus never misled people when He called them to faith in Him. Neither must we.

FURTHER STUDY

Acts 4:32–37;
Phil. 3:3–11

1. What were the early believers prepared to give up?

2. What did the apostle Paul give up?

**My Father and my God, help me, I pray, not to hold anything back or withdraw from any commitment I have made. I long to fully trust You, be fully surrendered to You and be fully Yours.
In Jesus' name. Amen.**

Newness – a must

For reading & meditation – Luke 5:1–11

'Simon Peter... fell at Jesus' knees and said,
"Go away from me, Lord; I am a sinful man!"' (v8)

Luke's account of Jesus' calling of the disciples focuses mainly on Simon Peter. Picture the scene with me. The Saviour had been speaking by the Sea of Galilee. As the crowd pressed towards Him, eager to hear His words of wisdom, He got into Simon Peter's boat, sat down, and continued teaching. When He finished He turned to Peter and said, 'Put out into deep water, and let down the nets for a catch' (v4). That must have struck Peter as rather odd, don't you think, especially as Jesus' trade was carpentry, not fishing? Peter explained that he had fished all night and caught nothing but, at Jesus' command, he did not hesitate to do as he had been told. Instantly, the fish that had been eluding him all night suddenly filled his nets, so much so that the nets began to break. Clearly this was something beyond the ordinary. Simon Peter had witnessed an amazing miracle.

And what was his response? He turned to Jesus and said, 'Go away from me, Lord; I am a sinful man!' There was something about Jesus' moral majesty that revealed, by contrast, the guilt and sin in Simon Peter's heart. Doubtless it dawned upon him that contact with Jesus means that one does not stay the same person but begins on a new path. Something radical took place in the heart of Simon Peter that moment which led him from fishing in the comparative isolation of the Sea of Galilee to fishing for people in the ocean of the world. That call to discipleship involves newness – becoming a new person and walking a new path.

FURTHER STUDY

Acts 5:17-21,
27-32;
Rom. 6:1-7;
7:4-6;
2 Cor. 5:14-21

1. What is Peter's message of this new life?

2. Where does Paul say this newness comes from?

Lord Jesus, how can I thank You enough for making me a new person, giving me a new nature and promising that one day I will even have a new name? I am grateful beyond words. Amen.

A taxman's transformation

For reading & meditation – Mark 2:13–17

'"Follow me," Jesus told him, and Levi got up
and followed him.' (v14)

Taxmen are often characterised as some of the most unpopular
people on earth. All the more so in the time of Jesus. Levi, the tax
gatherer, put himself in a strategic spot in Capernaum so as to collect
the taxes of those going to and from Galilee. Capernaum was the
crossing point between the territory governed by Antipas and that
governed by one of Herod the Great's other sons – Philip. Missing
no opportunity to raise revenues, these local lords, backed by the
occupying Romans, exacted tolls on anyone entering their domain.

Tax collectors were the victims of much abuse
and were used to people either shouting at them or
cursing them as they grudgingly paid their taxes.
One day Jesus came along, stopped at Levi's booth,
looked him in the eyes and simply said, 'Follow me.'
Immediately he got up and followed Jesus. What
happened to the money he had collected? Who would
replace him? Was he under contract? These questions
lie unanswered. We can be sure, however, that Jesus would not
have encouraged Levi to do anything inappropriate or irresponsible.

FURTHER STUDY

Acts 16:22-34;
1 Tim. 1:12-17

1. Why was the
Philippian jailer
filled with joy?

2. Why was Paul
so grateful?

Once again this example highlights that when Jesus calls He
anticipates a response of a life given in relationship and trust.
Dietrich Bonhoeffer, the German pastor who was executed by the
Nazis just before the end of World War II, said, 'Had Levi stayed at
his post, Jesus would have been his present help in time of trouble,
but not the Lord of his whole life.' Levi sensed that he was being
called by a higher authority than Antipas and a greater king than
Caesar. He might have been unpopular with the people but Jesus
called him to be one of His disciples.

**Jesus, how glad I am that Your call came also to me. It was a call
that overwhelmed all my suspicions and conquered my heart's
antipathy. Again I am truly grateful. Eternally grateful. Amen.**

Jesus – boundary breaker

For reading & meditation – Matthew 9:9–13

'the Pharisees... asked his disciples, "Why does your teacher eat with tax collectors and 'sinners'?"' (v11)

We reflect on the call of Levi, or Matthew, again today because Matthew's Gospel brings out a particular emphasis not found in Mark's account. We are told that Jesus had dinner at Matthew's house in company with 'many tax collectors and "sinners"' (v10). Tax collectors were regarded by most people in Israel as the dregs of society because they colluded with the Romans. But what does the term 'sinners' mean in this passage? It is generally thought that here 'sinners' is used of a special class of

FURTHER STUDY
Jer. 7:1-11;
1 John 1:5-10
1. Who did Jeremiah say was acceptable to God?
2. What is given to those who acknowledge their sin?

people in Israel who had gone outside the acceptable boundaries of the Jewish religion. They had either failed or refused to practise the rituals of the Jewish faith. When Jesus sat down with such 'sinners' He was heavily criticised by the Pharisees, for they were keen to restore Israel to what they believed to be the true standards of Old Testament teaching. In doing so, the circle of who was accepted as a genuine member of God's covenant people became tighter and tighter with many excluded.

Jesus, however, was a 'boundary breaker'. His way of restoring the nation of Israel spiritually was to start with those who heeded His call and committed themselves to Him. When Jesus was alerted to what the Pharisees were saying about Him He declared, 'It is not the healthy who need a doctor, but the sick' (v12). The Pharisees were in the same condition as the taxmen and 'sinners' when it came to the matter of the heart. It is sad that they failed to recognise that fact, for we can change only that which we acknowledge.

My Father and my God, how thankful I am that You have sought me out even in my 'sinfulness'. This has led to such great changes in my life. All honour and glory be to Your peerless and precious name. Amen.

Why twelve?

For reading & meditation – Matthew 10:1-4

'He called his twelve disciples to him and gave them
authority to drive out evil spirits and to heal' (v1)

Jesus, as we know, gathered the Twelve around Him to be His first
disciples. We do not have the details of how every single one
was called, but there can be little doubt that each was personally
sought out and called by Jesus.

Why twelve diesciples? The number twelve would have carried
for the Jews of Jesus' day a special significance. They would have
known that the nation of Israel had been born of twelve tribes,
and so thoughtful Israelites would not have been left in doubt
as to the importance of Christ's selection of twelve
men to form His ministry team. He was symbolically
reassigning the leadership of the people of God to
artisans and fishermen!

What an outstanding act of authority this was.
Those who had the insight to see the Saviour's
strategy must have been astonished by it. The Twelve
had been chosen to form the nucleus of a new and
restored people of God. Who but God could do such
a thing? Later these ordinary men chosen by Jesus
to be His disciples became apostles and helped to
lay down the doctrinal foundation on which the Church of Jesus
Christ was built and on which a whole new covenant family was
created. The Twelve had a mixture of personalities and at times
their temperaments clashed. Yet ultimately, under Jesus' masterly
supervision and guidance, and with one sad exception, all of them
became the men God intended them to be. One has only to think,
as an example, of how volatile, unpredictable Peter became a solid
rock in the early Church.

FURTHER STUDY

Eph. 2:12-22;
Rev. 21:5-14

1. Who make up
the members
of God's
household?

2. How does
John describe
the holy city,
Jerusalem?

**Lord Jesus, how wonderful it is that You gather men and women
with so many differences of personality and temperament and they
become followers with one purpose. I count myself happy to be
among them. Thank You, dear Saviour. Amen.**

Plugged into truth

For reading & meditation – John 6:60–71

'On hearing it, many of his disciples said,
"This is a hard teaching. Who can accept it?"' (v60)

W e move on now to consider Jesus' approach to those outside
of the Twelve whom He also called to become His followers.
It seems clear from the Gospels that many were attracted to
Jesus not just because of His words but also because of His ability
to work miracles. No doubt the miracle recorded in the earlier
part of John 6 – the feeding of the five thousand – led many to
possibly think: if we follow this man He can give us bread and
we will not have to work for it. If this was the kind of thinking

FURTHER STUDY

Phil. 4:14-20;
3 John 1-12

1. For what
commitment
does Paul
commend the
Philippians?

2. In what ways
is Gaius plugged
into the truth?

going on in people's minds you can be sure that Jesus
was well aware of it. That is probably why He would
often prick the bubble of applause with statements
intended to cause people to consider carefully what
it meant to follow Him. News of the miracle of the
feeding of the five thousand spread like wildfire, and
in the passage before us now we hear Jesus saying
some challenging things to the people, so much so
that we read: 'From this time many of his disciples
turned back and no longer followed him' (v66).

One thing is clear about His approach to recruiting
His followers: He never sold them short. The Saviour always told it
as it was. Jesus was well aware that there were many fair-weather
followers in the crowds that gathered to listen to Him, who wanted
to see what they could get rather than what they could give. Few
were willing to enter into a long-term commitment to Him and put
Him before everyone and everything. It is one thing to be caught
up with the electric atmosphere that surrounds Jesus but it's quite
another to be plugged into the truth.

**Gracious God and loving heavenly Father, save me, I pray, from
becoming a fair-weather follower of Your Son. If You are calling me
to a deeper commitment, then help me respond to that challenge.
In Jesus' name I pray. Amen.**

A true follower's heartbeat

For reading & meditation – John 2:12–25

'But Jesus would not entrust himself to them,
for he knew all men.' (v24)

Yesterday we explored how Jesus knew in His heart that some were drawn to Him not because of His message but because of His miracles. This is made clear in the passage before us now.

When Jesus came to Jerusalem and saw the Temple being desecrated, He took a whip and drove out the sheep and cattle and overturned the tables of the money-changers. Following that, He continued to stay in Jerusalem and work many miracles. Many, we are told, 'believed in his name' (v23). But then we read these interesting words: 'Jesus would not entrust himself to them, for he knew all men.' The Saviour knew full well how fragile was the people's interest in Him and how changeable were their feelings. He saw deep into the human heart and was completely aware that the admiration of the crowd and celebrity status they gave Him could quickly change. It may not have been the same crowd that later in His life cried for Him to be crucified but it was the same human nature. People are perfectly capable of wanting to give Christ a crown today and a cross tomorrow.

FURTHER STUDY

John 6:60–71;
Acts
8:9–13,18–23

1. Why did some disciples desert Jesus and others not?

2. What was wrong with Simon's response?

Just as in New Testament times, so now there are those who join the Church in the hope that their needs will be met by Christ – for increased finances, for healing, or for employment. Then, when things don't go the way they expect, they turn away from Him. Jesus may well answer prayers of people for the things we have mentioned (and often does) but the heartbeat of Jesus' true followers is a relationship that is not dependent on Him meeting our expectations, but one that seeks to meet His.

Lord Jesus, forgive me if I regard my expectations of You as being more important than Your expectations of me. I know You delight in answering prayer but not always in the way I expect. Help me to accept that – to trust You no matter what. Amen.

Counting the cost

For reading & meditation – Matthew 8:18–22

'Foxes have holes and birds of the air have nests, but the Son of Man has nowhere to lay his head.' (v20)

Even the most casual reader of the Gospels cannot help but notice that Jesus never missed an opportunity to make clear to people the cost of being one of His disciples. The Saviour never disguised the fact that there is a price to be paid if we follow Him.

In today's passage Jesus makes clear to a would-be disciple the possible cost to be considered in following Him. Any evangelism that plays down the cost of discipleship betrays Jesus. Dietrich Bonhoeffer called this 'cheap grace'. We cannot smooth away the rough edges of the cross for the sake of gaining easy converts. Nor can we attempt a road-widening scheme on the 'narrow… road that leads to life' (Matt. 7:14) in order to make the gospel more accessible to people of any generation. Discipleship is always on His terms, not ours.

FURTHER STUDY

John
3:1-10,16-18;
21:18-19;
Acts 9:11-19

1. What terms of discipleship did Jesus spell out for Nicodemus?

2. What cost did both Peter and Paul face?

Sometimes the gospel is presented in our churches in ways that remind one of a free trip to Disneyland. 'Come to Jesus', certain preachers say, 'and all your troubles will be over.' Really? Many find that when they come to Jesus they have more troubles than they had before. A large number of Christians will tell you that when they became believers they found that their families and friends ignored them; they were ridiculed and in some cases disinherited for the sake of the gospel. Some have even found misunderstanding in their closest relationships because of their commitment to the Saviour. It is always best in the long run to make clear to new Christians that there is a cost to knowing Jesus.

Gracious God, forgive us that so often in our eagerness to win people to You we hype up Your gospel and sugar-coat its costs. Help us be honest in everything we do for You, especially our evangelism. In Jesus' name. Amen.

'Evanjellybabies'

For reading & meditation – Luke 9:57–62

'No-one who puts his hand to the plough and looks back is fit for service in the kingdom of God.' (v62)

This passage presents even more clearly the need for honesty when sharing with people what is involved in following Christ. The account shows us three men who wanted to follow Jesus. Eugene Peterson, in *The Message*, captures the force of what Jesus had to say to each of them. To the man who said, 'I will follow you wherever you go,' He gave this somewhat blunt reply: 'Are you ready to rough it? We're not staying in the best inns, you know.' To the man who claimed he had to first go and bury his father Jesus said, 'First things first. Your business is life, not death. And life is urgent: Announce God's kingdom!' And to the man who said that he had to straighten things out at home before committing himself to becoming a disciple Jesus said, 'No procrastination. No backward looks. You can't put God's kingdom off till tomorrow. Seize the day.'

Significantly, Luke notes that this happened 'as they were walking along the road' (v57). The road on which they were walking led to Jerusalem – the place where Jesus would be put to death. To follow Him on that road is not always a rosy prospect. One church leader said that if we were as honest as Jesus was when presenting the gospel and made clear the cost of discipleship, we might well have fewer converts but the ones we had would be true disciples. Much of today's evangelism softens the cost of answering His call, of sugar-coating the gospel to make it more palatable. Someone has described this as 'evanjellyism' which produces only 'evanjellybabies' – people who bend easily in the moment of testing.

FURTHER STUDY

Acts 9:19–28;
Col. 3:1–10

1. In what ways did Saul seize the day?

2. How did Paul exhort the Colossians to put first things first?

Lord Jesus, while we can never accuse You of mis-selling the gospel, sometimes in our eagerness to win people to You we come very close to doing that. Help us be clear and balanced when calling people to commitment. Amen.

A dawn but no sunset

For reading & meditation – Mark 2:18–22

'How can the guests of the bridegroom fast while he is with them? They cannot' (v19)

The people who questioned Jesus about fasting must have been quite surprised by His answer, especially if they were of the religiously legalistic type. Eugene Peterson paraphrases Jesus' reply in this way: 'When you're celebrating a wedding, you don't skimp on the cake and wine. You feast. Later you may need to pull in your belt, but not now. As long as the bride and groom are with you, you have a good time.' On the surface Jesus' words appear to disparage the practice of fasting, but we know from other statements He made (Matt. 6:17, for example) this was not so. John's disciples may have been fasting as an expression of repentance intended to hasten the coming of the Messiah, whereas the Pharisees often fasted in order to impress people.

FURTHER STUDY

Rom. 14:16–17;
Phil. 1:3–11,14–19;
1 Pet. 1:1–9

1. What made Paul rejoice?

2. What gives joy to those who believe?

Jesus explained that in His Person the kingdom of God was already present, and the image He chose to illustrate that a Jewish wedding – an event that sometimes lasted a whole week and was always full of joy. I believe He is saying that fasting is not appropriate when the circumstances call for feasting. And you can't easily mix the old with the new either. If you sew a patch of new fabric onto old cloth to cover a hole, the fabric will shrink and tear away, making matters worse.

Jesus used these figures of speech to show that His coming to this world was a time for breaking with the old and ushering in the new. When the sun comes up, what need is there of candles? To be a disciple of Jesus is to be part of a dawn which will never end in a sunset. Hallelujah!

Lord Jesus, once again, I thank You that You have called me to participate in this revolution which You brought to the world. My gratitude is Yours for ever. Amen.

Not a spectator sport!

For reading & meditation – Matthew 9:35–38

'Jesus went through all the towns and villages, teaching in their synagogues, preaching the good news' (v35)

What an amazing time it must have been when Jesus was here on earth and the first waves of the kingdom of God broke upon the shores of this tired world. Good news, never before heralded, is brought to weary and disconsolate men and women. Sickness and disease gives way to the power that flows from God to the infirm and afflicted. Today's passage, brief though it is, records how God's truth was preached with heart-stopping authority.

To be called by Jesus is far more than to be someone who has made 'a decision for Christ' or been 'smitten with religion'; a disciple is someone who has become involved in a glorious revolution. In the words of theologians Glen Stassen and David Gushee: 'Jesus taught that as His disciples obey Him and practice what He taught and lived, they participate in the reign of God that Jesus inaugurated during His earthly ministry, and that will reach its climax when He comes again.' Even though we are not literally walking with Jesus in the way the first disciples did, it remains true that Christians are being used to bring God's saving rule to the world.

FURTHER STUDY

Luke 10:1-11;
Acts 14:1-4,8-17

1. How did Jesus' disciples participate in the reign of God?

2. How were Paul and Barnabas caught up in God's plans?

Discipleship is not a spectator sport! We become caught up in the feelings and desires that flow through the heart of the Trinity. We long that lost sheep will find the Shepherd; that workers will be sent into the harvest; that injustice will be put right. Sharing the compassion of God, we find that not only do our hearts ache over a lost world but that He works through us to make us part of the answer.

Lord Jesus Christ, the more I realise that I am a participant in Your plan to bring Your saving rule to the world, the more my heart yearns to show its gratitude. May I do so not only with my lips but also with my life. For Your name's sake. Amen.

'Under instruction'

For reading & meditation – Matthew 10:5-25

'A student is not above his teacher, nor a servant above his master.' (v24)

I n the chapter before us today Jesus spelt out in the clearest fashion His expectations of those who have chosen to follow Him. As He sent out the Twelve, He gave them instructions on how to represent Him and His kingdom before the people they would meet. In today's text, He makes clear that a student is not above his teacher, nor a servant above his master. Disciples need always to remember that this relationship is a permanent state of affairs. We never rise above the Master and Teacher so as to dictate to Him. In Christ's school of discipleship no one ever graduates with a 'Master's Degree'!

FURTHER STUDY

Acts 14:19-28;
1 Pet. 2:18-25

1. Notice how Paul and Barnabas display long-term commitment.

2. How did Peter encourage slaves to follow in Christ's steps?

When the famous Watchman Nee came to the UK in the 1930s, he was fascinated to see that learner drivers displayed an 'L-plate' on their cars. This conspicuous red letter 'L' on a white background tells everyone that the driver is under instruction. Disciples are always 'under instruction'. At best we can aspire to be like our Master and Teacher; we will most certainly never reach the stage where we no longer need to be instructed by Him.

When disciples become like their Master they may well find themselves being treated as He was. Jesus drew the scorn of those whose godless lifestyle He challenged, and we can expect similar treatment when we do the same. As His disciples, we share His companionship and leadership, and we may also share His fate – rejection, opposition, misunderstanding, ostracism, perhaps even death. No matter what, He will never leave us, and no matter what, may we never leave Him.

Father God, help me understand that to be Your disciple means I am in the faith for the long haul. There is to be no turning back. I'm in this no matter what. I'm Yours all the way. Amen.

No secret disciples

For reading & meditation – Matthew 10:26–32

'There is nothing concealed that will not be disclosed, or
hidden that will not be made known.' (v26)

It is often said that the most frequent exhortation in Scripture
is not 'Do not sin' but 'Do not be afraid'. This is just what Jesus
urged and reminded His disciples in the verses before us today. The
reason He gave, however, seems somewhat strange. 'Nothing will
remain concealed,' He told them, 'but all will be disclosed.' How
was that to help them not to fear?

Jesus was saying that one day everything about Him would be
out in the open and the whole world will know that He is the one
true Lord and Saviour. For that reason alone there is
no need to fear going public now. Jesus does not want
us to be secret disciples. What greater incentive do
we need to live faithfully and fearlessly for Him than
to know we are part of a cause that will ultimately
prevail?

Jesus then went on to warn them that there is
Someone of whom they should be afraid: 'But rather
fear Him who is able to destroy both soul and body
in hell' (v28, NKJV). Commentators differ as to
whether Jesus was talking here about God or the
evil one. However the thrust of the passage implies
that though we may fear the devil in the same way
we exercise caution in crossing a road, the One whom we should
have fear and reverence for is the One who can destroy both
soul and body in hell. Yet, at the same time, for the disciple, this
reverence for God is combined with a trust in a loving Father who
is concerned about the smallest details of our lives.

FURTHER STUDY

Phil. 2:5–11;
1 Pet. 3:8–18;
Rev. 1:4–8

1. What will
happen when
everything
about Jesus is
out in the open?

2. How does
Peter suggest
we overcome
fear?

**Loving Lord, help me absorb this truth that ultimately Your cause
will prevail throughout the whole universe. Nothing is outside
Your love and care, so I need never be afraid of what happens to me.
I am so thankful. Amen.**

'Insider knowledge'

For reading & meditation – Matthew 11:25–27

'you have hidden these things from the wise and learned, and revealed them to little children.' (v25)

Followers of Jesus are the most privileged people in the universe. We are privy to things that others struggle to understand. The Father, we are told, has revealed the mysteries of His kingdom, not to the worldly wise and the intellectually great but to 'little children'. It may not be flattering to be called 'little children' but the fact is that the truths of the kingdom cannot be discovered through intellectual probing alone but by revelation. If they were not revealed to us then we would never understand them, since worldly knowledge and wisdom cannot lead us to them.

FURTHER STUDY

1 Cor. 1:26-31;
2:6-12;
Eph. 3:2-12

1. In whom should we boast and why?

2. What, according to Paul, is hidden and what is revealed?

Those who try to figure out the truth about Jesus and His kingdom simply by using their intellectual ability are unlikely to progress very far. But when they come to Christ in the attitude of childlike trust and receive Him into their hearts as their Saviour, then that humble dependency opens them up to seeing and understanding things they could never glean through intellectual reasoning alone.

Self-assured intellectuals just don't 'get it' when it comes to understanding the things of God. They will never comprehend, without the operation of divine grace on the heart, that this Galilean carpenter, Jesus of Nazareth, is none other than the Son of God to whom God has entrusted 'all things'. As such, He has a unique 'inside knowledge' of His Father which He shares with His disciples. As we said – Jesus' followers are the most privileged people in the universe.

Heavenly Father, there are just not enough words to express my appreciation that you have revealed to me the truths of Your kingdom. Why I should be chosen for this privilege is beyond me. But I shall rejoice in it now and through all eternity. Amen.

Homesickness

For reading & meditation – Matthew 11:28–29

'Come to me, all you who are weary and burdened,
and I will give you rest.' (v28)

Calvin Miller, in his wonderful allegory of Jesus' life entitled The Singer, intriguingly suggests that Jesus was singing a song no one else knew. What was even more shocking was that those who professed to be well versed in the knowledge of God showed no desire at all to learn His tune. Only the 'little ones' – the least, the last, and the lost, the tax collectors and 'sinners', the sick and the poor – seemed to understand the enchanting melodies He sang. And the more they followed Him and listened to Him and felt His loving acceptance, the more they heard in Him the music of eternity.

It is the purpose of God to restore fallen human beings into fellowship with Himself. Someone has commented, 'There is only one sickness – homesickness.' Those outside of the kingdom, whether they realise it or not, are homesick. They have one foot in time and one foot in eternity, and they are not at home in either. In fact, they are afraid of both. They are afraid because they can't put the two together and, in trying to make sense of things, live a restless existence here on earth.

Discipleship may involve laying things down, but we gain something far more valuable through Christ – rest. Those who are prepared to take His yoke upon themselves and join themselves to Him may think they are burdening themselves with religious obligation, but in reality they discover that His yoke is no more a burden than wings are to a bird. When the soul commits itself to God, it finds what it has always longed for – perfect peace and rest.

FURTHER STUDY

Phil. 4:4–9;
1 John 5:1–12

1. How does Paul echo the words of Jesus?

2. How does John highlight the unity of the Father, Son and Spirit?

Father, I am so glad that I have found my way home. But when I realise that there are so many who have not yet found that way, my heart aches. May many this day, all over the world, discover the joy of homecoming. In Jesus' name I pray. Amen.

Breaking more boundaries

For reading & meditation – Luke 8:1–3
'These women were helping to support them out of their own means.' (v3)

Although Jesus called twelve men to be His disciples, He nevertheless readily accepted women into His immediate circle also. In fact, they became His closest friends. Joanna, the wife of Chuza, the manager of Herod's household, was just one of several women who supported His ministry and who almost certainly put both their money and their homes at His disposal. They took enormous social risks in doing this, but doubtless His words had struck home to such a degree that they were willing to give up everything to follow Him.

FURTHER STUDY

Acts 12:5, 11-14;
16:11-15,40;
Rom. 16:1-16

1. What part did women play in the life of the Early Church?

2. For what did Paul commend women in the church at Rome?

Previously we said Jesus was a 'boundary breaker' and this was certainly true in His relationships with women. Of course, He never overstepped the bounds of propriety ordained by God but He did take many cultural risks in breaching social and traditional conventions to display God's respect and concern for women. Israel at that time was a strongly patriarchal society, and even to stop and talk to a woman – as Jesus did with the 'woman at the well' (see John 4) – broke normal conventions. We can well imagine what gossiping tongues said about the fact that Jesus attracted women to His cause. But that did not deter Him. It was right to treat women as equal to men, and Jesus never failed to do that which was right, even when it went completely against the social customs of His day. Over the centuries, the Church, generally speaking, has not earned itself a good record as regards its treatment of women. One thing is certain: it has not got its poor attitude to women from Jesus.

Lord Jesus, help us, we who follow in Your footsteps, to be 'boundary breakers' too. Whenever we come across a custom that clearly is contrary to Your will, give us the courage to do the right thing. Amen.

No greater family

For reading & meditation – Mark 3:31–35

'Whoever does God's will is my brother and sister
and mother.' (v35)

If Jesus' respect for the dignity of women caused some people to be astonished, then His attitude to His own natural family must have produced a similar reaction. In the modern Western world we are used to having our family dispersed, with siblings and children in far-flung places, living independent lives. But in Eastern societies, then as now, things were very different. The family was/is a close-knit unit – an extended group of people of all ages living in close proximity to each other and supporting each other financially and emotionally. To threaten this would cause quite a stir. But here Jesus appears to put the claims of the kingdom before family loyalty. In response to the news that His mother and brothers were outside, Jesus looked around and said to everyone within the sound of His voice: 'Right here, right in front of you – my mother and my brothers. Obedience is thicker than blood' (*The Message*).

This, however, should not be regarded as an attack upon the family. Far from it. Jesus reserved strong words for those who neglected their family obligations under the guise of religious duty. Nevertheless, He was placing the family in the larger context of the claims of God's kingdom. A new day was dawning. No one could escape its challenge by hiding behind domestic conventions. Jesus was creating a new covenant family for His Father, and every allegiance – whether family, tribal or national – takes second place to this. Visit a Christian church anywhere in the world and you will find yourself part of a family.

FURTHER STUDY

Gal. 3:26–29;
Col. 3:11;
1 Pet. 1:22–2:6

1. How does Paul describe God's new covenant family?

2. What kind of family does Peter describe?

My Father and my God, I am so glad that now I am in Christ I belong to everyone else who is in Christ. Though I am thankful for my earthly family, I am even more grateful for the wider family with whom I am destined to spend eternity. Amen.

The point of the parables

For reading & meditation – Mark 4:1-12

'Then Jesus said, "He who has ears to hear, let him hear."'
(v9)

The contrast between Christ's 'little children' and those who think they understand the Christian message by intellect alone becomes apparent once again, as Jesus explained the reason behind His parables to the disciples. What Jesus actually says contradicts the commonly held view that He spoke in parables to make it easy for us to understand the truth. Parables, we are told, are like illustrations preachers use to help make their message clear. But this seems to be the exact opposite of the case as Jesus presents

FURTHER STUDY
2 Sam. 12:1-10,13;
Acts 11:1-12
1. How did Nathan's parable get past David's mental defences?
2. What means did God employ to slip past Peter's defences?

it here. Jesus spoke in parables not to simplify the truth of the kingdom but almost, it seems, to conceal it from those who resisted God's claims upon them. The NIV Study Bible states that the words 'so that' found in verse 12 show 'Jesus likens His preaching in parables to the ministry of Isaiah, which, while it gained some disciples (Isa. 8:16), was also to expose the hard-hearted resistance of the many to God's warning and appeal.' Parables have another purpose also: they are designed to tease, challenge, and get behind our mental defences. They are intended to make us ask 'What does that mean?' or 'What can He be getting at?' or even 'How dare He say that?'

The parables Jesus told were understood only by those who wanted to know the truth. Understanding His illustrations was not so much a matter of the head as of the heart. Eugene Peterson says: 'Parables aren't illustrations that make things easier; they make things harder by requiring the exercise of our imaginations which, if we aren't careful, becomes the exercise of faith.'

My Father and my God, how glad I am that by Your Holy Spirit You found a way to slip past my defences and invade my soul with the truth about Jesus. Now I find myself a new person in a new world. Thank You, my Father. Amen.

A friendly invasion

For reading & meditation – Mark 4:30–34

'He did not say anything to them without using a parable.'
(v34)

There is little doubt that Jesus' favourite way of teaching was through parables. This was because His intention was to be subversive – to overturn people's lives. As they listened to Jesus sharing parables they did not hear any mention of God and so there was no challenge to their own independence. Their defences were relaxed and this allowed His words to enter their hearts. Without them realising it, the parables lodged in their imagination. And then, perhaps weeks, months or even years later, the truth would explode like a time bomb in their unprotected hearts. They would realise that even though Jesus had not specifically mentioned God and the things of the kingdom, this was really what He had been talking about. Those whose hearts were soft towards God no doubt gave themselves deeply to Him, whereas those who resisted His words were being warned that if they persisted in their hard-hearted defiance they were heading for spiritual personal disaster.

FURTHER STUDY

Amos 7:1–13;
Mark 12:1–12;
1 Pet. 2:7–10

1. What reaction did Amos' stories produce?

2. What reaction resulted from Jesus' parable?

Some might regard this as a kind of invasion, but that is not so. 'God's truth is not an alien invasion,' says Eugene Peterson, 'but a loving courtship in which the details of our common lives are treated as seeds in our conception, growth and maturity in the kingdom. Parables trust our imaginations, which is to say, our faith.' Human integrity is preserved because the truth does not overpower the will but rather seeks to overcome it by entreaty and persuasion. If you are a disciple of Jesus, you became one – not because you were overpowered but because you were loved. You are the object of a friendly invasion.

Yes, heavenly Father, yes. I am so grateful for this 'friendly invasion' that brought my soul into living fellowship with You. In You, my Father, I have found everything my heart ever longed for – and more. Amen.

A bigger vision of Jesus

For reading & meditation – Matthew 8:23–27
'You of little faith, why are you so afraid?' (v26)

We come to one of the most important matters for a disciple of Jesus – the nature of faith. While Jesus and His disciples were crossing from one side of the Sea of Galilee to the other, a fierce storm came down on the lake causing the disciples to fear for their lives. Matthew, Mark and Luke each tell the story from their own perspective but all three make it clear that there was great fear in the hearts of every one of the disciples that day. There was not just one storm on Galilee but thirteen – one on the lake and

FURTHER STUDY

Mark 9:2-10;
2 Tim. 1:7-12;
2 Pet. 1:16-21

1. What gave Peter a bigger vision of Jesus?

2. What vision of Jesus did Paul remind Timothy of?

twelve in the hearts of the disciples! Jesus, however, was asleep and apparently unperturbed by what was happening. When He is awakened by the frantic and fearful disciples, His first response is to challenge their 'little faith' and question why they are so afraid. 'Little faith' is what we demonstrate when we are just hanging on by our fingertips. That kind of faith is easily swamped by the waves of doubt and fear.

The degree of our faith is measured by our understanding of the stature of the One in whom we believe. Years ago, J.B. Phillips wrote a book entitled *Your God is Too Small*. It highlights that you will never rise higher in your Christian life than your concept of God. If you have a small concept of God, then your faith will be correspondingly small. The twelve disciples on the lake that day were about to discover the stature of the One they were following. As He rose and commanded the waves to be still, they gained a far bigger vision of His greatness and power. The treatment for 'little faith' is always a bigger vision of Jesus.

Heavenly Father, I see that to grow in faith is not to try to boost my faith through self-effort but to gain a bigger vision of Jesus. Open my eyes, I pray, so that I see even more clearly the majesty of Your beloved Son. Amen.

He cares

For reading & meditation – Mark 4:35–41

'He said to his disciples, "Why are you so afraid? Do you still have no faith?"' (v40)

As we look at another account of the storm on the lake, we notice that Mark places a different emphasis on the conversation between Jesus and His disciples. Whereas Matthew has Jesus saying 'You of little faith,' Mark reports Him as saying, 'Do you still have no faith?' Jesus challenges the disciples, saying that they responded with not just 'little faith' but 'no faith'. Rather, they had panicked at the situation. They could not see that He slept so peacefully in the midst of the storm because He trusted implicitly in the Father's sovereignty and care.

The disciples, it seems, misinterpreted Jesus' sleep as indifference to their fate. 'Don't you care if we drown?' (v38). 'Don't you care?' I wonder how they reached the point where they believed Jesus did not care about them. This surely is the saddest unbelief of all. To doubt Jesus' power is one thing, but to doubt that He cares is the worst character assassination of all. Some of you will be aware of Rabbi Kushner, who wrote the bestseller *When Bad Things Happen to Good People* – interesting but it is off-beam biblically. Kushner doubted that God has the power to change things, but at least he did not doubt that God cares.

The disciples were the men who had been sharing their lives with Jesus, had been taught by Him and cared for by Him; but now they were overcome by what they saw around them rather than trusting in Jesus Himself. From time to time doubts may arise in our hearts, but let us not doubt the truth that Jesus cares. He has done too much for us to ever entertain that idea.

FURTHER STUDY

Eph. 2:3-13;
Titus 3:3-8

1. How does God demonstrate His love for us?

2. What saying is worthy of our trust?

Lord Jesus, if ever a doubt about Your love and care for me arises in my heart, please help me to see it immediately. You have done so much for me. Let me not allow such a doubt to linger in my mind, let alone take possession of it. Amen.

Always in control

For reading & meditation – Mark 4:35–41

'Jesus was in the stern, sleeping on a cushion.' (v38)

S ailors say that the worst possible place to be in a storm is the stern of a boat. Yet here was Jesus in the worst possible place, enjoying what must have been the best possible peace. What a lesson that was for the panic-stricken disciples. Confidence in His Father's love and care of Him allowed Jesus to sleep and let His Father deal with the storm. This is not to be taken to mean that when we find ourselves in a storm we close our eyes in denial and hope everything will be all right. If there is something that needs to be done, then we pay attention to it. As people sometimes say: God helps those who help themselves. In this situation, however, the disciples could do nothing to help themselves; they were entirely at the mercy of the storm. What they learnt was that when you have done all that you can and there is still no change, you continue to trust God to bring you safely through.

FURTHER STUDY

Rom. 5:6-11;
1 John 2:28-3:3;
3:21-24

1. What confidence did Paul have in God's love?

2. How did John encourage his readers to have confidence?

A story is told of a man by the name of John Bentley who was prone to worry. One night as he struggled to get to sleep, troubled by something that he could not deal with using his own wit and wisdom, he thought he heard the Lord say to him, 'John, why don't you go to sleep and I will stay up and do the worrying?' Well, we can question whether God really did say that to him, and we certainly know God does not worry, but let's not miss the point: if there is something to worry about, we turn the matter over to God. He worries over nothing because He is able to handle everything.

Heavenly Father, when I have done everything I need to do, please help me to relax and rest in the sure knowledge that You are in charge. Help me to trust You all the way. In Jesus' name. Amen.

If only...

For reading & meditation – Luke 8:22–25

'"Where is your faith?" he asked his disciples.' (v25)

A lready we have looked at one incident – the storm on the lake – through two different pairs of eyes. Today we take another look at the same incident – this time through the eyes of Luke. We do so because we shall discover another aspect of faith that every disciple of Jesus ought to understand.

Luke's understanding of the situation is that after He was awakened Jesus asked His disciples, 'Where is your faith?' For Luke, the concern in the heart of the Master was not so much that they had no faith but that the faith they had was not being put to use. Frequently there is talk about having a mid-life crisis; here the disciples were in a mid-lake crisis. And when they needed their faith most, they could not find it. We should be careful not to criticise the disciples too enthusiastically, for if we were to look into our own hearts we might realise that we too have a tendency to mislay our faith. It is so easy to feel full of faith in a Sunday worship service, but when we hit a mid-week crisis we wonder where the faith we had on Sunday has gone.

FURTHER STUDY

Acts 13:42–52;
Heb. 12:1–3

1. How did God's Word spread in a time of crisis?

2. On whom should we fix our eyes so as not to lose heart?

The way to develop and sustain faith is to listen attentively to what Jesus says to us. The disciples had heard Jesus say, 'Let's go over to the other side' (v22), but for some reason they overlooked or forgot what He had said. They should have known that if Jesus said, 'We're going over to the other side of the lake,' then that is where they would finish up. The storm could not possibly sink the boat in which Jesus was sailing. If only they had remembered that Jesus is true to His word. If only…

Father, help me to learn this lesson also – that You always keep Your word. Not one of Your promises has ever been broken. I rest my faith and confidence on that glorious fact. Amen.

A stretched faith

For reading & meditation – Mark 6:35–44

'"How many loaves do you have?" he asked. "Go and see."'
(v38)

On almost every page of the Gospels we see Jesus putting His disciples into situations which stretched their faith and understanding to the very utmost. The miracle of the feeding of the five thousand mirrors the provision of manna in the wilderness at the beginning of Israel's history. The message reconfirms that in Jesus, Israel's God is bringing about a new and greater exodus.

There are many who wonder why, since Jesus could feed five thousand, He does not end the world's hunger at one stroke. Miracles like this took place not as acts of arbitrary power but as signs of the presence of God's kingdom in Jesus. Most probably the disciples had a hard time coming to terms with this. Everything that happened was outside their previous experience, and so we can forgive them for being slow on the uptake.

First of all, they were understandably concerned about the practicalities of the situation: 'It's late,' they said. 'Send the hungry crowd home to eat.' 'You give them something to eat,' Jesus told them. 'It would cost eight months of our wages to pay for that,' was their hasty reply. Somewhere in the crowd they managed to find five loaves and two fish and watched while Jesus offered these up and the miraculous multiplication took place.

The life of discipleship is often like that. We come on the scene with our limited understanding and then try to convince Jesus with our arguments about how impracticable and impossible things are. Then we stand amazed as He takes what we give Him and works the most astonishing miracles. Amazing!

FURTHER STUDY

Luke 24:13-27;
John 20:24-31

1. What happened to the disciples who were slow on the uptake?

2. Why did John write his Gospel?

**Lord Jesus, forgive us that we are so slow to understand, and even remonstrate with You. Increase our faith, dear Lord, we pray.
For Your own name's sake. Amen.**

Afraid - of Him?

For reading & meditation – John 6:16–24

'But he said to them, "It is I; don't be afraid."' (v20)

Here again the disciples were out of their depth in a boat on the Sea of Galilee. As it got dark, a strong wind started to blow, with the result that they found themselves toiling and rowing but getting nowhere. Then Jesus came to them, walking on the water. They were afraid, thinking He was a ghost (see Matt. 14:26). But as He spoke to them they let Him into their boat and, reassured by His presence, they immediately reached their destination.

Is that not typical of the life of discipleship? So often we strive for what seem unreachable goals, and what we do seems to end in futility. We toil in rowing, 'up against it', and get nowhere. Then Jesus comes and what happens? We are afraid of Him; He is not like us and seems at home in the impossible. This is our first reaction. Then eventually we let Him in and before we know it, we are at the place we intended to go. We read that when Jesus first came to this world 'King Herod... was disturbed, and all Jerusalem with him' (Matt. 2:3). He was disturbed at the coming of the Deliverer! E. Stanley Jones said concerning this fear expressed by Herod and others in Jerusalem that 'they were naturalised in their lost-ness'. The disciples, too, sensed they were caught up in something bigger, and because they couldn't understand it they were afraid of it. Should we be afraid of Jesus when He comes to us in ways that are beyond our understanding? Should the heart be afraid at the coming of love? We will never fully understand Jesus. It's best to accept whatever He does as always being the right thing at the right time.

FURTHER STUDY

Acts 10:9-10;
Rev. 1:9-18

1. How was Peter reconciled to something beyond his understanding?

2. How was John reassured when faced with the supernatural?

Gracious and loving Lord, may I never keep You at a distance because of fear or misunderstanding. Make me as comfortable with the supernatural as You are. For Your own dear name's sake. Amen.

'Mountaintop intercession'

For reading & meditation – Mark 6:45–52

'After leaving them, he went up on a mountainside to pray.'
(v46)

We continue considering the story of the miraculous appearance of Jesus to His disciples during a storm on Galilee. Mark draws our attention to something very significant: after the disciples set out in the boat, Jesus went up onto a mountain to pray. Mark tells us also that when the boat was in the middle of the lake, Jesus was alone on the land (v47). Presumably, from His vantage point on the mountain, Jesus could see the disciples toiling in rowing and He might well have still been watching their progress as darkness fell. What thoughts were in the mind of the Saviour at that moment? What was He praying about during His time alone with His heavenly Father? We can only speculate, but did He, during His prayer time, realise that the wind was getting up, become aware of His disciples' problems and arrive at a plan to come to their aid through a miracle?

It has been suggested that, for us, the most significant part of this story is not so much the miracle on the water but Jesus' prayer time on the mountainside, for following that prayer time came an incident that gave the disciples a new revelation of His majesty and His love. Every one called by Jesus can rest in the knowledge that as we venture out on the lake of life He is watching over us and is engaged in mountaintop intercession. In our Christian life the greatest thing is not our own prayer life but the fact that Jesus prays for us (see Heb. 7:25). In the end, our deepest comfort is not that God answers our prayers but that God answers His.

FURTHER STUDY

Luke 22:31–32;
John 17:20–26;
Rom. 8:32–39;
Heb. 7:23–25

1. What did Jesus pray for Simon Peter?

2. What did Jesus pray for us?

Dear Saviour, what comfort and peace it gives me to know that You are watching over me and praying for me through every hour of every day. Your intercession is my heart's consolation.
Thank You dear Master. Amen.

Get out of the boat

For reading & meditation – Matthew 14:22–36

'But when he saw the wind, he was afraid and, beginning
to sink, cried out, "Lord, save me!"' (v30)

We reflect further on the incident we have been looking at
over the past two days – the miraculous appearance of Jesus
as He walked on the Sea of Galilee. Matthew adds an important
detail to the narrative also told by John and Mark. From him we
learn that when the disciples see Jesus walking on the water, Peter
– no surprise here – boldly urges Jesus to invite him to do the same!
'Come on, then', Jesus replies. The rest, as we say, is history. Peter
walked on the water for a while, but when he looked down and
saw the waves beneath his feet, he lost his nerve
and began to sink. When he called out, 'Lord, save
me!' Jesus didn't hesitate. He reached out, grabbed his
hand and said, 'Faint-heart, what got into you?' (*The
Message*). Simon Peter was saved from drowning by
the gracious intervention of Jesus.

FURTHER STUDY

Luke 11:5-13;
Acts 4:23-31

1. What does
Jesus teach on
praying with
boldness?

2. How did
God answer
the believers'
prayer?

Let's not forget, though, that the central focus of
this story, quite rightly, is Jesus Himself. Everything
that happened was intended to reveal to the disciples
new aspects of Jesus' personality and to show to
them that He was who He said He was – God in
human form. Thankfully they grasped some of the truth that Jesus
intended them to learn for we read: 'Then those who were in the
boat worshipped him, saying, "Truly you are the Son of God"' (v33).

Jesus responds positively to those who answer His call and
venture forth boldly for the sake of the kingdom. Before Simon
Peter started to sink, he actually did walk on water. The waves
became like a pavement beneath his feet. If we want to walk on
water then we have to get out of the boat.

**Gracious Lord, can it be that there are things not happening in my
life because I am afraid to step out? Though I know You don't want
me to take reckless risks, perhaps I need to be bolder.
Please help me dear Saviour. Amen.**

Do you believe in miracles?

For reading & meditation – Mark 6:45–56

'Then he climbed into the boat with them, and the wind died down. They were completely amazed' (v51)

For one more day we consider the moments when Jesus appeared to His disciples walking on the water. The verse chosen as our text tells us that the disciples were amazed at what they had witnessed; they just could not understand what was going on. Eugene Peterson paraphrases part of today's reading in this way: 'They didn't understand what he had done at the supper. None of this had yet penetrated their hearts' (*The Message*).

It says a great deal for the integrity of the Gospel writers that they so endearingly and honestly record their own flaws and failures. The fact that they did not understand what Jesus had done at the feeding of the five thousand suggests they had not yet fully grasped the Saviour's mission, hence their further confusion at Jesus walking on the water and His calming of the waves. We read 'their hearts were hardened' (v52), and at that moment they were no different from some of His outright opponents (see Mark 3:5). Scepticism and rationalism still seemed to play a strong part in the disciples' thinking even though they had witnessed some most amazing events.

FURTHER STUDY

1 Cor. 1:18–25;
Heb. 3:12–14

1. What does Paul tell us about man's wisdom?

2. What does the writer to Hebrews warn us about?

There are many in today's Church who struggle over the issue of miracles. The belief in miracles seems to me to be an important part of being a disciple of Jesus.' Why are we reluctant to believe in miracles? Conversion itself is a miracle. And when we become Christians we experience one miracle after another. The power of Jesus exceeded the rational abilities of His disciples. It always does.

Lord Jesus Christ, forgive us if our hearts are so hardened by rationalism and scepticism that we cannot see that which is beyond the scope of our natural minds. Help us dear Saviour. Amen.

A class by Himself

For reading & meditation – Mark 8:27–30

"'But what about you?" he asked.
"Who do you say I am?'" (v29)

In today's passage Jesus is seen with His disciples near the cool and pleasant town of Caesarea Philippi, which was on the northern boundary of Israel. In effect, He took them on a 'retreat'. Drawing the disciples aside from the hustle and bustle of the crowds attracted by His ministry, Jesus asks them what people were saying about Him. They report the popular rumours sweeping through Galilee that a remarkable prophet had arisen or even been reincarnated.

It was not surprising that people had reached these conclusions. In some ways Jesus behaved like the prophets of Israel's history. What is more, His message was a double-edged sword of both justice and grace. And there can be no doubt that He Himself had a keen sense of following in the prophetic tradition, which He revealed when He began to anticipate the fate that awaited Him in Jerusalem (see Luke 13:33). There were many people then, as now, who were prepared to recognise Jesus as a prophet but who were unable to see that He was more than a prophet.

FURTHER STUDY

Acts 2:22-24,
32–41;
10:36-43

1. In what ways is Jesus more than a prophet?

2. In what terms does Peter preach this to Cornelius?

It's interesting that this matter was raised by Jesus in the vicinity of Caesarea Philippi, for history records that the town had been recently renamed in honour of the Roman emperor and the local ruler, Philip, brother of Herod Antipas. Its original name was Paneas because it hosted a shrine to the Greek god Pan. Does Jesus fit into a pantheon of gods? The disciples needed to learn, as does the whole world, that Jesus belongs in a class all by Himself.

Lord Jesus Christ, when will the world wake up to the truth that You are more than a prophet? You are the eternal Son of God – true God of true God. I am so grateful that my eyes have been opened to that great and glorious truth. Amen.

'Watch this space!'

For reading & meditation – Matthew 16:13–20

'Then he warned his disciples not to tell anyone that he was the Christ.' (v20)

When Jesus talked with His disciples to discover their true thoughts about Him, Simon Peter, the most outspoken disciple in the group, blurted out, 'You are the Christ, the Son of the living God' (v16). The Holy Spirit brought from the Father's heart to Peter's heart the revelation of who Jesus really is.

The Saviour then went on to talk about the crucial and foundational role that Peter's confession would have in the Church. We need have no fear about acknowledging that Peter was a founding apostle of the Church, since Peter's great sermon on the Day of Pentecost undoubtedly demonstrates this to be the case. What we are talking about here has nothing to do with tracing papal lineage back to Peter. Every true Christian church remains faithful to the confession given by Peter that day: Jesus is the Christ, the Son of the living God. It is important to note that this revelation, and not Peter's personality, was the rock on which Christ said He would build His Church.

FURTHER STUDY

Acts 3:11–16, 18–26; 4:8–14; Rom. 4:16–25

1. How does Peter give his listeners the fuller picture?

2. How does Paul preach the same gospel as Peter?

Jesus cautioned His disciples about telling others who He was because at that point in His ministry it would have been easy for the crowds to get a totally wrong idea of His role as the Messiah. In order to get a clear picture of His mission they needed to wait until after His death and resurrection. Jesus was saying in effect: 'Watch this space! In due time you will come to see the fullness of my mission here on earth. Then you will be able to tell the world who I really am.'

Lord Jesus, how wonderful that we can now tell people who You really are. Forgive us when we are so slow to make known the good news that You are the Christ, the Son of God, the Saviour of the world. Forgive us and restore us. Amen.

Whose voice?

For reading & meditation – Matthew 16:21–23

'Peter took him aside and began to rebuke him. "Never, Lord!" he said. "This shall never happen to you!"' (v22)

We are staying with the passage recording Peter's confession and Jesus' first prediction of His death in order to draw from it some further insights that will help us understand discipleship. How amazing that the disciple who had just been commended for receiving the unique revelation from the Father was now being told he was doing the devil's work! With one ear he had listened to the voice of the Father in heaven; with the other he had listened to the voice of the devil.

Without doubt, a wrong and misleading thought had been planted in Peter's mind when he tried to dissuade Christ from talking about going to a cross. This caused Jesus to say to Peter, 'Get behind me, Satan… you do not have in mind the things of God, but the things of men' (v23). The devil would have used everything in his power to keep Christ from the cross because he knew that Jesus' death there would bring his ultimate defeat. But there was no other way Christ could establish the kingdom of God without the suffering of the cross.

. We do people a disservice when we misrepresent the gospel and deceive potential disciples into thinking that the Christian life is all a bed of roses. Regrettably, there are some churches which write the cost of discipleship in small print in the hope that it will escape people's attention. Some churches now talk less of repentance, because it might be too off-putting for today's seekers. But repentance is where our transformation begins!

FURTHER STUDY

Rom. 6:8-12;
1 Pet. 4:12-19

1. What does discipleship require according to Paul?

2. What does Peter say should be our attitude to suffering?

Gracious and loving Lord, one truth seems to be coming at me from all directions: true discipleship requires not just a part of me but all. Help us as Your Church not to water down the gospel. For Your name's sake. Amen.

The divine 'must'

For reading & meditation – Matthew 16:24–28

'Then Jesus said to his disciples, "If anyone would come after me, he must deny himself"' (v24)

For one more day we consider this passage in which Jesus predicts His death and laid down in strong language what He asks of His followers. The 'must' of divine necessity which motivated Jesus also motivates those who become His disciples. We are to bear the yoke of discipleship in the same way that He bore the cross upon His shoulders. There is a 'must' in the heart of a disciple, just as there was in the heart of the Saviour. We must deny ourselves, we are told, take up our cross and follow Him. But what does it mean to 'deny' oneself?

FURTHER STUDY

Rom. 12:1-3, 9-19; Heb. 10:32-39; 13:20-21

1. What kind of lifestyle is pleasing to God?

2. What confidence does the writer of Hebrews want his readers to have?

Let's try to clear a few things up for there are many strange and misguided ideas about the subject of self-denial. It involves much more than giving up chocolate or desserts for Lent! Some have even taken Jesus' instruction to mean that we must hate ourselves. True self-denial, however, has nothing to do with self-hatred or self-denigration. Rather, in this case it is the bold and courageous act of fully giving over our lives to Jesus and letting Him lead us. In other words, we surrender our lives into His hands and allow Him to shape and determine our destiny – for the whole of our lifetime.

Those who hesitate at what Jesus said need to consider carefully His words: 'What good will it be for a man if he gains the whole world, yet forfeits his soul?' (v26). What is the alternative to rejecting the claims and appeal of Jesus? It is the loss of one's soul. In the words of Jim Elliot: 'That man is no fool who gives up what he cannot keep to gain what he cannot lose.'

Lord Jesus, may the same 'must' – the same energy and love that drove and motivated You – govern my life also. Help me be consumed with You to follow your call, to work for You and to honour You in every part of my life. In Your name I ask it. Amen.

'Take up the cross'

For reading & meditation – Mark 8:34–37

'If anyone would come after me, he must deny himself and take up his cross and follow me.' (v34)

On different occasions, when explaining what it meant to answer the call of discipleship, Jesus openly said that they would have to 'take up the cross'. Just as people have misunderstood the command 'deny yourself', so too has this instruction been misconstrued. In the days of Jesus, the phrase 'to carry the cross' had a quite specific and significant meaning. Under the ruthless rule of the occupying Romans, you would often have seen the frightening spectacle of a procession of people dragging their heavy cross-beams to the place of execution. And crucifixion – which was considered to be the most agonising and humiliating death – was reserved exclusively for revolutionaries and those convicted of crimes of violence. In other words, taking up the cross for the men and women of Jesus' day could mean quite literally having to give their lives for His cause.

FURTHER STUDY

Phil. 1:19–26;
2 Tim. 4:6–8;
Rev. 12:10–12

1. How did Paul face the possibility of death?

2. How do Christians overcome the accuser?

As followers of Jesus, we can certainly expect to face public hostility and social discomfort as a result of answering His call to discipleship. To carry our cross is to lay down self-will and pick up God's will, and where the two collide we choose His will over our own. In some parts of the world, even as you read these lines somebody will be facing imprisonment torture and perhaps death for Jesus' sake. At present, those of us who live in the Western world mostly do not have to face that possibility, but what would happen if we did? Would we put Jesus first, even though our own lives were threatened by our doing so?

Lord Jesus, it is so easy to answer 'Yes' if I know I am not likely to be in that position, but I pray with all my heart that my love for You will be greater than the love I have for myself or even the love I have for life. Help me, dear Saviour. Amen.

'My way'

For reading & meditation – Luke 9:23–27

'For whoever wants to save his life will lose it, but whoever
loses his life for me will save it.' (v24)

An aspect of discipleship we have yet to consider is Jesus'
challenge to us to lose our lives in order to find them. In *The
Message*, Eugene Peterson paraphrases Jesus' words here like
this: 'Self-sacrifice is the way, my way, to finding yourself, your
true self.' Notice the words 'my way'. Jesus did not hesitate to put
aside His own interests and He looks for the same in His disciples.
We can be sure that He will never ask us to do what He was not
prepared to do Himself.

FURTHER STUDY

Gal. 5:19-26;
1 John 3:16-20;
4:7-16

1. What
characterises
those who
belong to
Christ?

2. Of what
level of self-
sacrifice does
John speak?

By His baptism and during the wilderness
temptations, Jesus led by example in setting aside His
own comfort to do His Father's will. In baptism He
identified with sinners – and just in case anyone who
saw Him entering the waters might have thought He
was a sinner, God opened the heavens and said, 'This
is my Son, whom I love; with him I am well pleased'
(Matt. 3:17). In the temptations He refused to satisfy
His hunger by using His name to turn the stones into
bread, and turned down the offer of the kingdoms of
this world on easy terms (see Matt. 4:1–?11).

But what did Jesus mean when He said that if we
lose ourselves we will find ourselves? People are
desperately trying to find themselves – through work, money,
entertainment, sport, relationships, and so on. But mostly, they
find a fictional self, not the real self. No one can find their true
self until they lose it for the sake of Christ and His kingdom. And
having lost it, they find a self with which they can live, as we say,
happily ever after.

Lord Jesus, I do not want to live with a fictional self; I want to live
with my real self, the self You want me to be – my true self. Lead me
deeper into an understanding of this I pray. In Your name I ask it.
Amen.

The 'how-much-more' God

For reading & meditation – Luke 12:22–34

'Therefore I tell you, do not worry about your life, what you will eat; or about your body, what you will wear.' (v22)

Jesus' instructions to His disciples here are ones that we, His twenty-first-century disciples, need to take to heart. 'Don't fuss about what's on the table at mealtimes,' He tells them, 'or if the clothes in your closet are in fashion' (v22, *The Message*). Of course, it is one thing to accept that we shouldn't fuss; it is another thing to practise it. So how do we break free from the habit of worrying over everything? One way is by learning about the 'how-much-more' God. If God can take care of the ravens and the lilies and provide for them, how much more is He committed to His disciples. He calls us on this basis – the fact that we mean more to Him than birds or flowers – to trust Him. Our Father knows what we need.

How often have you been in difficulty, wondering how you would fare, when suddenly something happened and the need was met? If we had more confidence in our Father's ability to intervene at every stage of our lives, we would spend less time worrying and more time praising. Living each day with resilience and a deep trust in the Father to provide for our needs is a powerful, if unglamorous, testimony to all who are seeking God. *The Message* puts it like this: 'People who don't know God and the way he works fuss over these things, but you know both God and how he works. Steep yourself in God-reality, God-initiative, God-provisions. You'll find all your everyday human concerns will be met' (v30).

Are any concerns troubling you at this moment? Trust God. Don't worry – He will meet with you in your need.

FURTHER STUDY

Rom. 15:13;
Heb. 13:5-8;
1 Pet. 5:7-11

1. Meditate on Paul's prayer.

2. Why should we be content with what we have?

Lord Jesus, You are speaking to me again. You know my tendency to worry over so many things. Forgive me, I pray, and give me an ever-growing consciousness of Your ability to take care of everything. Amen.

Lessons from a little child

For reading & meditation – Mark 9:30–37

'If anyone wants to be first, he must be the very last, and the servant of all.' (v35)

Once again Jesus highlighted for His disciples the upside-down nature of life in God's kingdom, as He taught them an important lesson about status and power. Isn't it astonishing that while He was conscious of having to suffer and die for their sakes they were arguing about which of them was the greatest? When He asked them what they are arguing about, there was an embarrassed silence!

Of course, it's all too easy to criticise the disciples, but how

FURTHER STUDY
1 Cor. 9:19-23;
Gal. 5:13-14;
1 Pet. 2:11-17;
5:1-6

1. In what ways did Paul serve others?

2. How does Peter encourage both service and humility?

often are we, too, caught out in our pride and competitiveness and power struggles? Like them, how slow we are to learn that the first shall be last and the servant of all. As He did so often, Jesus surprised the disciples with a timely object lesson. He took a child and stood him in their midst. Many people are puzzled by Jesus' action here, as children are seldom humble or angelic – except when they're asleep! Jesus, however, was illustrating that a child is someone with a humble status who was absolutely dependent. In infancy a child depends on his parents for everything I believe it is John Stott who said,

'Children are rightly called "dependants"; for what they know they depend on what they have been taught, and for what they have they depend on what they have been given.' Humility and dependence are to be the pre-eminent characteristics of those who are followers of Jesus Christ. If these are absent in those who call themselves disciples then they have not fully understood the nature of His call. They may carry the name but not the nature.

Lord Jesus, help me examine my heart in these moments to see whether or not these characteristics of humility and dependence are part of my personality. I long to be a disciple, not just in name but in nature also. In Your name I ask it. Amen.

What a leader!

For reading & meditation – Mark 10:32–34

'the disciples were astonished, while those who followed
were afraid.' (v32)

Many have wondered what it must have been like to walk and talk with Jesus. Many years ago, the singer Johnny Cash fronted a film of the life of Jesus called *Gospel Road*. One scene that grabbed the attention of viewers was a shot taken from a high angle looking down on the 'disciples' as they wandered along a lane together. It showed a bunch of young men good-naturedly joking and laughing and jostling each other. At one point the group even tried to throw 'Simon Peter' over a wall! The film gave a vivid impression of the sheer humanness of life among the disciples. Here, however, in the passage before us now, there is no hilarity, no laughing or pushing – for those who are travelling with Jesus are aware He is on the road that will lead to His death.

FURTHER STUDY

John 11:55–57;
12:12–15,20–28

1. How did Jesus face what lay ahead?

2. How did people respond to His arrival?

We read that the disciples were 'astonished' and others who followed were 'afraid'. Probably those who followed and were afraid were pilgrims on their way to the Passover in Jerusalem who had heard that Jesus was going there to die. It is interesting to watch how Jesus handles the situation. Knowing what lies ahead of Him, He does not draw back, but strides ahead of them, leading the way. What a graphic image this is of the Saviour's determination to be, as the writer to the Hebrews says of Him, 'the author and perfecter of our faith' (Heb. 12:2). Over the past weeks we have seen Him in so many different situations, but the more we see of Him, the more astonished we are at His courage, determination and self-giving love. He is the One who goes ahead of us into the eye of the storm to bear the judgment that really was meant for us.

My Saviour and my God, give me the courage to face whatever lies ahead no matter how threatening or unpleasant it may be, knowing that nothing can ever happen that we cannot handle together. In Your name I pray. Amen.

What shows on your face?

For reading & meditation – Luke 9:51–53

'but the people there did not welcome him, because he was heading for Jerusalem.' (v53)

Every face, it is said, tells its own story. A blush, a furrow of pain, or the steady gaze that comes from inner peace – these things can reveal what is going on deep inside us. Luke tells us that as the time came for Jesus to face the cross, He resolutely set out for Jerusalem. The New King James Version puts it like this: 'When the time had come for Him to be received up... He steadfastly set His face to go to Jerusalem' (v51). Although geographically Jesus moved in several different directions after this, His overriding purpose was always to go to Jerusalem, there to suffer and die for us.

FURTHER STUDY

Acts 6:8-15;
7:54-60;
2 Cor. 3:12-18;
4:5-6,13-18

1. What story did Stephen's face tell?

2. What should our faces reflect?

The disciples were annoyed because the Samaritans refused them hospitality but Jesus did not share their irritation. Little did they realise it but Jesus, far from being frustrated with the inhospitable Samaritans, was on His way to die for them. The closer Jesus got to the cross, the more His determination to do the will of God showed in His countenance. God's will for Him was to walk straight into the firestorm of judgment in order to take it upon Himself and spare the lives of not just the Samaritans but anyone who will answer His call.

You, amazingly, are not heading for a cross but a crown. But can people see as they look at you that you are, in the words of the old hymn, 'marching upward to Zion, beautiful, beautiful Zion'? Every day something registers on our faces – anxiety, surprise, concern, anger, frustration. How wonderful it would be if people saw in our countenance something of our eternal destination.

Jesus, may I be so consumed with You that this will be apparent in everything I say and do. Your determination to do the will of God showed on Your face. May my determination to do Your will be seen on my face also. Amen.

A thing most beautiful

For reading & meditation – Matthew 26:6–13

'Jesus said to them, "Why are you bothering this woman?
She has done a beautiful thing to me."' (v10)

DAY
102

The account of the woman anointing Jesus' head with her most precious perfume has been described as the sweetest and most moving scene in the whole of the Gospels. She ministered to Jesus in more ways than she imagined, for He interpreted her action as an anointing for His burial, days before His crucifixion.

The disciples reacted badly to this outpouring of love, objecting to the waste, and arguing that funds were being diverted from the poor. They were technically right, but spiritually wrong. Jesus never once played down the need to care for the poor. What mattered to Jesus at that moment was not how correct she was in terms of Old Testament law but how passionate was her devotion. That's what He defended; that's what He called 'beautiful'. And that's the picture He has ensured is remembered for all time, and the one He holds out for all His disciples. Wherever the gospel is preached, Jesus said, the story of what this woman did will be told.

There are many other events Jesus could have selected to be retold again and again. So why did He choose this one? Because the issue that matters to Jesus, the one that He holds dear to His heart, the one that brings a smile to His lips or a tear to His eye, is not how much we know, but how much we love. I once read in a devotional: 'Maybe this is why, when Pharisees were fighting over theology [and, we may add, the interpretation of Old Testament laws], prostitutes were falling at the Saviour's feet and slipping into the kingdom of God on their tears.'

FURTHER STUDY

Luke 7:39–50;
23:50–24:3

1. What did Jesus say distinguished the sinful woman from the Pharisee?

2. What devotion was shown to Jesus after His death?

Precious Saviour, thank You for showing me that what You enjoy most about me is not how much I know, but how much I love. I love You Lord Jesus. Help me to love You even more. Amen.

When the going got tough...

For reading & meditation – Matthew 26:47–56

'Then all the disciples deserted him and fled.' (v56)

These words are some of the saddest in Scripture. What kind of disciples were these who deserted their Master in His hour of need? Had Jesus failed to detect the faithlessness in His friends? Or, was it the case that they had not really heeded His challenges that a true disciple should be ready to lay down their life for Him and the gospel? Most likely it was the latter.

Judas, we read, betrayed Jesus with a kiss, even though Jesus called him 'friend'. Simon Peter betrayed the Saviour differently, by drawing and using his sword (see John 18:10), fuelling the suspicion that the cause of Christ was based on violent revolution, which, of course, it was not. Jesus explicitly renounced violence as the way to bring in the kingdom. Nor would He reach out for a spectacular deliverance. There in the Garden of Gethsemane He surrendered the right to divine intervention to spare His suffering just as He had done earlier, during the temptations.

When the going got tough for that band of disciples, the tough got going – in the opposite direction. At that moment in the Garden of Gethsemane Jesus had as much trouble with His followers as He did with His enemies. Yet, despite the confusion of His disciples and arrest by His enemies, the Saviour submitted Himself to the Father's will, which had already been spelt out in the Scriptures (vv54–56). How amazing that He did this this for you and me. Had there been no cross there would have been no salvation.

FURTHER STUDY

Gal. 1:1-10;
2 Tim. 1:13-18;
4:9-18

1. What does Paul reaffirm in the midst of desertion?

2. What sort of loyalty did Paul expect and receive?

Jesus, You are so wonderful. Among the confusion, while You were experiencing desertion and disloyalty, You thought not of Yourself but of those You were set on saving. I am so glad that that included me. Amen.

'Were you there...?'

For reading & meditation – Mark 15:16–20

'Then they led him out to crucify him.' (v20)

Although so far in this issue we have been thinking about the call and cost of discipleship, today we focus on what our salvation cost the Saviour. In simple terms, it meant that He took on Himself the punishment for sin which we ourselves should have borne. An illustration might help.

Many years ago in India, a young boy was adopted by a headmaster and his wife. The boy became increasingly wayward and rebellious. One day after the boy had committed a wilful act of disobedience, the headmaster took a cane and told the boy to hold out his hand. The boy stood there defiant and full of bravado but stretched out his hand. The headmaster brought down the cane heavy and hard... not on the boy's hand, but on his own. Seeing what had happened, the boy cried out with inner pain, fell at his father's feet and asked for forgiveness. After that the boy was completely different and later became a bishop in India. Every Good Friday he would tell that story to illustrate how his father's suffering broke something inside of him and freed him from himself.

FURTHER STUDY

1 Tim. 2:1-7;
1 John 2:1-6

1. For whom did Jesus give His life as a ransom?

2. For whose sins did Jesus atone?

Gaze once again on the cross. Appreciate afresh the central and most glorious truth of the Christian gospel, that God in the person of Jesus bent to deal with mankind's predicament and on the cross paid the full penalty for our sin. The sins which nailed Him to the tree – prejudice, selfishness, blame-shifting, arrogance, and so on – are the same sins that we have committed. In that sense, it can be said of us that we also crucified the Son of God. Yes, we were there when they crucified our Lord.

Dear Saviour, I realise afresh that You were put to death not by one or two monstrously malicious sins but by an accumulation of ordinary sins – the sins I myself have committed. For that I am eternally grateful. Amen.

Man's worst – God's best

For reading & meditation – John 19:28–37

'Jesus said, "It is finished." With that, he bowed his head and gave up his spirit.' (v30)

The question is often asked by those who know something of the life of Christ: How can it be that a being so true, so loving, so perfect, was done to death while still comparatively young? He was only in His early thirties when He died. Surely it borders on the incredible that the human race should treat Christ, the most perfect man who ever walked on this earth, in the way it did. Many regard His crucifixion as the greatest felony in history.

This greatest of human crimes became the greatest of heaven's blessings. Jesus took upon Himself our sins and bore them all away. But people ask: couldn't God have forgiven our sin without sending His Son to a cross? Would God have allowed it had there been any other option? In a righteous universe there is always justice. Even our own blunted conscience has enough sharpness in it to tell us that. Sin is so contrary to God and to His holiness. It is so awful, so affronting that no human mind can grasp just how opposed it is to the nature of God. Only holiness can perceive holiness. There was only one way for God to overcome sin: He had to bear the punishment Himself. On that green hill outside the city wall (to use the words of an old hymn) God in the Person of His Son drew sin to battle – and won. Something was completed at Calvary which never needed to be repeated.

FURTHER STUDY

Isa. 53:3–11;
Heb. 9:11-15

1. What part did God play in the death of Jesus?

2. How did Jesus obtain redemption?

No human mind can fully comprehend how the price of sin was paid on the cross, but the fact that it was is the message of the whole New Testament. We may not be able to fully understand it but we most certainly can fully stand upon it.

Jesus, Son of God and Saviour of my soul, I am humbled by Your willingness to come to earth, die on a cross, all in order to save me. My soul has been won by You. I worship forever at Your feet – Your humble and obedient disciple. Amen.

The most glorious dawn

For reading & meditation – Matthew 28:1–10

'at dawn on the first day of the week, Mary Magdalene
and the other Mary went to look at the tomb.' (v1)

We now turn our thoughts to the glorious resurrection of our
Saviour! The women who loved Jesus and followed Him
were anxious to offer their last expression of devotion to Him by
anointing His body with spices. It is only a small ministry that
can be exercised upon the body of a loved one who has died, but
love always insists on offering it.

The Gospel writers tell us that the women hurried to the tomb
just as dawn was breaking. There was no man in the party, as this
kind of ministry was usually performed by women,
and women alone. They knew the tomb was sealed
with a great stone, and Mark says they murmured
to one another as they walked there, 'Who will roll
the stone away from the entrance of the tomb?' (Mark
16:3). But when they arrived they found that the stone
has already been rolled away. A white-robed youth
addressed them: 'There's nothing to fear here. I know
you're looking for Jesus, the One they nailed on the
cross. He is not here. He was raised, just as he said...
Now, get on your way quickly' (vv6–7, *The Message*).

FURTHER STUDY

Acts 13:26-37;
1 Cor. 15:12-25;
Col. 1:9-14

1. How important
is Jesus'
resurrection
to Paul?

2. What kind of
kingdom has
Jesus brought
us into?

Some years ago, a programme on television
entitled *The World's Most Glorious Dawn* dealt with the landing of
the Allied Forces on the Normandy beaches, which led ultimately
to the end of World War II. But I believe the most glorious dawn in
history was when the Son of God stepped from His garden grave in
the power of an endless life. The radiance of that dawn has spread
its golden glow over the whole of history. There was never a dawn
like it before and there will never be a dawn like it again.

**Lord Jesus Christ, the radiance of that glorious dawn when You
rose again from the dead lights up my soul. Because You live, I live
also. And not just in time but also in eternity. I am so thankful.
Amen.**

The real thing

For reading & meditation – Luke 10:23–24

'Then he turned to his disciples and said privately,
"Blessed are the eyes that see what you see."' (v23)

Ｗe can only speculate as to how clear it was to the early
disciples that they were some of the most privileged
people on earth because they rubbed shoulders every day with
Jesus Himself. What bliss it must have been for the disciples to
walk with Jesus day after day and be part of His revolutionary
programme.

If the disciples did not realise how privileged they were, then
they must have been really out of touch with the world around

FURTHER STUDY

Acts 5:41-42;
Eph. 1:3-14;
1 Pet. 1:10-12

1. What privilege
did the apostles
rejoice in?

2. What are
the privileges
of salvation?

them. World history had reached the turning-point;
they were living through God's saving revolution,
the arrival of His kingdom. It was for this day that
the kings and prophets had longed. Surely some of
the disciples must have grasped the significance of
what was happening, though sometimes when we
look at their behaviour, we wonder.

Of course, living as we do in this day and age
when the Spirit has come to illuminate our minds
and hearts, we have the advantage over them. And
we also have the true witness of these first disciples, written in
hindsight after the resurrection, on which to base our faith. Living
now, as we do, on this side of Easter, we are even more privileged.
It would have been wonderful to have lived in the days of Jesus
– the other side of Easter – but surely as Jesus Himself said to
Thomas: 'Because you have seen me, you have believed; blessed
are those who have not seen and yet have believed' (John 20:29).
Do you realise how blessed you are?

....

**Lord Jesus, I can never know just how privileged the disciples felt
to be close to You but I know how privileged I feel to be called as
one of Your disciples. Nothing that has ever happened or could
happen can be more wonderful. Amen.**

Little prayer - little power

For reading & meditation – Mark 9:14–29

'He replied, "This kind can come out only by prayer."' (v29)

This ninth chapter of Mark's Gospel contains an amazing contrast. It begins with Christ's glorious transfiguration on the mountain top and then moves to the scene of confusion down in the valley. Mark describes vividly what we meet there: chaotic crowds, argumentative religious types, hand-wringing do-gooders, puzzled sceptics, muddled half-believers, out-of-control children and desperate parents. And there, too, we meet the disciples of Jesus who seem unable to make a difference. Three of the disciples had witnessed Jesus' transfiguration but the disciples appear powerless and paralysed.

No amount of subtle editing can disguise how the Church can on occasions seem paralysed by its own sense of helplessness, lack of understanding and prayerlessness. The reason why the disciples couldn't cast out the evil spirit, explained Jesus, was because they 'come out only by prayer'. He did not mean that they had not prayed enough immediately before attempting to exorcise the demon, but rather that any effective ministry must be underpinned by a lifestyle of prayer. Thankfully we are not alone in these situations, and like the father of the child we can say, 'I do believe; help me overcome my unbelief.' Our authority lies not in us alone but in the One who has called us – Jesus.

FURTHER STUDY

Eph. 6:10-20;
1 Thess. 5:16-28;
2 Thess. 1:11-12;
3:1-5

1. What must we do to be 'strong in the Lord'?

2. What is Paul's prayer for the Thessalonians?

We can begin to see from Jesus' statement why He spent so much time in prayer. In those times, He waited upon His Father for the spiritual strength He needed for whatever He wanted Him to do. Little prayer, little power. A lot of prayer, a lot of power.

Heavenly Father, I understand that the more time I spend with You in prayer the more I perceive Your will. Forgive me if I am prone to rely on my own strength rather than Yours. Help me be willing to spend more time with You in prayer. Amen.

Prowess in prayer

For reading & meditation – Luke 11:1-13

'When he finished [praying], one of his disciples said
to him, "Lord, teach us to pray"' (v1)

Someone once defined a disciple as a person who has learned to
pray the Lord's Prayer. They meant, of course, not just reciting
the words but praying with a full understanding of it. However, to
call this the 'Lord's Prayer' is really a misnomer as Jesus was not
saying, 'This is how I pray,' but 'This is how you can pray.' Jesus
would never pray, for example, 'Forgive us our sins,' for He had no
sins to be forgiven although, of course, other aspects of the prayer
we can well imagine Him praying.

FURTHER STUDY

John 5:16-23;
1 Cor. 15:27-28;
2 Cor. 1:8-11

1. How did Jesus
describe His
dependence on
His Father?

2. In what
circumstances
did Paul learn
the secret of
dependence?

It is interesting that although Jesus was the
greatest teacher the world has ever known, the
disciples never asked Him, 'Lord, teach us to preach'.
But there was something about His prayer life that
arrested their attention. What was it? Perhaps more
than anything it was that it showed His total reliance
on God His Father for daily strength and direction.
They must have sensed it was this Father–Son
relationship which sustained Jesus in everything. A
quick overview of the life of Jesus, from His baptism
to His suffering on the cross, reveals that at every
step of the way He relied on the Father's presence
and power being there for Him.

Examine the prayer closely and you will see that it breathes an
atmosphere of dependence. It begins with recognising that God
is our Father. Then follows an admission of dependence on Him
for our daily bread and our protection against temptation. Only
prayerful trust in our heavenly Father will enable us to live the
life of discipleship and sustain us in all we do.

**Lord Jesus, the more I learn about You the more I see that Your
strength while here on earth was Your absolute dependence on
Your Father. I long for that strength to be mine also. Please teach me
to be a more dependent disciple. Amen.**

The Father-Son relationship

For reading & meditation – Matthew 6:5–15

'This, then, is how you should pray: "Our Father in heaven, hallowed be your name"' (v9)

The disciples had been nourished by the great uplifting prayers of the prophets – Isaiah, Jeremiah, Ezekiel, and others – but recognised that the prayer life of Jesus was in a league of its own. They had never heard anyone pray like Jesus, hence their request, 'Lord, teach us to pray' (Luke 11:1). As we explored yesterday, the one thing above all others that would have struck the disciples about the prayer life of Jesus was that it revealed His absolute dependence on His Father for everything. And it is this Father–Son relationship that He wants also for us.

We, of course, are not 'sons' in the same sense that Jesus was God's Son, but in Christ we are sons and daughters having the same rights of access to the Father as He did. Following Jesus, then, is a life of dependence on the Father's goodness in the service of His kingdom and in obedience to His will. It may involve us in forgoing many of the securities we have come to rely on, which the world promises to provide. In laying down this model of prayer for His disciples, Jesus lovingly welcomes us into His own warm and shatterproof fellowship with His Father.

FURTHER STUDY

Eph. 2:14-22;
3:7-13;
Heb. 2:10-13;
4:14-16; 5:7-9

1. What attitudes did Jesus express in His own prayer life?

2. How are we to approach God?

What a gift our Lord gave us when He framed this prayer. One sentiment that has always spoken to me is: 'We don't choose the prayer; it chooses us. It reaches out to us, forms us, invites us into the adventure called discipleship.' But it is not just a form of prayer; beneath lies a whole philosophy about prayer. God save us from merely reciting it without realising what underlies it.

Lord Jesus, every time I recite the Lord's Prayer help me to remember what lies beneath the words and teach me, I pray, to have the same dependence on the Father that You so wonderfully demonstrated. In Your name I ask it. Amen.

Our family tree

For reading & meditation – John 19:17–27

'he said to his mother, "Dear woman, here is your son,"
and to the disciple, "Here is your mother."' (vv26-27)

In times of deep crisis it is a great comfort to be surrounded by those we love and those whom we know love us. Jesus, in His death, must have derived some comfort from seeing His mother and His closest disciple at the foot of the cross. Characteristically, He thought more of them than of Himself, and in His dying words provided for a relationship of mutual support and commitment for the remainder of their lives. Speaking to His mother, He said, 'Dear woman, here is your son,' and to the disciple, 'Here is your mother.'

FURTHER STUDY

Matt. 5:38-48;
Eph. 4:1-5,14-16;
4:25-5:2

1. Why does Jesus ask us to love our enemies?

2. How does our love overflow for one another?

This bond, formed on the level ground at the foot of the cross, has characterised Christ's Church throughout the centuries. Commentators Richard Bauckham and Trevor Hart put it like this: 'Just as Jesus' mother and the Beloved Disciple would not otherwise have been related had not Jesus at His death brought them together and charged them with being mother and son to each other, so the Church is the community of people who would not otherwise be related, but whom the crucified Jesus brings together, forging new relationships through His death for us.' This is why we say that there are no strangers in the Body of Christ, just brothers and sisters we may not have met yet.

In the shadow of the cross John was bound to Mary and Mary to John in a new relationship. That same cross binds all those called disciples together in a way that is beyond anything natural. It is by Christ's love for us and His love flowing through us to one another that others may know we are His disciples. The cross is our family tree.

Lord Jesus, this truth challenges me deeply: that I am bound not only to You but to everyone else who is bound to You. May the love You have for me and the love I have for You overflow both to those who love You and those who don't. Amen.

Shock tactics

For reading & meditation – Luke 14:25–35

'If anyone... does not hate his father and mother...
he cannot be my disciple.' (v26)

Several times over the past few weeks we have seen how Jesus shocked His hearers with the most challenging statements. Many people think that the words found in today's reading are among the most shocking and sensational He had ever spoken. . Unless we understand what Jesus was getting at when He spoke these words we can easily run away with the erroneous idea that He did not support family values.

Jesus was emphasising, once again, that our relationship with Him takes precedence over every other relationship. The words 'hate his father and mother', and so on, are not be taken to mean that disciples are to feel anger towards or detest their parents or any other of their relations, but rather that they are to put Jesus, His cause and His kingdom above and before everyone else to whom they relate.

FURTHER STUDY

2 Cor. 4:7-12,
16–18; 6:4-10;
1 Tim. 6:11-16;
2 Tim. 2:1-8

1. How did Paul show he was in a battle?

2. How does Paul encourage Timothy to be a fighter?

Jesus has come not to hold a party but a rescue mission – a rescue mission to save the world. The mission is so important that, like invasion troops before going into any major conflict or perilous mission, His followers may have to write their last letters home, set aside their own possessions and put their lives at risk. If we really understood the real emergency, He seems to be saying, brought on by the arrival of God's kingdom in our midst, we would be willing to go without our most precious things and rally to His cause. As Dallas Willard puts it, 'As long as one thinks anything is really more valuable than fellowship with Jesus in His kingdom, one cannot learn from Him.'

Lord Jesus, I understand that You are on a mission, a rescue mission, that will ultimately usher in Your kingdom. By Your grace I am with You. Thank You for Your calling and the strength that You provide to walk with You. Amen.

Upset families

For reading & meditation – Matthew 10:34–39

'I did not come to bring peace, but a sword.' (v34)

The passage before us today once again reveals something of the drastic and dramatic way in which Jesus upset the normal fabric of domestic life. Because He came as Messiah to establish God's sovereign rule, Jesus will not only bring peace but at times division also. Families will be split in their response to the challenge He brings. Those who become His disciples sometimes find their family members may not understand what they are doing, and may be misunderstood or even rejected by them. Just as Jesus puzzled His own family at times, so His disciples will sometimes baffle and confuse theirs.

FURTHER STUDY

John 15:9–17;
Rom. 15:5–9

1. What is love measured by according to Jesus?

2. Why do we pray for a spirit of unity?

Has responding to His call caused you to be misunderstood, perhaps even disowned, by your family? Take heart. You belong now to a new family – the family of the redeemed – and you may even begin to feel closer to them than you do to your blood relations. Having said that, however, there are sad stories of men and women who, having become Christians and been outlawed by their blood family, found that their new family, the Church, failed to welcome them and give them the nurture and support they needed. This not only grieves the heart of God but surely is far from the picture the New Testament presents of what a loving church family should be. If we do not love our brother whom we can see, says the apostle John, how can we love God whom we cannot see (1 John 4:20)? God forbid that those who lose their families because of their loyalty to Christ should then find the family of God unfriendly and unwelcoming.

Father, forgive us if we are insensitive to the plight of Christians who, because of their loyalty to You, have been rejected by their families. Help us to love and welcome them into their new family. For Your own dear name's sake. Amen.

Receiving Christ

For reading & meditation – Matthew 10:40–42

'He who receives you receives me, and he who receives
me receives the one who sent me.' (v40)

Here Jesus places great responsibility on those who are
unwelcoming to His disciples. 'The way in which people
treat you,' He told them, 'is the way they are treating me.' Dietrich
Bonhoeffer, in *The Cost of Discipleship*, said: 'The bearers of Jesus'
word receive a final word of promise for their work. They are now
Christ's fellow workers and will be like Him in all things. Thus they
are to meet those to whom they are sent as if they were Christ
Himself. When they are welcomed into a house, Christ enters with
them. They are bearers of His presence. They bring
with them the most precious gift in all the world,
the gift of Jesus Christ.' We are bearers of Christ's
presence in our homes, in our church, at school, in
our place of work, in the whole world.

FURTHER STUDY

1 Cor. 4:14-17;
1 Thess. 2:1-12;
Heb. 6:10-12;
13:7-8

1. In what ways
was Paul a true
representative
of love?

2. Who is worth
imitating?

Some people have taken these words of Jesus and
applied them inappropriately. One man, a professing
Christian, who was experiencing great difficulty in
his family relationships because of his own difficult
and demanding behaviour, confronted the members
of his family with this text and accused them of
being 'Christ crucifiers'. They were deeply offended, as they had no
wish to fall foul of the Christian gospel. The reality of the situation
was that this man, anxious to cover up his unchristian behaviour,
was trying to turn Jesus' statement to his own advantage.

How different is the description in today's verses of a true
disciple who shows hospitality to Jesus' servants. Even the smallest
act of kindness done in His name will not go unrewarded by Jesus.

**Lord Jesus, I see that as Your disciple I can bring to people the gift
of Your presence. Help me to be conscious of this and truly
represent Your love. Help me to be aware also when others bring
Your presence to me – and rejoice. Amen.**

'Celebrity-ism'

For reading & meditation – Matthew 19:16–30

'Jesus answered, "If you want to be perfect, go, sell your possessions… Then come, follow me."' (v21)

A new status has appeared among us, claims the Christian writer Larry Crabb. That new condition, he says, is 'Celebrity-ism'. He defines it as 'looking up to people just because they are in the public eye'. In today's world, people become celebrities on the flimsiest of pretexts. Jesus, however, was never overawed by the status of those with whom He came into contact. He saw people in their true light, irrespective of their position in life.

The man in our story today who met with Jesus was, we are told, young and rich (v22). He appeared to be honest, respectable and God-fearing. However, he collected commandments in the same way that some people might collect stamps! Jesus offered to help him to complete his collection by giving him another command: 'Sell your possessions… Then come, follow me' (v21). To his ears those words would have sounded more startling than they do now to ours, as in those days it was generally assumed that people with money, land and prestige were especially blessed by God.

FURTHER STUDY

Luke 21:1-4;
Col. 1:24-27;
2:9-15;
James 1:9-18

1. What have we been given in Christ?

2. From whom do perfect gifts come?

Characteristically, Jesus turned such an idea on its head by saying that it is as hard for a rich man to enter the kingdom of God as it is for a camel to go through the eye of a needle. In other words, all human ideas about the priority of wealth or fame count for nothing when it comes to entering into the kingdom. In God's new order there is a reversal of all normal notions of greatness and wealth and fame. Disciples are rich in the things that really matter.

Lord Jesus, how can I thank You enough for transforming my view of life? Help me see clearly now that one thing and one thing alone matters – my relationship with You. Having You I have everything. Thank You my Saviour. Amen.

The first prerequisite

For reading & meditation – Luke 10:38–42

'but only one thing is needed. Mary has chosen what is better, and it will not be taken away from her.' (v42)

Today's reading is one of the best-known incidents in Jesus' life. At one level it shows Jesus' humanity in that He wanted to be with friends, a home to which He could retreat from the pressures of ministry, and 'sisters' who no doubt fussed over Him. But even in this relatively everyday scene, the revolutionary characteristics of the kingdom of God become evident.

In the story, domestic harmony began to fracture when Martha, feeling overburdened by her workload, resented her sister's failure to help. But the issue was not, as is often suggested, an imbalance between the active and the contemplative life, between those that do and those who are quiet before God. A deeper drama was unfolding here. The real scandal was that Mary was behaving like a man! According to the conventions of the time, women were meant to stay in the kitchen. Martha knew her place and kept to it. But Mary did something which was socially risky. For a woman to be at ease in the company of men was regarded in those days as shameless behaviour.

FURTHER STUDY

Deut. 6:4–8;
Mark 12:28–34;
John 21:13–17;
1 John 4:20–21

1. What gives the greatest commandment its significance?

2. How does Jesus link love and service?

Even more disturbing was the fact that Mary sat at the feet of the teacher. This indicated much more than that she was hanging on Jesus' every word; this was the classic ancient posture of a disciple. And Jesus accepted Mary in this stance. Amid all the distracting demands of life, Mary seized the 'kingdom moment' and showed that she wanted more than anything to be a disciple of Jesus. The first prerequisite for being a disciple of Jesus is attentiveness to the Master. Service takes second place to that.

Jesus, my Saviour and my God, thank You for reminding me again that what You long for in our relationship is not just service but love. I would put my heart up against Your heart, feel its beat and catch its rhythm. Amen.

No place for sentimentality

For reading & meditation – Luke 11:14–28
'He replied, "Blessed rather are those who hear
the word of God and obey it."' (v28)

Among the crowd who gathered to hear Jesus' life-changing words in today's reading was one woman who, obviously impacted with what He had been saying, suddenly shouted out to Him, 'Blessed is Your mother!' The remark sounded innocent enough, but Jesus responds by saying, 'Blessed rather are those who hear the word of God and obey it.' It was a moment of sentimentality that He could easily have let pass, but J.B. Phillips, in his translation, as a heading for verses 27 and 28, wrote 'Jesus brings sentimentality down to earth'. Following Jesus and being His disciple is much more than sentimental feelings. The stakes are too high for that. He wants lasting disciples who hear and obey God's Word. That's the way to receive true blessing.

I believe it was Oswald Chambers who said that 'sentimentality consists of emotions that you have never worked out in practice or obedience'. How easy it is in Jesus' presence to be 'moved', but 'moved' to what ends? Feelings have to be translated into action, into response.

In their book *Kingdom Ethics*, Glen Stassen and David Gushee put their finger on this problem: 'People congratulate themselves on their being forgiven, without repenting; that God is on their side, without their following in the way of God as revealed in Jesus; that they are Christians, without it making much difference to their lives.' When we respond to His call to true discipleship, we don't just admire Jesus from the sidelines; we follow Him on the road.

FURTHER STUDY

Rom. 6:13–18;
1 Thess. 2:13–16;
2 Thess. 2:13–16;
3:6–10

1. What results from our obedience?

2. How does Paul link the word of men with the Word of God?

Lord Jesus, You make things very clear. Your blessings come to
those who do more than just hear Your Word, they obey it also.
Your mother was such an example of that. May I be an example too.
Amen.

Love and obedience

For reading & meditation – John 14:15–31

'I love the Father and... do exactly what my Father
has commanded me.' (v31)

In many ways – and this is meant reverently – Jesus Himself
is the best model of a disciple we could ever hope to find. He
demonstrates in His own relationship with the Father the kind of
relationship He longs and hopes for with us.

Jesus was governed by two powerful motivations: love and
obedience. Frequently today, love and obedience are regarded
by some as incompatible. It is a sign of our times that the pledge
to 'love, honour and obey' is absent in many wedding services.
It is suggested that to talk about obedience in the
marriage ceremony is to confuse issues, because
the commitment to love ought to be enough. An old
song says, 'Love and marriage, love and marriage,
go together like a horse and carriage.' But love
and obedience? People seem to have difficulty in
tying the two together. Jesus, however, understood
obedience as the evidence of love. For Him, love and
obedience were joined together by God and should
not be put asunder.

FURTHER STUDY

John 16:22-28;
1 Cor. 13:4-7;
Heb. 2:14-3:6

1. How does
Jesus model
the love Paul
talks about?

2. In what ways
is Jesus our
apostle and
high priest?

By acting out the part of a true and loving 'disciple'
Jesus, of course, clarified for us what love is all about.
Divine love is tender but tough; it both feels and acts, and it blends
fierce intensity of emotion with firm commitments. This kind of
love is passionate and faithful. It never lets us go or lets us down.
It doesn't just utter fine words but expresses itself in self-giving,
as demonstrated on the cross. 'The world must learn,' said Jesus,
'that I love the Father like this.' Just as Jesus models a love that is
expressed in obedience, we can safely do the same.

**Lord Jesus, just as You demonstrated Your love for Your Father
through Your obedience, so may I demonstrate my love for You in
the same way. Save me from thinking there can be any other way.
Amen.**

Long-term obedience

For reading & meditation – Matthew 28:18-20

'go and make disciples of all nations, baptising them in the
name of the Father... Son and... Holy Spirit' (v19)

We return now to the deep concern that prompted this theme.
It is well expressed by Glen Stassen and David Gushee
who write: 'When Jesus' way of discipleship is thinned down,
marginalised or avoided, the churches and Christians lose their
antibodies against infection by secular ideologies that manipulate
Christians into serving the purposes of some other lord.'

Today's text forms what we might call the standing-orders or, if
you like, the mission statement of the Christian Church. We need
to be continually reminded of it. Biblical evangelism
is not just a matter of winning people to Christ but
of making disciples for Christ. When you think of
it, there is no other way the Church can be built up.
Imagine the Church without committed disciples,
living merely on the vagaries of feelings. Such a
movement would have become extinct years ago.
Responding to His call means committing ourselves
to long-term learning and obedience, whereupon we
find ourselves immersed in the glorious love and life
of the Trinity – Father, Son and Holy Spirit. Then we
embark on the continued teaching and training that
makes us mature.

FURTHER STUDY

Eph. 1:17-23;
3:14-21;
Col. 1:15-23

1. Immerse
yourself in the
Trinity life of
God as you pray
Paul's prayers.

2. About what
was the apostle
Paul passionate?

Where do you stand in relation to this mission statement? Are
you committed to following Jesus wherever He leads you? Do you
enjoy your Christian life and experience, or are you just enduring
it? Disciples are passionate people whose passion is nurtured by
the most passionate being in the universe.

**Lord Jesus, whatever passion I have for You – today I open my heart
to receive more of You. Let Your passion ignite my passion. Help me
always to receive more of You. In Your peerless and precious name
I pray. Amen.**

'The Christ Person'

For reading & meditation – Acts 11:25–30

'The disciples were called Christians first at Antioch.' (v26)

In today's reading Barnabas and Saul, seeing the great need of these new disciples at Antioch, 'taught great numbers of people'. Now, as then, new Christians need teaching in the great truths of the gospel and in practical Christ-like living.

It was not enough to profess faith in Christ; converts learnt to demonstrate over time how they were learning to live and behave like Jesus. Decisions were not enough; making disciples was what mattered. So Barnabas and Saul taught the believers in Antioch for a whole year. What a wonderful experience to be taught personally by these great men. These were not just Bible studies for the curious: their teaching was intended to shape the hearers' lives.

Eventually, when those inside the Church had grown to live like Jesus, to act and react in Christ-like ways, then those outside the Church, perhaps rather mockingly or possibly affectionately, started to call them the *Christianos* – the Christ people! Was there something in the lives of these Christians at Antioch that reminded people of the self-giving love of Jesus. Many years ago A.W. Tozer, aware of the trend to water down the claims of Christ in his day, wrote in an article titled 'The Old Cross, and the New' these challenging words: 'God offers life, but not an improved old life. The life He offers is life out of death. It stands always on the far side of the cross.' If at times it feels as if we have failed in our calling, I thank God that, knowing our frailties, He reaches out, takes our hand and calls us further up and further in.

FURTHER STUDY

Acts 28:16-24;
28:28-31;
Rom. 16:25-27

1. What is our final glimpse of Paul as a committed disciple?

2. Join Paul in his benediction and give thanks.

Thank You, Lord Jesus, for what You have taught me about being a true disciple. From this day forward help me to be a more deeply committed follower of You than ever before. For Your honour and glory I pray. Amen.

Our True Identity

Two identities

For reading & meditation – Ephesians 1:1–14

'For he chose us in him before the creation of the world to
be holy and blameless in his sight.' (v4)

Today we begin a series of devotional meditations that I pray
will lead us to a deeper understanding of what it means to
enter into our true identity in Christ. A Christian is a person with
two identities. One is our natural identity, which we grow into,
and the other is the one given to us by God. Our true identity is
the second one – the one that becomes ours when we give our
lives to God. According to the dictionary, identity is 'a sense of
one's distinctiveness'.

I was once challenged by someone who claimed
that as the word 'identity' is not found in the Bible, I
should not be discussing it. With my response, I was
able to bring to his attention the many terms we use
as Christians that are not found in Scripture – 'the
Trinity' and 'the attributes of God', to name just two.
The truths they define, however, are clearly laid down
in the Bible.

We frequently hear people speaking about an
'identity crisis' – and this term does not solely apply
to adolescents who are wrestling with the questions of who they
are and their changing role in life. Interestingly, Christians can
experience a similar identity crisis. It is possible to be a Christian,
experience God's forgiveness and be sure of your future in heaven,
but – as far as your life on this earth is concerned – not understand
the unique role that God has planned for you. Yet, as the text for
today tells us, God had plans for us 'before the creation of the
world'. There remains a confusion and tension living in two worlds.
Is it possible that the world has not yet seen the real you?

FURTHER STUDY

Deut. 7:6–9;
Matt. 25:31–34

1. Why did God
choose the
Israelites?

2. When did
God prepare a
kingdom for us
to inhabit?

**Father, take me deeper into You, I pray. Help me come to a greater
understanding of who I really am – the person You intend me to be.
In Jesus' name. Amen.**

Why couldn't you be you?

For reading & meditation – 2 Corinthians 5:1–10

'For we must all appear before the judgment seat of Christ that each one may receive what is due to him' (v10)

After a lifetime of observing Christians and trying to help them with their life struggles, I have to say that it has always distressed me to find Christians who have no clear understanding of their new identity in Christ and of God's unique purpose for their lives. An apocryphal story recounts how an elderly rabbi named Zusya died and went to stand before the judgment seat of God. As he waited for God to appear, he grew nervous, thinking about his life and how little he had done. He started to persuade himself that God was going to ask him, 'Why couldn't you have been like Moses or Solomon or David?' But when God did appear, He simply asked, 'Why weren't you Zusya?'

FURTHER STUDY

Matt. 25:14-30

1. How did the servants handle what was entrusted to them?

2. What are the rewards of faithfulness?

Imagine appearing before God and discovering, when it is too late, that the real you – the person God intended and longed for you to be – never saw the light of day. In his play *As You Like It*, Shakespeare famously wrote: 'All the world's a stage, and all the men and women merely players... one man in his time plays many parts.' But what if those parts are the parts that others expect us to play, rather than the life God wants us to be able to live? So many spend their days standing centre-stage in life, living up to other people's expectations; trying to be something they are not, when they could be discovering their true identity and being the people God meant them to be. It's important to understand that, whatever identity you have formed for yourself since you came into this world, that is not your true identity. Your true identity is the one that is found in Jesus.

Gracious Lord and Master, I sense that I am on the verge of amazing discoveries about who I am in You. Give me, I pray, an understanding mind and heart to grasp the things You want to reveal to me. Amen.

You are... you will be

For reading & meditation – John 1:35–42

'Jesus looked at him and said, "You are Simon son of John.
You will be called Cephas"' (v42)

A favourite passage of mine is the one before us today. I have
preached on it and commented on it hundreds of times over
the years. Jesus looks into the heart of Simon Peter and foresees the
man he would eventually become. 'You are Simon,' He said. 'You
will be... Cephas.' References to Simon Peter often cause confusion.
That is because we are dealing with four languages. We find the
Hebrew name Simon, the Aramaic name Cephas, the Greek name
Petros, and the English name Peter.

When Jesus said to Simon Peter, 'You will be called
Cephas', He used the Aramaic word for 'rock' (which
is *petros* in the Greek language). I wonder how those
who knew him would have described Simon Peter's
identity – his friends and family, for example. We
rarely see ourselves as others see us. Others would
no doubt have said that he was outspoken; impulsive;
generous; a good leader. At times he was even loud-mouthed, and
certainly knew how to curse and swear (see Mark 14:71). I wonder,
too, how Simon saw himself. Perhaps he viewed himself in a more
generous way – a caring family man and a loyal friend. But Jesus,
when looking into the heart of Simon Peter, saw his true identity. He
saw him not as he was but as he would become – a rock. 'That
is the man I will make you,' Jesus was saying, 'the man I plan for
you to be.' The disciple who would deny all knowledge of Jesus in
His hour of greatest need, would go on to become the courageous
leader whose fearless preaching led to the conversion of 3,000 souls
on the day of Pentecost (see Acts 2:14–41). The reed who was so
easily shaken by the wind became a rock – the man God intended.

FURTHER STUDY

Acts 9:1-19

1. What was
Saul like?

2. What was Saul
to become?

**Lord Jesus, I wonder what You see as You look deep into my life.
Help me come to a clearer understanding day by day of the person
You plan for me to be. Amen.**

As solid as a rock

For reading & meditation – 1 Peter 1:1–12

'Praise be to the God and Father of our Lord Jesus Christ!
In his great mercy he has given us new birth' (v3)

Whenever I read of Simon Peter in the Acts of the Apostles, I wonder if the person I am reading about is really the blustering, hot-headed fisherman we meet in the Gospels! The man who had once caved under pressure did indeed become what Jesus intended him to become – a rock. In Acts we see Peter healing a crippled beggar (Acts 3), preaching with great power to the people and the Sanhedrin (Acts 4), receiving a vision that resulted in him ministering to Gentiles in Cornelius' house (Acts 10), and being miraculously delivered from prison (Acts 12).

FURTHER STUDY
John 18:15–18, 25–27;
Acts 5:27–29, 40–42
1. How did Peter respond to persecution before the resurrection?
2. How did he respond afterwards?

But perhaps the most overwhelming evidence that Peter truly became the man God intended him to be is seen in the two letters he wrote. These show that he became as solid as a rock not only in the practice of the Christian life, but also in doctrine. Reading the opening chapter of 1 Peter, we find him first of all affirming that God is the source of new life and a living hope brought about by Jesus' resurrection (v3). Second, that God is the source of a faith that is more precious than gold (v7). Third, that in God is found inexpressible joy (v8). Fourth, that God judges with fairness and impartiality (v17). We could go on to examine at least another dozen or so great affirmations that he makes in the subsequent chapters of his two letters, but suffice to say that Peter's solid grasp of truth and his loyalty to Christ leaves no room to doubt that the man Jesus said he would be was indeed the man he became.

Lord Jesus, my desire is to be the person You created me to be.
Forgive me if I have been satisfied with staying with my natural
identity, rather than reaching out and finding my
true identity in You. Amen.

X-ray vision

For reading & meditation – Luke 19:1–10

'Look, Lord! Here and now I give half of my possessions to the poor' (v8)

Over the past couple of days we have seen how Jesus looked at Simon, the reed blowing in the wind, and saw Peter, the rock. Jesus sees with x-ray vision – He sees past who we are to who we can become.

Some years ago I was visiting a zoo with one of my grandsons when he suddenly started to cry. What prompted this was the sight of an eagle in its cage. Because of his great love for birds and animals, he felt sad that this wonderful bird, made for the skies, was confined to a cage. So many of us are like that eagle – made for the skies, but surrounded by bars. We have never understood or entered into our true identity.

I have asked you to read today the story of Zacchaeus' meeting with Jesus because it reinforces the impact that an encounter with Jesus can have on our personality. Zacchaeus changed in moments from being a mean, tight-fisted individual to a person who was generous and large-hearted. In his novel The Robe, Lloyd Douglas imagines: 'Perhaps he [Jesus] looked Zacchaeus squarely in the eyes until the man saw – reflected there – the image of the person he was meant to be'. Douglas is using artistic licence here, of course, but if we could all look steadily into the eyes of Jesus and see there the vision He has for us, we would not be content to remain as we are. Instead, we would gain new energy to be the men and women He sees us to be. The poet Ralph Waldo Emerson wrote: 'Could'st thou in vision see

Thyself the man God meant, Thou never more could be, The man thou art – content'

FURTHER STUDY

Matt. 4:18–22; 9:9–13

1. How did Christ see the disciples with double vision?

2. How did they respond to His call?

Gracious Father, please give me that vision – the vision of the person You long for me to be. Then I know I will never be content with the person I am. Grant it, dear Father, I pray. In Jesus' name. Amen.

Less, not nothing

For reading & meditation – John 3:22–36
'He must become greater; I must become less.' (v30)

When Jesus looks at us, He sees us not as we are but as we can be. Jesus looked at Saul the zealot and saw Paul the apostle. He looked at Augustine the sensualist and saw Augustine the saint. As He looks at you, what does He see, I wonder? Of this you can be sure: He sees you not just as you are, but as you can become.

Earlier we said some Christians might think that because the word 'identity' is not found in the Bible, we should not even consider the issue. Other Christians object to the word 'self' (another word for identity) being mentioned in connection with spiritual issues. They argue that any focus on self is dangerous because it turns our attention from Christ to ourselves. We are to think of ourselves as nothing, they say, and of Christ as everything. Well, it is true that Jesus is everything, but it does not follow that we are to think of ourselves as nothing – as nobodies.

I once heard a preacher speaking on today's passage, who claimed that just as John the Baptist decided he must become nothing, so also must we. However, John did not say he wanted to become nothing, but less. John had in mind the truth that his ministry as the forerunner of Jesus was coming to an end, because the Saviour was about to take over. I would go as far as to say that the idea that we should focus on God and Christ alone – and not seek to understand ourselves and our identity as new creations in Christ Jesus – is not Christian, and is in fact anti?Christian. Understanding ourselves and our new identity in Jesus is an important aspect of our spiritual journey.

FURTHER STUDY
Acts 26:4-23
1. Where did Saul find his identity before his conversion?
2. How did Paul view his new identity in Christ?

Lord Jesus, help me understand more clearly that although You are everything, that does not mean I am to be nothing. You do not see me as a nobody, so please help me not to see myself as one either. Amen.

'Double knowledge'

For reading & meditation – 1 Timothy 4:9–16
'Watch your life and doctrine closely. Persevere in them'
(v16)

If, as we have been saying, one of our goals on the Christian journey is to become the people God intends us to be, then it is vital that we know something about ourselves as well as knowing God. I would go as far as to say there can be no true Christian spirituality without what theologians describe as 'double knowledge'. The need to know both God and the new self in Jesus is, I believe, something that the contemporary Christian Church may not have emphasised properly or even recognised.

Many of the great saints of the past have understood this, and if you study Church history you will find numerous statements made by Christian activists and scholars who recognised the importance of this 'double knowledge'. John Calvin, in his famous book, The Institutes of the Christian Religion, wrote: 'There is no deep knowing of God without the deep knowing of self, and no deep knowing of self without the deep knowing of God.' Augustine, a great leader of the Church in the fifth century, composed a prayer which has been prayed over the centuries by multitudes of Christians: 'Grant, Lord, that I may know myself as I know Thee.' Thomas Merton, a more recent writer, has expressed a similar thought in this way: 'There is only one problem on which all my existence, my peace and my happiness depend; to discover myself in discovering God.'

Any attempt to know more about God without desiring to know more about ourselves and our true identity will result in unbalanced Christian living.

FURTHER STUDY

Phil. 3:2–14;
2 Cor. 12:9–10

1. What was Paul's ambition?

2. What did Paul understand about himself and God's power?

Father, I see that this 'double knowledge' is necessary for my development as a Christian. Help me not to focus on the one and ignore the other. For Your honour and glory I ask it. Amen.

Shipwrecked lives

For reading & meditation – Proverbs 2:1–15

'For wisdom will enter your heart, and knowledge will
be pleasant to your soul.' (v10)

The statement with which we ended yesterday – any attempt
to know more about God without desiring to know more about
ourselves and our true identity will result in unbalanced Christian
living – needs some explanation. Today's verses from Proverbs
talk about the moral benefits of the wisdom that comes from God.
But that wisdom, I believe, enables us not only to know God but
ourselves also.

Dr David Benner, a well-respected author and lecturer, says

FURTHER STUDY

Matt. 23:1-7,
23-28;
1 Tim. 1:18-19

1. How did the
Pharisees lack
self-awareness?

2. Why may
people
shipwreck
their faith?

that 'focusing on God while failing to understand
ourselves may produce an external form of piety
which is not earthed in reality'. He tells of one
particular minister known to him, who was the
pastor of a very successful church and appeared to
have a deep knowledge of God. However, this man
knew little about himself, and eventually this lack of
awareness about himself and his weaknesses paved
the way for him to commit a sin that ruined his
ministry. His inner self was largely unknown to him.

My own experience of dealing with the many
ministers and Christian leaders who have come to me for
counselling over the years confirms David Benner's findings. I,
too, have been surprised that those in positions of leadership in
the Church, through their lack of self-knowledge and awareness
could fall into sin, when they seemed to have studied the Bible and
know so much about God. And inevitably, their life and ministry
has been shipwrecked as a result of their actions. Knowing God,
is not enough; we must know something about ourselves as well.

**Father, save me from being spiritually shipwrecked by an
unwillingness to look at what may be going on within me. Guard
me from this danger, I pray. In Jesus' name. Amen.**

A staggering statement

For reading & meditation – Matthew 18:1–9

'it would be better for him to have a large millstone hung
around his neck' (v6)

DAY
129

Yesterday we spoke about Christian leaders who have a
knowledge of God but understand little about themselves
and their own identity. Sadly, such short-sightedness means that
our lives are unbalanced and can cause our spiritual downfall. I
particularly mention those in Christian leadership because of Jesus'
teaching about the dangers of the blind leading the blind (Matt.
15:14). It is so easy for both to fall into the pit of failure and despair.

How many churches have been wounded by leaders who
profess to know God but know little or nothing about
themselves? And how many young Christians have
become disillusioned and then faltered in their faith
because of disappointment in a spiritual leader?
The importance of this cannot be overemphasised
for, as Jesus says in today's text, it would be better
for a person who causes young believers (young in
years as well as young in faith) to sin to have a large
millstone hung around his neck and be drowned in the depths of
the sea. Wen you consider the damage that can be caused by a
leader who falls into sin, and the wounds he inflicts on those whose
faith is just being formed, these words are quite understandable.

FURTHER STUDY

Matt. 15:10-20;
1 Cor. 9:27

1. What did the
Pharisees fail
to understand?

2. What was
Paul's concern?

Although I have been focusing on Christian leaders, what I have
been saying applies to every Christian. The consequences of seeking
to know God but deliberately ignoring a biblical understanding of
the self results in broken marriages, family upheavals, and a whole
host of other problems. John Calvin's statement bears repeating:
'There is no deep knowing of God without the deep knowing of self,
and no deep knowing of self without the deep knowing of God.'

**God my Father, I pray today for every Christian leader and ask that
You will help them in this important matter of knowing themselves
as well as knowing You. And I pray the same for myself also.
In Jesus' name. Amen.**

The peril of distraction

For reading & meditation – Psalm 139:17-24

'See if there is any offensive way in me, and lead me in the way everlasting.' (v24)

I have found that when dealing with the matter of understanding the self, it is so easy to be misunderstood. I want to emphasise that when I talk about the importance of understanding who we are and our true identity, I am not suggesting that it is necessary to enrol in a course in psychology. We simply need to open our minds to biblical teaching on the subject.

The Christian leader known by Dr Benner, to whom we referred two days ago, fell into sin because, in the words of Dr Benner,

FURTHER STUDY

Psa. 26:1-3;
Prov. 17:3;
Isa. 1:10-17

1. Why should we ask God to examine our hearts?

2. Why would God not hear Israel's prayers?

'he dared not expose the reality of his inner world to God'. This leader accepted and understood the truth that sin is to be brought before God and His forgiveness sought when we deviate from God's plan, but he made sure that the sins he exposed to God were small sins (if, of course, there is such a thing as a 'small' sin) – ones that did not have a great effect on others. He did not allow the searchlight of God's Word to show him the deep root of sin in his heart, and this superficial knowledge contributed to his downfall.

But before we judge this man too quickly, we ought to examine ourselves to see if we are acting similarly. Do we, for example, ask God to forgive us for not working harder in His kingdom (something most of us might often need to confess) simply as a distraction, in the hope that our confession will keep God's focus, and ours, off the deeper issues that lie in our hearts? May the peril of distraction not hinder God's gracious work in us to help us find our true identity.

Father God, help me to be honest with You in all things. But when I see the deceitfulness of my heart, help me to always remember that I have a risen, ascended Lord who is able to save me completely when I come to God through Him (Heb. 7:25). Amen.

An oft-practised ploy

For reading & meditation – Psalm 51:1–19

'Surely you desire truth in the inner parts; you teach me wisdom in the inmost place.' (v6)

Today we continue considering the possibility that we might sometimes confess minor issues to God in the hope that this will distract our attention, and God's, from the much more damaging issues that need to be confessed. I have often seen this played out as I have counselled Christians over the years. A person might acknowledge issues such as laziness, or neglecting to spend time with God in prayer. After a while, however, it becomes apparent that talking about these 'minor' issues is an attempt to avoid the more major issues in their lives – issues that lie at the root of their behaviours, and which are the underlying reason why they are disinclined to pray or read the Scriptures.

FURTHER STUDY

1 Sam. 15:10-24;
Jer. 17:9-10

1. What is better than sacrifice?

2. Why may we be deceived?

How easy it is to be self-deceived. The psalm we have read today shows us that it is not enough for us to be true outwardly – in the self we project to others. We must be true also on the inside – in the inner parts of our being. But it is not easy to be honest, either with God or with oneself. I have to put myself on the line here and say that I have found one of the greatest difficulties in my life is being honest about what is going on in my heart. Sometimes, as I have looked into my heart, I have been astonished at the realisation of just how self-deceived I can be. There is, perhaps, no deception as dangerous and damaging as self-deception.

The second half of today's text says, 'You teach me wisdom in the inmost place.' Only God can provide us with the true wisdom that enables us to realise the reality of who we are, both to ourselves and to Him.

My Father and my God, give me that wisdom I pray – the wisdom that affects not only my mind but the deeper expanses of my heart also. This I ask in Jesus' name. Amen.

Subjective knowledge

For reading & meditation – Psalm 36:1–12

'Continue your love to those who know you, your righteousness to the upright in heart.' (v10)

Experience has shown me that people who are unwilling to look closely at themselves are equally unwilling to look closely at God. They cling to ideas about God, often using them as a substitute for direct experience of Him. Knowing God and knowing one's self are, as I have been emphasising, interdependent. God and self are best known in relation to each other.

Often, for example, I have talked with Christians who said they know God is forgiving. Yet their understanding of His forgiveness was limited because they were unwilling to open their hearts fully to Him and ask Him to forgive all their sin. Sadly, because they were unwilling to acknowledge matters such as wrong thinking in their lives, they were unwilling to accept God's instructions given in Scripture, such as His insistence on allowing truth to penetrate our inward parts, which we mentioned yesterday. Similarly, some people say they believe and understand that God is love, but in listening closely to them I have found their understanding of God's love to be superficial. And why? Because to truly understand the love of God we must receive it in an undefended state, just as we are.

FURTHER STUDY

2 Sam.
11:26–12:13

1. How did David despise God?

2. How did Nathan help David to deepen his knowledge of himself and God?

If we do not allow ourselves a degree of vulnerability with a wife, a husband, children and close friends, then we will also be guarded when we approach God. If we are honest, often our understanding of God is more objective than subjective.' Objective knowledge is something we acquire from a distance; subjective knowledge is gained by experience.

Father, I ask myself if I am guilty of this. Is my knowledge of You merely objective and not subjective? Search my heart, Lord, and please help me to come clean. In Jesus' name. Amen.

Superficial knowledge

For reading & meditation – Psalm 7:1–9

'Judge me, O LORD, according to my righteousness,
according to my integrity, O Most High.' (v8)

We reflect further on the subject we raised yesterday – the difference between objective and subjective knowledge. If the knowledge of our self is objective, then we will carry this over into our relationship with God. If, on the other hand, it is subjective – involving our feelings and experience – then we will carry this over into our understanding of God and our relationship with Him. The more deeply we know ourselves, the more deeply we will know God. This cannot be overstressed, for my reading of Christian books and magazines published at the time of writing these notes tells me this is largely a forgotten factor in contemporary Christian society.

FURTHER STUDY

Dan. 4:24-37

1. Why did God take away the king's authority?

2. How did the king come to know God more deeply?

Dr David Benner, the Christian professor whom I mentioned a few days ago, recounts how he once listened to a man talking about his knowledge of God. As this man spoke, Dr Benner sensed that though he used a lot of words, his knowledge of God was nevertheless superficial. This was confirmed when the man began to talk about his personal life. Dr Benner said: 'Listening to the things he told me about his life was like reading a throwaway paperback novel or watching a B-grade movie. The role he was playing lacked depth and reality. It was two-dimensional. As he told me about himself, he was describing someone he had been watching from a distance. The knowledge he had of his person was objective and remote.' Dr Benner makes the point that because this man's knowledge of himself was superficial, so also was his knowledge of God. The prayer of Augustine was this: 'Grant, Lord, that I may know myself as I know Thee.'

Father, I take this prayer spoken by Augustine on my own lips today and pray it most sincerely: 'Grant, Lord, that I may know myself as I know Thee.' In Jesus' name I ask it. Amen.

A humble self-knowledge

For reading & meditation – 1 Corinthians 8:1–13
'Knowledge puffs up, but love builds up.' (v1)

Thomas à Kempis, in his book *The Imitation of Christ*, said: 'A humble self-knowledge is a surer way to God than a search after deep learning.' Notice the phrase, 'a humble self-knowledge'. It is always a pleasure, as I am sure you have found, talking with someone who has a great deal of knowledge but does not show it off in an arrogant and boastful manner. Humility is a very attractive virtue, especially in those who are extremely knowledgeable.

I have come across people – and doubtless you have too – whose knowledge has inflated their ego. Knowledge for its own sake can easily lead to conceit. This is what Paul is talking about in the passage before us today – a knowledge that puffs up but does not build up. The knowledge that builds us up, he says, is the knowledge that has love at its heart. Of course, when Paul talks about love, he has in mind the love that is deposited in our hearts by God. That love enables us to take whatever knowledge we gain and use it to achieve good and godly outcomes. When love is absent, self-knowledge can lead to problems such as self-preoccupation.

FURTHER STUDY
Micah 6:8;
Luke 14:7-11

1. What does God require of us?
2. What was the advice of Jesus?

Some theologians like to use the term 'transformational knowledge' when talking about the kind of knowledge under discussion here (that is, knowledge of the self that leads not to self-preoccupation but to loving concern for others). The puzzling paradox is that there are many Christians who are not short of knowledge about either God or themselves, and yet, because there is little love guiding that knowledge, it seems not to do them any good or enable them to grow spiritually.

Father, protect me from the kind of knowledge that breeds arrogance. May love be the underlying motive that guides me in everything I do. In Jesus' name. Amen.

It is always personal

For reading & meditation – Matthew 15:1–9

'They worship me in vain; their teachings are but rules taught by men.' (v9)

We will benefit, I believe, from dwelling further on the thought with which we ended yesterday, namely that some Christians are not short of knowledge about God or themselves, and yet it seems not to help them relate well or grow spiritually. It is possible for our minds to be full of information about God and ourselves that does not help us to really know either. Knowing about God objectively does not transform the soul any more than having information about love and not experiencing it.

Today's reading tells us that the Pharisees knew a great deal about God and His law, but knew nothing of His heart: 'These people honour me with their lips, but their hearts are far from me' (v8). They possessed objective knowledge that had never been made personal. Transformational knowledge is always personal. It involves not merely knowing about something, but knowing it personally and relationally. When my wife was alive, I knew that she loved me because I experienced that love. To really know God's love, we need to receive that love and allow it to reach the depths of our being.

FURTHER STUDY

Luke 11:46–54;
2 Tim. 3:15

1. What is the key to true knowledge?

2. What is the purpose of wisdom or knowledge?

At the time of writing, I still find that the more open and honest I am to God and myself, the more deeply I know both. People who have never developed a personal knowledge of God through His Son Jesus will find a limit in their understanding of themselves. If we fail to know God subjectively, we will not know ourselves subjectively for, as someone has said, 'God is the only context in which the human personality can make sense of itself.'

Father, help me not to be content with merely knowing about You objectively, but to yearn and seek to know you more – personally and relationally – each day, and transform my relationships with others too. In Jesus' name. Amen.

Knowing – yet not knowing

For reading & meditation – Luke 5:1–11

'Simon Peter... fell at Jesus' knees and said, "Go away from me, Lord; I am a sinful man!"' (v8)

To illustrate our discussions over the past few days, it is helpful to take another look at the life of Simon Peter. When the 'Big Fisherman' (as Lloyd Douglas called him) first met Jesus, he came to understand that He was the Messiah (see John 1:41). In the passage before us today, we find Peter witnessing a miraculous catch of fish. This miracle, no doubt, strengthened his belief that Jesus was the Promised One. At this stage, his knowledge of Jesus as the Messiah was built on the testimony of his brother, Andrew,

FURTHER STUDY
2 Kings 5:9-27

1. What did Gehazi know about God?

2. How do we know his knowledge of God was incomplete?

and his own brief contact with Jesus. That is about as much as he knew of Him. But what did he know about himself? He certainly knew he was a sinner (as our text for today indicates), but it is unlikely he knew the depth of his fears or the extent of his pride. This level of understanding awaited a deeper experience of Jesus.

As Peter followed Jesus, however, and learned more about Him, it becomes clear that he started to know more about himself. His experience of walking on the water with Jesus no doubt taught him that he could take a bold step of faith, but also that he could quickly capitulate to fear (Matt. 14:22–33). But then, later, Jesus told him that the hour would soon come when he would deny all knowledge of Him (Matt. 26:34). Peter was shocked by such a revelation. Doubtless he thought to himself, 'Doesn't Jesus know of my loyalty and the strength of my commitment to Him?' Peter found it easier to doubt Jesus than to doubt himself. He had not yet encountered either the intense pride or great fears that were lurking in his heart.

Gracious Father, I am seeing more clearly that however much I know of You, my heart awaits a knowledge that is deeper still. As I prayed at the beginning of this series, please take me deeper into You. In Jesus' name. Amen.

Growing in self-understanding

For reading & meditation – John 21:15–25

'Jesus said to Simon Peter, "Simon son of John, do you truly love me more than these?"' (v15)

We continue pursuing the thought that God and self are best known in relation to each other, and we are seeing this illustrated in the life of Simon Peter. Reflect on Peter's reaction when Jesus knelt to wash the disciples' feet (John 13:6–9). What might we say of Peter's knowledge of Christ and of himself at this point? Then, following his denial of Jesus, Peter was overwhelmed with anguish. A word from a young girl drew from him a degree of disloyalty that he did not know was in his heart. He had discovered a part of himself of which he was unaware, and it filled him with shame and regret (Matt. 26:69–75).

Today's reading reveals a significant development in Peter's life as he comes to learn more about the Saviour's love for him, and in turn gains a deeper knowledge of himself. In Jesus' questioning of Peter two different words for 'love' are used. In His first two questions to Peter, Jesus used the strong Greek verb for 'to love' – *agapao*: 'Do you love me?' But when Peter replied, he used the lesser Greek verb *phileo*, which conveys affection and friendship. However, the third time Jesus questioned Peter, He asked, 'Are you my friend?' (v17, Phillips), as if suggesting, 'Peter, is this all I mean to you? Do you not love me in the way I love you?' It would have been good to read that Peter abandoned the lesser verb *phileo* and said, 'Yes, Lord, I love You,' using the same verb as Jesus used – *agapao*. But he didn't. Had the knowledge of his previous failures prepared him for a more honest facing of himself? If so, he was growing in his understanding of Christ and also of himself.

FURTHER STUDY

John 14:1–6;
20:19–29

1. What did Thomas discover about himself?

2. What did he discover about Jesus?

Lord Jesus, in my relationship with You, help me not to be content with using the lesser words, but to say without any awkwardness or embarrassment, 'I love You'. Amen.

How well are you growing?

For reading & meditation – 2 Peter 3:10–18
'But grow in the grace and knowledge of our Lord and Saviour Jesus Christ.' (v18)

What, I wonder, did Simon Peter reflect on after the post-resurrection encounter with Jesus that we looked at yesterday? How I wish we had a record of Peter's thoughts in the days between that time of questioning and the descent of the Spirit at Pentecost. If we could have interviewed Peter during that period, and asked him some questions about his understanding of Jesus and himself, I imagine he would have said something like this: 'I have come to see how little I knew about either myself or the Master. Following my denial of Him and my refusal to be recognised as one of His disciples, I did not deserve to be forgiven. But the fact that He did not hold this disloyalty against me and continued to show me His love, has truly amazed me.'

FURTHER STUDY

1 Pet. 2:2;
2 Pet. 1:2-8

1. How do we grow in the Christian faith?

2. What are the qualities of a mature Christian?

This is only conjecture, of course, but I imagine it's pretty close to what was really going on in his mind. Our observation of the way in which Simon Peter acquired a deeper knowledge of both God and himself shows us how genuine knowledge of God and self is gained. Peter came to know himself more deeply in relation to Jesus. He did not know himself until Jesus showed him who he was, but as he learned about himself, he also came to learn more about Jesus and, as today's text shows, it was his desire that we should grow too.

Before moving on, pause and reflect on what you may have learned about yourself from your encounters with God, and also what you may have learned about God when you have examined your deeper self. How well are you growing?

Father, I hear Your call to have a closer personal encounter with You, and to move beyond objective knowledge to personal knowledge. Take me there I pray. In Jesus' name. Amen.

God longs to be known

For reading & meditation – Hosea 6:1–11

'For I desire mercy and not sacrifice, and the knowledge of
God more than burnt offerings.' (v6, NKJV)

Having demonstrated that our knowledge of God depends on
our knowledge of ourselves, and our knowledge of ourselves
depends on our knowledge of God, we move on now to consider
how we can develop our knowledge – first of God and then of
ourselves. I say deepen our knowledge of God, for I am talking
here to those who have already entered into a relationship with
Him by putting their faith in Jesus Christ.

The starting point of all true knowledge of God is the knowledge
of oneself as a sinner, and the need to be rescued
from our sin through the forgiveness and new start
offered to us by Jesus' sacrifice for us on the cross.
This means we need to repent of our sin. When we
have done that and put our faith in Christ, God then
gives us the spirit of wisdom and revelation so that
we may know Him better and have the eyes of our
heart enlightened (Eph. 1:17–18).

It is a curious spiritual paradox that as committed
Christians we come to know God best – not by
looking at God exclusively, but by looking at God, then at ourselves,
and then at God again. Ever since I became a Christian, I have
been astonished by the thought that God desires to be known by
His human creation. But apparently, as today's text shows, this
brings Him immense pleasure. Revealing Himself to the men and
women He created, it seems, gives Him great delight. However,
we are not to draw from this the conclusion that God created
us because He had a need to be known. God may not need to be
known, but He does want to be known.

FURTHER STUDY

Isa. 1:2-4;
Hosea 4:1;
1 John 2:3-6

1. What was
God's charge
against Israel?

2. What is
the result of
knowing God?

**Loving Father, it is quite astonishing to me that You long to be
known by Your human creation. And what joy it is to me to know
You in the measure I do. Yet there is much more to be known.
So lead on, my Father. Amen.**

God - a caricature?

For reading & meditation – Acts 2:14–41

'For David... said, "The Lord said to my Lord: 'Sit at my right hand'"' (v34)

Knowing God more deeply involves us first and foremost having a clear idea of who He is. Over the years I have come to see, through my ministry of personal counselling, how a faulty understanding of God can suppress or restrict our spiritual growth. It may surprise you to know that almost every spiritual problem I have had to deal with in the counselling room had its roots in a faulty concept of God. This is why I believe that our concept of God is one of the most important elements of our Christian life.

FURTHER STUDY

Acts 17:22–30;
Rom. 1:18-23

1. How did the Athenians worship a caricature of God?

2. Why did people become fools?

Today we remind ourselves that from its very beginnings, the Christian Church's view of God is based on the revelation of Himself in the Bible. From his first sermon at Pentecost, we can see what a transformation has taken place in Simon Peter's life, as he uses with complete confidence the Word of God as his base to teach the people about Jesus (Acts 2). From my experience of helping people with their problems, I have found that if your concept of God is rooted in Scripture then you will be better equipped to overcome life's struggles on your spiritual journey.

In the early days of my ministry, I was rather surprised by the number of times I asked a person how they saw God, and they described Him in terms of their parents. One woman told me she always imagined God sitting behind a newspaper. As you have no doubt guessed, in her formative years, whenever she wanted to talk to her father, she always found him more interested in his newspaper than in her. Consequently, the God she worshipped was not the true God but a caricature.

Heavenly Father, clear from my mind all wrong thoughts of You. Help me to see You as You really are – the God of the Bible, not the God of my imagination. In Jesus' name. Amen.

'Christian idolaters'

For reading & meditation – Luke 11:1–13

'how much more will your Father in heaven give the
Holy Spirit to those who ask him!' (v13)

Yesterday, I mentioned that in the early days of my ministry I was quite surprised by the number of times that, when I asked a person how they saw God, they described Him in terms of their parents. I once asked a woman, 'How do you see your father?' and she replied, 'Distant, cold and uncommunicative.' Half an hour later I asked her, 'How do you see God?' She used the same three words to describe Him: distant, cold and uncommunicative.

The many hours I have spent talking with people in the counselling room have given me a deep conviction that our progress in the Christian life is determined by the way we see God. There is a lovely story about a little girl whose parents told her that her baby brother came from God in heaven. When she heard that, she rushed to the cot where he was lying and said, 'Quick, tell me what God is like.' By some mysterious law of the soul, we are shaped by the image of God we hold in our hearts. If idolatry is bowing down to a god who is not the true God, then it follows that those who do not relate to God as He really is could well be described as 'Christian idolaters'. So many people, when they approach God, have in their minds a caricature of Him and do not see Him as He really is. Their picture of God is constructed out of the childhood fears, guilt and misconceptions of their early developmental years.

FURTHER STUDY

Matt. 6:26;
Luke 15:11-23

1. How did the prodigal son think about his father?

2. How did the father think about his son?

In today's reading, Jesus shows us that the best in us is multiplied a million times in the heart of God. The true God is a God who delights to give good things to His children.

Father, thank You for revealing Yourself in Your Word as large-hearted, magnanimous, and the one who delights to give good gifts to His children. Help me keep that picture ever before me. Amen.

Inventing an impossible God

For reading & meditation – Hebrews 7:11-19

'a better hope is introduced, by which we draw near to God.' (v19)

We have concluded that we cannot have a true knowledge of God without a true concept of Him. A faulty view of God can affect us in at least three ways. First, it can affect the way we worship Him (as you cannot give yourself to someone of whom, deep down, you are unsure). Some view God as a policeman, who is waiting to catch them out and come down heavily upon them for any minor mistakes they may have made. How can you truly worship a God like that?

FURTHER STUDY

Exod. 20:18-21;
Luke 9:51-56

1. Contrast the
response of
Moses and of
the Israelites to
God's presence.

2. How did
James and
John view God
in heaven?

A faulty view of God can affect us also in the way we relate to Him. Some see God as a tyrant whom they serve as slaves, and not as His sons and daughters. I have known some Christians come close to breakdown because they invented an impossible God, whose demands were so high and whose opinion of them was so low that there was no way for them to live except under His frown. Dr Joseph Cook, an American missionary to Thailand, was forced to return home from the mission field because of stress and anxiety. He attributed this to a faulty concept of God. In his book Free for the Taking he wrote, 'I believed that the day-to-day acceptance I longed for from God could only be mine if I let Him crush everything that was really me.' Is it any wonder he struggled?

Third, a faulty concept of God can affect us in the way we witness for Him. If we do not know Him and see Him as the one who loves us eternally, then this will become apparent when we talk about Him to others.

Loving Father, I see how flawed is my concept of You. Once again I ask You to clear from my mind all wrong ideas I have of You and leave intact only those that are based on the revelation of You in Scripture. In Jesus' name. Amen.

Keeping a safe distance

For reading & meditation – James 4:1–10

'Come near to God and he will come near to you.' (v8)

A popular Christmas song in the UK in the early 1990s includes the line, 'God is watching us from a distance'. The words may sound good, but the image of God that the song presents is rather sentimental and, frankly, not true to Scripture. People like the idea of a God who keeps His distance, who provides but doesn't intrude, who protects but never requests, who never judges and never meddles. There are thousands of 'Sunday Christians' who view God in this way. They like a God who is there but who doesn't encroach on their daily lives, except when they are in trouble.

Phil Greenslade talks about those who see church as the place where God dwells, and from which He never emerges. He writes in his commentary on Psalm 63: 'His place is usually a safe distance from us in what someone has described as God's game reserve, the national park of His churches. There God is allowed quietly to graze without disturbance and without interference from Monday to Saturday, then on Sundays the curious drive to see if God is still there and even to admire how well He is looking. So we treat Him as a comforting backdrop to life, the background music while business goes on as usual. He may be dutifully acknowledged, prayed to and even believed, but He is essentially a side show.'

The God of the Bible desires nearness to His people and, as today's text assures us, when we draw near to Him, He will draw near to us. He loves our trust and our intimacy. If we do not recognise this then we will never know Him as He truly is.

FURTHER STUDY

Heb. 4:14-16;
10:19-23

1. Why can we draw near to God without fear?

2. What do we receive before God's throne?

Father, more and more I am realising that I can know You only when I see You as You are. Please help me to search the Scriptures to discover the truth about You. In Jesus' name. Amen.

The Son is the message

For reading & meditation – John 14:1–14

'Anyone who has seen me has seen the Father.' (v9)

We continue reflecting on our need to know God as He is – a knowledge and experience based on Scripture and not on our own ideas about Him. The only way God can be known as He really is, is through Jesus, His Son. Our knowledge of God will never grow deep unless we have an ongoing relationship with Jesus. If the invisible God had not become visible, our knowledge of Him would have remained very limited. The Old Testament characters knew God, but the divine revelation was made complete in the person of His Son. To know Jesus is to know God, and to know God is to know Jesus.

FURTHER STUDY

Luke 7:18-23;
John 12:44-46;
Acts 2:22

1. What happens when we think about Jesus and believe in Him?

2. What do Jesus' miracles show us about God?

In the passage before us today we see Philip asking, 'Lord, show us the Father and that will be enough for us' (v8). Jesus' reply was simple but bursting with life-changing truth: 'Anyone who has seen me has seen the Father.' Here is the wonder and mystery of the Trinity – again, as Jesus said: 'I and the Father are one' (John 10:30). If we do not filter our ideas about God through Jesus, then we can easily reach conclusions about Him that are faulty. A teacher was once talking to some children and asked what they thought of Jesus. A little boy put up his hand and said, 'Jesus is the best photograph God ever had taken.' He is.

Dr E. Stanley Jones once commented, 'We see God in the face of Jesus Christ or we do not see Him.' The corollary of that statement is that if we have not seen God in the face of Jesus, we have not seen the Father. The ancient prophets brought the message, but the Son is the message. The gospel is in His person.

Lord Jesus, I see the Father in You – in who You are and what You do and what You say. You are the language of eternity translated into the speech of time. Above all, You are my God. Amen.

'The Great Simplification'

For reading & meditation – John 12:37–50

'Jesus cried out, "When a man... looks at me, he sees the one who sent me."' (vv44-45)

Though we must be careful not to devalue Old Testament Scripture, it is true to say that no perfect revelation of God came through it. Humanity awaited the advent of Jesus Christ. As stated yesterday, if we have not seen God in the face of Jesus then we have not seen the Father.

Suppose we want to know God (as many do) but we ignore Jesus. What happens? We will not be starting with God but with our ideas about God. However, generally speaking, if our ideas about God are not informed by Scripture, they are unfounded. We must start, if I might put it this way, with God's ideas about Himself. And to do that we need to look at the Bible. Here we see that He has revealed Himself to us in the person of His Son, Jesus Christ. Jesus is God breaking through to us – 'the Great Simplification', as someone has described Him.

FURTHER STUDY

John 1:1-14;
Col. 2:9

1. Contrast John and Jesus.

2. What was Jesus full of?

A physicist who was talking to his students said, 'There are two important things to be remembered: your centre and your circumference. They depend on each other.' If you have the wrong centre, you will have the wrong circumference. As far as the Christian faith is concerned, if Jesus is not the centre then we will not find the right circumference. If we do not start with Him then we will develop ideas about God that have no basis in reality.

Alfred Adler, the Jewish psychologist, was once asked, 'What do you think of Jesus Christ?' He replied, 'Whenever I hear His name I pause to revere the greatest character in history.' However, Jesus is not just the greatest character in history; He is totally unlike every other character in history.

Lord Jesus, You are not just the best humanity has ever seen, but the best it will ever see. I bow yet again before You and worship You as my Saviour and my Lord. Amen.

The power of the four Gospels

For reading & meditation – John 3:1–15

'Just as Moses lifted up the snake in the desert, so the Son of Man must be lifted up' (v14)

The better we know Jesus, the better we will know God, for as He Himself said, 'I am the way and the truth and the life' (John 14:6). Perfect knowledge of God comes through Jesus Christ. This begs the question: how do we get to know Jesus better? The simple answer is, by spending more time with Him in prayer, but also – and this is essential – by exploring the four Gospels.

Have you ever wondered why we have four Gospels? They provide not just eyewitness accounts but a fully rounded picture of Jesus. One of the things that surprises me is that many Christians are more eager to read the epistles than to explore the Gospels. And often, the time they do spend looking at the Gospels takes the form of a Bible study rather than a Spirit-guided meditation. However, I have found that immersing myself in the Gospels and asking the Spirit to guide my imagination has enabled me to come to know Jesus intimately.

One writer says, 'Spending time in Gospel meditation has begun to put flesh on the God I have been seeking to know for so many years.' Listening to sermons about Jesus is fine, and reading books about Him helps increase our understanding, but there is no substitute for meditating on the life of Jesus as recorded in the Gospels. Just as the Israelites looked at the bronze snake and were healed (Num. 21:4–9), watching, exploring and looking to Jesus in the Gospels allows the Spirit to take His life and make it ours. Believe me, meditating on the Gospels has tremendous transforming power.

FURTHER STUDY

Matt. 14:14;
15:32;
Luke 7:11-16;
Heb. 12:2-3

1. How did Jesus feel about sick, hungry and hurting people?

2. What prevents us becoming weary and losing heart?

Lord Jesus, forgive me if I spend little time focusing on the picture of You that is presented in the four Gospels. Help me see that it is vital for me to meditate on these Gospels if I am to know You better. Amen.

Make time to pray back

For reading & meditation – Hebrews 10:19–25

'let us draw near to God with a sincere heart in full
assurance of faith' (v22)

Another way to deepen our knowledge of God and our relationship with Him is to maintain a rich devotional life. The time, I believe, when the soul is most receptive – when we are most open to God – is when we worship Him and express our love for Him in the act of worship and prayer. 'We come to God best by love, not by navigation,' said St Augustine.

As we meditate on the Word of God, we begin to find reasons for which we can offer praise and be thankful to the Lord for what He has done for us. Early in my Christian life – just a few months after I came to faith – I attended a Bible study on the missionary journeys of the apostle Paul. Finding the discussion somewhat boring, I blurted out, 'What's the point of discussing these missionary journeys when we could make better use of our time by praying?' My pastor replied, 'If Paul had not been sent to the Gentiles then none of us would be sitting here now as redeemed men and women.'

FURTHER STUDY

Psa. 95:1–11;
1 John 3:1–3;
3:16–19

1. How do we approach God?

2. How can we know that we truly love God?

He continued, 'Now let's use that as a focus for our prayers and thank God together for the way He led Paul to reach out to us.' I have never forgotten that lesson, and ever since, when I read the Scriptures, my soul is alert to new discoveries – matters that cause me to turn to God in worship, thanksgiving and praise. *Every Day with Jesus* would lose much if the prayers at the end of each day's meditations were no longer included. These prayers give us the opportunity to pray back to God matters we have just considered, and this deepens our lives devotionally.

Father, thank You for showing me that the art of building my devotional life is to take what I am seeing in Your Word and pray it back to You in worship, thanksgiving and praise. Help me to make that a spiritual habit. In Jesus' name. Amen.

Theology leading to doxology

For reading & meditation – Romans 11:25–36

'Oh, the depth of the riches of the wisdom and knowledge of God!' (v33)

The devotional life is, I believe, key to knowing God more deeply. When we take a truth from God's Word – a truth that He has revealed to us – and pray it back to Him with thanksgiving, the soul is enriched in a way that is not possible through objective study alone. This is not to say that objective study of the Scriptures is unimportant, but we need to link what we know about God to the giving of thanks and praise to Him.

We find a classic example of this in the passage we have read today. Paul has been outlining in the previous chapters God's purpose for Israel. After dealing with complex theological matters, he then turns from theology to a devotional doxology, and there rises in his heart a song of thankfulness: 'Oh, the depth of the riches of the wisdom and knowledge of God!' Paul was a praising man. He was ready at all times to climb onto the raft of truth, and raise his hands to God in passionate prayer and praise (see 1 Tim. 2:8).

FURTHER STUDY

2 Sam. 7:16–24;
Psa. 92:1–4

1. How did David respond to hearing God's Word?

2. What is it good to do?

An Australian reader once wrote to me to say that he had been researching why *Every Day with Jesus* was so popular around the world. The number one reason, he concluded, was that the prayers at the end of each day's readings enabled people to express what they had been taking in, and, by expressing what they had learned in a prayer, they were impressing it more deeply on their minds. Ever since I set out to write these daily meditations many years ago, my focus has been to help fan the flame of devotion in the hearts of God's children. It's not just what happens in our heads that is important; it's also what happens in our hearts.

My Father and my God, help me know and understand this, for I see it can make the world of difference in my devotional life. Help me see – and see clearly – how to deepen my knowledge of You. In Jesus' name. Amen.

'Be still my soul'

For reading & meditation – Psalm 46:1–11
'Be still, and know that I am God' (v10)

There is a further matter we need to consider if we long to know God more deeply, and that is the willingness to quieten our souls. Let's read again today's text: 'Be still, and know that I am God.' It does not say, 'Be stirred, and know that I am God.' Or, 'Be surprised, and know that I am God.' Instead it says, 'Be still, and know that I am God.' There are some Christians who can't bear to be still. They feel they need to have the radio on or music playing in the background in order to get through the day. Blaise Pascal observed that many of the struggles of life spring from the fact that we are unable to sit still in a room. To know God, and know Him deeply, requires that the soul be quietened.

FURTHER STUDY

Isa. 30:15-18;
Hab. 2:20;
Zech. 2:13

1. How were the Israelites to experience salvation and strength?

2. What was their response and the Lord's continued longing?

In my opinion, though, God's instruction to us here has less to do with ensuring that we are not surrounded by noise, and more to do with entering into what Peter Kreeft calls 'the Job experience'. He observes that it was only when all his questions had been silenced by God that Job was ready to be transformed. One of the most significant sentences in Job, Kreeft says, is, 'The words of Job are ended' (Job 31:40). It is not wrong to question God as to why there are so many mysteries surrounding Him – why He allows such terrible things to happen in His world, for example. But in the end, are we prepared for the reality that God is under no obligation to give us answers to our questions? Then, when we remain surrounded by mysteries, the issue is whether or not we can continue to be still and keep our confidence in Him.

Father God, how I long to have a soul that remains still and tranquil even when surrounded by chaos and noise. Teach me more of this, I pray. In Jesus' name. Amen.

How Job experienced stillness

For reading & meditation – Job 19:1–22

'Then Job replied: "How long will you torment me and crush me with words?"' (vv1-2)

The need to quieten our souls before God is illustrated in the life of God's servant Job. God did not automatically provide answers to Job's many questions. In fact, in time Job found that when God responds, it is as Questioner, and not Answerer.

Peter Kreeft, the writer to whom I referred yesterday, asks this question: 'If we had the opportunity to talk to some great person... would we want to do most of the talking or would we want to listen most of the time?' Why do we talk so much to God when really we'd do much better listening? How patient God is with us as He waits for us to settle down and silence all our verbal and mental noise!

FURTHER STUDY

Job 37:2-5,14;
Psa. 62:5-8;
Eccles. 3:7;
Zeph. 1:7

1. When should we be silent before God?

2. When should we speak to Him?

In today's text we see Job push back against the fact that his three counsellors were so busy talking to him that they didn't listen to him. Yet, I wonder if he was guilty of the same thing with God. One writer asks his readers if they have ever kept silent for half an hour, speaking with neither their lips nor their mind. 'You are going to have to learn that art,' he says, 'if you want to enjoy heaven, because according to Revelation 8:1 there will be silence in heaven for half an hour.' It is interesting that in the vision of the future and all the heavenly activities there is mention also of silence.

God may have to respond firmly to silence us, as it is only when the soul is silenced that He is best able to reveal Himself. How sad that often God is not able to speak with us because we are too busy plying Him with questions.

Father, please continue to teach me how to be still before You and listen to what You want to say to me. I ask this in Jesus' name. Amen.

The answer to everything

For reading & meditation – Job 42:1-17

'My ears had heard of you but now my eyes have seen you.'
(v5)

Staying with the story of Job, consider for a moment what might have happened if God had answered all the questions Job had stored up. Job probably would have been satisfied for a while, but then more questions would have arisen – questions about God's answers to his questions. Each answer would have produced more questions. However, God never answered Job's questions; instead He answered the real need of the questioner and provided a deeper knowledge of Himself. Instead of answers to his questions, Job was given a new revelation of God. He received not just truths but the Truth – and that is the only experience that can truly satisfy the human heart. When we ask God questions, He knows that often the real issue is not the actual question of what is going on in the heart of the questioner; He knows what we are really asking for – and that is the nearness of His presence.

FURTHER STUDY
Psa. 73:12-28

1. What was bad for the psalmist?
2. What was good for the psalmist?

The most important verse in the book of Job is our text for today. This is the answer to everything. This ends our questions about the problem of evil, the meaning of life, and every other matter that perplexes us. Once we truly know God, we will not be troubled by the difficult questions that arise in life, for though we may not have the specific answers we seek, we know the answerer – and that is enough. Job did not get what he thought he wanted, but he received what he needed – to know God deeply, intimately, closely. Job had heard about God, but now he sees Him. 'I will not give you answers,' said God to Job; rather, it seems as if God were saying to Job, 'I will give you something better – I will give you myself.'

Father, help me to understand that knowing You is infinitely more important than answers to my questions, for the more I know You, the more I can trust You when no answers are provided. Amen.

Known and loved

For reading & meditation – 1 John 4:7–21

'This is love: not that we loved God, but that he loved us
and sent his Son as an atoning sacrifice for our sins.' (v10)

aving looked at some of the ways in which we can deepen
our knowledge of God, we move on now to consider how
we can deepen the knowledge of our own self and gain a greater
understanding of our true identity. Christians possess two
identities; the first one is of our own making and the second one
is the gift of God. Let's keep in mind that the only reason we can
know ourselves is because we are already known by God. He knows
every single person of His creation, and knows us far more deeply

FURTHER STUDY

John 3:16-17;
Rom. 5:1-8

1. How did God
demonstrate
His love for us?

2. What has God
poured into us?

than we know ourselves. There is nothing we can
discover about ourselves that is hidden from Him.
This is in part what David Benner is highlighting
when he says, 'If God does not know us, we do not
exist.' In his book Knowing God, the theologian Jim
Packer writes: 'What matters supremely, therefore,
is not in the last analysis the fact that I know God,
but the larger fact which underlies it – the fact that
He knows me. We are graven on the palms of God's
hands and never out of the Divine mind. All our knowledge of God
depends on God's sustained initiative in knowing us. We know God
because God first knew us and continues to know us.'

We cannot gain authentic self-knowledge and understand our
true identity simply by looking at God; authentic self-knowledge
comes by focusing on how God looks at us. And how does He look
at us? He sees us first through the eyes of love. A theologian of the
past commented that if every human being could see how much he
or she is loved by God, there would be no such thing as an unsaved
sinner in the world. How true.

**Loving Father, how incredible that though You know everything
about me, You loved me enough to send Your Son to die for me.
Help me to see that, though undeserving, I am an object of Your
eternal love. Thank You. Amen.**

Disciplined for the highest

For reading & meditation – Hebrews 12:1-13

'the Lord disciplines those he loves, and he punishes
everyone he accepts as a son.' (v6)

Yesterday we said that important though it is to look at God,
there can be no authentic self-knowledge and understanding
of our true identity by focusing on Him alone. Authentic self-
knowledge comes from understanding that God sees us through
the eyes of love. This love has nothing to do with what we do.
Neither our faithfulness nor unfaithfulness changes His love for
us in the slightest degree. This does not mean that He overlooks
our behaviour or our unfaithfulness. In fact, as today's text tells
us, it is because He loves us that He disciplines us.
He thinks so much of us that He will not let us get
away with anything that diminishes our character or
paralyses our potential. Divine love is unconditional,
unlimited and unending, but it also seeks to purify
and help us grow.

FURTHER STUDY
2 Tim. 3:16-17;
Rev. 3:14-22

1. What is
Scripture
useful for?

2. Why did the
Lord rebuke
the church in
Laodicea?

Our existence makes no sense apart from God's
love. This means that there is nothing in our lives,
however trivial it may seem, that He does not take
notice of. An ancient philosopher once asked: 'Can
the great cosmic mind concern itself with trifles? Does the God
who created the universe interest Himself in the unimportant
details of our insignificant lives?' My answer is an absolute 'Yes'.
Though God is far, far above our thoughts, He stoops to ask the
love of our hearts, and takes a father's interest in His children.
For centuries, men and women have journeyed on this path and
testified that God is as good as His word. God can no more stop
loving you or caring for you and me than He could stop loving His
only Son. You are more precious to Him than you can ever imagine.

**Father, I am so thankful that You love me enough to restrain me.
Your discipline leads to my development. Help me see that I am
being disciplined by the Highest for the highest. Amen.**

The basis of our identity

For reading & meditation – Galatians 3:26–4:7

'So you are no longer a slave, but a son; and since you are a son, God has made you also an heir.' (4:7)

The principles we have covered over the past couple of days are absolutely essential as a lead-up to understanding ourselves. Let me repeat them so that they are firmly fixed in our minds.

First, knowing ourselves begins with the recognition that God knows us. As David Benner has said, 'If God does not know us, we do not exist.' Thomas Merton, who wrote on spiritual issues, said in a somewhat tongue-in-cheek statement, 'To be unknown by God is altogether too much privacy.' Second, God sees us through the eyes of love. He cannot help it because He is love. He cannot do anything without love being the motive and inspiration. Third, He takes a perfect father's interest in all of His children. Every one of us is imprinted on His heart and is always before Him.

FURTHER STUDY
Rom. 8:28-39;
2 Cor. 6:18
1. What is God's purpose for us?
2. What cannot separate us from God's love?

To come to understand our identity in God, then, the first thing we accept is that we are known by God, loved by Him, and have the assurance of His personal interest in all the details of our lives. Sadly this is not the case for a large number of people. So many attempt to find their identity in what they do rather than who they are. If our identity is based on what we do, and not who we are, then what happens if, as the result of an accident, illness or old age, we can't perform any more? In such situations, people often fall apart.

Believe me, we live dangerously when we try to find our identity in our performance or contribution to life rather than in the truth that we are children of our heavenly Father, heirs of God and beneficiaries of eternity. It's not what you do but who you are that's important.

Father God, forgive me if I have tried to find my identity in what I do rather than in who I am in You. Write this truth across my heart: 'I belong by faith in God's Son to the creator of the universe.' Amen.

Who am I?

For reading & meditation – Ephesians 5:21–6:4

'Fathers... bring [your children] up in the training and instruction of the Lord.' (6:4)

So, how is our identity formed? We consider first our natural identity – the identity that is formed in our early developmental years. As soon as we enter the world, there is a question mark over the head of every one of us, metaphorically speaking. I am speaking metaphorically, of course. It can't be seen but it is there, clamouring for an answer. The question is: who am I? Psychologists say that we are not mature until we have a clear answer to that question. Sadly, some are never able to answer it clearly because those who nurtured them neglected to minister to them in the way necessary for them to come to an awareness of who they are.

Many times in the past I have written that every one of us, when we come into the world, has three basic needs. We need to know that we belong to someone who loves us, that we are worthwhile, and that our lives count for something. If these needs are met in a good and loving relationship then we begin to feel secure; we develop a sense of identity based on the realisation that we are loved, that we are seen as worthwhile, and that we can make a contribution to life. Let there be no doubt about it: the relationships we experience in the early years of our life play a vital part in the formation of our natural identity. Nothing contributes more to a secure sense of identity than knowing we belong to someone who loves us.

How sad when children grow up in homes where they receive little or no love. Is it any wonder such children have little or no sense of identity?

FURTHER STUDY

Gen. 25:21-23;
Psa. 139:13-16;
Jer. 1:4-5

1. When did God first know and care about us?

2. How did God reward Isaac?

Father God, I am so grateful that even if I never felt loved by human beings in the way my heart craved, I have found that kind of love in my relationship with You. Now I can live with a spring in my step and a song in my heart! Amen.

Three crucial building blocks

For reading & meditation – Colossians 3:18–25

'Fathers, do not embitter your children, or they will
become discouraged.' (v21)

I t has been said that 'the self is a series of reflected appraisals'.
In other words, the image of ourselves we construct is the one
we see reflected in the eyes of those who nurture us. The things
we think we see in their eyes become the building blocks on which
we construct our identity. If I see and sense that I belong to a
loving family, then building block number one is placed beneath
my feet. If I see I am valued for who I am and not what I can do,
then building block number two goes into place. If I see that those

FURTHER STUDY

Gen. 21:8-20

1. How was
Ishmael
rejected?

2. How did
God love and
care for him?

who nurture me consider I have a significant role to
play in the world, that's building block number three.
As far as our natural identity is concerned, we are
the products of those who either loved us, or failed
to love us. Those who regrettably do not have these
three building blocks put in place rarely know who
they are, and go through life with an incomplete
sense of identity.

In the days when I worked as a counsellor, I could
often sense when the building blocks we have just mentioned had
not been firmly established in a person's developmental years. They
may well have had a loving home, but for some reason or other
that person didn't perceive the love the parents had for them.

Our creator made us to be loved, and He gives parents the first
chance to pour love into a child's heart. Sadly, those who do not
consistently provide a loving environment (including of course
loving discipline as well as encouragement and affirmation) may
make it difficult (though not impossible) for a child, when they
become an adult, to receive the love that is offered to them in Jesus.

**God my Father, I cannot be at my best unless I know and feel I am
loved. Whatever failures in love I have experienced, I know You
will never fail me. Saturate me with Your love, I pray.
In Jesus' name. Amen.**

A homing beacon

For reading & meditation – Deuteronomy 32:1–6

'He is the Rock, his ways are perfect, and all his
ways are just.' (v4)

As we consider the subject of our natural identity (as opposed
to the identity we experience in Christ) it's important to
remember that no matter how loving parents may be, no parent
is perfect. No one is able to give us all the love that our soul craves.

Often I have heard people say, 'I had the most perfect parents.'
What they mean is that their parents gave them a high degree
of love and affection. But however good it was, it was not perfect
love – the kind of love we were created to experience. Only God
can truly give us that. By God's grace, parents may
have laid good foundations in their children's lives
but, because of our fallen nature, what parent can
say that self-interest has been totally absent in
their relationship with their offspring? The Bible
emphasises the role that parents can play in helping
children develop, but in the final analysis there is a
deep longing for love – a longing placed there by God
Himself that only He can satisfy. That longing is like
a homing beacon calling us back to God to have a relationship with
Him that will be far more satisfying than any human relationship.

FURTHER STUDY

Psa. 18:30–32;
1 Cor. 3:5–16;
Gal. 4:19

1. What did Paul
seek to do?

2. What could
he not do?

When studying adolescent psychology many years ago, I came
across this brilliant statement: 'Childhood is that period of life
when parents build the rooms of the temple in which God will
dwell later when the child is an adult.' And until God dwells in
those rooms, a person's sense of identity is not complete. Only
God can enter into those areas of our lives that imperfect parents
cannot reach. As I said the other day, we do not know who we are
until we know whose we are.

**My Lord and Master, I see that whatever knowledge I have gained
in life, I can only truly be myself when I know You. Above all
things I want to be the person You intended me to be.
In Jesus' name. Amen.**

Name-calling that lives on

For reading & meditation – Proverbs 26:18–28

'A lying tongue hates those it hurts, and a flattering mouth works ruin.' (v28)

As we have seen, our natural identity, is greatly influenced by those who relate to us in our early developmental years. But not only are all parents flawed human beings, so also are others to whom we relate – brothers, sisters, uncles and aunts. Our peers can also have a strong influence on us. Many children have been negatively influenced by questions they were taunted with in the school playground: 'Do you know that your ears stick out?' 'Why is your face always so red?' 'Are you stupid or something?'

FURTHER STUDY

Judg. 6:11-15;
1 Pet. 2:9-10

1. How did Gideon feel about himself? But what did the angel call him?

2. What names did Peter use to identify believers?

In our early years we are like containers into which people drop negative statements. Because of our inexperience and lack of discernment, we are unable to say, 'That is not who I really am,' and throw them out. We just don't know what to do with the negative things we hear, and can easily begin to believe what others think of us.

More than once I have sat with people in whose heart and mind a negative remark (made by someone in their past) still reverberated. A woman once told me that when she was at school a gang of cruel children would follow her home, shouting things after her. Their taunts continued to ring in her mind into her adult years. Eventually she became so tormented by it that she decided the only way to drown out those cries was to self-harm. A Christian counsellor was able to help her find release from the taunting voices, and led her to a deep relationship with the Lord. These negative statements and actions of others can affect us more deeply that we may think.

Father, if I have allowed the negative comments of others to dominate my life, then please help me break free of them now. Replace them with the knowledge of what You think about me. In Jesus' name I pray. Amen.

Blank slates?

For reading & meditation – Proverbs 22:1–16

'Folly is bound up in the heart of a child, but the rod of discipline will drive it far from him.' (v15)

Continuing our theme of how our natural identity is formed, we need to see that it is influenced not only by our parents and others to whom we relate, but also by our own sinful nature. The legacy that has come to us from Adam and Eve means there is a marred image within our personality that causes us to be estranged from God.

Our text for today tells us that or foolishness is bound up in the heart of a child. What does this mean? Our nature, with which we are born, causes us to foolishly believe that having our own way in everything will give us the life we want. The natural disposition of our hearts is to live our lives independently of God. Having to depend on another causes us to feel helpless, and helplessness is what our natural self resists more than anything else. There is an inbuilt self-reliance and independence, and of course our world reinforces this position. The text goes on to say, 'the rod of discipline will drive it far from him'. The assignment God gives every parent is to weed out foolishness and build in wisdom.

FURTHER STUDY

Psa. 51:1–5;
Rom. 7:18–25;
Col. 1:21

1. What was David's confession?

2. What was Paul's dilemma?

There is a theory, believed by many, that at birth we are like empty or blank pages, waiting for someone to write on us. But we are not blank slates. The Bible is very clear that in our nature there is a bias towards sin and a resistance to God. Paul points out that 'All of us… lived… at one time, gratifying the cravings of our sinful nature' (Eph. 2:3). Is it any wonder that we cannot have a true sense of our identity while our unredeemed hearts contain so much enmity towards God?

Lord God, it seems too good to be true – that with so much working against me from the day I arrived in this world, I have nevertheless been brought through to a knowledge of You. I am so grateful. Thank You, my Father. Amen.

Excessive attachments

For reading & meditation – Jeremiah 2:4–13

'My people have... forsaken me, the spring of living water, and have dug their own cisterns' (v13)

The writer Basil Pennington suggests that our natural identity is shot through with the dangerous idea that our value as a person depends on ourselves – what we have, what we can do, and what others think of us. Consequently, life becomes a series of excessive attachments. 'Seeking to avoid implosion and non-being,' he says, 'we grasp at things that appear to have substance and then cling to those things with the tenacity of a drowning man clutching at straws.' Perhaps we cling to our possessions,

FURTHER STUDY

Luke 12:13–21;
Col. 3:5

1. Why was the rich man foolish?

2. What are modern-day idols?

accomplishments, dreams, memories and friendships – and hold on to them so tightly that they become idols to us. These things can be a blessing to us when we hold them in open hands of thankfulness, but they become a curse when we grasp them in clenched fists of entitlement – when we view them as 'mine' and believe that possessing them gives us the life we seek.

Reading today's passage, we see that God was devastated that His people tried to find spiritual satisfaction by ignoring the fountain of living water (referring, to Himself), and digging cisterns of their own from which they drank lukewarm, dirty, bacteria-infested water. God is not against our enjoying attachments to legitimate things, but He wants us to hold such things loosely. Sometimes we may think the things to which we cling are innocent indulgences. However, without care, they can sabotage our spiritual lives because we may start to put our confidence in them rather than in God. Watch your attachments. They can very quickly turn into idols.

My Father and my God, I see that my life is fulfilled only when it is centred on You. Save me from excessive attachments, and help me to depend on You, and You alone, for my life to work in the way You intended. Amen.

No need for idols

For reading & meditation – 1 John 5:13–21

'Dear children, keep yourselves from idols.' (v21)

Today we build a little more on the idea that when we cling to things such as our possessions, accomplishments, dreams, memories and friendships, they become idols to us – substitutes for God. After Adam and Eve had sinned in the Garden of Eden, they grabbed the nearest external thing to cover up the internal feelings of vulnerability and shame that they now felt. In their case it was leaves. In our fallen state we do something similar – we hide behind the 'fig leaves' of a false self in order to escape the painful awareness of our spiritual nakedness. These 'leaves' help us forget that we are exposed to God's view. But God calls to every one of us over and over in life: 'Where are you?' He wants to show us that our attempts to cover up are a defence against our spiritual nakedness. Sadly, His call often goes unanswered. Defensiveness is one of the clearest evidences of our false self. (I am using the term 'false self' to describe the self we develop in our natural life as opposed to the new self we become in Christ.) But defensiveness is unnecessary in a heart that feels secure in God's love.

FURTHER STUDY

Prov. 30:12;
Isa. 59:6;
1 Cor. 10:6-14

1. Why is being pure in our own eyes not enough?

2. How does God view our attempts to cover our sins?

Touchiness, too, is a mark of our hidden self. Often, the more prickly a person is, the more he or she is using the defence of a false self. Some people bristle easily if they are not taken seriously, maybe betraying their need to cover up feelings of unimportance. Others take themselves too seriously and are unable to laugh at themselves. All these things suggest we are not comfortable with our inner selves. We are living falsely rather than truly.

Heavenly Father, I understand that I am to rely on You for my security, self-worth and significance. May I always do so, for then all the leaves of defensiveness and touchiness will fall away – no longer needed. In Jesus' name. Amen.

A second start

For reading & meditation – 2 Corinthians 5:11–15

'Therefore, if anyone is in Christ, he is a new creation; the old has gone, the new has come!' (v17)

It is clear from Scripture that every one of us starts life with an imperfect identity – a false self. This is largely because we ignore God's purposes for us and try to make it through life relying on our own devices. The writer James Finley puts it in this way: 'We are not our own origin, nor are we our own ultimate fulfilment. To claim to be so is a suicidal act that wounds our faith relationship with the living God and replaces it with a futile faith in a self that can only be described as a false self, the one that we construct from our own life experiences rather than the one God planned for us from all eternity.'

FURTHER STUDY

John 1:12–13; 3:1–8

1. Why do we need a new birth?

2. How does this happen?

In a sense, when we come into the world, we all go through our own Garden of Eden experience. As soon as our identity begins to be formed, Satan, who blinds our eyes to the person God wants us to be, whispers untruths that we foolishly listen to when he tells us that we can be more fulfilled by acting independently of God. We can't, but he persuades us that we can. By believing his lies we develop a false self in order to cover up the spiritual nakedness we talked about yesterday. Our first birth has tilted us in the wrong direction. We develop into adulthood with a false self, which is completely different to the self which God has in mind for us – our true self.

How good it is to know that through what the Bible calls being 'born again' (John 3:3,7) we can have a fresh start. Through this new birth, we enter into the kingdom of heaven where everything is new; we are given a new nature, a new hope, a new faith, a new confidence, and, of course, a new identity.

Gracious Father, help me grow into the person You planned me to be way back there in eternity. Forgive the wrongs I impose on myself when I try to be other than You intend me to be. In Jesus' name. Amen.

The model for our identity

For reading & meditation – Colossians 3:1–17

'For you died, and your life is now hidden with
Christ in God.' (v3)

Our life – our true self – is hidden, we are told, in God. Jesus
is the source of our true being and the ground of our true
identity. Because the true self can exist only in relation to Jesus
Christ, the best way to learn how our new identity is to develop
is to look at the life of Jesus when He was here on earth, and see
how His identity was formed. The scriptural basis for this is that
God's great and overall purpose for our lives is to make us like
Jesus Christ. The New Living Translation of the Bible puts it like
this: 'For God knew his people in advance and he
chose them to become like his Son' (Rom. 8:29). So
we ask ourselves: How did Jesus arrive at a sense of
His identity and discover His purpose in the world?
How did He come to learn who He was? Was it
through a blinding revelation, or did the awareness
come gradually?

FURTHER STUDY

Rom. 6:4–5;
Gal. 2:19–20;
Col. 2:9–14

1. How have we
been raised
with Christ?

2. What does
this mean for
our identity?

Some believe that Jesus was conscious of who
He was from the moment He was born. When He
was lying in the manger, they say, He already knew
He was God. I have difficulty believing that myself. The idea of
Jesus, on the day of His birth, contemplating where He had come
from and what He was doing on earth cannot be reconciled, in
my view, with the fact of His humanity. There is something rather
inconsistent and unsustainable about that idea. My belief is that
He gained an awareness of who He really was more gradually,
because Scripture tells us in Luke 2:52, 'Jesus grew in wisdom
and stature, and in favour with God and men.' To grow in wisdom
means one knows more today than one did yesterday.

**Lord Jesus, I am so thankful that You came into this world as a real
human being and lived out Your life in the conditions we ourselves
experience. Help us to model our lives on Your example. Amen.**

God's two books

For reading & meditation – Isaiah 61:1–11

'The Spirit of the Sovereign LORD is on me, because the LORD has anointed me to preach good news to the poor.'

(v1)

In his book *The Crises of the Christ*, Dr Campbell Morgan intriguingly suggested that God has written two books: one is called 'Nature' (or creation), and the other 'Scripture'. Because Jesus' mind was not tainted by sin, His intellect, Morgan claimed, was open to the two books that God has written in a way that our minds, because of the effects of sin, are not. I too, am convinced that Adam and Eve's sin has darkened our minds to such a degree that we use only a fraction of their potential.

FURTHER STUDY

Job 12:7-10;
Prov. 6:6-11;
Matt. 6:26-31

1. Why does God ask us to consider His creation?

2. What can creation teach us about God?

As Jesus studied the Scriptures and first read today's passage, I wonder if the Spirit drew near to Him and gave Him the assurance that He was the one being spoken about. It seems reasonable to me to assume that as Jesus looked at creation, read the Scriptures, and talked to His Father in prayer, the realisation that He was the promised Messiah slowly dawned upon Him. But in the midst of this growing revelation that He was the chosen one, the Messiah, there is no evidence that Jesus was gripped with a smug sense of entitlement, or attempted to go on what we might call a power play. He remained humble and obedient to the Father through it all. 'We are at our greatest and most authentic when we are humble,' said the writer Oswald Chambers. If this is so, then there has never been anyone greater or more humble than Jesus. As He came to an awareness that He was the Son of God, He did not allow that revelation to unbalance Him. He was great because He was humble, and He was humble because He was great.

Lord Jesus, the development of Your life as a human on this earth fascinates me. In You the authentic notes of eternity can be heard. May Your humble attitude be found also in me. Amen.

Parental influences

For reading & meditation – Luke 2:41–52

'When he was twelve years old, they went up to the Feast, according to the custom.' (v42)

Jesus' parents may also have helped Jesus in understanding His identity as the Son of God. We know little about His guardian, Joseph, except that he was a faithful and willing servant of God. Though somewhat stunned by the news that Mary would give birth to a son conceived by the Holy Spirit (Matt. 1:18–25), he obediently gave himself to the role of being a caring husband. Mary, too, showed a willing obedience to be part of God's eternal plan, and she was honoured by God. When the angel Gabriel told her that she was to become the mother of Jesus, he greeted her with these words: 'Greetings, you who are highly favoured! The Lord is with you' (Luke 1:28). No doubt Joseph and Mary, two very remarkable and God-fearing people, would, at appropriate times over the years, have told Jesus about the miracle of His birth, the visit of the shepherds, and the prophecy of Simeon and Anna on the day He was circumcised.

The events connected with Jesus' visit to the Temple in Jerusalem at the age of 12 give us an idea of how His awareness of His mission to the world was developing. After His parents had returned to the Temple, having missed Him on their journey home, He said to them, 'Didn't you know I had to be in my Father's house?' (v49). Jesus had come to think about Himself not only in relation to His earthly parents, but also to His Heavenly Father. Here again we get a glimpse of His astonishing humility when we read, 'He went down to Nazareth… and was obedient to them' (v51). No power struggle – just an obedient and servant spirit.

FURTHER STUDY

1 Kings 2:1-4;
Acts 16:1;
2 Tim. 1:5

1. What parental advice did Solomon receive?

2. How could Timothy trace a parental influence in his faith?

Lord Jesus, in You no flaw can be found. How wonderful that You, the Son of God, my Saviour, deliverer and constant friend, were willing to humble Yourself as a man. My gratitude knows no bounds. Amen.

Two critical events

**For reading & meditation – Matthew 3:13–17;
Luke 4:1–13**

'This is my Son... with him I am well pleased.' (Matt. 3:17)

From the time Jesus visited the Temple at the age of 12 until the time when He was baptised by John in the River Jordan, we have no record of what went on in His life. These are often referred to as the 'silent years'. It is clear, however, that by the age of 30 (see Luke 3:23) Jesus knew the specifics of His divine mission and submitted Himself to water baptism by John. As He stepped out of the River Jordan, God made it clear that He was not like the others being baptised. As the heavens above Him opened, God declared, 'This is my Son, whom I love; with him I am well pleased.'

FURTHER STUDY

Matt. 17:1–5;
John 5:36–37;
12:27–29

1. What did God say about His Son?

2. What testimonies confirmed Christ's identity?

Immediately following His baptism, Jesus was led by the Spirit into the desert to be tempted by the devil. Here, His deceitful adversary attempted to get Him to adopt a false self. Satan's goal was for Jesus to abandon His God-given mission and thus avoid the cross. The three temptations aimed at Jesus were an appeal to get Him to base His identity on power ('tell these stones to become bread'), possessions and prestige ('if you worship me, it will all be yours'), and popularity with the people ('throw yourself down from here').

Jesus navigated those fierce temptations with His identity intact. He would not allow anything to deter Him from the path God had planned for Him. Luke's Gospel says that He went into the desert full of the Holy Spirit (Luke 4:1), and came out in the power of the Spirit (Luke 4:14). All that temptation was able to do to Him was to turn fullness into power.

Lord Jesus, help me to draw strength from You in the same way that You drew strength from the Holy Spirit and from the Scriptures. May I too come through every temptation deepened and not dismayed. Amen.

A bold assertion

For reading & meditation – Luke 4:14–30

'and he began by saying to them, "Today this scripture is fulfilled in your hearing."' (v21)

We continue looking at key moments in Jesus' three years of ministry – moments that show us how sure He was concerning His identity. Today we look again at His reading of Isaiah 61, which talks of the Messiah's ministry. When Jesus had finished, He sat down and declared, 'Today this scripture is fulfilled in your hearing.'

The fact that Jesus sat down is significant because in those days it was customary to stand while reading the Scriptures, but to sit down when teaching. As Jesus sat down, we are told, 'The eyes of everyone in the synagogue were fastened on him' (v20). Why? We cannot be sure, but probably those in the congregation were so eager to hear what He had to say because of His growing reputation. From verse 14 we learn that news about Him had already spread throughout the whole countryside. It is hard for us to imagine the amazement felt by those in the synagogue when Jesus began His sermon by saying, 'Today this scripture is fulfilled in your hearing.' These words must have caused such astonishment because Jesus was applying Isaiah's prophecy to Himself. He was telling them that He Himself, at that very time, was ushering in God's kingdom through the work He was doing.

The more we read of Jesus' ministry in the Gospels, the clearer it becomes that He had no doubts as to who He was and His mission on this earth. What is more, the passage we have focused on today shows us that He was not going to allow anything to divert Him from the path to which God had called Him.

FURTHER STUDY

Mark 10:45;
Luke 22:66–23:3

1. How was Christ's identity linked with His life's purpose?

2. How boldly did Christ assert His identity?

Lord God, give me, I pray, a clear sense of my identity and of the purpose You have for my life. And please help me to give my will to Your larger will. May I be willing to lose my life so that I might find it again. In Jesus' name. Amen.

Jesus defines His mission

For reading & meditation – Matthew 16:13–28

'Jesus began to explain to his disciples that he must go to Jerusalem and... be killed' (v21)

Over the past few days we have looked at some passages in the Gospels that show how Jesus became aware of His identity and how, during His public ministry, He was completely clear about His calling. Several times Jesus affirmed His divine Sonship, and declared His purpose for being in the world. In today's reading, we have what is perhaps the clearest declaration of them all.

In this passage Jesus asks His disciples, 'Who do people say the Son of Man is?' (v13). He did not ask this out of an uncertainty about His own identity: this would have been a dangerous question if He did not already know who He was. His identity was never shaped by others' opinions, because He was sure about who He was. And as a result, He was not pulled, as many of us are, in different directions by the desire to live up to others' expectations.

FURTHER STUDY

John 1:29–36;
Matt. 11:2–6

1. What did John think of Jesus?

2. How did Jesus resolve John's later doubts?

Some wanted Jesus to be a political saviour and rescue Israel from Roman tyranny. Others wanted Him to be a miracle worker and satisfy their physical and material needs. Still others wanted Him to be a teacher and open up the Scriptures to them. Even His disciples had different views about the role He should play in the life of Israel. However, as He went on to outline in the clearest terms the purpose of His mission, and make it plain that He would give His life on a cross, they could no longer be in any doubt about it.

The Saviour did not rely on the expectations of others to define His identity because He was already sure of that through His communion with His Father and by His meditation on Scripture.

Heavenly Father, forgive me if I have sought to live up to the expectations of others instead of finding out who I am through communion with You. Help me understand that the more I know You the more I will know myself. In Jesus' name. Amen.

An eternal perspective

For reading & meditation – John 13:1–17

'I tell you the truth, no servant is greater than his master'
(v16)

Of all the incidents in the life of Jesus that reveal the confidence He had in His identity, the one we are about to consider probably gives us the greatest insight into how complete His sense of identity was. I once heard an eminent psychiatrist say that a clear understanding of one's identity rests on four things: (1) a sense of belonging, (2) a healthy attitude to one's death, (3) a willingness to confront issues, and (4) a loving spirit that reaches out to others. As I listened to him say those words, my mind turned to the passage before us now. It struck me very forcibly that Jesus exemplified every one of those four things when He was here on earth – and to the most perfect degree. As Jesus is the model for us, His sons and daughters, I think it will be helpful for us in understanding our true identity to consider these four things one by one, and see how they fit into our own lives.

FURTHER STUDY

John 8:54-58;
17:1-5

1. How did Jesus show an eternal sense of belonging?

2. What is eternal life?

First, a sense of belonging. Picture the scene in the upper room. He is getting close to the hour of His death. Inside, the atmosphere is tense. Outside, a storm is about to be unleashed. But look at Jesus, and how secure He seems to be. The account says, 'Jesus knew… that he had come from God and was returning to God' (v3). Can you see the sweep of those words? John is painting an eternal perspective here. He steps off the platform of time and goes back to the truth that Jesus knew He had come from God and was now returning to Him. His sense of belonging was complete. He belonged not just to time but to eternity and, more importantly, to the God of eternity.

Loving Father, I see so clearly how important a sense of belonging is to my new identity. Help me walk through life with a new sense of confidence, knowing that I belong not to time but to eternity. And, most important of all, to You. Amen.

In the mind of God

For reading & meditation – Psalm 139

'My frame was not hidden from you when I was made
in the secret place.' (v15)

To be really and truly known is one of the most wonderful experiences of life, and in this psalm, we can enter into David's amazement, awe and incomprehension bordering on disbelief as he seeks to fully apprehend the true depth and bandwidth of God's thoughts towards us; more numerous than the grains of sand! God knows our comings and goings, our beginning and our end. He is familiar with us. God is thinking about you all the time. The thought of God's infinite knowledge and loving care of us, from the moment of conception, is brought out powerfully in *The Message*'s paraphrase of verse 15: 'You know me inside and out, you know every bone in my body; You know exactly how I was made, bit by bit, how I was sculpted from nothing into something. Like an open book, you watched me grow from conception to birth.' To live in the truth of this revelation of being known and loved by God, even from before the creation of the world (see v16 and Eph. 1:4), changes everything.

FURTHER STUDY

2 Tim. 1:7-10;
Titus 1:1-2;
1 Pet. 1:18-21

1. When was grace given us?

2. When was Christ chosen to die for us?

I shall never forget, as a young man, writing in the front of my Bible these words: 'Selwyn Hughes, 17 Martin Street, Fochriw, Bargoed, Glamorgan, South Wales, the United Kingdom, Europe, the World, the Universe'. When my pastor happened to see what I had written, he took out his pen and added these four words: 'The mind of God'. The impact of those four additional words has not left me to this day. In a sense, my life began not in my mother's womb but in eternity. My natural identity began in the womb, but my eternal identity began in the mind of God.

God my Father, I am so thankful that I was in Your thoughts before I was formed in the womb and that one day I will enjoy Your presence and be completely conformed to the image of Your Son forever. Amen.

Victory at the place of fear

For reading & meditation – 1 Corinthians 15:50–58

'Where, O death, is your victory? Where, O death,
is your sting?' (v55)

Before we move on, I would like to underline that if our identity
is not rooted in the eternal, then we are just children of the
temporal. Our new identity in Jesus means we have an eternal
context within which to think of ourselves. Eternity is our real
home. We are children who were conceived in the mind of God
before we were conceived in the womb of our mother.

Let's consider now the second thing on which a clear sense of
identity rests: a healthy attitude to one's death. Jesus had predicted
His death since early in His ministry, so it is not
surprising that He saw the end approaching. John
begins his account of what happened in the upper
room with these words: 'Jesus knew that the time
had come for him to leave this world and go to the
Father. Having loved his own who were in the world,
he now showed them the full extent of his love' (John
13:1). In the hours before His death, Jesus' heart was
not filled with fear but with perfect love. And perfect
love, John tells us, is so powerful that it drives out
every fear (1 John 4:18).

FURTHER STUDY

Job 1:13–21;
Psa. 49:10–15

1. How did Job
view personal
loss and his
own death?

2. What was
the psalmist's
view of death?

I do not believe that Jesus was free of all apprehension as He
thought about His imminent death, but certainly there was no
fear in His heart. The painful experience He went through in the
Garden of Gethsemane was, I believe, not caused by a fear of death
but by the knowledge that He had to bear the consummate weight
of human sin and, in consequence, be temporarily forsaken by
the Father. It was the prospect of that which caused Jesus such
tremendous turmoil in the garden.

*Lord Jesus, if there is a fear of death in my heart – or any other fear
– sweep through my soul with Your perfect love and cause all fear to
dissipate. In Your precious name I ask it. Amen.*

'A cordial for our fears'

For reading & meditation – Hebrews 2:5–18

'and free those who all their lives were held in slavery by their fear of death.' (v15)

For many people, even some Christians, the fear of death dominates their lives. It is a basic fear of all humankind. The older we grow, the more this fear is brought to the forefront of our mind. Some people are quite unwilling to face it. They push it away and believe any consideration of it is 'morbid'. William Cory, the poet, was haunted by the fear of death. In one of his books, Dr W.E. Sangster writes about how William Cory was once in a room where there was a small caged bird, bursting with song. A little girl who was also in the room clapped her hands together in great delight. Cory said gloomily, 'Yes, he's happy; he doesn't know that he will die.'

FURTHER STUDY
2 Sam. 12:16–23;
Phil. 1:21–26

1. Why could David look forward to death?

2. What did death mean for Paul?

Regular readers may remember I did a study on the fear of death and found three basic elements underlying this fear. First, the fear of the physical act of dying. Will it be painful and drawn out? Second, the fear of finality. Is death the end of everything? Third, the fear that beyond death one might have to face judgment. No one who knows Christ need fear these things. He will be with us in the physical act of dying, and we have the assurance that death is not final but the crossing over from the temporal to the eternal – from knowing Jesus' presence to seeing Him in person. And, for a Christian, there need be no fear of judgment. To us He has said, 'Your sins are forgiven you.' Jesus Christ is our Saviour, Surety, Ransom, Redeemer, Friend. He stands, like a great wall, between penitent sinners and their sins. He is, in the words of one poet: 'A sovereign balm for every wound, a cordial for our fears.'

Lord Jesus, I am so thankful that when I have You I have everything. Death cannot alter that fact. Please give me the strength and grace not only to live well but to die well. For Your own dear name's sake. Amen.

A denial of reality

For reading & meditation – Hebrews 9:11–28

'man is destined to die once, and after that to face
judgment' (v27)

We are exploring how one of the components of a clear sense
of identity is a healthy sense of one's finitude. Of course,
there are many people who aren't Christians who say they have
a healthy attitude towards their death, but I wonder about that.
Those I have talked to over the years who have made this claim
have based their attitude on the belief that death ends all, that
there is no final judgment, or that God is too good to let people go
to a lost eternity. But all these things are a denial of reality.

I am convinced that the truth of judgment is laid
deep in human consciousness, and finds support in
the iron law of cause and effect in the material world.
The apostle Paul talks about those who 'suppress the
truth' (Rom. 1:18). The human mind is capable of
pushing away things it doesn't want to accept, and
though the psychological mechanism of suppression
may at times help people through a difficult phase
in their lives, it can have very serious repercussions.
It is certainly dangerous when it causes us to ignore our eternal
welfare. A healthy attitude to one's death is best gained as a person
looks to Jesus as their Saviour and Lord.

FURTHER STUDY

Luke 23:39–43;
1 Thess. 4:13–18;
1 John 2:1-2

1. Why should we
not fear death?

2. Why should
we not fear
judgment?

Some time ago newspapers reported the case of a man who
appeared in court charged with a serious offence and found
that his counsel was not there to plead for him. Thankfully, no
pardoned sinner will be in that plight. Our counsel appears before
the throne of God, and is willing to plead for us. He will bring about
an assurance in our hearts that we are forgiven. But only if we
have asked for forgiveness.

**Lord God, help me not to deny reality. Your Word says there is a
judgment to be faced, and I can face that by trusting in You. I do so
now. Please forgive me and save me. In Jesus' name. Amen.**

Stooping to conquer

For reading & meditation – Luke 22:7–30

'a dispute arose among them as to which of them was considered to be greatest.' (v24)

Now we look at the third building block on which a clear sense of identity rests: a willingness to confront difficult issues. It is clear from the passage we have read today that at the time when Jesus celebrated the Passover, His disciples were arguing about which of them was considered the greatest.

Jesus never hesitated to tackle thorny issues that arose among His disciples. Sometimes He would reproach them; at other times He would patiently teach them through a parable. But when it

FURTHER STUDY

Phil. 2:1–8;
1 Pet. 5:5

1. How did Christ humble Himself?

2. What does God give to humble people?

came to the matter of which of them was considered the greatest, not only did Jesus teach them with words, as we see in today's reading, He also taught them by example what humility means, by washing their feet. The account in John's Gospel says: 'Jesus knowing that the Father had given all things into his hands, and that he was come from God, and went to God… laid aside his garments; and took a towel… and began to wash the disciples' feet' (John 13:3–5, KJV).

The consciousness of His greatness was the secret of His humility. All things had been placed in His hands so He used those hands to minister to His disciples in an act of great humility.

The preacher Phillips Brooks said: 'The true way to be humble is not to stoop until you are smaller than yourself, but to stand at your real height against some higher nature that will show you what the real smallness of your greatness is. Stand at your very highest, and then look at Christ, then go away and be forever humble.' The most essential quality when confronting difficult issues, either in ourselves or with others, is humility.

Lord Jesus Christ, You who showed what was right by getting down on Your knees in prayer, please give me the same humility so that I can follow Your example. I pray this in Your holy name. Amen.

A bridge not too far

For reading & meditation – John 17:20–26

'May they be brought to complete unity to let the world
know that you sent me' (v23)

Yesterday we saw that Jesus dealt with the issue of pride in the
hearts of His disciples by stooping to wash their feet. I wonder
how the disciples must have felt as they watched Jesus, the Lord
of glory, take a towel and bend down to wash their feet.

Often in our relationships with other Christians, issues can arise
that need to be dealt with. Many Christians will go through today
knowing there is an unresolved issue with a fellow Christian, and
yet they fail to deal with it. A friend of mine once said, 'A failure to
confront an issue that arises between one Christian
and another is a failure in love.'

Many years ago when I was a pastor, I drew up
a list of issues that, based on my experience up
to that time, I found Christians were reluctant to
deal with. The three that headed the list were these:
estrangement in their relationships with others, an
unwillingness to face the fact that they were not
just victims but agents (I will explain this later), and
third, a reluctance to truly and fully repent.

FURTHER STUDY

Matt. 5:21–24;
Eph. 2:11–18

1. Why is
reconciliation
more important
than sacrifice?

2. What is
the basis of
reconciliation?

Take the first – estrangement in relationships. Is there anyone
with whom you are out of fellowship because of some past
disagreement? Then take the initiative and seek to be reconciled.
The other person may not want to be reconciled, but that is not
your responsibility. You make the first move. The carpenter of
Nazareth will help you build a bridge across the divide between
you and those with whom you are estranged. Walk over it. It will
take courage, but as you now are in Christ, courage is one of the
marks of your new identity.

**Gracious and loving heavenly Father, I see that a failure in love is a
denial of my new identity. Help me to do everything that love
requires. In Jesus' name I pray. Amen.**

Agents for change

For reading & meditation – Revelation 2:1–7
'Repent and do the things you did at first.' (v5)

Today we continue the discussion of issues that Christians often find difficult to confront.

The second issue is an unwillingness to accept that we are not just victims but agents. Many reading these lines will have been victims of deep hurt and damaging maliciousness during their developmental years. They travel through the rest of their lives holding on to their hurt and thinking of themselves as victims. This is the way they perceive themselves, and they approach the whole of their lives from that perspective. Sadly, you can't change your past; but you can change what you do about it now. You are not just a victim; you are also an agent. By that I mean you have the power, provided by the indwelling Spirit, to change. Don't live in the past. Lift up your head and realise you have a new identity. Leave past baggage behind instead of carrying it around with you day after day.

FURTHER STUDY

Acts 2:36-39;
17:24-30;
1 John 1:8-10

1. What does God command us to do?
2. When might we be deceived?

The third issue people often fail to confront in their lives is the need to repent of any sins or lapses. Those who belonged to the church at Ephesus lost their first love. One would think the answer to that problem would have been to regain their first love and then go on as they did at first. But Jesus, their Counsellor, told them that they first needed to repent. Any spiritual dislocation, whether small or large, first needs to be dealt with by repentance. If we fail to do so, we will be seeking to bring about spiritual repairs in our own strength and without dependence on God. There are several other issues that Christians frequently fail to confront, but the three I have mentioned are, without doubt, crucial.

My Father and my God, as I go through life hand in hand with You, give me, I pray, an increasing sense of my new identity. May the image of Your Son continue to take shape within me. In Jesus' name. Amen.

Improve your serve

For reading & meditation – 1 Peter 4:1–11

'Each one should use whatever gift he has received to serve others, faithfully administering God's grace' (v10)

Now we move on to look at the fourth mark of a healthy sense of identity: a loving spirit that reaches out to others. The passage in John 13 (which, as we have already seen, shows how complete Jesus' sense of identity was) begins with these words: 'Having loved his own who were in the world, he now showed them the full extent of his love' (John 13:1). And what was 'the full extent of his love'? It was serving His disciples, even though He faced the prospect of being crucified within the next 24 hours. True love goes on demonstrating concern for others even when one's heart may have reasons to become self-preoccupied.

FURTHER STUDY

Matt. 25:34–40;
Acts 9:36–40;
Gal. 5:13

1. How can we minister to Christ?

2. How did Dorcas show her love for people?

Luke, in his account of the Last Supper and the dispute that arose among the disciples as to which of them was considered to be the greatest, tells us that Jesus interrupted this self-centred conversation with the words: 'I am among you as one who serves' (Luke 22:27). From John's account we know that He gave a visual demonstration of His words by wrapping a towel round His waist and washing the disciples' feet. Then, when He had resumed His place at supper, He said, 'I have set you an example that you should do as I have done for you' (John 13:15).

Every Christian is called to serve somebody. Yet I have to say that some of the people known to me who are most dedicated to serving others are those who, though struggling with illness or limited in some way, forget their difficulties and move with a loving spirit into the lives of others.

God my Father, forgive me if my life is not being stretched in service to others on Your behalf. Help me find a need, and in Your strength seek to meet it. In Jesus' name. Amen.

The true motivation

For reading & meditation – 2 Corinthians 5:11–15

'For Christ's love compels us, because we are convinced that one died for all' (v14)

Jesus understood Himself not as someone who came to be served, but as someone who came to serve. Everyone who is in Christ and seeks to enter into their new identity will find they have the same energy and drive to serve others. If we are not involved in serving others, then we are limiting the potential God has for us. As I said yesterday, we're called to serve somebody.

A great danger we face, however, when we set out to serve others is that we do the right thing for the wrong reason. It is possible, for instance, to serve others because of the good feelings we get from doing so. There is a big difference between feeling good because we have served others, and serving others in order to feel good. People who fall into the latter category are sometimes termed 'rescuers'. One pastor tells of a woman in his church who was always seeking to rescue others in the congregation from their troubles because of the buzz she got out of it. She would look around the church for someone to help and latch on to them. 'You could always tell her victims,' he said, 'by their hunted look.'

FURTHER STUDY

John 13:34-35;
15:12-13;
Heb. 6:9-12

1. How will people know our faith is genuine?

2. Why did Jesus lay down His life?

It is also possible to be drawn to serving others in order to be distracted from unhealthy issues in our own lives that we are unwilling to face. Such motivation is just another form of deception. Are we willing to look into our hearts and ask ourselves this question: 'Is my desire to serve others a veiled attempt to serve myself and meet my own needs, or, like the apostle Paul, am I compelled by the love of Christ?' When we serve, let's serve others with the love that flows from God to us, and not the love of self.

Heavenly Father, help me understand that the degree of my receptivity reflects the degree of my maturity. Help me to open myself more and more to Your love so that what flows from me to others is love of You, not love of self. Amen.

A heart at peace

For reading & meditation – John 20:19–23

'as my Father hath sent me, even so send I you.' (v21, KJV)

In today's verses we see Jesus presenting His disciples with a challenge: just as He was sent by His Father, so now He is about to send them – 'As… so.' What was the great mission of Jesus' life? He was sent to serve. Therefore our mission, like His, is to be one of service. He emptied Himself of status and took the form of a servant, and in that great passage in Philippians 2, Paul tells us that Jesus' humble mind ought also to be evident in us (Phil. 2:5–11).

Please allow me to give a personal testimony here. I shall never forget the time when I first entered the ministry and thought that now I was a minister I would have elders, deacons and others serving me. I saw myself as the boss rather than a servant. However, Jesus spoke to my heart and said: 'This is not the way it is to be. You are there not to be served but to serve.' His gentle words to my heart changed my attitude completely, and I came to realise that the greatest in the kingdom of God are not those who are served by the largest number but those who serve the largest number.

FURTHER STUDY

Luke 17:7-10;
22:24-27

1. What is the attitude of a good servant?

2. How is greatness measured in the world and in God's kingdom?

Why did Jesus equate greatness with service? Is it not because of the intrinsic worth of human beings? If all men and women are made in God's image then, as John Stott says, 'they must be served, not exploited, respected and not manipulated'. I lay no claim to spiritual greatness but it has strengthened my heart to have had the privilege of serving others every day through these notes. From experience I know that I am at my best when I am serving others, either through teaching or writing. A heart set on loving service to others is a heart at perfect peace with its Lord.

Lord Jesus Christ, we look in Your face and we see the meaning of love. It is a love that reaches out not only in words but also in deeds. As love functions in You, so let it also function in me. For Your own dear name's sake. Amen.

Maximum effectiveness

For reading & meditation – Romans 12:1–8

'We have different gifts, according to the grace given us.'
(v6)

Having looked at what an eminent psychiatrist once described as 'the four marks of a healthy personality', and seen how they were exemplified in the life of Jesus, we ask ourselves if they are present in us also.

Am I saying that these four things alone form the elements of our new identity? Of course not. There is much more that comprises our true sense of identity. Take, for instance, the passage before us today, which follows on from the thought we have

FURTHER STUDY

1 Cor. 12:12–31

1. Why is everyone vital in Christ's body?

2. What is your role in Christ's body, and are you fully functioning?

been considering over the past few days – namely that it is God's perfect will that we serve others. It shows us that everyone is gifted in a special way to serve others. For many years I have been saying in the pages of *Every Day with Jesus* that one of the greatest tragedies in contemporary church life is that so many do not operate within their giftedness. They are like square pegs in round holes. This is what I had in mind when I raised the question at the beginning of these meditations: Is it possible that the world has not yet seen the real you?

If you haven't yet discovered the basic gift God gave you, and you're looking for a place to start, a free resource is available from CWR ('Discovering Your Basic Gift', available on the website). Thousands have used this tool to discover and develop their basic spiritual gift, and have gone on to function in the role that God planned for them before the foundation of the world. Unemployment may be a problem in some societies, but there is no unemployment in the body of Christ!

Father, if I am failing to fit into the role You have designed for me in Your body, please help me discover it without delay. I long to be maximally effective, not minimally useful. In Jesus' name. Amen.

Co-heirs with Christ

For reading & meditation – Romans 8:1–17

'Now if we are children, then we are heirs – heirs of God and co-heirs with Christ' (v17)

What now is our conclusion as we complete this present issue on the subject of 'Our True Identity'? The four elements we have looked at over the past two weeks which, as we have seen, were part of Jesus' identity, can be replicated in us too. God wants to shape us into the image of His Son, and these four elements are an important part of that image.

As I said yesterday, there is much more that comprises our new identity in Christ, but these elements are foundational. One writer describes displaying them as putting on a tailor-made suit or dress after having spent all your life wearing clothes that have been bought 'off the peg'. Our new identity in Christ Jesus means that we can know who we are, to whom we belong, need have no fear of death, possess the courage to confront every issue that arises in our lives, and move out in loving service to others.

FURTHER STUDY

Gal. 3:26–4:7;
Rev. 21:7;
22:3-5

1. Who are we?
2. What will we inherit?

But finally, a word of caution: although when we come to Christ our new identity is there, deep within our spirits, the understanding and application takes time to develop. Be aware of this. Let me tell you my own experience. In the years immediately after entering the Christian ministry, my identity was wrapped up in being a preacher and a minister. If someone had asked me in those days, 'Who are you?' I would probably have said, 'I am an ambassador of Jesus Christ.' But as I came to know more of the Lord, I also came to see my identity not in terms of what I do, but of who I am. The answer to the question, 'Who are you?' through God's transforming grace became, 'I am a child of the living God, an heir of God and a joint heir with Jesus Christ.' Nothing is more wonderful than that!

Gracious Father, help me base my sense of identity on who I am in You. Never let me forget that my new identity is not something that has come through my accomplishments, but through divine grace. Thank You, my Father. Amen.

Persued by Grace

Learning from failure

For reading & meditation – 2 Kings 14:23–29

'the word of the LORD... spoken through his servant Jonah
son of Amittai, the prophet from Gath Hepher' (v25)

Today we begin a devotional study of the book of Jonah. Most children know something about Jonah, as do adults – whether Christian or not. He is best known, of course, for the dramatic encounter he had with 'a great fish'. One preacher said: 'Put Jonah in the middle of a bunch of anglers and you can be sure of one thing – his story of the one that got away will beat all the others!'

Many who have read or heard the story of Jonah consider it a fictitious tale or a parable designed to correct unspiritual attitudes. They put it in the same category as such stories as *Moby Dick*, *The Adventures of Pinocchio* or the *Arabian Nights* – fascinating but fictional. That is why we start our study with the reference to him in the books of Kings. It shows us that Jonah was a real person – a prophet who lived during the days of Jeroboam II (793–753 BC) and predicted the expansion of the Northern Kingdom of Israel. A grave near Nazareth is still pointed out to tourists as being Jonah's.

FURTHER STUDY

2 Chron.
32:24-26;
1 Cor. 10:1-13;
Rom. 15:4

1. Why were people's failures included in the Old Testament?

2. What can we learn from them?

Although Jonah eventually did what God asked of him, many aspects of his life were not praiseworthy. So if Jonah is not a role model, why are we studying his life and why is his story included in the Bible? I believe it's to provide us with lessons in how God is constant and consistent in His pursuit of relationship with us, that we might enjoy restored relationship with Him. Though we are focusing on a man whose life is complex and on one level seems to fail, the lessons we learn from his attitudes and actions will help us to fail less.

Father, I see that just as I learn from the successes of Your servants,
so I can learn from their failures also. Give me a teachable spirit,
I pray. Speak Lord, Your servant is listening. Amen.

Saying 'no' to God

For reading & meditation – Jonah 1:1–2

'Go to the great city of Nineveh and preach against it,
because its wickedness has come up before me.' (v2)

The Jonah narrative begins with the fact that he is given a job to perform by God that he doesn't want. Having received a prophetic call to go to Nineveh, he plans to head in the opposite direction. Jonah didn't object to preaching, but he wanted to choose his own pulpit! Nineveh was the great capital of the ancient Assyrian Empire and was built on the banks of the Tigris River in northeastern Mesopotamia, which we know today as Iraq.

The Assyrians were enemies of Israel, and their brutality and wickedness was such that it offended the sensitive heart of God. God says to Jonah to go to Nineveh and, 'Preach to them. They're in a bad way and I can't ignore it any longer' (v2, *The Message*). Why should God worry about one of Israel's fiercest enemies? Jonah is nonplussed by God's sudden interest in Nineveh and fails to understand why He should attempt to save such godless people. But shouldn't a prophet obey God's commands without question or quibble? We would think so, but Jonah is adamant.

FURTHER STUDY

Luke 9:23-27;
14:15-24

1. What is required of a disciple?

2. Identify some of the reasons why people say no to God.

Put yourself in Jonah's place. Would you be willing to follow God's clear command if He asked you to do something that to you didn't seem to make sense? How many of us, I wonder, if we are being honest, identify with his response, especially when we don't readily understand. However, we who commit ourselves to serving God must come to grips with this most important fact: we are not always called to understand but to stand. Those who can't or won't at least grapple with this truth make little progress along the path of discipleship.

My Father and my God, whenever Your words to me are contrary to my natural inclinations and desires, may I take my stand for You and against my feelings. Help me, dear Lord, for in my own strength I am so prone to fail. In Jesus' name. Amen.

'Where ego is...'

For reading & meditation – Jonah 1:3
'But Jonah ran away from the LORD and headed
for Tarshish.' (v3)

We move slowly through these opening verses of Jonah's
account because there is so much truth that needs to
be drawn out from them. Today we reflect further on Jonah's
surprising refusal to obey God's command to deliver His message
to Nineveh. What were the reasons for his noncompliance? Did
he fear for his life? Was he overcome by cowardice? Personally, I
think that his disinclination to follow God's instructions was almost
certainly due to being overly concerned for his own reputation. A
later statement indicates this was indeed a factor (4:2).

FURTHER STUDY

Gal. 2:11-21;
Phil. 2:3-8

1. How was Peter
concerned about
his reputation?

2. What is Jesus'
example?

The people of Israel had seen many prophets come
and go. On more than one occasion in the nation's
history men had claimed to be prophets even though
they weren't. In Moses' time God had warned that
this would happen, and had given instructions on
how to differentiate between the false and the true:
'If what a prophet proclaims in the name of the LORD
does not take place or come true, that is a message
the LORD has not spoken' (Deut. 18:22). I have no doubt Jonah
pondered the fact that if, after prophesying against Nineveh, the
people repented, causing an outpouring of God's mercy and grace,
then some might conclude he was not a true prophet. His concern
was not for God and His glory but for his own reputation.

Sin has been described by some as putting our ego in the place
where God wants to be. Sigmund Freud said his whole philosophy
could best be summed up in the phrase: 'Where Id [the sum total of
our instinctive impulses] is, let Ego be.' The Christian worldview, I
believe, is best summed up in this phrase: Where ego is, let God be.

**Loving heavenly Father, forgive me if, like Jonah, I put my interests
before Your interests. From now on may You be central and my ego
marginal. In Jesus' name I pray. Amen.**

What God delights in

For reading & meditation – Psalm 86:1–17

'But you, O Lord, are a compassionate and gracious God, slow to anger, abounding in love and faithfulness.' (v15)

W e pause to look at a text that shows the contrast between Jonah's attitude and the compassionate and forgiving nature of God. As the events of Jonah's story unfold, it becomes quite clear that he was more interested in shouting judgment than in announcing the offer of divine forgiveness. Many Christians I have met are like that; they are fiery in their denunciation of sin but fail to emphasise the fact that the thing God delights to do is to forgive.

Some time ago I gave a lecture for the Bible Society in Dublin on

FURTHER STUDY
Ezek. 18:21-23;
John 8:1-11
1. What does
God delight in?
2. Describe
the attitudes
of Jesus and
the Pharisees.

the subject 'The Bible – God's Word for Today'. After I had completed my lecture a priest commented on the statement I had made concerning the truth that God delights to forgive. He said: 'If an angel came down into this room tonight and told us that the Trinity had decided to abandon the fact of hell, many of us would be very disappointed, as we all know people we would like to see finish up there.' The audience laughed, but they identified with the point he was making.

How many of us, I wonder, gain a sense of moral satisfaction from the thought that godless people deserve judgment when we should be concentrating on their need for forgiveness? Let us be quite clear about this: God is against sin – all sin – and promises that the unrepentant will face the consequences. But what He loves to do is forgive. Listen to what God says through the prophet Micah: 'What does the LORD require of you? To act justly and to love mercy' (Micah 6:8, my emphasis). Perhaps we ought to still our hearts for a moment and ask ourselves this crucial question: Am I as concerned about mercy as I am about judgment?

Father, You have challenged me to consider whether I love mercy or prefer judgment for others. Please change me to bring my nature in line with Yours so that I may act justly but love mercy. Amen.

The Tarshish illusion

For reading & meditation – Jonah 1:3

'He went down to Joppa, where he found a ship bound for that port.' (v3)

It is interesting to notice that in response to God's command Jonah sets off, but in the totally opposite direction. He could have ignored God's call and remained where he was, but instead he sets out for Tarshish. Why Tarshish?

Well, for one thing, Tarshish was a much more interesting proposition than Nineveh. The 'Tarshish' spoken of here was most likely the Spanish town called Tartessus, which was famous for its silver, iron, tin and lead. The city exported these minerals to such places as Joppa and Tyre. Ezekiel speaks of the trade that the people of Tyre had with Spain: 'Tarshish did business with you because of your great wealth of goods' (Ezek. 27:12). Nineveh was an ancient city with an unhappy history; Tarshish promised adventure. My Bible dictionary says that in Old Testament times Tarshish, in the popular imagination, became a kind of distant paradise – a Shangri-La.

FURTHER STUDY

Psa. 139:1-24

1. What did the psalmist acknowledge?

2. What was his concluding desire?

I wonder, am I talking today to someone who has been called by God to do something that seems difficult? Do you find yourself thinking about going in the opposite direction to that which you have been called? Are you just about to buy a ticket to 'Tarshish'? If so, I have this message: your attempt to run from God's call is just not worth it. You can run but you can't hide. God knows your end from the beginning and, though He loves you as you are, He loves you too much to let you stay as you are. Jonah ran, but God went with him. Whenever you find yourself in circumstances that seem to aid you in your flight from God, be aware that conducive conditions are not necessarily indicators of the divine will.

Loving Father, thank You for reminding me that pleasing circumstances are not always a sign that I am doing the right thing. Help me always listen to Your Word, which is guaranteed to lead me in the right direction. Amen.

Jonah on his way

For reading & meditation – Jonah 1:3

'After paying the fare, he went aboard and sailed for Tarshish' (v3)

The ticket that Jonah purchased from Joppa to Tarshish was, without doubt, one of the costliest ever acquired. He went in the opposite way to that specified by God and finished up in the deep – literally! Let's remind ourselves of the circumstances. God sends Jonah to Nineveh, a city over 500 miles northeast of Jerusalem. Instead, Jonah sets t in the opposite direction.

This just demonstrates the fruitlessness of resisting God's good and perfect will. A motto on the wall of the Bible College where I trained read: 'To be in the will of God is better than success'. Some students met one evening and had a discussion. 'There is something not quite right about that statement,' they commented. 'It would be better to say: "To be in the will of God is success".' Everyone agreed, and, after approaching the principal, the motto was changed. Had Jonah reached Tarshish he might have had a seemingly successful life, but it would have been 'success' that lay outside the will of God, therefore unsuccess. Success is knowing the will of God – and doing it.

Jonah paid heavily for running away from God. And so will we. On the outside we may appear to be confident and carefree, but on the inside we will pay the price often in the form of guilt, anxiety and so on. Someone has said we are not so much punished for our sins as by our sins. When we ignore something God has called us to do we cannot really escape – either from God or ourselves. All that results is that we cannot live with God. And if we cannot live with God then we won't be able to live with ourselves.

Lord, save me from thinking that escaping from Your will and ways gives me freedom. When I do so I am free only to go from one entanglement to another. Help me see that when I play truant with You, I play truant with myself. Amen.

God is everywhere

Did you notice that the verse we are looking at (v3) begins and ends with the statement that Jonah was running away from the Lord? It starts, 'But Jonah ran away from the LORD', and it finishes: 'and sailed for Tarshish to flee from the LORD. The two statements beg the question: Why would anyone want to run away from the Lord? Or: Can anyone really run away from the Lord?

It seems Jonah had an imperfect view of God and His presence. The prevailing opinion in many nations during Old Testament times was that each country's god was limited to its own land. Sometimes people would carry soil from one country to another in the belief that the god of that country would travel with them. The account of Naaman's quest for healing demonstrates this kind of thinking (2 Kings 5:17). Some Israelites believed that God was confined to the Temple in Jerusalem, or, at most, to the territory of Israel. So perhaps Jonah thought that when he sailed away from the shores of Israel he would be leaving God behind. Or he may have thought that when he got far away from Israel, then the impact of God's presence would be diminished in his life, in the same way that a radio signal fades the further one gets from the transmitter. Jonah would learn, as we must learn, that there is nowhere where God is not.

I once read the story of a vehement atheist who wrote on a wall: 'God is nowhere.' But unwittingly he left a space between the letters 'w' and 'h'. As he stood back and looked at what he had written he read: 'God is now here'. It brought about his conversion.

FURTHER STUDY

1 Kings 20:23-30;
2 Chron. 16:8-9;
Isa. 54:5

1. What was wrong with Aramean thinking?

2. Where is God's focus?

Father, I am reminded of the psalmist who said: 'Where can I flee from your presence?' Help me live in the consciousness that wherever I go, You are there too. I can never go anywhere where You are not. Amen.

Saved by a storm

For reading & meditation – Jonah 1:4

'Then the LORD sent a great wind on the sea' (v4)

Jonah, on his voyage to Tarshish, finds himself in stormy weather. The hurricane ruined his plans to go to Tarshish; his vacation was spoiled but his vocation was saved. None of us likes to find ourselves caught up in a storm, but at times it is the only way God can get our attention. The poet George Herbert wrote these lines: 'Poets have wrong'd poor storms; such days are best, they purge the air without, within the breast.' A storm may bring chaos and cause great damage but it also clears the air.

FURTHER STUDY

Job 1:13-22;
2:7-10;
42:1-17

1. How did Job respond to the storm he experienced?

2. How was Job blessed by God after the storm?

I once talked to a man who told me that he had gone through a period of deep depression. He described this time as like being in a storm. My curiosity was aroused when he further concluded: 'Now I can thank God for my depression.' I found this surprising so I asked him how he could thank God for depression, and his reply went something like this: 'The storm I was facing that caused my depression was due to wrong patterns of living. I needed those wrong patterns and ideas shaken up and challenged, for they were sending my life in the wrong direction. The depression was a message that said: "You are not thinking right, or living right. I am going to turn your life upside down and inside out. You won't like it for a while, but it will be for your ultimate good". I came out of the storm a new man.'

Though it may be difficult for us to admit it, the truth is that some of us cling to things that will be loosened only by a storm. Another of the lines from George Herbert's The Country Parson that I love is this: 'Storms are the triumph of His art.' They are.

Father, I don't like being caught up in a storm but I see that sometimes tempests are necessary to move me from wrong patterns of thinking to right ones. The next time I find myself in one help me to remember this. Amen.

All knees on deck

For reading & meditation – Jonah 1:5

'All the sailors were afraid and each cried out
to his own god.' (v5)

The sailors on board the ship bound for Tarshish had to encounter two storms: one was on the sea, the other was in their hearts. These sailors no doubt would certainly have had plenty of experience at sea and no doubt had been buffeted by many storms, but this one's constitution was entirely different. As they listened to the wind and the sound of the creaking timbers, and saw the huge waves breaking over them, the text tells us they were terrified. But what could they do in such a desperate situation? Well, they could pray. We will never know if the captain ordered 'all knees on deck', but each one, we are told, cried out to his own god.

The sailors were not only a praying party but a practical group also. Perhaps they believed in the old adage that God helps those who help themselves. Across the howling hurricane they shout to each other: 'Let's lighten the load.' And in order to lessen the danger, they throw the cargo overboard. After all, what is the value of corn when compared to human lives?

FURTHER STUDY

Neh. 4:7-9;
Matt. 9:36-10:8

1. How is prayer
and action
linked?

2. What were the
disciples to do?

We must remember, of course, that these men were praying to non-existent gods, but the point that prayer goes hand in hand with action is still an important one. There is a passive side to prayer and an active side also. The taking hold of God must lead to undertaking for God. The quiet must quicken. These lines by Gay McNitt make the point most effectively: 'You must use your hands while praying, though, if an answer you would get, for prayer-worn knees and a rusty hoe Never raised a big crop yet.'

**Heavenly Father, give me wisdom, I pray, to know not only when to get down on my knees but also when to get up. Let me not linger too long in the passive when I ought to be moving into action.
In Jesus' name. Amen.**

'Flurried and worried'

For reading & meditation – Jonah 1:5
'And they threw the cargo into the sea to lighten the ship.'
(v5)

W e continue reflecting on the issue we touched on yesterday, namely that the sailors were not only a praying party but a practical group as well. They prayed and threw the cargo into the sea to lighten the load. A definition of prayer I have always liked is this: prayer is receptivity. But if prayer were only receptivity then we would be left leaning too much towards the passive side of life. We would be left with the attitude of taking without undertaking. I would remind you again that, although the sailors were praying to non-existent gods, they put 'hands and feet' to their prayers. They were prayerful but creative.

We should and can find prayer to be creative, for when our lesser life touches the Life it becomes alive. Frequently I reflect on the passage in the New Testament that tells of Jesus getting up early, while it was still dark, and going off to a solitary place to pray. Simon Peter searches for Him, and when he finds Him says: 'Everyone is looking for you!' Jesus replies: 'Let us go... so that I can preach' (Mark 1:35–38). Jesus' praying was preaching in incubation. The praying stimulated the preaching, the receptivity became response, the impression of prayer became the expression of proclamation.

The most godly Christians in the world are those who wait quietly before God in prayer and then rise to put their hands to the practical tasks that await them. The poised, prayerful person becomes sure of directions, sure of their resources and moves from task to task with calm confidence. The prayerless are hurried, flurried and worried, wearing themselves out.

Father, help me not to linger on the passive side of life so that I fail to deal with the active side. Help me know when to stop and when to go. I long to be a balanced Christian. In Jesus' name. Amen.

Oranges versus diamonds

For reading & meditation – Colossians 3:1–17
'Set your minds on things above, not on earthly things.'
(v2)

For one more day we reflect on the fact that the sailors on the ship headed for Tarshish thought nothing of tipping the whole cargo into the sea when their very existence was under threat. 'Trouble,' it has been said, 'helps us more than anything to see things in their true perspective.' Possessions don't count for much when one's life is at stake.

Many years ago, on the night of 14 April 1912 to be precise, the Titanic, the largest vessel then afloat, collided with an iceberg in the mid-Atlantic, and almost three hours later sank to the bottom. Much has been written of what took place in those four hours. Survivors spoke of the calm heroism of the captain, the officers and the crew. They told of the courage of the bandmaster, who led the playing of 'Nearer my God to Thee'. They told another story, less courageous but equally interesting. A certain wealthy woman, who had been allotted a place in one of the lifeboats, asked if she might run back to her cabin to get something, and was given three minutes to go. She hurried along the corridors, already tilting at a dangerous angle. When she reached her cabin she saw money and costly gems littering the floor. She saw them, but she paid no attention. Snatching at two oranges, she ran back to the lifeboat. Hours before, who would have said the moment would come when she might prefer two oranges to valuable jewels. But death had boarded the Titanic, and with one blast of its awful breath reversed her values. Oranges were worth more than diamonds.

Trouble forces us helps us to things as they really are.

FURTHER STUDY

Mark 4:18–19;
Luke 12:13–21;
1 Tim. 6:17–19

1. Why are riches deceitful?

2. What are true riches?

Loving Saviour, I need to have the right perspective on everything. Teach me the art of weighing all things in relation to eternity, of seeing things as they really are, not as I would like them to be. In Jesus' name. Amen.

Jonah the escapist

For reading & meditation – Jonah 1:5

'But Jonah had gone below deck, where he lay down and fell into a deep sleep.' (v5)

It's intriguing that while the sailors were trying to keep the vessel afloat, Jonah was below deck – fast asleep. Jesus, you will remember, was also in a boat when a storm blew up (Mark 4:35–41). And He, too, fell asleep. His sleep was due to physical tiredness but Jonah's was, we might speculate, due to a psychological defence mechanism known as escapism.

Escapism has been described as 'the attempt to avoid difficult situations or uncomfortable feelings... by withdrawing or engaging in thoughts or behaviours which tend to draw the mind away from the thing feared.' Some people escape and distract themselves with hobbies and other positives – others favour more destructive patterns of addictions and other isolating behaviours. People whose life issue was the result of escapism have said to me: 'Why would I retreat into this when the consequences are destructive and troublesome for those around me?' The answer is that we divert attention from emotional pain by producing a different circumstance and situation. Psychologists have a term for this: conversion. The mind converts a mental health or emotional issue to a physical one.

FURTHER STUDY

1 Kings 19:1-19;
Psa. 55:1-8

1. Describe how Elijah's emotions prompted his actions.

2. What was the psalmist's response to conflict?

A man I once knew complained that he couldn't wake up in the mornings. After nine or more hours' sleep he had to be woken by his wife. Yet his doctor told him there was no physical reason for this. He was carrying a lot of unresolved conflicts. One by one they were dealt with and he returned to a normal sleep pattern. When he had nothing to retreat from he woke up eager to face the day.

Loving heavenly Father, deliver me from any escapist attitudes. I would make no evasions, have no subterfuges in my life. May I be open, honest and not willing to dodge anything. Help me to face everything with You. Amen.

A prayerless prophet

For reading & meditation – Jonah 1:6

'The captain... said, "How can you sleep? Get up and call on your god!"' (v6)

In a storm it is a matter of 'all hands on deck', but two hands, at least, were missing – Jonah's. The prophet's hands were folded, not in prayer, but to form a cushion on which to sleep. He was discovered by the captain, who woke him and said: 'What's this? Sleeping! Get up! Pray to your god!' (*The Message*).

Though the captain's rebuke must have brought Jonah to his feet, there is no record of him calling on God in prayer. How could he explain to the captain that he was not on speaking terms with his God? How different from Jesus who, when He was woken by His disciples in the midst of a fierce squall, rose to His feet, prayed to His Father and commanded the storm to cease (Mark 4:39). We said the other day that storms reveal what we value in life, and in this storm Jonah is exposed as a man who is most likely ashamed and trying to avoid God. A friend of mine used to define prayer as 'revision' because, as he put it, 'a revised version of your life is put out every time you pray – really pray.' When we open up our heart to God then more and more of our life is brought in line with His will and ways.

FURTHER STUDY

Psa. 32:1-7;
Luke 23:26-34

1. How did the psalmist experience revision?

2. How did Jesus avoid harbouring negative emotions?

A Christian psychologist once undertook some research into the matter of what causes Christians to lapse into prayerlessness. He found that the chief reason was that they were harbouring things in their hearts they did not want to give up. They thought prayer would give God the opportunity to challenge them. There is no need to hold on to guilt, self-pity, resentment. We need to learn God is for us: when we give things over to Him we find more freedom.

God my Father, save me from becoming a prayerless person. Help me bring more and more of my life under the shadow of Your wing so that more of You can be seen in my life, and my will aligned to Yours. Amen.

Being educated in being

For reading & meditation – Jonah 1:6
'Maybe he will take notice of us, and we will not perish.'
(v6)

Yesterday we said that the storm revealed Jonah as a prophet who was still trying to avoid God. Before progressing any further with the Jonah narrative permit me to linger on this matter of prayerlessness. One aspect of prayer, we began to explore yesterday, is that of revision: a revised version of our lives is put out every time we pray – really pray. When we open up our heart to God in prayer then we are aligning more of our life with His. Consequently, as channels of receptivity are opened, our whole life, will and purpose is brought into alignment with the will of God and so consequently and somehow counter intuitively, yet miraculously, we are wonderfully transformed, renewed and invigorated.

FURTHER STUDY

Psa. 1:1-3;
John 15:1-16

1. What makes us fruitful?

2. Why and how does God prune us?

Education has been defined as change. If this is so, then prayer is life's greatest form of education, for through prayer we are being educated, at the very centre of our lives. We are being educated in being what it means to live in a restored relationship with God, others and ourselves and these three lines are wonderful ones to pray daily: 'May I know Thee more clearly, love Thee more dearly, follow Thee more nearly.'

If prayer is revision, then also prayer involves pruning: 'every branch that is grape-bearing he prunes back so it will bear even more' (John 15:2, *The Message*). Prunes it of what? He takes off suckers that sap the life of the branch, suckers that bear no fruit, that only keep the branch from bearing fruit. It is because of this that when people say to me they are too busy to pray I respond: 'Then you are busier than God intends you to be.'

Father, search me and see if there is any hidden thing in me, anything about which I do not want to pray. In these few quiet moments now, as I pause before You, bring it to the light. In Jesus' name. Amen.

A non-functioning conscience

For reading & meditation – Jonah 1:7

'Then the sailors said... "Come, let us cast lots to find out
who is responsible for this calamity."' (v7)

When Jonah is persuaded to come on deck he sees the sailors
engaged in heated discussion with each other. For all their
prayers to their different gods, there is no let-up in the storm. So
many people are praying, but the storm does not ease. What is
the reason for this, they ask themselves. Eventually they conclude
that someone is responsible for the storm. But who? They cast lots
to find out. For ancient Near Eastern people it was customary,
when the use of reason and logic failed to settle an issue, to mark
a pebble and put it in a bag along with several
unmarked pebbles. The individual who drew out the
marked pebble was viewed as being responsible for
the matter in question.

FURTHER STUDY

Rom. 2:12-16;
1 Tim. 4:1-3

1. What is the
purpose of the
conscience?

2. Why may
people be
hypocrites?

While the drawing of lots is being organised, Jonah
holds his peace. He knows something that nobody
else knows, but he stays silent. Why doesn't he own
up and say: 'There is no need to cast lots. I'm the one
responsible for this storm?' Was it cowardice? I don't
think so. Rather it seems a combination of childish petulance and
a conscience dulled by self-pity and self-centredness.

I can think of nothing more injurious to our spiritual life than
having a conscience that does not operate in the way it was
designed. King David deceived himself to such an extent that his
conscience failed to function correctly until God brought Nathan
to him with a stinging parable that penetrated his defences and
helped him see himself as he really was (2 Sam. 12:1–14). Anyone
whose conscience does not move with speed and certainty is like
a ship at sea without a compass.

**God, forgive me if I am slow to recognise issues and deal with them,
or if I stand by and let things happen because I have lost my
sensitivity to that which is right. Strengthen me so that I become
the person I should be. Amen.**

Lying to yourself

For reading & meditation – Jeremiah 9:1–16
'Friend deceives friend, and no one speaks the truth.
They have taught their tongues to lie' (v5)

Today we reflect further on why it was that Jonah, knowing he was responsible for the storm, failed to own up and allowed the sailors to cast lots. We suggested that Jonah's conscience had been dulled and did not work in the way it was designed. But I also believe that Jonah was lying to himself.

Deception of any kind is to be strongly avoided as it inevitably results in spiritual loss. But if I were forced to decide which kind of deception is worst, I would unhesitatingly declare that it is deception

FURTHER STUDY
Gen. 3:9-13;
Isa. 44:12-20

1. What lie did Adam and Eve tell?

2. How may people deceive themselves?

of oneself. This leads by scarcely perceptible degrees to the worst state into which a man or woman may fall. I once heard Dr Sangster, one of Methodism's greatest preachers, say this: 'At first it might sound absurd to speak of lying to oneself. Men and women lie to deceive somebody who is unacquainted with the facts. It is usually a cowardly device for concealing the unpleasant truth from a person at present in ignorance, and hence it seems possible only to lie to somebody who has less information upon the point than you have yourself. If they knew the truth as you knew it, you couldn't deceive them. How, then, can a man or woman lie to themselves?'

Sadly, Jeremiah 17:9 tells us 'the heart is deceitful above all things' and we often hide things from ourselves and others. The truth is that we can and do lie to ourselves, and I suspect we all know something of the danger from personal experience. Jonah stood on the deck with a dulled conscience, believing a self-imposed lie. And what was that lie? Perhaps this: 'I am not the only one to blame... others are bad too.'

Thank You Father that I do not have to hide things from myself. You know me better than I know myself: help me to accept this truth. In Jesus' name. Amen.

Outrun by God

For reading & meditation – Jonah 1:7

'They cast lots and the lot fell on Jonah.' (v7)

DAY
198

How do we engage with people who lack insight and who have deceived themselves to such an extent that they cannot see their precarious predicament? It is a big problem. If you argue with them, they argue back. And usually they are not lacking in specious arguments. From the start they are on the defensive, and they fight every step of the way. If you fall back on flat affirmation and exclaim, 'Surely you can see what is happening to you,' they will say something along these lines: 'There is more than one way of looking at things,' or, 'I'm only human... everybody fails from time to time.' And if you still persist, they turn away from you with an air of injured dignity.

In the case of King David, as we have mentioned, God eventually brought to him the prophet Nathan, whose carefully God-crafted story got beneath his defences and exposed his self-deception (2 Sam. 12:1–14). Runaways from God and His truth are still loved by Him. If Jonah would not own up to his spiritual condition and admit that the storm was God's way of bringing him to his senses, then God would find some other way to deal with him. God watched as the sailors cast lots and intervened at the right moment to make sure that 'the lot fell on Jonah'. The action was human but the outcome was divine.

FURTHER STUDY

2 Sam. 11:2–5,
14–17,26–27;
12:1–4

1. How did
David try to
outrun God's
commands?

2. How did God
outrun David?

Jonah must have thought that his chances of getting away from God were high, but what a shock he had when the lot fell to him. An interesting verse in the book of Proverbs says: 'We toss the coin, but it is the Lord who controls its decision' (Prov. 16:33, TLB). When will we learn that there is just no way we can outrun God?

Father, if I am self-deceived about anything then do whatever is necessary to expose what is wrong, I pray. The health of my soul is too important to be left untreated. In Jesus' name. Amen.

Let me tell you a story

For reading & meditation – Psalm 139:1-24
'Search me, O God, and know my heart' (v23)

We pause to look at a psalm that Jonah would have done well to consider. If he had prayed 'Search me, O God... test me... See if there is any offensive way in me' then he would have saved himself a great deal of difficulty. Jonah is a curious man – his knowledge and doctrine of God was first class but he resisted an intense personal encounter. Have your feet wandered on that same perilous path as Jonah's? Are you deceiving yourself? Let me warn you against doing so, and tell you a story.

FURTHER STUDY
John 8:4-9;
21:17-22

1. Why can we see others' failings but not our own?

2. Why do we try to deflect the truth of God's Word on to others?

There was once a man who was brought up in a good home, understood the way of righteousness and had the reputation of being a mature and upright Christian. But gradually things began to change and he found himself becoming more concerned about his work than what pleased God; spiritual matters began to take second place. He kept up the duties of the Christian life, said a prayer at the end of the day, faithfully read *Every Day with Jesus*, but never admitted that what was being said applied to him. Are you that man?

There was once a young woman who was a bright and shining light for Jesus. Then she got married and had children. Gradually she began to lose her interest in spiritual matters, the fire in her life burned low, and she settled for spiritual mediocrity. She, too, read *Every Day with Jesus* but neatly deflected the truth on to other people. She thought of others who needed spiritual renewal, never herself. Are you that woman? If so, then I commend you to God who forgives, cleanses, restores, redeems and renews.

Father, I ask myself: Am I the one You are talking to here? If so, forgive me for deflecting Your truth on to others instead of receiving it for myself. I accept it now – humbly. Forgive and restore me. Amen.

Questions galore

For reading & meditation – Jonah 1:8–10

'This terrified them and they asked,
"What have you done?"' (v10)

As soon as Jonah is known to be the cause of the storm he is plagued by one question after another from the sailors. They fire them at him fast and furiously: 'Confess. Why this disaster? What is your work? Where do you come from? What country? What family?' (v8, *The Message*). Jonah tells them that he is a Hebrew and a worshipper of the true God who made the sea and the land, and that he is running away from Him. This made them more afraid than ever, for they realised that they were harbouring a fugitive from the One who could, within minutes, turn a calm sea into a terrifyingly turbulent one. Why Jonah was running from his God they did not yet know, but they saw clearly from the howling hurricane and the raging sea that He was a God to be reckoned with.

When we look at God's ways from the vantage point of the whole of Scripture we see that what drives Him is not the desire to battle with the human will and win, but benevolence and love. When we're wanting to be something other than what God wants us to be, the chances are we're wanting something that will not actually make us happy. God knew that Jonah would never be fulfilled outside His will, and He set about doing for Jonah what he needed, not what he wanted. Some might consider it petulant of God to have chased Jonah when he wanted to get away, but a great tragedy would have occurred if God had allowed him to keep running. We can often find ourselves in a storm of our own making and try to blame God. We need to remember that we can trust God to work out His purposes for our lives.

FURTHER STUDY

1 Kings 19:1–18;
Psa. 136:1–12

1. How did God chase and minister to Elijah when he ran away?

2. What drives God in His relationship with His people?

Father, once again I am sorry for running from You. Stop me, I pray, from pursuing any path that leads me away from You. I am so thankful that I can trust You – even in the storm. Amen.

God's loving disciplines

For reading & meditation – Hebrews 12:7-13

'God disciplines us for our good, that we may share
in his holiness.' (v10)

W̱e pause once more to focus on a passage that reminds us
God loves us too much not to help us grow in faith and trust.
Personally, I have doubts about using the word 'punishment'; a
better word, I think, is 'discipline'. God was not so much punishing
Jonah for the mentality that led him to run away but disciplining
him so that he could still fulfil all that God had planned for him.

Some might see the whole story of Jonah as an expression of
God's anger and petulance. But that is not so. Steven Covey, in

FURTHER STUDY

Prov. 3:11-12;
Rev. 3:14-22

1. What
motivates God
to discipline us?

2. Why
does Jesus
discipline us?

his book *The Seven Habits of Effective People*, talks
about the difference between a win-lose approach to
life and a win-win attitude. The win-lose approach
is evident when one person tries to get the better of
another; the win-win approach is apparent when one
person wants to win but is equally interested in the
other person winning. God's approach to Jonah was
that of win-win. He was not spelling out the message
to Jonah: 'See how much bigger than you I am.' No,
He wanted him back in the prophetic ministry and carrying His
message to Nineveh.

In *The Problem of Pain*, C.S. Lewis says: 'God has paid us the
intolerable compliment of loving us in the deepest, most tragic,
most inexorable sense.' Sometimes God's ways may seem harsh
and unkind, but behind them is a heart that beats with love. He
loves us too much to let us get away from Him. The next time you
might feel that God is on your case remember this: if He didn't love
you so much He would not pursue you in the way He does. It may
seem uncomfortable to you but really it is a divine compliment.

**Father, I am so thankful for the thought that You love me too much
to let me get away from You. Help me never forget that You
discipline me in order to develop me. Amen.**

Another form of escapism?

For reading & meditation – Jonah 1:11–12

'The sea was getting rougher and rougher. So they asked him, "What should we do to you...?"' (v11)

As the fury of the storm increases, the sailors want desperately to remedy the situation. If the storm is the result of a dispute between Jonah and his God then surely, they think, he will know what should be done. So the sailors ask Jonah: 'What should we do to you to make the sea calm down for us?' (v11). Jonah knows that if the crew want to rid themselves of the trouble, they have to rid themselves of him: 'Pick me up and throw me into the sea,' is his reply (v12).

Isn't it interesting that though Jonah was not willing to go to Nineveh, he was willing to be thrown overboard! What was in his mind, I wonder, when he made this statement? Regret at putting the sailors' lives at risk? A desire to have his life ended? Can Jonah's decision to be a scapegoat be compared to Moses' plea: 'blot me out of the book you have written' (Exod. 32:32)? I don't think so. Jonah was not yet repentant and was feeling sorry for being found out. One commentator suggests that Jonah's request to be thrown overboard was actually an act of penance. That may be so, but it was not penance that was needed at that moment, it was repentance. Was this just another attempt to dodge the real issue by substituting another?

An act of penance may be appropriate after receiving forgiveness, but it can never be thought of as earning forgiveness. There was only one way for Jonah to be restored, and that was not by being cast into the sea but by casting himself into the arms of a loving and merciful God. If only...

FURTHER STUDY

Luke 18:9-14;
2 Cor. 7:8-11

1. How can religious observance dodge the real issue?

2. What is the difference between sorrow and repentance?

Gracious and loving heavenly Father, how sad it is when we try everything except the one thing that leads to restoration – full confession and repentance. Help me to take Your way always, for Your way always works. Amen.

'Full speed astern'

For reading & meditation – Jonah 1:12

'I know that it is my fault that this great storm
has come upon you.' (v12)

Yesterday we saw that though Jonah was not willing to go to
Nineveh, he was willing to go overboard. He was willing to do
anything except the right thing – repent. We pause here to look at
what repentance really is. As frequent readers will recognise, the
word 'repent' in Greek is *metanoia*, which means 'a change of mind'.

C.S. Lewis described repentance as a movement of the soul that
is 'full speed astern'. It is not fun to repent, and it is much more
than eating humble pie, says Lewis. He describes it as 'unlearning'
the self-conceited behaviours we have spent years
learning; in a way, killing off a part of ourselves that
has been there for many years. He points out also that
this 'kind of death' is not something God demands
of us before He will take us back; it is simply a
description of what going back to Him is like. If we ask
God to take us back without it, he says, then we are
really asking Him to take us back without going back.
Like Jonah, we are relating to God on our own terms.

When I was once in India I saw a man who had
bound himself in chains sitting outside the tent where I was due to
speak. I asked the pastor who was escorting me why he was sitting
there like that. 'He is attempting to pay a penance for his sins,' he
explained. If he had come into the tent he would have heard that
penance is not enough. Penance without repentance is mere self-
punishment. Perhaps that is what Jonah wanted to do – he wanted
to provide his own atonement. Penance has a place in the Christian
life but it always comes after repentance – never before it.

FURTHER STUDY

Luke 19:1-10;
Eph. 2:1-10

1. How did
Zacchaeus
go full speed
astern?

2. What are the
roles of works
and faith?

Father, may I get this clear in my mind, for I see if I take a wrong
step here I will land up in difficulty. Help me see I am saved not by
what I do, but by what You have done for me on Calvary's tree.
I am eternally thankful. Amen.

A reversal of values

For reading & meditation – Jonah 1:13

'the men did their best to row back to land.' (v13)

We know little about the sailors who manned the ship, but our text for today shows them to be good God-fearing men who wanted to do everything in their power to avoid throwing Jonah overboard. Instead of acceding to his request, they concentrate on rowing as hard as they can towards the shore. You can imagine the sweat pours from their brows, their arms ache as they pull on the oars, but the wind continues to blow more fiercely than ever.

To Jonah, the crew were heathens, 'foreigners to the covenants of the promise' (see Eph. 2:12), but as they showed their concern for him, he was sharing, whether he felt it or not, a common bond with them – the bond of humanity. I wonder, did Jonah realise as he saw them toiling in their rowing that their concern was not only for themselves but also for him? Jonah was fleeing from God because he did not want to carry the message of God's loving concern to Gentiles. Yet here, before his very eyes, a group of Gentiles were showing more concern and compassion for him than he had for them. They were closer in character to God and to what was right than he was.

FURTHER STUDY

Acts 28:1-2;
Rom. 2:14-15;
5:6-8

1. Why do the ungodly act in a godly way?

2. Why is it so hard to believe God loves the ungodly?

Before we begin to feel too smug about Jonah's failures, perhaps we ought to take a long look at our own attitudes and ask ourselves: do those around us show more compassion and concern for us than we do for them? God wants us to be concerned about all who live in His world. The former principal of a Scottish Bible College once asked his students: 'Why is it so hard for the godly to believe that God also loves the ungodly?' Why indeed.

My Father and my God, deliver me from all exclusiveness, all pride, all prejudice, and help me obey the commission to move towards others in the name of Him who loves the world. Amen.

What irony

For reading & meditation – Jonah 1:14

'Then they cried to the LORD, "O LORD, please do not let us die for taking this man's life."' (v14)

Despite the best efforts of the sailors to reach the shore, the storm proves too much for them and they abandon the task. Now they have no choice except to do what Jonah suggests. But first they pray to this strange new God. Eugene Peterson, very effectively, translates their prayer in *The Message* thus: 'O GOD! Don't let us drown because of this man's life, and don't blame us for his death. You are GOD. Do what you think is best.'

It is clear from both their actions and their prayer that they are pinned on the horns of a dilemma. This God is awesome and has tremendous power. He has already caused a fierce storm to blow up because of an act of recklessness by one of His people. Clearly He is a God to be reckoned with. These 'heathen' sailors appear to have shown more respect for Jonah's God than Jonah did himself. The prophet was so caught up in self-protection that he was unable, in my opinion, to realise that the very thing he was trying to avoid at Nineveh – helping the Gentiles find salvation – is happening before his eyes. The men are slowly but inexorably being drawn to the Lord God Almighty.

FURTHER STUDY

Ruth 1:1-22;
4:13-17;
Phil. 1:15-18

1. Who does
God choose to
serve Him?

2. How might
God use
unbelievers
to help others
come to
know Him?

Jonah's name, by the way, means 'dove'. And a dove, as you know, ironically symbolises peace. The prophet was experiencing very little peace in his own heart at this moment, but God was using his circumstances and his situation to bring peace to the hearts of the sailors. God is able to use our setbacks to help others come to know Him. His ways are more wonderful than we can truly understand.

God, though You can work through my setbacks and my mistakes, help me never to use this as an excuse. Keep me true to You, dear Lord, in everything I do and everything I say. In Jesus' name I pray. Amen.

God – a Promise-Keeper

For reading & meditation – Jonah 1:15–16

'Then they took Jonah and threw him overboard,
and the raging sea grew calm.' (v15)

Once the sailors have prayed and thrown Jonah overboard, the sea immediately becomes strangely calm. The crew can only look at the tranquil sea and each other's faces. It seems too good to be true. Now what will they do? If we suspected that their prayer to Jonah's God was an attempt to get them out of a hole and that they would forget all about Him when their prayer was answered, then we were wrong. Jonah's God has shown He can still the sea. They are in awe of Him.

All kinds of emotions must have arisen within them: astonishment, gratitude, respect, wonder and relief. What will they do now? We read that 'the men greatly feared the LORD... offered a sacrifice to the LORD and made vows to him' (v16). Notice the phrases 'feared the LORD and 'sacrificed to the LORD'. The repetition of God's covenant name makes it clear that the sacrifices were not to the god of the sea but to the God of Jonah. Ships often carried live animals to provide both the crew and passengers with fresh meat, so it would have been quite easy to offer this sacrifice.

FURTHER STUDY

Matt. 28:20;
Heb. 6:13-20;
13:5-6

1. What has God promised you?

2. Why can we have confidence in God's promises?

But in addition to the sacrifice, they made a vow to serve the Lord. How serious were they in making those vows, I wonder? We will never know – this side of eternity at least. Since Jonah was a prophet, no doubt at one time he had made a similar vow to serve God, but he had defaulted on his promise. It is one thing to promise to serve the Lord 'in a moment'; it is another to keep that promise. Though sometimes we find it hard to keep our promises to God, He never fails to keep His promises to us.

My Father and my God, how can I thank You enough for the fact that You have never broken one of Your promises to me? Forgive me for the times when I have broken promises to You. Forgive me and strengthen me. In Jesus' name. Amen.

A whale of a tale

For reading & meditation – Jonah 1:17
'But the LORD provided a great fish to swallow Jonah' (v17)

Now we come to the issue that poses doubts and problems for many Christians: the 'great fish'. C.S. Lewis, for example, could not accept that the story of Jonah was true, and considered it to be nothing more than an Old Testament parable. He described it as having few historical attachments, grotesque in incidents, and not without a distinct though edifying view of Jewish humour. I even heard one so-called Bible preacher refer to the story of Jonah as 'a piscatorial conjuring trick'.

FURTHER STUDY

Matt. 17:24-27;
Luke 5:4-11;
John 6:5-13

1. What lessons do Bible fish teach us?

2. How did Jesus work miracles of timing and sustenance with fish?

Personally, I believe the things we read in the book of Jonah actually happened. The Bible does not tell us (despite many children's songs and stories) that Jonah was swallowed by a whale. The Hebrew term used is *dag gadol*, which means 'a big fish'. It could have been one of the whale family or it might have been another large fish. The NIV Bible Commentary says: 'Cases are occasionally cited of men recently lost overboard being recovered by whalers, still alive inside their catch.' Whether you believe it to be fact or fiction, it's interesting that Jesus referred to the story of Jonah and regarded it as being true. He said: 'For as Jonah was three days and three nights in the belly of a huge fish, so the Son of Man will be three days and three nights in the heart of the earth' (Matt. 12:40).

When we read the Jonah account we must remember that God works miracles. First, we see a miracle of timing – God arranging for a great fish to be at the right place at the right time. Second, a miracle of sustenance – Jonah being kept alive for three days.

My Father and my God, if I have difficulties here then help me to remember that all Scripture is God-breathed and has been given to instruct us. Grant that I may hear what You are telling me through this account. Amen.

Nothing is impossible

For reading & meditation – Psalm 95:1–11

'The sea is his, for he made it, and his hands formed the dry land.' (v5)

I feel constrained to spend another day discussing the subject of the miraculous. Yesterday we said that the matter of Jonah being swallowed by a great fish was a miracle of timing and of sustenance. God prepared a great fish to swallow him, and kept him alive within its stomach for three days.

I confess that I fail to understand why people who accept the Old Testament miracles such as the crossing of the Red Sea, the provision of manna in the wilderness and Elijah ascending to heaven in a chariot drawn by horses of fire, then struggle at the story of Jonah being swallowed by a whale. (By the way, from now on I may refer to the 'great fish' as a whale because it makes for easier reading.) If we look back on the account after having read the New Testament, with its description of such miracles as the feeding of the 5,000, the healing of the blind, the stilling of the storm and, of course, the most incredible miracle of all – Christ's resurrection – it becomes difficult to gainsay it.

FURTHER STUDY

Matt. 22:23-33;
John 9:1-16

1. Why were the Sadducees in error?

2. List different reactions to the miraculous healing.

One writer says that if you believe in a personal God then you have to believe that He can act upon His creation in a way that changes things. He can suspend the laws of nature or speed them up at will. Every year water is turned into wine in wineries all over the world – a natural process. But one day Jesus speeded up the whole process and did it in minutes at Cana (John 2:1–12). If God in Christ could do that then quite frankly I do not find it difficult to believe that God could cause a man to be swallowed by a whale and sustain him there for three days and three nights!

Father, this question of miracles is not an easy one to understand. Yet clearly You are a God of miracles. You entered my life and changed it. That in itself is a miracle. 'Lord, I do believe; help me overcome my unbelief.' Amen.

The 'three days' difficulty

For reading & meditation – Jonah 1:17
'and Jonah was inside the fish three days
and three nights.' (v17)

I t is explained in this section of our text that Jonah was inside the whale for a period of three days and three nights. As we think about this it might be helpful to consider that Jonah found himself inside the great fish for three reasons. First, to save him from drowning. Second, to give him time to come to his senses. Third, to prefigure the death and resurrection of our Lord.

Jesus, as we have mentioned, referred to the story of Jonah when talking about His death and resurrection and said: 'For as Jonah was three days and three nights in the belly of a huge fish, so the Son of Man will be three days and three nights in the heart of the earth' (Matt. 12:40).

While reflecting on this time span of three days and three nights it is important to understand the usage of this term in historical context. The expression did not necessarily refer to three full days. On occasion it was used to denote one full day and part of two others. Some commentators believe that this explains the difficulty a number of people have over the question of how Jesus could be in the tomb three days and three nights when He was put to death on a Friday afternoon (the Sabbath began as the sun went down) and rose again the day following the Sabbath. The explanation offered is that the three days would have included part of Friday afternoon, all of Saturday and part of Sunday morning. Similarly several Jewish festivals last eight days. Though people like to point out apparent contradictions in the Bible, what they alight upon are simply questions that need thinking through.

FURTHER STUDY

Gen. 4:1-10;
Acts 5:1-11

1. Think through why God allowed innocent Abel to die.

2. How can we reconcile Ananias' death with a God of love?

Father, give me an ever-growing confidence in Your Word. Help me see that though there are seeming contradictions, the problems are not in Your Book, but in my understanding of Your Book. Deepen my understanding of it, I pray. Amen.

On talking terms again

'From inside the fish Jonah prayed to the LORD his God.'
(v1)

The very first thing the prayer-avoiding prophet does when he discovers himself inside the whale is to pray. But when you think of it, there is very little else one can do there except pray. Do not let this thought, however, detract from the fact that he opened up his heart once again to God.

Interestingly as we consider Jonah's prayer we see that his prayer is not a prayer for deliverance, but one of thanksgiving. The prophet's heart overflows with gratitude for the spectacular way in which he has been saved from certain drowning. Some might consider Jonah contemptible for crying out in prayer only when he was in trouble. However such is the mercy and goodness of God that He listens to prayers made in such circumstances nevertheless. Isaac Bashevis Singer, quoted by William Barrett in *The Illusion of Technique*, says: 'Whenever I am in trouble I pray. And since I'm always in trouble, I pray a lot. Even when you see me eat and drink, while I do this, I pray.' It's sad, however, if prayer is limited only to times of trouble. A little boy was asked by his vicar if he prayed every day. 'No,' responded the boy, 'as there are some days when I don't need anything.'

FURTHER STUDY

Matt. 6:9-15;
1 Tim. 2:1-4

1. What are key elements of prayer?

2. List some of the different types of communication with God.

The main purpose of prayer is not petition but communion. Jonah had not been doing this for some time, but now things have changed. He communes with God from inside the fish and is once again on talking terms with the Almighty. He doesn't have much earthly comfort but there is no comfort like the comfort of a restored relationship with God.

Father, as I think of Jonah I have to ask myself: Do I pray only when I need something or when I am in trouble? Forgive me if this is so. Help me increasingly to see prayer not only as petition, but as communion. In Jesus' name. Amen.

Confined by God

For reading & meditation – Psalm 88:1–18

'You have taken from me my closest friends...
I am confined and cannot escape' (v8)

Confined in the whale's stomach, Jonah became a different man. In confinement, I believe, God does some of His greatest work. Have you ever found yourself in a situation that you can't move one way or the other and you give yourself to God? Why does God put us in such a situation? This is sometimes the only way that He can get our attention; it is because only then will we stop trying to work things out for ourselves and begin to listen to Him.

All of us are tainted with the terrible tendency to insist on getting our own way. We prefer to act as a god rather than worship the true God. What happened in the Garden of Eden is re-enacted every day in our homes, offices, factories, shops, boardrooms, schools and colleges. The tempter is at work telling us what he told our first parents in Eden: 'You will be like God' (Gen. 3:5). Sometimes God needs to hem us in on all sides – confine us to a 'God space'.

FURTHER STUDY

Lam. 3:1-26

1. How did the prophet feel?

2. How did his confinement deepen his awareness of God?

When I was a pastor I would hear people say: 'I have been unable to get out for weeks' (perhaps due to an accident or illness). Then they would add: 'It is the best thing that has ever happened to me.' Pressing them for an explanation, I would discover that in the confinement they had woken up to the fact that they had lost touch with God and kingdom matters. Suddenly, instead of routinely pursuing inconsequential matters such as the accumulation of possessions, they came face to face with the reality of who God is. Our lives are not diminished by God's confinement, but deepened by it. Some of the most profound passages in the New Testament were written by Paul from a prison cell.

Father, how sad it is that sometimes I am so preoccupied with the 'now' that You have to confine me before I give time to eternal realities. Help me take some deliberate steps now to rid myself of the illusion that I am my own god. Amen.

Prayer that is learned

For reading & meditation – Jonah 2:2
'In my distress I called to the LORD,
and he answered me.' (v2)

Now we come to the words of the prayer Jonah spoke from inside the whale. Having briefly considered that the surprising thing about this prayer is that it is a prayer of thanksgiving and not a prayer of repentance, does that mean that Jonah had not repented of his truculence? Was he trying to substitute praise for repentance?

Commentators agree that though there is no mention of repentance in this prayer, Jonah had actually come to the point where he had turned back to God. This conclusion is based on the fact that Jonah uses words which are in the past tense: 'In my distress,' he says, 'I called to the LORD, and he answered me.' Clearly something significant had happened in his soul, though we have no record of it. Again: 'From the depths of the grave I called for help, and you listened to my cry.' What we shall find now as we go through Jonah's prayer verse by verse is that it is closely aligned to the prayers of the psalmists. Almost every verse has words that are mirrored in the vocabulary of the psalms. The book of Psalms, as you know, has two dominant themes: lament and thanksgiving. The writers either cry out in pain or burst forth in praise, and Jonah echoes their thoughts.

FURTHER STUDY

Psa. 23:1-6;
121:1-8; 150:1-6

1. What do the psalms affirm?

2. Why should we praise God?

Jonah, it seems, had been nourished by the book of Psalms, and in the midst of a crisis he prayed in the way that others before him had prayed. We, too, would do well to study the intercessions of some of the great prayers of the past. Then, when we can't pray or don't know how to pray, the prayer language of others will come to our aid.

Father, so often I feel I need assistance in deepening and developing my prayer life. Help me recognise the importance of nourishing my soul through the prayers of others, and not only recognise this but practise it. In Jesus' name. Amen.

A school of prayer

For reading & meditation – Psalm 18:1-19

'I call to the LORD, who is worthy of praise, and I am saved from my enemies.' (v3)

We pause to reflect further on the fact that Jonah's prayer was not so much spontaneous as set. It was clearly furnished with the stock vocabulary of the psalms. The opening words are taken from the psalm we have read today (18:6). They can be found also in Psalm 120:1. Eugene Peterson has studied the phrases used by Jonah in his prayer, and notes them to be exact quotes from more than a dozen different psalms. Following his study Peterson made this statement: 'Jonah got every word – lock stock and barrel – out of his Psalms book.'

FURTHER STUDY

Psa. 28:1-9;
93:1-5

1. How did the psalmist change fear to faith?

2. How did the psalmist overcome tumultuous seas?

If we want to learn to pray effectively, then we need to consider undertaking some apprenticeship in prayer. After all, even the disciples asked Jesus to teach them to pray. I thank God for my pastor who told me over and over again in my youth: 'If you want to learn to pray then you need to soak yourself in the book of Psalms. It is the best school of prayer you will ever attend.' And I pass on to you the advice I was given: saturate yourself in the psalms, and when you find yourself in a crisis and don't know how, or what to pray, the words of the psalmists will provide a framework for you. When interviewers sometimes ask me what is the best advice I have ever been given, this is what I often tell them: to soak myself in the psalms.

There is no doubt that Jonah's prayer was triggered by his plight, but it wasn't sullied by it. He found himself praying a prayer that brought him in touch with the largeness and adequacy of God – a prayer he had learned at the feet of the psalmists.

Father, I am convinced. I need a deeper prayer life. Right now I enrol in the school of prayer that You have opened up to me and all Your children through the book of Psalms. Guide me as I prepare to soak myself in the psalms. Amen.

'Here's the text'

For reading & meditation – Psalm 30:1–12

'I will exalt you, O LORD, for you lifted me out of the depths'
(v1)

The psalm before us now is another from which Jonah borrows as he gives thanks to God for his protection. The words 'O LORD, you brought me up from the grave' (v3) are similar to those Jonah uses twice in his prayer: 'From the depths of the grave I called for help' (2:2), and 'You brought my life up from the pit, O LORD my God' (2:6).

A view held by many Christians today is that prayer is true and real only when it is spontaneous. That view needs to be challenged. For 20 centuries the Church in general has used the text of the psalms to teach people and encourage them to pray. Our Christian forefathers explained that fundamentally prayer is our response to the God who speaks to us. His Word becomes the basis of everything we do. He must get the first word in – always. Eugene Peterson expresses it like this: 'We come to consciousness in a world addressed by God. We need to learn how to answer, really answer – not merely say Yes sir, No sir... How do we do this? We don't know the language. We are so under-developed in this God-addressed world. Israel and the Church put the psalms in our hands and say, "Here, this is the text; practise these prayers so that you will learn the full range."'

FURTHER STUDY

Psa. 86:1–17;
89:1–2

1. How does
the psalmist
combine
confession,
praise and
request?

2. What is the
psalmist's
commitment?

Every Christian desires to pray. Many echo the words of the Samaritan woman: 'We have nothing to draw with and the well is deep.' The good news is we have – the psalms. Use them as your bucket and you will, I promise you, pull up new strength and inspiration for your prayer life.

Father, once again I come to thank You for providing me, through the psalms, with the resources that can add greatly to my prayer life. Help me draw from them all that has gone into them. In Jesus' name I ask it. Amen.

The waves are His

For reading & meditation – Jonah 2:3
'all your waves and breakers swept over me.' (v3)

We continue now with Jonah's prayer. The words that form our text for today are again found in the psalms – Psalm 42:7. Jonah reflects on the fact that he had been hurled into the deep and was in a desperate situation. But as he muses further he says something quite remarkable: 'all your waves and breakers swept over me'. Notice the words again: 'all your waves and breakers swept over me'.

When we find ourselves in the midst of a storm or buffeted by waves of trouble we are often in danger of misunderstanding the meaning of our circumstances. We can view the situation as the refutation rather than the confirmation of God's faithfulness. We would do well not to regard the storm or raging wind and waves as an expression of divine displeasure but as the proof of His concern – that we become the people He wants us to be. When plunged into adversity's icy waters we are apt to forget that it is His waves and His breakers that are sweeping over us. And because of this they cannot harm or hinder, but contribute to the purposes God has for our lives.

FURTHER STUDY
Acts 27:9-44

1. How did God meet with Paul in the storm?

2. How did God prove His concern for people?

Let's remember to be discerning and not to foolishly charge God with neglect or imagine that we have been removed from His keeping when the waves wash over us. Though we might think the waves have been sent to bring us down to death, they are, in fact, meant to bring us into life. The waves God sends will not carry us off course, but sweep us into His arms.

Father, help me understand that the waves You allow to buffet me are not intended to destroy me, but to develop me, not to hurt me, but to help me. May the waves carry me closer to Yourself. In Jesus' name. Amen.

Need a new start?

For reading & meditation – Jonah 2:4

'I said, "I have been banished from your sight; yet I will look again towards your holy temple."' (v4)

The words 'banished from your sight' are a further indication that Jonah has actually changed his attitude, and is now experiencing once again a close relationship with God. Just as entering a relationship with God isn't possible without repentance, so restoring a broken relationship with Him isn't possible without repentance either. The evidence that Jonah had turned back to God is very clear in this verse. He tells us that his eye is turned towards the light that he had spurned: 'yet I will look again towards your holy temple.'

One of the effects of independence is that the soul is filled with a sense of shame. And when we feel shame two things happen. First, we find it difficult to look into the face of the one we have wronged, and second, we find it equally difficult to be looked upon by the one we have wronged. Shame has been described by one Christian psychologist as the 'haemorrhaging of the soul'. Our soul bleeds when it is filled with shame and stains every other emotion. Yet there is no sense of shame now in Jonah's soul. For the first time in a long while he admits he is able to look towards God's holy Temple – a statement that implies he is again looking to God for His strength and support. His heart is filled with hope; it is a new day.

FURTHER STUDY

Psa. 32:1-7;
51:1-19

1. Describe the psalmist's emotions prior to his confession.

2. What happened when the psalmist confessed his sin?

Turn now towards God, ask Him to forgive you and I promise that through divine forgiveness the shame will be dispelled from your soul and you will look once again into His eyes with joy.

My Father and my God, Your Word pierces my soul like a sword. Forgive my sin, cleanse my heart, sweep away all shame and restore to me the joy of my salvation. In the name of Your Son, my Saviour, I ask it. Amen.

A strange prayer chamber

For reading & meditation – Jonah 2:5
'The engulfing waters threatened me... seaweed was
wrapped around my head.' (v5)

The imagery Jonah uses in this part of his prayer – 'the engulfing waters threatened me, the deep surrounded me' – leads our minds to some of the well-known Bible texts that recount how God's people were menaced by turbulent waters. Think, for instance, of the flood that covered the earth in the time of Noah, the crossing of the Red Sea and the River Jordan, the squall on the Sea of Galilee, the severe storm that resulted in Paul being shipwrecked on Malta. All these incidents show us that though the waters were a threat to God's people, they were not allowed to harm them. In each instance God undertook the protection of His people, and did not permit them to be swept away. This is what Jonah is rejoicing in as he realises that the thunder of the waves and the roar of the sea were powerless to harm him because they were part of God's plan to restore their relationship.

FURTHER STUDY

Psa. 18:1-19;
Isa. 43:1-13

1. How did the psalmist overcome death and destruction?
2. What is God's promise?

When we read the Scriptures we find that God's people offered prayer to Him from some strange places and in some strange circumstances. Paul prayed in a prison. Jesus prayed on a cross. Daniel no doubt prayed when he was in the lions' den, and Jeremiah is certain to have prayed when he was thrown into an empty cistern. But no one before or after (in Scripture, at least) prayed from the belly of a large fish with seaweed wrapped around his head! Not a very comfortable prayer position... But prayer, as we said earlier, can be made any time, in any circumstances. Nothing can stop our communication with God. He loves nothing more than to be known and be with those He knows.

Heavenly Father, how I magnify Your name that though You discipline me You never desert me. The waters of Your chastisements are designed not to sweep me off course but to draw me closer to Yourself. Thank You my Father. Amen.

But...

For reading & meditation – Jonah 2:6

'To the roots of the mountains I sank down; the earth
beneath barred me in for ever. But you' (v6)

'Where would we be,' said Dr Martyn Lloyd-Jones on one
occasion, 'were it not for the "but"s of the Bible.' He was
preaching on Romans 5:8 at the time: 'But God demonstrates his
own love for us in this: while we were still sinners, Christ died for
us.' So often in Scripture this little conjunction becomes a bridge
by which we cross from pain to peace, from spiritual poverty to
spiritual plenty.

When Jonah said he went to 'the roots of the mountains' what
did he mean? Historically people used to think that,
like trees, mountains had roots, and that those roots
went down into the sea bed. He uses another strange
expression also: 'the earth beneath barred me in for
ever'. The Living Bible conveys the thought in these
words: 'I was locked out of life and imprisoned in the
land of death.' Jonah is dwelling here on how close
to death he came. But... just as death reached out to
grasp him, God provided him with a way of escape.

I wonder where you and I would be today but for
the mercy and goodness of God. It was this knowledge
that God would intervene in their lives that saved
so many Bible characters from despair. To them, God was ever
present – the great Environing Reality. They never let go of the fact
that though God might let them sink down to the very depths of
depression, He would lift them out of it. 'But God.' These two words
viewed in their context suggest the thoughtfulness of God as well
as the power of God. It mattered not whether Jonah knew God; God
knew him. Jonah was always in His thoughts. So are you.

FURTHER STUDY

Gen. 50:20;
Rom. 6:15-23;
1 Cor. 2:5-10;
Eph. 2:1-10

1. Why does
God intervene
in our lives?

2. Contrast a
person before
and after God's
intervention.

**Father, how my life is reassured by the words but God. Were it not
for You, dear Lord, the story of my life would be very different. How
can I thank You enough for the change You have made in my life?
I bow in humble adoration. Amen.**

Illuminated memory

For reading & meditation – Jonah 2:7

'When my life was ebbing away, I remembered you, LORD
(v7)

'**R**ecollection,' it has been said, 'is often the first step towards realisation.' 'When my life was ebbing away,' confessed Jonah, 'I remembered you, LORD.' Frequently this God-given sense of memory is what redeems the soul from despair. Many a sorely tried person has been brought back to confidence in God's intervention by recalling some spiritual experience or memory. Often it is because we forget that we faint. Jonah had been running away from God, and no doubt had attempted to push God out of his

FURTHER STUDY

Psa. 77:1-20;
1 Cor. 11:23-26

1. What is the connection between faith and memory in the psalm?

2. What are we to remember?

thoughts. But as he sinks into the turbulent ocean, his memory is illuminated by his knowledge of God and his experience of His intervention and work in his life.

This verse impacted me shortly before I wrote these notes: 'After he was raised from the dead, his disciples recalled what he had said. Then they believed the Scripture and the words that Jesus had spoken' (John 2:22). Notice that it was when the disciples recalled what Jesus had said that they believed. Here is a powerful spiritual concept:

recollection and belief. The two form a powerful and fruitful partnership that can be responsible for incalculable good in the life of us all. Quickened memory often propels the soul to a place of faith. This happens to Jonah. He remembers God, turns his thoughts once again to Him, reflects on his relationship with Him and the prayer that had previously dried up begins to flow again. This is what an anonymous poet wrote: 'How oft in hours of threatened loss, when heart was numb with many fears, has come a flash of light and truth, across the interspace of years.'

Gracious Lord, teach me so that I may with joy draw water out of the wells of inspired meditation. Help me understand clearly how spiritual memories can assist in creating a new and nobler reaction to the challenge of the present. In Jesus' name. Amen.

The truth about idolatry

For reading & meditation – Jonah 2:8
'Those who cling to worthless idols forfeit the grace
that could be theirs.' (v8)

The more Jonah prays, the more profound we see his theology becoming. Here he thanks God that he does not belong to the ranks of idolaters whose gods are worthless and who deprive themselves of the blessing that could be theirs. One commentator says that this verse is pivotal, for in it Jonah identifies the biggest single hindrance to knowing God – idols.

Jonah was probably thinking of the idols used by the heathen – idols of wood and stone. But idols can take many other forms too. Self can be an idol. Possessions can be an idol. People can be an idol. Anything that becomes a centre of love and attention greater than that which we give to God is an idol. Idolatry has been described as 'substitution' – substitution of the marginal for the important, the unreal for the real. Anything or anyone we treat as the object of our absolute loyalty and love takes the place of God. In this sense Jonah, too, was an idolater, for he put his own interests before God, and, as we shall see later, continued to do so, despite the seeming sincerity of his prayer.

FURTHER STUDY
Psa. 118:8-9;
Col. 3:1-7;
1 Tim. 6:17-19;
1 John 2:15-16

1. What do we substitute for dependency on God?

2. Why do we have substitutes?

One of the devil's deceits is to entice us to believe that because we do not bow down, as some pagans do, to idols of wood and stone, we are free from idolatry. So often we offer prayers similar to Jonah's and thank God we don't worship idols, and then depend on something other than God! John Calvin saw the human heart as a relentlessly efficient factory for producing idols. Sadly we find it easier to trust in our own fear-inspired ingenuity rather than trust the One who loves us continually with grace and mercy.

Father, illuminate my heart today and expose any idols that might be hidden there. Help me to receive anew your love, grace and mercy. In Jesus' name I ask it. Amen.

The gift of God

For reading & meditation – Jonah 2:9

'But I, with a song of thanksgiving, will sacrifice to you.'
(v9)

Jonah's mind is made up – apparently. He pledges to go on singing a song of praise to God and promises that when the opportunity arises, he will offer a sacrifice to God and renew his vows. It all sounds so promising but, as we shall see later, Jonah is not as good as his promise. What a mercy it is that God blesses us for what we are today, and does not hold the failures of tomorrow against us.

The climax of Jonah's prayer, when he cries 'Salvation comes from the LORD', is one of Scripture's most wonderful statements.

FURTHER STUDY

Psa. 118:13-24;
Eph. 1:1-14

1. What are we
saved from?

2. What are
we saved to?

This was one of the great texts used during the Evangelical Revival of the 18th century, and is the cornerstone of evangelical truth. I imagine thousands, if not millions, have been brought to faith through hearing this text. It was one of Martin Luther's favourite verses. And it was said that if C.H. Spurgeon was ever called upon to preach unexpectedly, he would base his sermon on this text.

The words have been described as the marrow of the gospel because through them we learn that God is the One who saves us. We can do absolutely nothing to save ourselves. Always the initiative is with God. This is an amazing truth, the fact that 'We love because he first loved us' (1 John 4:19). He reaches first to us. He doesn't wait for us, He is ever active in pursuit of bringing us back to Himself. The very faith by which you take hold of Him is not yours; it is the gift of God. If you have never accepted the salvation that is offered then I ask you to do so now. This is the good news Jonah sounded out from inside the whale. This is the heart of God's mercy: salvation comes from the Lord.

Heavenly Father, I acknowledge that salvation is not something I achieve, but something I receive. I open my heart to You right now. Come into my life and save me. I repent of my sins and accept Your forgiveness. Thank You for hearing my prayer. Amen.

The patience of God

For reading & meditation – Jonah 2:10
'And the LORD commanded the fish, and it vomited
Jonah onto dry land.' (v10)

God decides that the prophet has spent enough time inside the whale, and commands it to vomit Jonah up on dry land. One thing is certain: Jonah emerged from the fish's stomach a better man than when he went in. But was Jonah a completely changed man as a result of his time inside the big fish? Clearly, his confinement had resulted in some positive results. It had rid him of the delusion that he could run from God's commands without suffering the consequences. It had brought him to a place of repentance and restored his relationship with God. But deeply ingrained characteristics remained unaltered: he was still self-concerned and self-justifying.

Sanctification is an ongoing process. There are many things God can do in a moment: Jesus could give sight to the blind – instantly. He could turn water into wine – instantly. He could bring the dead back to life – instantly. But it took time to turn His disciples from vacillating personalities into mature sons and daughters of God.

What we can be glad about, however, is that God does not wait until we are perfect before He uses us. If He did, then many of us would have been disqualified years ago. Embedded like splintered glass in Jonah's heart (and also in ours) is a stubborn commitment to independence. God finds some further resistance in His prophet, and He sets about working on that with him. But in the meantime He still has work for him to do. There is nothing more amazing than the patience of God.

FURTHER STUDY

2 Cor. 6:14-7:1;
Phil. 2:12-16;
2 Pet. 1:3-11

1. What is the difference between sanctification and salvation?

2. How does sanctification happen?

Father, if it were not for Your infinite patience I would be washed up. Keep Your hand upon me, dear Lord, despite all my frailties and imperfection. But help me overcome them and be drawn still nearer to You. In Jesus' name. Amen.

A second chance

For reading & meditation – Jonah 3:1–2

'Then the word of the LORD came to Jonah a second time.'
(v1)

Inside the fish, Jonah had made some pretty big promises. Now God is going to take him at his word. The command comes again the second time: 'Go to... Nineveh and proclaim to it the message I give you' (v2). If Jonah thought that God would change His mind he must have been disappointed! This is the genius of God's Word – it is always the same. It's amazing to realise that the grace of God, which accepts a repentant heart, seals the act of acceptance with the gift of a new opportunity. The runaway prophet is given a second chance.

FURTHER STUDY

Acts 13:1–5;
15:36–41;
2 Tim. 4:11

1. How did Paul feel about John Mark?

2. How did he give him a second chance?

How many of us would be where we are today if God had not given us a second (third or fourth) chance to participate in His work? Perhaps you are in the situation right now of having wandered off course and are wondering if God will ever accept you or use you again. You feel disqualified from future service because of past mistakes. Take heart my friend, serving God is not an honour that is earned. None of us qualifies for God's service by merit. It is His mercy, not our merit, which enables us to do anything for Him.

If you feel I am describing you at this moment then this message from the Lord is for you: God is giving you another chance. So many of the people we read about in Scripture were given significantly more than just one chance: David, Elijah, Simon Peter, John Mark, to name just a few. So open your heart now and have done with all self-pity and self-derogation. Tell God you are sorry and be restored to the God-of-the-second-chance.

Father, how grateful I am that it is Your mercy and not my merit that enables me to serve You. Forgive me all my failures and restore me to Your service. In Jesus' name I pray. Amen.

Grudging obedience

For reading & meditation – Jonah 3:3

'Jonah obeyed the word of the LORD and went to Nineveh.'
(v3)

The man who said 'No' now says 'Yes'. God doesn't have to repeat Himself; this time Jonah doesn't argue. He has had enough of resisting for the time being, so he sets off for Nineveh in obedience to the word of the Lord. But what sort of obedience was it? Most commentators feel, as I do, that it was somewhat reluctant. At this stage, though, we need not be too harsh; at least he is heading for Nineveh now.

There is a type of obedience offered by some Christians that is grudging and reluctant. Perhaps that kind of obedience ought not to be called obedience at all. I came across this statement in my research, written by an unknown writer: 'Obedience accepted with delight and authority and exercised with humility provides the very lines along which our spirits best travel.' Obedience enthusiastically and consciously given reverses the scenario that took place in the Garden of Eden. The first humans ignored what God had said to them and their actions introduced chaos into a perfect world. When we obey God we do the opposite and enable God to work out His purposes – perfectly. Our obedience demonstrates our trust in God – for we wouldn't follow the commands of someone we didn't ultimately trust.

FURTHER STUDY

Deut. 6:24-25;
1 Sam. 15:7-29

1. Why should we be obedient to God?

2. Can we be partially obedient?

What God longs for is authentic relationship, but as we saw the other day, He remains patient even when our co-operation is shot through with imperfection. Obedience is one of the keys to effective living; feelings come and go. As one theologian said, 'To know God is to know that our obedience is due to Him.'

Gracious and loving heavenly Father, the more I know You the more clearly I see that what You ask of me is always the best – the best for You and the best for me. May Your requests always delight me. In Jesus' name. Amen.

'All ears'

For reading & meditation – 1 Samuel 3:1–21

'Speak, LORD, for your servant is listening.' (v9)

We reflect another day on this question of co-operation with God. The great Archbishop William Temple said: 'Every revelation of God is a demand, and the way to knowledge of God is by obedience.' Once Jonah decided to resist God, he stopped knowing Him; when he decided to co-operate, then his knowledge of God increased. To know God is to obey Him, and to obey Him is to know Him.

A missionary translator was trying to find a word for 'obedience' in the language of the tribe he was working with.

FURTHER STUDY

Phil. 2:5–8;
Heb. 5:7–10

1. What did obedience cost Jesus?

2. What was Jesus' reward for his obedience?

There was no word in their language for this virtue as it was seldom practised. One day while walking through the village the missionary's dog went missing. So putting two fingers in his mouth he gave a loud whistle. Almost immediately the dog appeared and ran to his master's side. A villager looking on said in the local tongue: 'Your dog is all ears.' The missionary knew he had found the word for 'obedience'. Are we 'all ears' when it comes to listening to God and doing what He asks of us?

While preaching in a church in Dublin, I noticed a woman in the congregation with her hand cupped behind one ear. Afterwards she said to me: 'I have been a reader of *Every Day with Jesus* for years, but this is the first time I have ever heard you speak. I didn't want to miss a word.' This is what it means to incline our ears towards God. We cup our hands behind our ears, spiritually speaking, so that not a sound or syllable is missed, and say with eagerness and enthusiasm: 'Speak, Lord, for your servant is listening.'

Dear Lord, may I be 'all ears' at the sound of Your voice as You speak to me daily through Your Word. Help me not to miss out on a single sound or syllable. In Jesus' name I pray. Amen.

A culture shock

For reading & meditation – Jonah 3:3

'Now Nineveh was a very important city - a visit required three days.' (v3)

Doubtless as Jonah approached Nineveh his mind was full of questions. How would he be received? What would the citizens say when he told them they were about to be destroyed? And what if they repented and God forgave them? How would he react if people then turned round and accused him of being a false prophet? He did not have long to wait for the answers for the city lay right in front of him.

Nineveh is first mentioned in the Old Testament as one of the cities established by Nimrod (Gen. 10:9–12), and it became, as we said earlier, the capital of the ancient Assyrian Empire. The book of Jonah describes it as a 'great city', 'a very important city', and also tells us that a visit required three days. In other words, it would take three days to cover the whole city on foot. Some believe the phrase 'a visit required three days' refers to the administrative district of Nineveh, which included the cities of Hatra, Nimrud and Khorsabad as well as the capital. Whichever these is true, I imagine Jonah experienced a culture shock as he first set foot in Nineveh. One commentator, H.L. Ellison, says: 'To the provincial Galilean familiar with the small, tightly packed Israeli towns on their tells, the wide expanse of Nineveh, including even open land within its walls, must have seemed enormous.'

FURTHER STUDY

Exod. 3:7-4:5;
Mark 16:15-20

1. How was Moses' task from God power related?

2. How is our task from God power related?

Jonah had a massive task ahead of him, but God's enabling is always equal to the task. I saw this once on a poster outside a church: 'The task ahead of you is never as great as the power behind you.' I hope it is a word that speaks directly to you now.

My Father and my God, let the thought grip my spirit that no matter what lies ahead of me this day, it is not as great as the power that lies behind me. I am so thankful. In Jesus' name. Amen.

The shortest sermon

For reading & meditation – Jonah 3:4

'On the first day, Jonah started into the city.' (v4)

How, I wonder, did Jonah begin his preaching tour of Nineveh? Did he stop at each street corner as he went along? Did he go to the places where crowds gather, such as the markets? Or did he just grab people as they passed him on the street and say: 'God is going to destroy this city in 40 days – that is as much time as you have to repent'? We are not told how he did it, but we are told he began to preach on his very first day in Nineveh. Jonah was there to preach and he got on with the task as soon as his feet hit the streets.

FURTHER STUDY

Acts 1:1-8;
19:1-20

1. What two things did the disciples have through the Holy Spirit?

2. How important is the Holy Spirit in evangelism?

Imagine someone walking the streets of any of today's great cities – London, Berlin, New York, Mumbai, Abuja, Sydney – and shouting: 'Forty more days and this city will be destroyed.' What do you think would happen? The last time I was in London I saw a man with a placard on which was written: 'This city is doomed. Get out of it as fast as you can.' People smiled as he passed and totally ignored him. They are used to seeing this kind of thing. But the people did not smile when Jonah proclaimed his message. And why? Because it was a message that carried with it the convicting power of God's Holy Spirit. All that Jonah was required to do was to speak the words; God's Spirit then took over and applied the message to the hearts of the people.

Nowadays we would describe these circumstances as a 'revival', or an 'evangelical awakening'. Indeed, what we are about to see in Nineveh is one of the greatest evangelical awakenings recorded in the Old Testament.

Father, I see that the effectiveness of words does not depend on their length but on their strength. Empower every word I speak for You. Give them weight and give them wings. In Jesus' name. Amen.

The significant forty

For reading & meditation – Jonah 3:4
'He proclaimed: "Forty more days and Nineveh
will be overturned."' (v4)

Today we ask: is there any significance in the fact that Nineveh was given 40 days to repent? Why 40? In Scripture, 40 is a significant number. 'It is a stock biblical phrase,' says one writer, 'that has hope at its core.' The number 40 is usually used in connection with a period of testing, a time of examination.

The 40 days when the rain fell, creating the flood that Noah and his family escaped in the ark, was a period of cleansing, a washing away of moral pollution. The 40 years in the wilderness was a probation period for the Israelites, providing them with a training course in discipline and trust. The 40 days when Elijah was on the run from Jezebel following the contest with the priests of Baal swept away the dangerous thoughts that had come into his mind as a result of her threats and intimidation. The 40 days of Jesus' fasting and temptation in the wilderness tested His resolve to do the will of God. Then also there was the 40 days following His resurrection when He demonstrated through numerous appearances to His followers the shape of life in the new kingdom.

FURTHER STUDY

Matt. 24:36-44;
Rom. 13:11-14;
1 Thess. 5:1-10

1. How are doom and hope shown in these verses?

2. When will the end come?

In Nineveh the 40-day period of grace had a salutary and sobering effect. It concentrated people's minds on the fact that time was running out. It spelt out doom, but it also spelt out hope. The old Nineveh was to go, but a new Nineveh was possible – a Nineveh whose citizens put their trust in the living God. They didn't have to go on living the way they did. Hope was at hand if they turned their eyes to the living God. Perhaps we need to bring back into proclamation evangelism the emphasis that time is limited...

Father, forgive us if we, Your Church, are failing to emphasise in our evangelism the truths concerning future things. Forgive us and show us how to apply the future to the present. Help us reach the lost at any cost. In Jesus' name. Amen.

Facing the future

For reading & meditation – Jonah 3:5

'The Ninevites believed God.' (v5)

Billy Graham said at a conference at which I was present: 'Evangelism devoid of eschatology [the doctrine of judgment and the last things] will get us nowhere fast.' In Nineveh, the announcement that the citizens had 40 days to decide whether or not they would turn to God achieved its aim. Notice that Jonah did not go about denouncing their sin or taking them to task for their worship of non-existent gods; he focused their eyes on the future. He introduced eschatology into the picture.

FURTHER STUDY

John 16:7-8;
Acts 24:22-25;
2 Pet. 3:3-18

1. How important is eschatology in evangelism?

2. How should we embrace the future in the present?

The Ninevites were obsessed with the present, taken up with the way things were, but Jonah pointed them to what was to be. Billy Graham is very perceptive – evangelism devoid of eschatology has little bite. Too often people ignore it, getting on with life's busy daily demands. The thing that concentrates people's minds is the question: What is the future without God like? Inevitably one day we will all die and the day is coming when the whole world will be weighed by God. This is the message of grace and truth we are to share with our friends, neighbours, streets and communities.

'The future,' said George Macdonald, 'has its effect on the present.' There is no doubt that an awareness of what lies ahead greatly influences our behaviour in the present. The men and women of this world think the future is in some way magical; they cling to the illusive hope that things will get better, forgetting that ultimately we all face an end to this life.

Father, I am so grateful that I am Your child. I have no fear of what the future holds because I know who holds the future. I pray for those whose future is bleak and hopeless because they do not know You. Save them, dear Lord. Amen.

A sign for all to see

'The Ninevites believed God. They declared a fast,
and all of them... put on sackcloth.' (v5)

Was there ever so much contained in such a short sentence:
'The Ninevites believed God'? How amazing was the message
that Jonah preached. And as a sign that they had truly repented
the people declared a fast and put on sackcloth.

Historically, in this region people would go without food or drink
for various reasons. If they had done wrong they believed that
fasting showed whatever god they worshipped how sorry they
were. The Israelites, God's chosen people, would sometimes fast in
order to get closer to God, to find out what He wanted
them to do or to demonstrate to Him that they were
desperate for His help. The fasting entered into by the
people of Nineveh was undertaken to show Jonah's
God that they felt remorse for their godless lifestyle
and wanted His forgiveness. Often when people
fasted they put on sackcloth – a coarse cloth that was
meant to symbolise the shame they felt for their sin.
Can you imagine a whole city engaged in a fast – the
whole population covered in sackcloth? Can you imagine, too, what
would happen if one of the major cities I named the other day were
to proclaim a fast and announce that the entire population was
turning to God? What a news item that would make.

FURTHER STUDY

Matt. 3:1–8;
Eph. 4:17–32;
James 2:19

1. What indicates
true belief?

2. Contrast
'belief' and
'conversion'.

Ancient records also indicate there was a religious conversion in
Nineveh. But we have no need for independent evidence because we
have Jesus' words to assure us that the Ninevites' conversion was
genuine: 'The men of Nineveh will stand up at the judgment with
this generation and condemn it; for they repented at the preaching
of Jonah, and now one greater than Jonah is here' (Matt. 12:41).

**Lord God, is it too much to ask that You save a whole city as You did
in Jonah's day? My faith staggers at the possibility. But with the
little faith that I do have I cry out: 'Do it again, dear Lord.
Do it again.' In Jesus' name. Amen.**

Not too proud to repent

For reading & meditation – Jonah 3:6–7

'By the decree of the king and his nobles: Do not let any
man or beast... taste anything' (v7)

It isn't only the people of Nineveh who turn from their
independence to put their trust in Jonah's God; the king is
converted too. He rises from his throne, takes off his royal robes,
covers himself with sackcloth and sits down in the dust. He
recognises the truth in Jonah's words, and submits his kingship
to God – acknowledging that only God is all-powerful.

In response to Jonah's message, the king issues a royal
proclamation. *The Message* paraphrases his command in this
way: 'Not one drop of water, not one bite of food for
man, woman, or animal, including your herds and
flocks! Dress them all, both people and animals, in
burlap, and send up a cry for help to God. Everyone
must turn around, turn back from an evil life and
the violent ways that stain their hands. Who knows?
Maybe God will turn around and change his mind
about us, quit being angry with us and let us live!'

The messengers deliver their desperate message
to the people, who immediately do as they are asked to. Days of
inconvenience are as nothing when great issues are at stake. The
royal decree set the stage for repentance among the Ninevites. The
people were obliged to obey the king's decree outwardly, but there
was no way the king could legislate for inward obedience. The people,
however, did not need a royal decree to repent; the Spirit of God had
already been at work in their hearts and brought them to the point
of recognising their need for Him. It is this change of heart that
brought the change for their future. Our nations desperately need
the same kind of heart change in all the people – including leaders.

FURTHER STUDY

1 Kings 21:17–28;
Acts 16:13–15

1. How did Ahab
avoid God's
judgment?

2. Why did Lydia
respond to
Paul's message?

**Father, visit our world with a great supernatural revival and cause
thousands, if not millions, to enter Your kingdom. You did this in
Jonah's day, in Jesus' day and at various times in history.
Come again Holy Spirit. For Jesus' sake. Amen.**

Taking the lead

For reading & meditation – Jonah 3:7–9

'Let everyone call urgently on God. Let them give up their evil ways and their violence.' (v8)

DAY
232

We spend another day reflecting on the implications of the royal proclamation. The messengers go off to deliver the king's decree to everyone in the city. They find of course, as we have seen, that the people are already fasting and are clothed in sackcloth. But the royal proclamation commands that all the animals are to be deprived of food also. Why? Surely animals have no consciousness of idolatry and sin. Withholding food from the animals would have brought grief to their owners and served as an added penance. The inclusion of animals in the fast underlined the depth of sincere repentance, and thus reinforced the seriousness of the moment.

If only present-day kings, presidents and political leaders had as much concern for the spiritual wellbeing of their people, and would likewise encourage them to turn to God. But if it is too much to expect kings, presidents, and political leaders to take a lead in turning to God, it is not too much to expect it of the Church. When we Christians demonstrate to the world our serious following of the one true God and His ways, when we adopt measures that are uncompromising, when we decide that we will take a lead in this matter and put righteousness first, then though we cannot legislate for righteousness we will, I believe, see a tremendous move of the Spirit of God across the world. We cannot force salvation on people but, by reaching out to people with grace and truth, we can make it possible for God to act. All He asks is for His people to provide Him with an opportunity – then He will make His move.

FURTHER STUDY

Jer. 29:10-14;
Dan. 9:1-16;
Rev. 3:14-22

1. How did Daniel interpret Jeremiah 29:13?

2. Why might the Church need to repent?

Father, how can we expect people to turn from their independence to You, when so often those of us in Your Church struggle to do so? Forgive us, restore us and help us to reveal Your grace, mercy and truth through our own lives. Amen.

No hope?

For reading & meditation – Jonah 3:10

'When God saw... he had compassion and did not bring upon them the destruction he had threatened.' (v10)

I t's deliverance day in Nineveh! The king is delighted, the people are filled with joy. Indeed, everyone in the city is relieved because God has had compassion on them and has forgiven them for their godlessness and sin. How, I wonder, did they receive the news that God had forgiven them? Some commentators believe that God instructed Jonah to tell them the good news, while others believe that He produced in each of the repentant people an awareness that they had been forgiven, in much the same way that those who are truly repentant today experience peace and freedom.

FURTHER STUDY

Dan. 9:17-19;
Titus 3:3-7

1. What did Daniel rely on?

2. What do we rely on?

This might be a good moment to consider that Jonah had simply said that in 40 days Nineveh would be destroyed – not that in 40 days the city would be destroyed if the people did not repent. A number have speculated that Jonah deliberately made no reference to the need for repentance because deep down in his heart he wanted to see the people of Nineveh destroyed. We cannot be sure of this, of course; however, it does seem strange that there is no record in Jonah's encounter with the Ninevites of a message of hope.

This begs the question: If Jonah did not qualify his message to the people of Nineveh and announce that they could escape impending judgment by way of repentance, then why did the king and his subjects do so, so willingly? My guess is that when the Spirit of God is at work in the human heart exposing sin, then that same Spirit, because He is guided by love, also gives the understanding that the way to find freedom is to confess all wrongdoing and throw oneself upon the mercy of a gracious God.

Gracious Father, I am reminded of Your Word: 'God's kindness leads you towards repentance' (Rom. 2:4). I rejoice that because You are kind, You are concerned not only to expose wrongdoing but to forgive it. I am eternally grateful. Amen.

Blocked goals

For reading & meditation – Jonah 4:1

'But Jonah was greatly displeased and became angry.' (v1)

We come now to the last scenes in Jonah's biblical narrative. Everyone is happy except the prophet. In fact, he is not just unhappy, he is decidedly angry, and enters into an argument with God over the fact that He has seen fit to forgive the Ninevites. In this final chapter the word 'anger' is mentioned four times in the New International Version and six times in some other translations. It is clearer now than ever that deep down in his heart Jonah wanted the Ninevites destroyed, not forgiven.

Anger, as I have suggested before, is usually the result of a goal we are pursuing becoming blocked. Let me give you an example. You are all alone in your house and you are woken in the middle of the night with a painful headache. You make your way to the medicine cabinet to get an analgesic and find that the cabinet is locked. You have no idea where the key is and your goal, which is to get a painkiller, is blocked. The likelihood is that to your headache will be added another problem – the problem of anger.

FURTHER STUDY

Psa. 30:1-12;
Luke 9:51-55

1. Contrast God's anger with His favour.

2. Contrast Jesus' and the disciple's reactions to the blocked goal.

What was Jonah's goal? I think it was to see the Ninevites wiped out. He wanted God's goodness to be shown only to Israel. God, in granting forgiveness to the Ninevites, had blocked this goal. Jonah, it seems to me, although fully aware and knowledgeable of God and His ways of love and compassion, was not a generous and forgiving person. God had made Jonah in His image, but Jonah had made God in his image – he projected on to God his own mean and parsimonious nature and wanted Him to act in the way he saw fit.

God forgive me, I pray, if, like Jonah, I tend to project on to You my own feelings instead of allowing You to impress into me the lineaments of Your own divine character. I want to become more and more like You. In Jesus' name. Amen.

Jonah's real problem

For reading & meditation – Jonah 4:2

'He prayed to the LORD, "O LORD, is this not what I said when I was still at home?"' (v2)

Anger can be an effective diagnostic tool. Just like a red light on the dashboard of a car, it warns us that something is wrong. Jonah became angry with God because He had blocked his goal of seeing the Ninevites destroyed by offering them His free and full forgiveness. Because things didn't go Jonah's way he became angry and petulant. He prays once more to God, but his prayer is vastly different from the one he prayed inside the whale. Here we see even more clearly his underlying motives and his true spiritual condition. *The Message* paraphrases his prayer in a most effective way: 'GOD! I knew it – when I was back home, I knew this was going to happen!... I knew you were sheer grace and mercy, not easily angered, rich in love, and ready at the drop of a hat to turn your plans of punishment into a program of forgiveness!' Interestingly, he again includes in his prayer excerpts from the Psalms – words from Psalm 86 verses 5 and 15 and Psalm 103 verse 8, which first appear in Exodus and Numbers. Jonah appears to have been a good theologian but a poor son. He was well versed in Scripture but immature in his personality.

FURTHER STUDY

Luke 11:37-54;
James 1:22-25

1. Why were the Pharisees biblically literate but immature?

2. How can we be self-deceived?

One of the things that has interested me down the years is that some Christians who are good at quoting Scripture are not necessarily good at applying it. They understand the dogmatics of Scripture but don't seem to understand the dynamics of their personality – how they tick. Looking at Jonah I would say he exemplifies some Christians today: biblically literate but somewhat immature.

Father help me, I pray, not simply to hold Scripture in my head but to let it reach deep into my heart. Teach me how to apply Your Word to my life daily so that I might be rid of all immaturity. Help me to grow up into You in all things. Amen.

Spiritually immature

For reading & meditation – Jonah 4:2

'I knew that you are a gracious and compassionate God, slow to anger and abounding in love' (v2)

Yesterday we concluded that there was nothing wrong with his knowledge of Scripture but there was a lot wrong with his knowledge of himself. The great preacher and commentator John Calvin, in the opening statements of his famous Institutes (his defence of his theological beliefs), makes the point that the better we know God the better we will know ourselves, and the better we know ourselves the better we will know God. In my experience most Christians are eager to know God but are not so eager to learn anything about themselves.

Jonah's problem, we said, was immaturity; he had never grown up. The part of him that wanted his own way had not only survived but thrived. He was more concerned about what the people of Nineveh thought of him than how God evaluated him. He wanted his own way more than His heavenly Father's ways. Clearly, he had never reached the stage that Paul refers to in 1 Corinthians 13: 'When I was a child, I talked like a child, I thought like a child, I reasoned like a child. When I became a man, I put childish ways behind me.' The Greek word Paul uses here for putting away is a powerful one – *katargeo*. It means to render inoperative, to lay aside, to put to rest. Though Jonah's problem appears to have been a spiritual one, its roots were psychological in the sense that it arose because he was the kind of person who wanted his own way. The temper tantrums he may have displayed in childhood were with him still. We are looking here at a man with a child's attitude; grown up physically but immature spiritually.

FURTHER STUDY

1 Cor. 3:1-4;
13:1-13

1. How may childishness be revealed?

2. What replaces childish ways?

Loving Father, help me to assess how much of my outlook and behaviour comes from childish ways I haven't yet put down. I open my heart to You for inspection. May I be childlike but never childish. In Jesus' name. Amen.

'The depressive triad'

For reading & meditation – Jonah 4:3

'Now, O LORD, take away my life, for it is better for me
to die than to live.' (v3)

Jonah's inner turmoil now leads him to the stage where he wants his life to end. When anger is not traced back to the goal that is being blocked and properly dealt with by changing that goal then it can quickly find expression in self-pity and depression. Many psychologists and counsellors understand that certain types of depression are the result of anger turned inwards on one's self. This is sometimes referred to as 'retroflexed rage'. People who recognise, face and address their anger rarely get depressed, but if anger is internalised then it can become a trigger for depression. One psychologist has coined the phrase 'the depressive triad' to illustrate a certain type of depression. He has found that depressed people, generally speaking, have a jaundiced and negative view of themselves, others and the future.

FURTHER STUDY
Num. 11:14-15;
Job 7:1-16;
Psa. 43:1-5

1. How do we see
'the depressive
triad' in Moses
and Job?

2. What is the
antidote?

Jonah, as we see him now, is suffering from 'the depressive triad': he is unhappy with the Ninevites because they had found forgiveness, he is unhappy with himself because his goal has been blocked, and as he looks into the future he sees nothing but trouble working for a God who is eager to forgive. In this condition he pleads with God to take away his life. God's mercy to the Ninevites meant an end (in his view) to Israel's favoured standing. How could he continue in such a situation? Just a little while before, while in the whale's belly, he was rejoicing because he had been delivered from certain death; now he prays to die.

Never forget that one of the greatest barriers to depression is seeing yourself, others and the future from God's point of view.

**Father, teach me to look at all things – myself, others, and the future
– from Your point of view. Deliver me from all negative thinking and
fill my mind with the truths that flow from You.
In Jesus' name I pray. Amen.**

Sulking Jonah

For reading & meditation – Jonah 4:4

'But the LORD replied, "Have you any right to be angry?"'
(v4)

Though Jonah wants his life to end, clearly God has other plans. God has just shown great love and kindness to the people of Nineveh, and now Jonah is about to get a taste of this God-filled grace treatment himself. How wonderfully God comes alongside Jonah. He doesn't respond to Jonah by becoming judgmental (a common issue, albeit unconsciously, in people helping), by saying: 'You shouldn't be angry.' Instead He questions him in this way: 'Have you any right to be angry?' God brings objectivity to the situation by asking a question rather than making a statement. Jonah, however, does not reply. He is not willing to face up to the roots of his anger and turns away from God as a sulking child would turn away from the concerned questions of his or her parents. Clearly, he is in no mood for a question-and-answer session with God, and becomes one of the most reluctant individuals He ever stood beside.

Sulking, Jonah goes off to the eastern part of Nineveh and waits to see what will happen. He is not there long before he finds the sun is a good match for his temper. What is he waiting for as he sits there overlooking the city? Perhaps he is hoping that Nineveh will be destroyed after all. If God had changed His mind once then perhaps He might change it again. I myself am convinced that if fire and brimstone had fallen on Nineveh, Jonah's self-pity would have lifted immediately because his goal would have been reached. How tragic that one of God's prophets should put his own interests before those of his Lord.

FURTHER STUDY
2 Kings 6:8–23;
Luke 22:49–51;
Rom. 12:14–21

1. Why do believers want unbelievers punished?
2. What does God want?

My Father and my God, show me, I pray, where my life conflicts with Yours. Help me lay down all self-will, all self-interest and walk in what You want for my life. You always give the best to those who leave the choice to You. Amen.

Grateful but not changed

For reading & meditation – Jonah 4:5–6

'he made himself a shelter, sat in its shade and waited
to see what would happen to the city.' (v5)

Despite having been given the awesome honour of presenting
God's gospel to a Gentile city, Jonah ends up peeved and
petulant. The man who has been saved from certain death and seen
a whole city turn to God, is left feeling sorry for himself. However,
something happens that pleases him: he finds some shade.

Sitting under a makeshift shelter he has made, he looks out over
the city, and this is where we see God's love once more go into
action. A plant nearby, which most commentators suggest was a

FURTHER STUDY

Gen. 4:1–8;
Matt. 18:21–35

1. Why did God
fail to root out
self-pity in Cain?

2. Why are
some people
unchanged by
God's blessings
and love?

castor oil plant, miraculously grows until its broad
leaves provide Jonah with shade and comfort. He has
some physical relief at least, if not spiritual solace.
I find it interesting to see how often God ministers
to the physical needs of His servants as He seeks
to bring home to them some important spiritual
truth. He did that for Elijah, you remember, when
He provided food and water for him at the time of
his depression (1 Kings 19:1–9). I think also of Simon
Peter in the post-resurrection encounter recorded for
us in John 21. Having been out all night on the lake,
and having initially caught nothing, he was invited by Jesus to
enjoy the breakfast He had provided for him. Before confronting
him with the important spiritual question, 'Do you love me?', Jesus
catered for his physical needs.

Jonah, we read, was 'very happy about the vine' – he was
grateful but not changed. How sad that even in the presence of a
miracle Jonah is still peeved and petulant. Self-pity can sometimes
get such a hold on us that not even God can root it out.

**God my Father, I pray that I may never get into the position where I
sit beneath the shade of Your merciful provision and remain
unchanged. Give me a heart that is alert and responsive to all the
overtures of Your love. In Jesus' name. Amen.**

Danger!

For reading & meditation – Jonah 4:7–8

'But... God provided a worm, which chewed the vine
so that it withered.' (v7)

Jonah's physical and spiritual discomfort is not over. As a new day dawns God arranges for a worm to destroy the plant, and within a short time it withers and dies. To cap it all, God sends a hot east wind across the plains, and soon Jonah grows faint and once again pleads with Him to take away his life. One of the saddest things I think I have come across in life is to see a servant of God in such despair that he or she cries out to die, and I have seen this many times. It's interesting, isn't it, that a man who has witnessed a whole city turn to God now pleads with that same God to end his existence. His message brought miraculous success, but he himself felt a failure. Can you imagine any evangelist in modern times sitting down after an entire city has been converted and wanting to die? Clearly, God's ministry to him physically and spiritually has not been allowed to touch the core of his life. He is still the same Jonah – self-centred, childish, and self-indulgent.

The only explanation for Jonah's continued resistance to God can be that he felt there were things on his agenda that were more important to him than the items on God's agenda. He was a runaway and an escapist when we met him in chapter 1, and he is a runaway and an escapist still. He separates himself from God by his petulance and pride. Whenever we resent and resist God's work in our lives, seeking only the prominence that comes through serving Him, we are in great spiritual danger. Surely we need no other warning than that of Jonah.

FURTHER STUDY

1 Sam.
2:12–17,22–25;
18:5–11

1. How did Eli's sons resent and reject discipline?

2. How did petulance and pride destroy Saul?

Father, there are so many lessons to learn that I feel somewhat overwhelmed. Help me not to resist Your way, even if I may need to put aside my own plans and agendas. May Your purposes always come first. In Jesus' name. Amen.

A time-honoured practice

For reading & meditation – Jonah 4:9

'But God said to Jonah, "Do you have a right to be angry about the vine?"' (v9)

For a second time God asks Jonah if he has a right to be angry. This time it is not in connection with Nineveh but with the shrivelled plant. Jonah, however, continues to argue with God. He's in good company, as many people in the Bible are seen disputing and debating with the Lord. Moses is one who did this. So is Abraham. So is David. So, too, is Job. And Jeremiah, one of the most faithful and loyal of all God's prophets, also reasoned with Him.

One writer I came across, Edward F. Campbell, made a statement in his book *Ruth* regarding this matter that at first I was not able to accept. Yet the more I pondered it, the more I realised that it was right. This is what he said: 'Not only is complaint tolerated by God but it can even be the proper stance of a person who takes God seriously.' When we think about it, we may find we frequently argue with God because He doesn't always do things the way we expect. A friend of mine, an Irishman, said (tongue in cheek) that God is Irish because 'Everything He says and does seems to be different from everyone else!' But when we come down to it, there is really no point in arguing with God because He is right in everything.

FURTHER STUDY

Gen. 18:16-33;
Isa. 1:18

1. Why should we debate with God?

2. What is God's invitation?

It is amazing to me that God permits us to debate with Him. He has the position and presence to consign us, puny creatures that we are, to utter oblivion, but He has the grace and patience to listen to our arguments, even to debate with us as He did with Jonah and others. I don't know about you, but I find this quite staggering. A God like this can have my heart and trust any time – all the time.

Father, it seems almost beyond belief that You do not just tolerate my complaints but You take each one of them seriously. I long to come to the place where I argue about nothing because I trust You in everything. In Jesus' name. Amen.

'Tell it slant!'

For reading & meditation – Jonah 4:10

'But the LORD said, "You have been concerned about this vine, though you did not tend it or make it grow."' (v10)

Though Jonah will not face the fact of his anger and seek to find the reason for it, God condescends to explain to Jonah why He caused the plant to wither. It was an attempt to provide Jonah with a visual aid, something that God could use to reveal to him his troublesome attitudes and ideology.

When it is not possible to help a person to see the truth, one has to try to slip past the defences by whatever means possible. Jesus, as we know, was expert at telling the truth but telling it slant. Few of His parables mention the name of God, but as people listened to them the truth of what He was saying sunk into their minds nevertheless. The withered plant was God's ploy to get Jonah's attention and to prise him out of the self-pity into which he had fallen. Listen to how the Living Bible paraphrases God's remarks: 'Then the Lord said, "You feel sorry for yourself when your shelter is destroyed, though you did no work to put it there, and it is, at best, short-lived. And why shouldn't I feel sorry for a great city like Nineveh...?"'

Jonah is full of pity for a plant, something that is here today and gone tomorrow, but he has no concern for the spiritual destiny of the people of Nineveh. Does Jonah show any signs of understanding the point God is trying to get across? Sadly not. And God will respect the right of a person to say 'No' to the last. With Jonah we do not know the final outcome. But we do know, because of Jesus, the lengths that God will go to to bring us back to Himself.

FURTHER STUDY

Luke 16:19–31;
20:9–19

1. Why can we be so self-centred while others starve or die?

2. Discuss some of the methods Jesus used in His parables.

Father, thank You for getting Your truth into my heart, even though at times You have to tell it 'slant'. Help me take down all my barriers so that ploys are never necessary. In Jesus' name. Amen.

God so loved...

For reading & meditation – Jonah 4:11

'Should I not be concerned about that great city?' (v11)

The Jonah narrative does not have a satisfying ending. It closes with an unanswered question. The chapter began with Jonah arguing with God under the short-lived plant and ends with God asking him this haunting question: 'Should I not be concerned about that great city?' Did Jonah ever answer this question, I wonder? If so, what did he say?

We will never know, for his answer, if indeed there was one, is not recorded. I would love to find out if Jonah ended his somewhat petulant discussion with God, if he ministered to God's people in Nineveh or if he returned to Joppa and boarded another ship bound for Tarshish. Why does the author not tell us? Some feel a part of the original manuscript is missing, hence the abrupt ending, but I think it is the intention of the author to leave the question hanging in the air. It is part of the author's storytelling device. The reason there is no answer is to leave us room to provide our own answer – a personal answer.

FURTHER STUDY
John 3:14-17;
2 Cor. 5:11-21

1. How concerned is God about the lost?

2. How concerned should we be?

So now we must stop being curious about how Jonah answered God's question and give our own response to it. How do we feel about a God who loves those whose lives are characterised with godlessness and sin? Are we more interested in seeing them get their just deserts than in finding pardon and forgiveness? Hopefully, through the life of Jonah, we have had a glimpse into the immense world of God's grace. The story focuses our gaze afresh on the fact that the God we serve and worship loves not just one particular race or group of people, but the whole wide world.

Father, with all my heart I answer, 'Yes, dear Lord, it is right that You should be concerned.' Thank you that your grace is directed towards all of us, and you never give up on us. Amen.

Standing Strong

Unsinkable!

For reading & meditation – 2 Corinthians 4:1–18

'We are hard pressed on every side, but not crushed;
perplexed, but not in despair' (v8)

The theme for this issue was prompted by the words of a well-known song entitled *(Something Inside) So Strong*. The song was inspired by those who lived through apartheid and the singer upholds that he knows he can make it through the hard times because there is something so strong inside of him. That 'something' was the conviction that apartheid was wrong and would topple because of people's determination and belief in good. Thankfully it did – although there is still much to do around the world on issues of equality.

There have been so many great changes in the world during the past few decades; many philosophies and ideologies have been dismantled. However, considerable problems still confront us. For me, one of the greatest problems is that of the disintegration of values and truth. Truth is seen by many to be subjective. Engage most people in a discussion about Christian issues and you are likely to hear: 'That may be the truth for you, but I view life from a different perspective.' Generally speaking, our culture and society has lost its sense of God, and all life feels the shattering effect. How do we as Christians find the inner strength to face the challenges of these fast-changing times?

FURTHER STUDY

Matt. 14:25-33;
Eph. 3:14-21

1. Why did Peter at first float and then sink?

2. How is our inner being strengthened?

We find it, of course, in God. But can we realise God within us in such a way that, no matter what occurs on the outside, we will remain strong and secure on the inside? If we can't, we are sunk; if we can, we will be unsinkable. Walk with me each day through the coming two months and we'll explore together how we can.

My Father and my God, I freely confess that whatever strength I have, I have because of You. I know, however, that more is available. My heart is open to all You want to teach me. Lead on and I will follow. In Jesus' name. Amen.

'Settling down in God'

For reading & meditation – Isaiah 26:1–6

'You will keep in perfect peace him whose mind is
steadfast, because he trusts in you.' (v3)

Yesterday we said that during the difficult years of apartheid
many pressed on believing that one day the system would be
overthrown; they had, as the song title put it: 'something inside so
strong'. Inner strength can come from many things: the conviction
that what one is fighting for is right, the steadying support of
others and so on. One man I met felt he had discovered the answer.
'I get inner strength from relaxation techniques,' he told me. 'They
give me inner peace.' However, when a tragedy struck his home,
the inner peace he thought he had gained went to
pieces. The 'something inside so strong' we are
going to explore is far more than human principles
or techniques and is based on the knowledge of God
and a loving relationship with the Creator.

How well do you know God? Well enough to rest
your whole weight on Him? 'How did you like your
first plane trip?' one businessman asked another. 'It
was all right,' was the reply, 'but I never did put my
whole weight down.'

Some may find a type of inner fortitude using
various ideological philosophies and programmes.
But this world provides nothing on which we can fully rest our
weight. The Quakers used to talk about 'settling down in God'. Have
you learned to 'settle down in God' – to trust Him so completely
that no matter what happens on the surface of life the depths
remain tranquil? An ocean appears turbulent when waves are
tumbling and crashing on the surface, but a few hundred feet
below all is calm. Can we be like that? In God we can.

FURTHER STUDY

Prov. 3:5-6,
21-26;
Dan. 3:13-27

1. What is the
basis of true
relaxation?

2. What was
the attitude of
the Hebrews
to impending
death?

Father, how can I sufficiently thank You for the privilege of being
able to 'settle down' in You? Teach me all I need to know to remain
tranquil when around me the waves of life are turbulent.
In Jesus' name. Amen.

An unshakeable kingdom

For reading & meditation – Hebrews 12:14–29

'Therefore, since we are receiving a kingdom that cannot be shaken, let us be thankful' (v28)

On the first day of our devotions we asked the question: can we realise God within us in such a way that no matter what occurs on the outside we will remain strong and secure on the inside? If that can't happen, we said, we are sunk; if it can happen, we will be unsinkable.

Some time ago I asked myself: 'Selwyn, what are the anchors in your life? When facing change, what holds you?' As I reflected on the elements that contribute to my own inner strength – an astonishing calmness that sometimes surprises me – I discovered a number of convictions and disciplines that have held me intact in all sorts of situations. Not only have they held me, but I have seen them work in the lives of countless others. So I know they will hold you also. You can have inner strength, grace and peace at all times and in all places.

The first principle is the one found in our text for today: recognising that we belong to an unshakeable kingdom. This text is one of the most steadying in the New Testament. All around us men and women are attempting to build on the basis of power, pride, position and learning, but these are shakeable. Throughout time, empires have been built on earthly values and ideologies alone – ideologies that were planned to last for a thousand years. Where are these empires now? Gone, for they were built on shakeable foundations. In the years that lie ahead we will witness many earthly kingdoms shaking and falling before our eyes. I don't know about you, but to me it means everything to know there is one unshakeable kingdom.

FURTHER STUDY

Matt. 7:24-29;
Acts 20:17-24

1. What can we build our lives on in order to be unshakeable?

2. Why was Paul not shaken from his purpose?

Heavenly Father, what comfort it gives to know that my feet are established in an unshakeable kingdom. Though I may shake, the kingdom in which I stand will not shake. For that I am deeply grateful. In Jesus' name. Amen.

Receiving the kingdom

For reading & meditation – John 18:28–40

'Jesus said, "My kingdom is not of this world."' (v36)

Whenever Jesus stood before Pilate, He said quietly but with deep assurance: 'My kingdom is not of this world.' Jesus' kingdom is not rooted in this world, and so the shaking of external events did not shake Him. He is the King of an unshakeable kingdom, and the ages testify to His everlasting surety. The powers that held Him, tried Him in a mock trial, condemned Him to death and crucified Him, have passed away. And yet He goes on from age to age, the only unshaken authority in a shaking world. The kingdom today is estimated to be followed by over two billion people (nearly twice the number of any other world religion).

FURTHER STUDY

Luke 23:39-43;
John 1:1-13

1. How could a dying criminal enter the kingdom?

2. How does believing precede receiving?

The passage we looked at yesterday includes these verses: 'since we are receiving a kingdom that cannot be shaken, let us be thankful, and so worship God acceptably with reverence and awe, for our "God is a consuming fire"' (Heb. 12:28–29). Notice the words 'receiving a kingdom'. The good news is that we don't have to strive to become part of God's kingdom – we simply have to receive it.

For many people, receiving Jesus is not easy. They want to earn their passage to heaven or do something to be saved. But the gospel of Jesus Christ, put simply, comes down to this: you have to remove the barriers of pride in your heart, recognise that you can do nothing to save yourself and receive Him into your life by an act of faith. You say to Jesus: 'Come into my life and have Your way.' Have you taken that step? If not, open your life to Jesus I ask you, and receive Him now.

God, I accept that to be led by You I must first let go of my unsurrendered self. I do so now, gladly and willingly. Come into my life, forgive my sins, and reign in every part of my life. In Jesus' name. Amen.

'Japanese lanterns'

For reading & meditation – Romans 10:1–13

'if you confess with your mouth, 'Jesus is Lord,'
and believe in your heart that... you will be saved.' (v9)

We said yesterday that the kingdom of God is not something we attain, but something we obtain. We receive the kingdom by giving our hearts to the King of kings.

An evangelist tells of holding a Christian meeting in a remote rural village in Japan. As he approached the church in the darkness he saw men standing at the various intersections holding lighted Japanese lanterns on which the shape of a cross was visible. These men were directing people to the church, encouraging them by means of the illuminated crosses to turn in and hear the Word of life.

We stand, as we all know, at one of the most fast-moving times in human history. One politician has described it 'on the verge of a nervous breakdown'. For many decades my main mission in life has been to lift up the cross of Jesus so that it might be seen, as those Japanese men waved their lanterns, to help guide disorientated and lost people to the kingdom – the one unshakeable kingdom in a shaking world.

You see, the cross of Jesus is the only way by which men and women can enter God's kingdom. God says: 'I will meet anyone, no matter what sins they have committed, but I will meet them at the cross.'

When you come by faith to the cross – the place where Christ died for you – and receive Him into your life as your Saviour then you will find your feet firmly planted on the solid foundations of a kingdom that can never be shaken.

FURTHER STUDY

John 3:14-17;
12:32-33;
Acts 2:37-41

1. How does the cross of Jesus draw people?

2. What do we do to receive Jesus?

God, I bow before Your cross in repentance and surrender. Come into my life and establish me in that unshakeable kingdom I have been reading about. This I ask in and through Jesus' saving name. Amen.

Why so guilty?

For reading & meditation – 1 Thessalonians 5:12–28
'pray continually' (v17)

Another principle to explore that will hold us strong is that of prayer – but what is it about prayer that makes so many people feel guilty? Even great and good men and women – people we would consider godly – have lamented the fact that they felt guilty about their prayer lives. Dietrich Bonhoeffer, the German pastor who was executed by the Nazis shortly before the end of the Second World War, once admitted that his prayer life was something of which he was ashamed. Martin Luther, too, confessed to being deeply dissatisfied with his ability to pray even though he spent many hours in prayer.

FURTHER STUDY

Neh. 1:1–2:5;
1 Tim. 2:1–2

1. What different types of prayer does Nehemiah show us?

2. List different types of prayer Paul encouraged.

In my library I have countless books written by people known for their godly impact on the world and on the Church. Yet though these devout individuals laboured in prayer and taught and preached about it, a large number were aware of their shortcomings. Some confessed to feeling guilty because they did not pray enough or because their prayers were not sufficiently powerful. So many of the biographies of notable Christians contain sentiments such as this: 'I read how so-and-so spent hours on his knees, and I knew if I was to draw close to God I must do the same.'

There has been a tendency throughout the ages for one generation to copy another in the practice of prayer. Let me suggest that as you develop your own prayer life (a devotional necessity) do not feel obliged to follow a pattern of prayer used by others, but instead find one that is right for you. Though we can learn from others, we must not allow their experiences to overawe us.

My Father and my God, I am so grateful for what I can learn from the saints of the past. But help me to develop a pattern and style of prayer that is mine and not that of someone else.
In Jesus' name. Amen.

Be yourself

For reading & meditation – 1 Samuel 17:32–58

'David fastened on his sword over the tunic... "I cannot go
in these... because I am not used to them."' (v39)

I have seen so many people become discouraged in their prayer
lives because they have tried to copy the style and pattern of
other people's prayers only to find that they did not suit their
personality or temperament. Like David in Saul's armour, they
are uncomfortable, uneasy and unprepared to wrestle with God
and resist the devil.

In the early days of my Christian life other believers told me
about the various approaches the saints of old used to adopt
whenever they prayed, the inference being that if
I wanted to be a 'saint' then I should follow their
example. We can learn from those who have
gone before but it is best if we find our own style
and pattern of prayer. Some people are extroverts
whose style of praying will differ greatly from that
of introverts. Great damage can be done to our
devotional lives when we try to copy others in this
matter of prayer. Time and time again I have heard
people say: 'I have tried to build my prayer life on
that of such-and-such a person (usually naming a remarkable
Christian whose biography they have read) but it doesn't seem
to work for me. I feel so guilty because I cannot rise to that level
of praying.'

In my experience, the biggest single reason why so many people
feel guilty about their prayer life is because of a failure to come
up to the expectations of others. So I say again: in this matter
of prayer – as indeed in all other things – be yourself and not
someone else. Nobody can pray your prayers better than you.

FURTHER STUDY

Matt. 6:5-13;
Luke 18:9-14

1. Why should
we not copy
the prayers
of religious
people?

2. How should
we pray?

**Gracious Father, I ask again that You will enable me to find a
pattern of prayer that is right for me rather than one that is based
on what others say or do. In Jesus' name. Amen.**

Divine acceptance

For reading & meditation – Romans 15:1–13

'Accept one another, then, just as Christ accepted you, in order to bring praise to God.' (v7)

W e are spending these few days reflecting on why it is that so many Christians feel discouraged – even guilty – about their prayer lives. One reason, as we have seen, is because people try to pattern their prayer lives on those of others. Today we think about another reason: a faulty view of God. On one occasion a woman said to me: 'I do not feel that God accepts me or is pleased with me unless I spend an hour in prayer every day, and that every part of that hour is filled with pleading, longing and straining to hear His voice – something I am never able to do.'

FURTHER STUDY

Luke 15:11-20;
John 8:3-11

1. When did the father accept the son?

2. Contrast the attitudes of Jesus and the Pharisees.

This woman, I discovered, had been brought up by parents who were impossible to please, and she was projecting her childhood experiences on to God – seeing God in the image of her father and mother. Many Christians do a similar thing – they allow their past experiences to govern their view of God and thus approach Him with fear and trepidation. They believe that in order to please Him they must do their very best, and when they can't, or believe they can't, they experience a sense of failure and guilt.

I have often said that if God allowed me ten seconds to address every single Christian in the universe with one message this is what it would be: God accepts you as you are. Of course He longs for your growth and development, but that is not a condition He makes for your acceptance. You may not feel, up to this moment, that you have taken great strides in prayer, but listen to me: you will never experience it if you become too tense. So relax. God accepts you as you are. Find space today to talk with Him.

Father, drive this truth deep into my spirit, for I am so prone to think that Your acceptance of me is based on my performance rather than on who I am in Christ. In Jesus' name I ask it. Amen.

Wow!

For reading & meditation – Luke 11:5–13

'how much more will your Father in heaven give the Holy Spirit to those who ask him!' (v13)

Hold fast to this truth: you are loved by God not because of your ability to pray or, for that matter, because of any other ability you possess; you are loved because He is love.

One of the members of a church in the north of England that I pastored for some years was a dear lady whose love for the Lord was unquestionable. One day when she talked to me about a problem in her life I asked her if we could pray about it together. 'Oh,' she said, 'I think the Lord is too busy to be bothered with my little problems. He has much more important things to deal with that require His attention.' This lady's concept of God determined her approach to God – a matter that I felt was too important to go unexplored.

Permit a personal question: How do you see God? Over the years I've put that question to many Christians and the answers have been surprising. 'I see God as distant, uncommunicative and judgmental,' said one. You don't need three guesses to know what kind of prayer life that person experienced. Look again at the text for today; it tells us that contrary to what many of us think, God is a Father who delights to answer prayer. God is not mean or stingy and gives us everything we need. Is there any parent reading these lines who does not delight to give their child something they know is good for them? Now multiply that feeling a million times and you get a faint picture of how God feels when we ask Him for the power to live the life He has called us to live. How much more. Wow!

FURTHER STUDY

Matt. 10:29-31;
Rom. 5:7-11

1. Why can we be sure that God is never too busy for our problems?

2. How has God revealed to us how much He loves us?

Father, I think I am beginning to accept that my concept of You determines my approach to You. Help me see You as You really are – as a God who delights to give me what I need. Amen.

Conversing with God

For reading & meditation – Exodus 33:1–23

'The LORD would speak to Moses face to face, as a man speaks with his friend.' (v11)

So far we have thought about the two main reasons people feel disappointed with their prayer lives. The first is that we try to imitate another person's approach to prayer rather than developing our own approach. The second reason is that we misunderstand the nature of God and fail to see Him as He really is – large-hearted and magnanimous.

Prayer first and foremost is conversation with God. My dictionary defines conversation as an 'informal exchange of ideas by spoken words'. Please keep in mind that I am not talking about the type of prayer we offer corporately but the kind of praying we do when we are alone with God. If prayer is conversation then it involves (as does all conversation) both talking and listening, and we may mark our progress by our increasing desire to hear God speak rather than to speak ourselves.

FURTHER STUDY
2 Sam. 5:18-25;
Jer. 1:4-14

1. Why was conversation with God vital for David?

2. How is prayer like conversation?

The chapter before us today gives us a wonderful picture of a divine–human conversation in which we are told that God spoke to Moses 'as a man speaks with his friend'. What a beautiful model this is of prayer as conversation. When we talk to God we need to express ourselves in the same kind of language we use when talking to our closest friends. If we shift our mental gears and attempt to use a different pattern of thought, this will hinder the natural expression of our minds. We are never to forget that when we talk to God we are talking to our heavenly Father. And God, like all good fathers, delights in the natural and uninhibited approach of His children.

Heavenly Father, may I never forget that when I approach You in prayer I am to come as a child to a loving Father. Teach me how to be as much at ease with You as You are with me. In Jesus' name. Amen.

The plea of Abraham

For reading & meditation – Genesis 18:16–33

'Far be it from you to do such a thing - to kill the righteous
with the wicked' (v25)

Yesterday we said that prayer is conversation with God in which we talk with Him as with a friend. This means that when we approach Him there need be nothing artificial, and we don't need to use clichés. We guard, of course, against becoming overfamiliar with God, never forgetting that we are talking to the Creator of the universe. But neither must we forget that He is also our Father.

The passage we have read today gives us another example of prayer as conversation. How respectful Abraham is in his approach to God, yet consider how he argues his case before Him with such incisive logic. And notice, too, that he uses down-to-earth language – the type of language used by a person who is speaking to someone with whom he or she has a close relationship. There is none of this 'Oh Thou that gildest the heavens and settest the stars in space' stuff. Can you imagine one of your children approaching you like that? As some of my readers will know, I lost my only sons David and John through death as adults, but when they were children had they come and talked to me in such high-sounding language I would have wondered what was wrong with them. Be natural in your conversation with God. Be you!

FURTHER STUDY

John 15:13-17;
James 2:20-24

1. How does Jesus refer to His disciples?

2. How do we become friends with God?

Have you ever listened to someone new to the Christian faith praying – those who are still fresh after their conversion and have not yet been around older Christians? They talk to God as if He's their friend. They use ordinary terms anyone can understand, and they occasionally laugh and cry as they pray. It's beautiful.

Gracious and loving Father, help me understand more deeply still that though You are my Creator, You are also my Father and my friend. Teach me how to maintain the balance between awe for You and friendliness with You. In Jesus' name. Amen.

Friend to friend

For reading & meditation – Psalm 17:1–15

'Hear, O LORD, my righteous plea; listen to my cry. Give ear to my prayer' (v1)

Before we leave this matter of prayer being a conversation, let me share something I have come across that impacted me greatly. It comes from François Fénelon, who lived in the seventeenth and early eighteenth centuries. This is what he wrote: 'Tell God all that is in your heart as one unloads one's heart, its pleasures and its pains, to a dear friend. Tell Him your troubles that He may comfort you; tell Him your joys that He may sober them; tell Him your longings that He may purify them; tell Him your dislikes that He may help you overcome them; talk to Him of your temptations that He may shield you from them; show Him the wounds of your heart that He may heal them; lay bare your indifference to good, your depraved tastes for evil; tell Him how vanity tempts you to be insincere, how pride disguises you to yourself and others. Tell Him – He's your friend.'

FURTHER STUDY

Gen. 15:1-15;
Luke 7:34

1. How did Abraham tell God all that was in his heart?

2. Who can be included as friends of Jesus?

The point François Fénelon was making is that if you are open and honest before God then you will not lack things to say to Him. Friends who have no secrets from each other never run out of conversation. They do not weigh their words for there is nothing to be held back. They talk out of the abundance of the heart; without needing to measure their words they say what they think. Like Hannah, we should pour out our heart to God (1 Sam. 1:15). In fact, in Lamentations we are told to 'pour out your heart like water in the presence of the Lord' (Lam. 2:19). Blessed is the man or woman who attains such intimacy with God and talks with Him as friend to friend.

Father, I long for greater intimacy and friendship with You. I know You are leading me gently on to see a new vision of prayer. Help me not to hold back. In Jesus' name. Amen.

Just ask!

For reading & meditation – Matthew 7:7–12

'Ask and it will be given to you; seek and you will find;
knock and the door will be opened to you.' (v7)

W e turn our attention now to an aspect of prayer referred to as
petition. As we see from today's passage, Jesus encouraged
us to ask the Father for things. Had He not done so we might
have hesitated to include personal petition in our prayer times.
Instead we may have deemed presenting our requests to God to be
unnecessary since He already knows what is best for us and can
be trusted to give it as and when He decides He will.

How grateful I am that it was Jesus Himself who encouraged
us to make personal requests. Not only that, He also
urged us to be persistent with our petitions. Ask, He
tells us and then, if you don't receive an answer, seek,
and if the answer still does not come then knock.
Three stages of intensity. Each one of us experiences
times when we are faced with considerable problems
and our hearts are so filled with anxiety that we
cannot prevent ourselves from asking God to help
us. At such times we can ask Him to remove the
anxiety and fill us with His perfect peace. God would
not have us silent in such an hour. His ear is always
open to His children's needy cries.

FURTHER STUDY

1 Sam. 1:9-20;
James 4:1-3

1. What
happened after
Hannah poured
out her heart
in petition?

2. What does a
failure to ask
God indicate?

Those who say that prayer should not be taken up with our
personal petitions do not get this idea from Scripture. Millions of
Christians all over the world will struggle through today, trying
to manage by using their own wisdom and strength rather than
kneeling before their heavenly Father and asking Him for His help.
The apostle James tells us: 'You do not have, because you do not
ask God' (James 4:2). Don't be so independent. Ask.

**Father, how grateful I am for this aspect of prayer. Help me be less
independent and become more dependent – dependent on You and
Your endless resources. In Jesus' name. Amen.**

Who is in charge?

For reading & meditation – James 5:7–20

'The prayer of a righteous man is powerful and effective.'
(v16)

Why present our petitions to God when He already knows what we need? If He is love then surely He will give us the things we need without us having to pray for them? It is true that because God loves us He orders and plans events for our lives that work for good whether we pray about them or not. But it is also clear from God's Word that His purposes are brought about by our prayers when our will is in line with His. Though it may stagger you, the truth is that God has given us the freedom to affect the course of events in His universe through our prayers. C.S. Lewis once compared history to a play in which the playwright has fixed the scene and general outline but left certain details for the actors and actresses to decide so that they can improvise. We live, says Lewis, in an open universe. Just as God has made certain things contingent upon the human will – things that will not be accomplished unless that human will decides to bring them about – so He has made certain things contingent on prayer.

FURTHER STUDY

2 Kings 13:14-19;
2 Chron. 7:11-16

1. How would Jehoash's actions affect events?

2. When would God intervene to bring blessing?

Then there is this other issue: God instructs us to petition Him. That alone should be sufficient reason for doing so. Kenneth Elzinga, a professor of economics in an American university, says: 'If it had been God's pleasure that we wiggle our ears we would be obliged to do it whether we see good reason in it or not.' Fortunately prayer is not a mindless exercise like wiggling our ears. We can see good reasons for petitioning God in prayer, one being the fact that it places us in the position of being dependent on Him. It reminds us who is in charge.

Gracious Father, if some things just won't happen in my life unless I ask for them to happen, help me to remember that I was created dependent on You and that You have invited and expect me to come to You with my requests.

Obedience – a key

For reading & meditation – Hebrews 5:1–14
'he offered up prayers and petitions... to the one who
could save him from death' (v7)

We spend another day looking at why we need to present our petitions to God. In my opinion there are several reasons. We have looked at three of them, the first being that God's purposes are accomplished through our prayers. The second reason is that God has said to us to make requests. We respond with obedience and do so simply because God has told us to. This is the paradox of the Christian life – we discover that when we act in obedience we demonstrate and develop trust and in turn become the beneficiaries. As we take these steps and open our lives to God He communicates more of His presence to us. A third reason is that it keeps us dependent on Him and helps us to realise who is in charge.

Here's another reason: when we come to God with our petitions He has got our attention and this gives Him an opportunity to guide us by answering or not answering our requests. One person has said: 'God answers every request that is put to Him. He says, "Yes", "No", "Wait" or "I will give you something better".' I certainly have been guided through God answering or not answering my prayers.

The following lines are some that I came across in my reading that I think put the matter extremely succinctly: 'If the request isn't right He answers "No", if the timing isn't right His answer is "Slow", if you aren't ready yet His answer is "Grow", when everything's ready and right... His answer is "Go".'

If all our requests were answered in the way we wished we'd have every reason to doubt the wisdom of God.

FURTHER STUDY

Luke 22:39–46;
2 Cor. 12:7-10

1. How did Jesus combine petition and obedience?

2. How did God answer Paul's prayers?

Father, thank You for wanting to share my life. Nothing is too trivial for You. Help me to be more open, more dependent – and more prayerful. In Jesus' name. Amen.

The last thing we do

For reading & meditation – Philippians 4:1–13

'but in everything, by prayer and petition, with thanksgiving, present your requests to God.' (v6)

Paul mentions several things here that are wanted by all true Christians. We all want to stand firm in our faith (v1). We all want to be joyful as we go about our duties (v4). We all want to have a mind that dwells on everything that is positive and beneficial (v8). We all want to apply God's principles so that our hearts are filled with His perfect peace (v9). We all want contentment and satisfaction (vv10–12).

We all want these things but how many of us experience them?

FURTHER STUDY

2 Chron. 16:1-13;
1 Pet. 5:6-7

1. Where did
Asa place his
reliance?

2. How is prayer
a humbling
experience?

Problems mount up, cares increase, worries escalate, irritation creeps in – and what do we do? Often the last thing we do is to pray and ask God to help us. An elderly Christian, when asked what advice he would like to pass on to the next generation, said: 'Make prayer the first thing you try, not the last.' The wording of today's text as found in the Amplified Bible helps to bring out its meaning: 'Do not… have any anxiety about anything, but… by prayer and petition (definite requests), with thanksgiving, continue to make your wants known to God. And God's peace [shall be yours...]' We might paraphrase Paul's message in this way: 'All those irritations and worries that bother you so much and the struggles that make you anxious or fearful will be dissipated and replaced with God's perfect peace, plus all the other qualities you want, if you will simply talk to God about them.'

Have you got the point? Through prayer, inner turmoil can be turned into perfect peace. It is not the last resort; it is the first necessity.

Father, help me understand why the first thing I should do when I am troubled – pray – is so often the last thing I do. Impress upon me that wishing things were better is no substitute for prayer. In Jesus' name. Amen.

First things first

For reading & meditation – Matthew 6:25–34

'But seek first his kingdom and his righteousness, and all these things will be given to you as well.' (v33)

Today we continue reflecting on the aspect of prayer called petition – making our requests known to God. Not all personal petitions are alike. Some requests pour out of our hearts in times of emergency, for instance when a loved one is desperately ill or a serious disease is diagnosed. The problem may not be related to health but possibly to finance – perhaps the realisation that there is not sufficient money for something essential.

When crises arise there is no time to think of worship, adoration or thanksgiving, and I do not think that God wants us to work through a pattern of prayer in moments such as these. Any theory of prayer that requires a person to express worship, adoration, praise and thanksgiving in a ritualistic way before bringing their request to God in a moment of desperation is to be avoided. Everything in me cries out against it. And in you, too, I am sure. I am certain that God does not want that either.

FURTHER STUDY

1 Kings 3:5–14;
Luke 11:13;
John 4:10

1. How did Solomon put first things first?

2. What should we ask for first?

There are other requests that do not come under the category of crisis prayers – requests for God's help in connection with family matters, personal issues, work, one's church and so on. Petitions, of course, are not always made for material things or benefits; they can be made for spiritual matters as well – for the gifts of the Spirit, for instance. We can be sure God is glad when we want those things. Nothing would be more advantageous to the world and to the Church than for Christians to avail themselves of the gifts and graces that God has in His storehouse in readiness for the time when we will ask for them.

Father, forgive me that so often my prayers are for material things rather than for spiritual things. Help me to get my priorities right – the spiritual first, the material second. In Jesus' name. Amen.

Asking amiss

For reading & meditation – James 4:1–10

'When you ask, you do not receive, because you ask with wrong motives' (v3)

One of the greatest problems in connection with petitioning prayer (crisis times apart) is that we can allow it to absorb all our moments of devotion. To me it is significant that those who have reached a stage of maturity in prayer say that the closer they get to God the less they are taken up with petitions. Another danger is that we make requests just for ourselves and forget the needs of others. It is quite astonishing how selfishness can rule our hearts even when we are on our knees. There are many Christians who use their moments of petition to plead for things that will not necessarily benefit them – more money, more influence, more popularity, more success. Surely it cannot be right to be filled with concern for our own needs and desires when there are those with much greater needs. God delights to bless us with material things, but He loves to give them, as yesterday's text highlights, to those who seek first His kingdom (Matt. 6:33). And even then He gives according to our need rather than our wishes.

FURTHER STUDY

Matt. 20:20–28;
Eph. 1:15–21;
3:14–19

1. Why might we ask for the wrong things?

2. What was the subject of Paul's prayers?

The writer George MacDonald said: 'There is a communion with God that asks for nothing, yet asks for everything... he who seeks the Father... is likely to have what he asks, for he is not likely to ask amiss.' A good guide with many, if not all, of our petitions is to ask ourselves: can I ask this in Jesus' name? Praying in His name does not mean attaching the name of Jesus to the list of our wants and desires, but seeking to know whether or not our desires coincide with His. When we pray in His name, we receive what He knows it is right for us to receive.

Lord Jesus Christ, help me be clear that praying in Your name is not attaching Your name to what I want but seeking to discover what is right. This is a prayer I know without doubt I can ask in Your name. Amen.

Asking in Christ's name

For reading & meditation – John 14:1–14

'You may ask me for anything in my name, and I will do it.'
(v14)

C.S. Lewis once said that prayer is request. And the very nature of a request is that it may or may not be granted – a request is not a command. And if the infinite and eternal God listens to the requests of humanity ('finite and foolish creatures), of course there will be some requests that He declines.

I mentioned yesterday that whenever we bring our petitions to God we ought to ask ourselves: can I ask this in Jesus' name? We need to be crystal clear on this point: it does not mean we simply end our prayers with the words 'In Jesus' name', because those words can be attached to the most selfish of prayers. Rather, praying in Jesus' name means praying in harmony with His will. Can we be sure that what we pray for is what He wants? Are we certain that we can ask in the Saviour's name for the course of action we want to take? Surely honesty compels us to admit that sometimes we pray for things that we are not certain God wants us to have. At such times it is wise to admit that uncertainty and say, as Jesus did: 'yet not my will, but yours be done' (Luke 22:42).

FURTHER STUDY

Acts 19:13-17;
1 John 5:13-15

1. Why is the name of Jesus not a magic formula?

2. How does John define 'ask anything'?

On the other hand, there are a multitude of things we know without any doubt that He wants to give us: health of soul, the mind of Christ, love, peace, joy and so on. If we have any doubt about these things, we are in doubt about matters that should not be doubted. Here the prayer of petition needs instead to be an affirmation; we should stop asking and start believing. It is God's will to bless you – so receive that blessing. Remember, as we said earlier, that God is more eager to give than you are to receive.

Gracious Father, help me from now on when I pray to seek to discover if my requests are in harmony with Your will rather than pushing for what I want. In Jesus' name I ask it. Amen.

Stop talking and listen

For reading & meditation – Psalm 85:1–13

'I will listen to what God the LORD will say' (v8)

Another element that ought to be present in our prayer time is listening to God. This is an aspect of praying that has been strangely neglected. Many believers fill every moment of their devotions by talking, never stopping to hear what God might want to say to them. Their prayer times are sadly one-sided.

Some Christians find it difficult to believe that the great God of the universe is willing to speak to them and convey His thoughts to their minds. But over and over again Scripture emphasises that although God is great enough to manage a vast universe He also takes a Father's personal care of His children. The very hairs of our head are numbered, we are told (Matt. 10:30), and that thought alone should lead us to conclude that every part of our lives is of the utmost concern to Him. John Stott says: 'Unlike heathen idols which being dead are dumb, the living God has spoken and continues to speak… and since God speaks we must listen.'

FURTHER STUDY

Jer. 29:10-14;
Dan. 9:1-19

1. How does
God say we will
hear Him?

2. How did God
speak to Daniel
and what was
his response?

But how does God speak to us? Well, He doesn't ordinarily speak in an audible voice as He did to Samuel, Abraham or Saul of Tarsus, though there are some today who have claimed to have heard Him speak in this way. God, of course, is able to do anything, but speaking audibly to men and women is, I think, the exception rather than the rule. The main way God speaks to us is through Scripture. Read a portion of the Bible slowly, preferably out loud. Let it soak in and if a verse strikes you, focus on it in meditation. Begin to listen. Ask: 'Father, have You anything to say to me?'

Father, I recognise that I need help in this area of prayer also. Teach me to listen. Give me a relaxed heart and mind so that I don't have to cover my anxieties with words. In Jesus' name I ask it. Amen.

He still speaks

For reading & meditation – Hebrews 4:12–16

'For the word of God is living and active. Sharper than any double-edged sword' (v12)

At present, we are focusing on the listening side of prayer, and that the principal way God speaks to us is through Scripture. One of the special ministries of the Holy Spirit is, as today's text tells us, to make God's written Word 'living and active' and 'sharper than any double-edged sword'.

In an amazing way God is able to 'quicken' a verse or passage of Scripture to us so that, though the Scripture is a written text, it also becomes a living message. He has not simply spoken once through His Word, the Bible, but speaks through it still. If we do not hear God speaking to us when we read His Word it is not because God is dead or silent but because we have not learned to listen. To quote John Stott again: 'If we are cut off during a telephone conversation we do not jump to the conclusion that the person on the other end has died. No, it is the line which has gone dead.' We need to adopt the attitude of Samuel, who said, 'Speak, for your servant is listening' (1 Sam. 3:10), rather than 'Listen, Lord, Your servant is speaking.'

FURTHER STUDY

Josh. 1:1–9;
2 Kings 22:3–13

1. What was Joshua's experience of listening to God?

2. How had the Israelites stopped listening to God?

George Muller, the man who established a great ministry among orphaned children in that city, told how beginning his prayer time by reading a portion of Scripture transformed his devotional life. Some like to begin and end by reading the Bible. This is the way I conduct my own prayer times. I find that after prayer my mind is more alert and ready to listen so that if I have missed anything of what God wanted to say to me at the beginning of my prayer time I am likely to hear it at the end.

Father, whenever I read Your Word help me to see if I am reading without listening. Honesty compels me to admit that often it is so. Help me to be not just a reader of the Word but a listener also. In Jesus' name. Amen.

'Turning eyes into ears'

For reading & meditation – Revelation 1:1-8

'Blessed is the one who reads the words of this prophecy, and blessed are those who hear it' (v3)

'Reading Scripture,' says Eugene Peterson, 'is not the same as listening to God. To do one is not necessarily to do the other. But they are often assumed to be the same thing.' The point he is making is one we hinted at yesterday. We should not only read Scripture, we should listen to it also. Peterson calls this 'turning eyes into ears'.

In reading we use our eyes; in listening we use our ears. We read marks on paper; we listen to a voice. That is why I often suggest reading the Bible out loud. Many a time as I have read the Word

out loud I have heard the voice of God through my own voice. Better still is to use one of the many audio resources now available so that you can hear the Word of God being read. Not long ago I talked to a man who said that as he listened to a recording of a Bible passage there was a moment when it seemed that God was speaking directly to him through a particular verse. Though he had read this verse many times he had never fully understood the message

the verse contained. The sound of a voice added a new dimension.

It is not without significance, I think, that when Christians in the seven congregations mentioned in the book of Revelation came together to consider the Word of God written to them by John from Patmos, they did not just read it with their eyes; they listened to it with their ears. Though I am aware that here I am emphasising the importance of listening to God in our private prayer times, I feel compelled to say that the practice in many churches of emphasising worship and praise in a service to the exclusion of the reading of God's Word aloud is something to be avoided.

FURTHER STUDY

2 Chron.
34:14-33

1. What was the effect when God's Word was read out loud?

2. What was the king's response?

Father, I realise that I have been taught to talk but have I been taught to listen? Teach me this art, I pray, lest I become preoccupied with hearing my own voice and fail to hear Yours.
In Jesus' name I ask it. Amen.

The inner voice

For reading & meditation – John 10:22–30

'My sheep listen to my voice; I know them,
and they follow me.' (v27)

Over the past few days we have been emphasising the listening side of prayer and the need to use our ears as well as our eyes when we are quietening ourselves before God. In other words, not just reading the Word of God but listening for the voice of the Holy Spirit, who speaks to us through that Word. It is not enough to read; we must learn to listen. Shakespeare's lines were not written to make the point I am stressing here but they are relevant nevertheless:

O learn to read what silent love hath writ.

To hear with eyes belongs to love's fine wit.

When I say that the principal way God speaks to us is through Scripture, no doubt all Christians would agree with this statement. However, when I say that God can speak directly to our hearts in words other than those of Scripture, we begin to enter controversial theological territory. Christians are greatly, even passionately, divided on this particular issue. Some even regard it as a dangerous doctrine to teach. So let me take the time to make my own position clear.

FURTHER STUDY

Acts 9:1–19;
16:6–10

1. How did
God speak to
Ananias?

2. How did God
speak to Paul?

I do believe that the principal way that God speaks to us is through Scripture. However, I also believe that it is possible for God to speak to our hearts directly in words other than those of Scripture, though what He says will always be in harmony with Scripture. Throughout the centuries spiritual men and women have testified that they have developed the art of listening to what they describe as the inner voice – the gentle impress of the Spirit that brings the message of heaven direct to the human heart.

Father God, how I long to hear Your voice speaking directly to my soul. Help me establish a listening post in my heart so that I can detect Your voice. In Jesus' name. Amen.

Listening – an art

For reading & meditation – John 10:1–21

'I am the good shepherd; I know my sheep
and my sheep know me' (v14)

People who have spent much time listening to God claim that they can distinguish between their own imagination and the quiet voice of the Spirit within their hearts. However, it must be made clear that those who have developed the art of listening to God's voice, and hearing it, stress that it comes only after practice.

It is essential to set aside time specifically for this purpose. In today's world where, as I have pointed out before, time seems to be something most people do not have, is it any wonder that the practice of listening to God is a lost art? Brigid Herman, a woman to whom I have referred many times over the years, says in her book *Creative Prayer* that the alert and adventurous soul making its first venture into the area of listening to God must learn to listen in silence. 'At first,' she writes, 'there will be the ghostly whisperings of the subconscious self, a dog barking in the distance, the sounds of traffic, a radio in the other room perhaps, the clamour of personal ambition, the murmur of self-will, the song of unbridled imagination, but one hour of such listening may give us a sure instinct for the Divine that a year's hard study or external intercourse with men will not.'

FURTHER STUDY

Mark 1:9–11;
Rev. 3:19-22

1. How did the Father encourage His Son?

2. What happens when we hear and heed Jesus' voice?

How I wish I could give you five steps that will enable you to listen to God, but as far as I am aware there is just one: take time to listen in silence. Those who do this say there are many occasions when nothing comes, but when something does, the sense that God is speaking in the soul is worth more than all the cost in terms of time and waiting.

Father, I come to this issue of time once again. Help me, without neglecting my family and my responsibilities, to rearrange my life so that I have more time to spend with You. In Jesus' name. Amen.

The Divine Shepherd

For reading & meditation – Acts 8:26–40

'The Spirit told Philip, "Go to that chariot
and stay near it."' (v29)

Does God talk directly to people today in the same way that the Holy Spirit spoke to Philip? Multitudes would testify that He does. Maybe not always in such dramatic circumstances, but certainly in a way that leaves a person in no doubt that it is the voice of the Lord that they heard.

However, many Christians have told me: 'I have prayed for years but have never heard God's voice speaking directly to my soul.' My response is this: 'Ah, but have you given time to waiting before Him, and have you done so believing He would speak to you?' It is possible to wait before God without any sense of expectation. I have been quite astonished to discover the part expectation plays in our spiritual development. It brings us to a state of spiritual alertness. Lack of expectation may be a defence that helps us not feel disappointed

Frequently I have been asked: 'What does the voice of God sound like?' The best way I can describe it is that it sounds like the voice of conscience, yet of course it is much richer and the message it gives is more positive. All of us have had moments when conscience has said to us: 'That was wrong,' or 'You shouldn't have done that.' But the voice of God does not merely approve or disapprove; it encourages, reassures, informs and instructs. The closeness of our walk with the Divine Shepherd (which Philip no doubt enjoyed) determines the degree to which we recognise His voice when He speaks to us. And when God speaks there is a quiet sense of authority. The trained ear recognises that it is the voice of the Shepherd.

FURTHER STUDY

Acts
10:1-23,44-48

1. How did God speak to Peter and Cornelius?

2. What was the result of their obedience?

Jesus, how I long to have a trained ear, but I accept that it does not come without cost. Draw me closer to You, I pray, so that my soul may become more sensitive to You and more receptive to the inner voice. Amen.

A word of caution

For reading & meditation – 2 Timothy 3:10–17

'All Scripture is God-breathed and is useful for teaching, rebuking, correcting and training in righteousness' (v16)

Before leaving this issue of listening to God I would like to give you one last word of caution. God will never contradict His written Word, and if we believe we have heard His voice telling us to do something that is contrary to what He says in Scripture, it is definitely not God's voice we have heard.

Some people who have claimed to have heard God's voice have engaged in actions that we know He would not commend. That, however, is no argument for abandoning the listening side of prayer. There is the possibility of error in all things human – or partly human – but the adventurous soul will not withdraw because of that. One preacher made the comment: 'One would need to abandon living if one wished to avoid the very chance of error.' Challenging and open to error as it may be, it is possible through close contact with the Chief Shepherd to be able to disentangle His voice from all other clamorous voices that speak within the soul and to know without any shadow of doubt that one has been spoken to by God Himself. Just to imagine it happening is wonderful, but to experience it is far more wonderful.

FURTHER STUDY

Psa. 19:7-14;
1 Cor. 2:9-16

1. How does God's Word affect us?

2. How may the Spirit teach us?

If in your prayer times listening to God is something you have neglected, make up your mind to remedy the situation. Start by learning to listen to the written Word, and then to the spoken word – the word spoken by the Shepherd directly to your heart. As I have said before, I shall never forget the moment I first heard the Lord whisper in my heart: 'Selwyn, I love you.' Since then He has said it to me quite often. But never too often.

Father, I realise the problem is not that You are unwilling to speak to me but rather that I have not prepared myself to listen. Through both the written Word and the spoken word may I hear the Living Word. In Jesus' name. Amen.

'Reverent listening'

For reading & meditation – Matthew 6:1–15

'But when you pray, go into your room, close the door and pray to your Father, who is unseen.' (v6)

Another spiritual principle we need to understand if we are to be men and women with inner spiritual strength is the need to cultivate a daily 'quiet time' (the time we set aside daily to be with God). Some people talk about building sacred spaces in secular society – whatever surroundings you choose it's about being with God without distractions. In the months following my conversion to Christ I noticed as I mixed with other Christians that some seemed calmer than others – more restful, more at peace – and they exuded an air of deep spiritual maturity. As I questioned them about this, I discovered the common denominator was that they all prioritised 'quiet time'. One of them made this comment: 'Those who say they can live in a state of prayer without definite times of prayer will probably find themselves without both. They are as short-sighted as those who say they can live in a state of physical nourishment without stated times for meals.'

Emily Herman has called quiet time: 'That tender and reverent listening at the feet of Wisdom which is the true and acceptable idleness.' It is an 'idleness' that results in renewed activity. You become alive all over. The great French philosopher Blaise Pascal, in his book *Pensées*, concluded: 'Nearly all the ills of life spring from this simple source that we are not able to sit still in a room.'

But what if in that stillness we met with God – how healing that would be.

FURTHER STUDY

Exod. 16:11–26;
John 6:47–51

1. What was the daily habit of the Israelites?

2. In what ways can our souls be nourished by Jesus every day?

Father God, help me see even more clearly the importance of daily time with You. May I cultivate those moments when I become 'open-doored to God'. In Jesus' name I ask it. Amen.

'A higher level'

For reading & meditation – Psalm 5:1–12

'O LORD, in the morning you hear my voice; in the morning
I lay my requests before you and wait in expectation.' (v3)

A traveller tells of his experience the first time he passed through
the Panama Canal. 'We who had sailed the oceans were
blocked, shut in, helpless, our freedom gone… We felt a lifting, great
fountains were opened from beneath, and to our astonishment that
great ship was lifted thirty-five feet in just seven minutes. Then the
gates opened and we glided out on a higher level, out on the bosom
of Lake Gatun.' The effect of regularly spending time with God can
be likened to that experience: it shuts you in with God, the door

FURTHER STUDY

Mark 1:35-39;
Luke 5:16-26

1. What was
the daily habit
of Jesus?

2. How did His
morning time
empower Him
for action?

closes upon you, and you may at first feel helpless,
so shut in, so inactive. And then infinite resources
begin to bubble up from beneath, and you are lifted,
without any noise or strain, to a more elevated level.
The door opens and you emerge on a higher level of
life. A poet, many years ago, wrote these lines:

Every morning lean thine arm awhile
Upon the window sill of heaven,
And gaze upon thy God;
Then with the vision in thy heart,
Turn strong to meet thy day.

I have found that it is best to have my time with God in the
first hours of the morning so that I can, as someone has put it,
'wash your thinking in the thoughts of Christ before you face the
challenges of the day'. If it is not possible to set aside time in the
morning then take any hour you can to draw close to Him. But
resolve that no day will go by without you attempting to spend
time with God. As you do so, patiently listen and intentionally
push past any distractions that try to pull you away from Him.

God my Father, give me the determination to 'take the pause that
refreshes', to drink from the living Fountain, the eternal Spring.
Help me gaze at You before my eyes meet the gaze of the world.
In Jesus' name. Amen.

A 'heart Lame'

For reading & meditation – Luke 8:40–56

'She came up behind him and touched the edge
of his cloak, and immediately her bleeding stopped.' (v44)

Yesterday it was suggested that we should choose the morning
for a quiet time, but if for some reason that is not possible then
we find any hour we can. But, as I said, I find the morning is best.
It's been said that: 'Those who do not provide for a quiet time in
the morning may have to provide for unquiet time throughout the
day.' This is not to say that when we miss our regular time with
God (sometimes this is unavoidable) He will set out to make our
day difficult. But we will have missed the opportunity to cultivate
an oasis of quiet within.

A poet has said: 'What a frail soul He gave me, and
a heart lame, and unlikely for the large events.' I
wonder, however, if 'a heart lame, and unlikely for the
large events' is more the result of our failure to take in
God's resources. He has infinite resources not only for
the asking but also for the taking. During a quiet time
the soul grows more receptive and, as someone has
put it, 'becomes the organ of spiritual touch' – that
touch becoming as rewarding as it was for the woman in our story
today as she reached out and touched the edge of Jesus' cloak. In a
regular time with God we exchange our impotence for His power,
our unrest for His rest, our grief for His joy. Quiet times produce a
quiet heart, which becomes a quiet confidence and a quiet power.
It is then that the soul becomes its best. It is then that you tune in
to God's wavelength.

As often as possible, begin the day with God. Let this be your
prayer: 'Without You, not one step over the threshold. With You
– anywhere.'

FURTHER STUDY

Psa. 27:8-14;
88:1-13

1. How can we
take strength
and heart
from God?

2. What was the
psalmist's habit?

**God, help me do what Your Son was so careful to do – have a regular
time of drawing close to You each day. Resources are so near at
hand. May I take the time that is necessary to avail myself of them.
In Jesus' name. Amen.**

'Don't leave home without it'

For reading & meditation – Luke 9:18–27

'when Jesus was praying... and his disciples were with him, he asked them, "Who do the crowds say I am?"' (v1)

Several decades ago, when the charismatic renewal was beginning to influence a large number of churches, many people began to develop a different attitude to daily time with God. Some argued: 'Now I am baptised in the Spirit I no longer need my daily quiet time. I have a perpetual "quiet time" – a moment-by-moment contact with God that extends through all my waking hours.' I was one among many leaders concerned about the consequences of such an idea, and reminded people that if Jesus needed to have stated times of quiet to be alone with God then we do far more.

One objection some raise with regard to the daily intentional setting aside of time with God is that it can contribute to guilt and legalism in the Christian life. This is a very real possibility, for I have known a number of people who believed that if they left home without first having their daily quiet time then God might cause some harm to come to them. Such a concept of God is just plain wrong. A daily quiet time is not a demand that God makes; it is a discipline that, when entered into, fortifies and enriches life.

FURTHER STUDY

Exod. 29:38–30:8; 36:1–3

1. What were the responsibilities of the high priest?

2. What delighted the people?

As we have already said, the morning works well, but if that is not possible then find some other time. The benefit of spending time with God first thing in the morning is that if we go out into the day with a God-reference rather than a self-reference then we are more likely to be calm within whatever pressures we face. The quiet time produces a quietness that becomes the atmosphere for the day.

Father God, give me the sense to guard the times of communion I have with You. May I increase them rather than decrease them so that I develop the inner strength that keeps me secure in an insecure world. Amen.

'Living off the surface'

For reading & meditation – Jeremiah 17:1-10

'blessed is the man who trusts in the LORD... He will be like a tree planted by the water' (vv7-8)

Billy Graham has said: 'If you are too busy to spend a little time with God each day in personal prayer and the reading of His Word, then you are busier than God intends you to be.' Over the past days I have stressed that it is preferable to set aside time in the morning; before we move on I would like to share this thought, which I came across in Dr E. Stanley Jones' *The Way*: 'A diver too busy to think about getting his line for air in working order before he descends to the depths would be no more foolish than the man or woman who descends into the stifling atmosphere of today's world without getting their breathing apparatus of prayer connected with the pure air of the kingdom of God above.' I wonder if one reason why so many Christians are spiritually anaemic is because they have done themselves the harm of self-inflicted asphyxiation.

FURTHER STUDY

Isa. 37:31;
Ezek. 31:1-9

1. What is the relationship between root and fruit?

2. Why was the tree majestic in beauty?

Consider for a moment the Japanese art of bonsai, whereby trees are dwarfed and grow no higher than a couple of feet. This is accomplished by tying up the taproot so that the tree lives off the surface roots; it thus remains a stunted thing. Don't do that in your Christian life – live off what is superficial. Surface roots draw from such things as the cultural, the educational, the social, the economic, the political or perhaps even the thin religious life of some churches. They draw sustenance from these things but the consequence is a life that is stunted spiritually. Only as our taproot goes deep down into God and draws sustenance from Him do we truly live. And a regular time with God is the best means to ensure this happens.

Heavenly God, You who sent Your Son to give us life in all its fullness, help me send my taproot down into Your resources and draw my energy, life and strength not from the surface but from the depths. In Jesus' name. Amen.

God's obligation

DAY 275

For reading & meditation – Isaiah 55:1–13

'so is my word that goes out from my mouth: It will not return to me empty, but will accomplish what I desire' (v11)

What can we do during our time with God? For many decades now I have studied the lives of men and women – both living and dead – noted for their devotional lives. Several features have become apparent. First, they began their times of devotion by opening up the Bible and sometimes reading several chapters, at other times just a single verse. George Muller, whom I mentioned earlier, had a rich devotional life and yet he said that for years he came to his daily quiet time with the sense of: 'This is what I should do as a Christian, but I will be glad when it is over.' Then someone asked him how he organised his quiet time. He said: 'I have a prayer list with me and begin to pray first for my friends and family, then for my own needs.'

'Try starting your quiet time by opening up the Scriptures and reading a few passages,' his friend suggested, 'and see what happens.'

FURTHER STUDY

Psa. 1:1-6;
Acts 8:26-38

1. Who will be spiritually fruitful?

2. How was the Ethiopian primed for salvation?

George Muller followed this advice and later admitted: 'It was one of the greatest secrets that had ever been imparted to me… it changed the whole atmosphere of my quiet time and brought a richness into it that is impossible to describe.'*

The reading of Scripture primes your spiritual pump, so to speak, and moves the soul towards God. Some need to be encouraged into thought by a help such as *Every Day with Jesus*, but it is important to remember that my comments are secondary, and not a substitute for first-hand contact with the Word of God. The Father is under no obligation to bless my words, but He has promised, as our text for today assures us, to bless His own Word.

Lord God, You have breathed into Your Word and it is a living book. Help me saturate my inner being with Your mind so that I will not be able to tell where my mind ends and Your mind begins. In Jesus' name. Amen.

'Speak, Lord'

For reading & meditation – Psalm 119:105–112

'Your statutes are my heritage for ever; they are the joy of my heart.' (v111)

We continue thinking about what we can do in our daily times with God. Though I am aware that I have made several of these points before, the fact is, as someone has put it, that: 'Everything that needs to be said has been said, but because we so easily forget we need to be told it again and again and again.'

A good suggestion to follow is to pause for a little while after prayerful contemplation of the Scriptures to see if God will say anything to you. Be silent before God. Pray this prayer: 'Father, have You anything to say to me?' Sometimes He will impress a thought on your mind of some act of kindness that is needed, or some insight from His Word. Or He may highlight something in your own life or behaviour that needs attention. If this happens, don't ignore it. Face the issue, ask God for His forgiveness and, if restoration or an apology is necessary, then do what you know is right.

When you become receptive in the way I have indicated then you will soon find that God will come close to you to guide, direct and develop your spirituality. He will take advantage of your receptivity to make you the best you can be. It is always helpful to have a notebook and pen with you during your times with God so that you can write anything that occurs to you or that He may say to you. The notebook and pen are signs of faith since they show that you expect some message to come to you. Once you have read the Word you will find your thinking and aspirations start moving in the right direction. And you will then pray prayers that are in harmony with the will of God.

FURTHER STUDY

Jer. 31:33–34;
Hab. 2:1–3;
2 Cor. 3:1–6

1. Why should revelation be written down?

2. What is the ultimate medium of the message?

Father God, amid all the hustle and bustle of life, help me to be silent. And in the silence speak words that will release me, heal me and make me more like Your Son. Reveal Yourself to me and cleanse me to the depths. Amen.

The power of pause

For reading & meditation – Psalm 37:1–17

'Be still before the LORD and wait patiently for him' (v7)

W e spend one last day considering what form a quiet time can take. The suggestions made so far have been these: first, spend some time reading God's Word. After reading, stay relaxed and receptive and ask God: 'Father, have You anything to say to me?' Learn to listen. Write down any message that comes. If you do not write down the inspiration or word of guidance it may fade as you go out and become immersed in the business of the day. 'The faintest ink,' said Confucius, 'is better than the strongest memory.'

FURTHER STUDY

2 Sam. 18:19–33;
Isa. 30:15;
40:28–31

1. Why should
Ahimaaz have
pressed pause?

2. How can
our strength
be renewed?

The final part of your quiet time could be taken up with the things that you want to say to God. Express your adoration of God. This is, after all, how the Lord taught us to pray: 'When you pray, say: "Father, hallowed be your name"' (Luke 11:2). God delights to be worshipped and adored. Always start there. Be ready also to thank God for the answers to prayer He has already given you. Remember, He always answers prayer by saying, 'Yes', 'No', 'Not just now' or 'I will give you something better'. Remember, too, that prayer is not a monologue but a dialogue, so be alert for anything the Lord may say to you concerning your petitions.

Another piece of good advice I once received concerning prayer is this: build pauses into your petitions. In other words, don't do all the talking. Pause to see if God wants to speak to you. That piece of advice has transformed my prayer life. Try it; it may do the same for you. Out of daily time with God comes quiet strength. People who walk through life with 'something inside so strong' are people, I assure you, who have cultivated quiet moments with God.

Father, to have the resources that will enable me to stand tall and strong in the midst of today's world I realise I must take time to be quiet alone with You. Please help me put what I have learned into practice. In Jesus' name. Amen.

Adjusting to change

For reading & meditation – Revelation 22:1-6

'On each side of the river stood the tree of life, bearing twelve crops of fruit, yielding its fruit every month.' (v2)

Another attitude we need to adopt if we are to stand strong is this: accept the fact of change, and allow God to make out of every phase of life something beautiful and good. Some people find it hard to adjust, settling for immaturity; refusing to grow older gracefully rather longing to be young again. We all look back at times – but when longing becomes an obsession it is a recipe for problems. On this subject, Dr E. Stanley Jones is particularly thought provoking. This is what he said: 'Every stage of life through which we pass has something peculiar to itself in possibility and achievement. Youth is not the only stage of possibility; each stage of life is crammed with possibilities of achievement and beauty.'

I have selected today's verse because of the interesting thought that the tree of life, situated on each side of the river that flows through the city of God, yielded its fruits every month. The 'tree of life' in the here and now – our natural life – youth, middle age and old age – yields something beautiful and good. Shakespeare talked about the seven stages of man – the infant crying in the nurse's arms, the boy creeping like a snail unwillingly to school and so on. Someone once said that there are really only three stages: youth, middle age and 'you're looking very well!' Whatever our age, we can always do something to make the time process beautiful. And it adds greatly to our spiritual inner strength and maturity if we know how to do so. So we're going to spend some time over the next few days unpacking what that means.

FURTHER STUDY

Exod. 17:8-16;
1 John 2:12-17

1. How did Israelites of different ages work together to win the battle?

2. What can characterise each stage of our lives?

Father God, give me the insight and imagination I need to make each phase of my life distinctive and beautiful. Help me adjust to all life's changes and enjoy the hours, days, months and years as they come and go. In Jesus' name. Amen.

Go, sell, give

For reading & meditation – Matthew 19:16–30

'Jesus answered, "If you want to be perfect, go, sell your possessions and give to the poor"' (v21)

O ur youth is often a challenging and formative period of life. Today we see Jesus giving three instructions to a young man who wanted eternal life: 'Go, sell… and give'. Perhaps Jesus has a similar message for us today. Go: be willing to identify the things in your life that are preventing you being the man or woman God wants you to be. As you finish reading this, make a list of the things hindering your spiritual life. No problem can be resolved until it is faced; then you can move on. Sell: get rid of whatever is preventing Jesus being centre of your life. For instance, throw out any books or magazines and delete websites or social media that draw you away from the things of God. Take time to develop your spiritual life through prayer, reading God's Word, spending time and sharing your life with other Christians. Give: change the orientation of your life so that you no longer are at the centre; instead, put others before yourself. God designed us as other-centred, not self-centred. You will function best when you are more concerned about others than you are about yourself. Here is some advice I was given when I was younger. Don't be impatient if you can't change the world overnight. However, if you can't do everything don't be tempted to do nothing. Do what is before you. Learn to serve others before striving for a position of leadership. Jesus' timing is always perfect. Remember to be faithful in the small things and God will build upon these. 'You have been faithful with a few things; I will put you in charge of many things' (Matt. 25:21).

FURTHER STUDY

Lam. 3:27;
Luke 16:10-13;
Acts 19:18-20

1. How can youth be a training period for greatness?

2. How did the Ephesians deal with spiritual hindrances?

Father, I would be a person committed to You and to caring for others. Help me be faithful in the small things so that I am trusted with the bigger ones. Build into my life good and godly values, I pray. In Jesus' name. Amen.

Keep on growing

For reading & meditation – 2 Peter 3:1–18

'But grow in the grace and knowledge of our Lord and Saviour Jesus Christ.' (v18)

Having thought briefly about youth, we now consider how to make the time process beautiful in our years of middle age. A saying that was once well known is this: 'Heaven lies about us in our infancy, and the world lies about us in our middle age.' There are many pressures to face in our middle age, not just from the world, but most cruelly and demandingly from ourselves.

It's not uncommon during this phase to begin to realise that life is not as one had expected or one has not achieved through the years all that one had hoped for. This often results in feeling downcast or experiencing profound feelings of loss. At these times, it is important to remember that our lives are woven into a much bigger story and that God's hand is at work bringing His purpose to pass. Several things that I set out to do as a young man I have not achieved, and I believe now that if I had done them it would not have been good for me at all. Don't wallow in self-pity – God is at work to achieve His purposes in your life. And, after all, it's His purposes that matter.

FURTHER STUDY

Num. 13:26-33;
Josh. 14:6-8;
Psa. 90:12-17

1. Describe Caleb's attitude at the age of 40.

2. How can we number our days aright?

One doctor said 'There are three great problems in middle age – baldness, bifocals and bulges.' Watch those bulges. Eat healthily but not excessively, and keep fit. Keep your mind active. Enrol in a course that adds richness to your life – why not a CWR course! You may have stopped physically growing during adolescence, but you need never stop growing spiritually.

The God who has led and cared for you will be there for you in the days ahead. Do not be afraid in the midst of change.

Great unchanging Jesus, thank You for what You have done for me in the past. You have led me in my earlier life and will also lead on into the future. Deepen my confidence and trust in You. In Your name. Amen.

When are we old?

For reading & meditation – Psalm 92:1–15

'The righteous... will still bear fruit in old age, they will still stay fresh and green' (vv12,14)

We now think about adjustments that we may need to make as 'older adults'. But at what stage of life are we called older adults? One comedian said you know you are at that stage when the candles on your birthday cake cost more than the cake! I personally believe this is not necessarily related to chronological age but a mentality of heart and mind.

However we define this stage, how do we adjust to the inevitable changes? If you have retired or when you retire, don't just stop. The human personality is made for creativity; when it ceases to create, it creaks, cracks and crashes! You may not be as prolific as before but do something, otherwise you will grow tired doing nothing. Get involved in your local community and church. Don't fight the fact of getting older; accept it and use the experience that you have gained.

Sadly as we grow older we are not always so physically robust and may need to be cared for by others. We need to learn to accept this with grace. Whether we are physically able or not, we can still pray and keep our minds active. The brain grows old but the mind can help prolong the vibrancy of the brain by keeping active. Try when possible to keep active. Exercise regularly (but not too strenuously!) and above all else fill your mind with thoughts and prayers from the Bible. Nothing is more wonderful than to be with an older person who has grown older gracefully. Constant companionship with Jesus will do this. Grow older knowing this truth: the best is yet to come.

FURTHER STUDY

Josh. 14:9-14;
Luke 2:25-38;
Titus 2:1-6

1. What was Caleb's attitude like at the age of 85?

2. How can older people contribute to the spiritual wellbeing of the church community?

Lord God, help me to so fill my mind with You that when physical energy fades, inner strength and beauty will take its place. Help me adjust to all change knowing that the best is yet to come.
In Jesus' name. Amen.

When things go wrong

For reading & meditation – 2 Chronicles 7:1–10

'they worshipped and gave thanks to the LORD, saying, "He is good; his love endures for ever."' (v3)

Now we turn our attention to another element that contributes to inner spiritual strength and security: a firm belief in the goodness of God. No soul can experience deep inner peace unless it rests ultimately in the goodness of God. I have written many times before of the impact this statement of Oswald Chambers had on me when I first came across it, but it was such an impact – please permit me to repeat it again: 'The root of sin is the suspicion that God is not good.' You see, up until that time I had always believed that the root of sin was disobedience. Oswald Chambers, with the lucidity that was characteristic of him, saw beyond that; he saw that every action is preceded by a thought, and when a thought contains doubts about the goodness of God then it is easy for sinful behaviour to follow.

FURTHER STUDY

Psa. 107:1–9;
Isa. 63:7–9

1. What is God's very nature?

2. How may this be expressed?

Permit me to repeat: no soul can experience deep inner peace unless it rests ultimately in the goodness of God. If I were to live for a thousand years I doubt if I could say anything more important than that. If you go through life harbouring doubts about the goodness of God then your inner strength and surety will quickly be undermined. Happiness, it has been said, depends on things happening happily. But what about when things don't happen happily? Can we still believe that God is good? If we believe that God is good only when things go our way then when things don't go our way, or God doesn't give us the answer to our prayers that we desire, we will quickly lose our peace and that 'something inside so strong'. And what good is inner strength and security if it depends on circumstances?

Father, help me drop my anchor into the reassuring and encouraging depths of the revelation that You are good. Help me hold this not as a mere opinion but as a conviction. In Jesus' name. Amen.

When Satan talks theology

For reading & meditation – Genesis 3:1–19

'"You will not surely die," the serpent said to the woman.'
(v4)

The aim of the very first temptation was to assassinate the character of God and suggest that He is not good. When Satan, in the form of a serpent, entered the garden in order to tempt Eve, he didn't say: 'Give me a few minutes of your time so that I can damn your soul.' He talked theology. 'Did God really say, "You must not eat from any tree of the garden"?' (v1). The devil knew it was impossible to cast doubt on the existence of God so he attempted to cast doubt on His goodness. His purpose was to put into Eve's mind the thought that if God loved her then He would not have prevented her eating fruit from the tree of knowledge of good and evil (2:17).

FURTHER STUDY

Num. 11:4-9;
Job 2:1-10

1. How did the people despise the goodness of God?

2. Contrast the attitudes of Job and his wife.

Oswald Chambers' said, 'The root of sin is the suspicion that God is not good.' The notion that God is not worthy of our absolute trust lies at the root of many of our problems. From counselling, I have discovered that a lack of confidence in the goodness of God is a major reason why people do not have inner strength and security. Time and time again I have asked Christians who were finding it difficult to cope with problems: 'Is God good?' Many would give the answer they thought was expected of them, but the more honest ones would say: 'I'm not sure.' To believe in the goodness of God when your life has been turned upside down is certainly not easy, but unless we find a way of being convinced of that truth we will not experience the inner strength that is necessary for us to stand up to this world. There can never be deep inner peace and harmony in the soul unless it rests ultimately in the goodness of God.

My Father and my God, I see that this is an issue I must settle once and for all. Help me develop a deep conviction that will keep me buttressed. This I pray in Jesus' name. Amen.

All is well

For reading & meditation – Psalm 34:1–22

'Taste and see that the LORD is good; blessed is the man
who takes refuge in him.' (v8)

Two days ago I wrote that if I were to live for a thousand years, I doubt that I could say anything more important than this: no soul can experience deep inner peace unless it rests ultimately in the goodness of God. And this is the thought I would like us to continue considering.

These meditations were written just after returning from ministering in Nigeria. People struggled to get to the meetings despite all kinds of obstacles and difficulties. For instance, because of a fuel shortage some had to wait at petrol stations for as long as 24 hours – in a few cases even for days. And the traffic jams created by those able to obtain petrol meant that in order to arrive at a meeting on time, people had to set out several hours in advance. Yet in the services I found the Christians calm and composed and ready to laugh. They packed the building in which I was speaking, and at almost every meeting a leader would stand and call out: 'God is good.' The congregation would respond with these words: 'All the time.' Then the leader would take that statement and say questioningly: 'All the time?' Again the congregation would affirm: 'God is good.' One well-known hymn they sang brought tears to my eyes:

FURTHER STUDY

Exod. 14:10-28;
Psa. 36:5-10

1. Contrast the attitudes of Moses and the people.

2. Why can we find refuge in God?

> '*When peace, like a river, attendeth my way,*
> *When sorrows, like sea-billows, roll,*
> *Whatever my lot, Thou hast taught me to say,*
> *It is well, it is well with my soul.*'

**Father, help me live over my circumstances, not under them. Give
me the faith that looks not at the panorama but at a Person – Your
Son Jesus Christ. 'Change and decay in all around I see; O Thou who
changest not, abide with me.' Amen.**

'If not' faith

For reading & meditation – Daniel 3:1–30

'I see four men walking around in the fire...
and the fourth looks like a son of the gods.' (v25)

If God is good then why does He not deliver us from the tribulations we sometimes have to face? Why does He not respond to our requests for His help in escaping from overwhelming sorrows and difficulties? Love and goodness may deny the thing asked for only because there is a wiser and bigger purpose.

Look again at the story of the three Hebrew young men. They said: 'If we are thrown into the blazing furnace, the God we serve is able to save us from it... But even if he does not... we will not serve your gods or worship the image of gold you have set up' (vv17–18). Notice the words: even if he does not. In effect they were saying: 'Even if our confidence in this immediate deliverance is proved false, nevertheless our confidence in the love and goodness and purposes of God will not be destroyed.' They hoped for an immediate rescue, and were sure God could save them from the burning fiery furnace. But their confidence in God did not depend on the outcome of their situation. That is faith.

FURTHER STUDY

2 Cor. 1:3-11;
12:7-10

1. How did suffering deepen Paul's faith?

2. How did he respond to unanswered prayer for healing?

Faith does not depend on a particular thing happening. It is not wrong to hope for it, to long for it, even to pray for it. If you do rest your faith on a particular happening then your faith will increase or decrease according to whether or not that happening takes place. But if your faith is placed in the character of God and His goodness then it will remain constant whether what you long for happens or not. The faith that says, 'I believe God,' is good. Better by far, however, is the faith that says: 'But even if He does not do it, I will still believe He is good.'

Help me, my Father, to trust Your goodness even when I cannot trace it. I rest not in the immediate but in the Ultimate – in You. The last word is always spoken by You, and that last word is always good. I am so thankful. Amen.

A loving hand on the helm

For reading & meditation – Isaiah 30:1–18

'in quietness and trust is your strength' (v15)

In 1987 a now notorious severe storm hit the British Isles, and not far from my home a whole row of beautiful trees was brought down. A local paper interviewed a tree specialist and asked him why those particular trees were uprooted when others nearby were not. This was his reply: 'The water in that area was too near the surface and so the trees did not have to put their roots down deep to find water; hence the tragedy.' It is a parable. Sometimes God denies us a shallow answer in order that we may put our roots deeper into eternal reality, and consequently stand tall and strong in any future storm. A person with the inner strength of which we are speaking expressed it like this:

Nothing that happens can hurt me.
Whether I lose or win.
Though life may be changed on the surface,
I do my main living within.'

FURTHER STUDY

Rom. 8:28-39;
2 Cor. 4:11-18

1. What is our confidence?

2. Where did Paul look?

A wise Welsh preacher I knew used to say: 'We must learn to live in time and eternity simultaneously.' If the time side of life seems to be full of trouble then the eternity side holds us steady. When a missionary to the Chinese people was asked for the secret of his peace and inner strength he answered: 'Confidence in the goodness of God.' Pressed to expand on that statement, he added: 'I have come to the place in my Christian life where I am convinced that in the midst of the worst thing that can happen there is a good and wise purpose at work. Thus I can go on, knowing that love is at the helm of my life. God loves me too much to let anything happen to me that will not work out for good.' In the words that Moffatt uses to translate our text for today: 'Your strength is quiet faith.'

Father, I too rest in the ultimate, not in the immediate. In You I am impregnable. I view the panorama of life in quiet confidence, knowing that a loving hand is at the helm of my affairs. I trust You and rejoice in Your goodness. Amen.

Made for worship

For reading & meditation – Job 1:6–22

'At this, Job got up and tore his robe and shaved his head.
Then he fell to the ground in worship' (v20)

Maintaining our belief that God is good is not easy. It's easy
enough when the sun is shining and everything is going
well, but what about when God allows a tragedy to overtake you?
Can you say with deep conviction at such times: 'Yes, God is good'?
Many Christians still utter the words, but without conviction.

In the passage we have read today Job is presented to us as a
fabulously wealthy and successful man, the father of a large and
happy family. Then all at once, like a bolt out of the blue, tidings
of disaster come crashing in upon him. Hot on the
heels of one another come the messengers of woe.
The reports are desolating. His oxen and donkeys are
gone, his sheep and camels are gone, his servants are
gone, his sons and daughters are gone. With a single
stroke he is bereft of almost everything. But think of
the moral splendour of this: Job, hearing the numbing
news, falls down on the ground and worships.

FURTHER STUDY

2 Sam. 12:15-23;
Job 13:15

1. What was
David's
response when
his child died?

2. What was
Job's ultimate
statement
of faith?

Another observation I have made is that those who
struggle with the idea that God is good find it difficult
to truly worship. Whenever I have been aware that
a person was struggling with the matter of God's goodness I have
asked: 'What does the word "worship" mean to you?' Some have
not responded, afraid that God would be angry with them if they
replied in the negative; others have been more forthright and said:
'Not a great deal.' After all, how can you worship a God in whom
you do not have confidence? Any conflict concerning the goodness
of God must be resolved, for while it remains it will be impossible
to truly worship. And worship is what we were made for.

**Father God, if I have any doubts that interfere with my worship of
You then show me how they can be dissolved. You made me for
worship, designed me for praise. Help me become what You planned
me to be – a true worshipper. Amen.**

No apologies

For reading & meditation – Psalm 86:1–17

'You are forgiving and good, O Lord, abounding in love to all who call to you.' (v5)

Yesterday we began to explore that it is not always easy to believe in the goodness of God when tragedy arrives on our doorstep. Rabbi Kushner, the author of the bestselling book *When Bad Things Happen to Good People*, tried to resolve this problem when his 19-year-old son died of a dreadful disease that had made him look like an old man of 90. The rabbi, wanting to believe that God is good, but unable to reconcile that fact with the death of his son, came to this conclusion: 'God is good, but sin has so upset His universe that although He longs to intervene and stop bad things happening, He is largely powerless to do so.'

That idea gave him some consolation, and it is easy to see why his book became a bestseller. And yet I cannot accept his explanation, however comfortable it may feel, because we are taught in Scripture not only that God is good, but that He is all-powerful also. The presence of sin in His universe has not blunted His power one iota. What He was He is, and what He is He was, and what He is and was He ever will be – all-powerful, all-knowing and ever-present. Christians are called to take God on trust, to believe that He allows bad things to happen not because He is powerless to prevent them but because a sovereign purpose is at work that we, in our present state, cannot comprehend.

FURTHER STUDY

Gen. 45:4-8; 50:15-21; Acts 7:54-8:3; 26:12-18

1. How did Joseph see his misfortunes?

2. What sovereign purpose was at work when Stephen was martyred?

Nowhere in the Bible does God ever apologise for allowing what we call tragedies or disasters to occur. Instead, He asks us to trust Him, to believe that 'in all things God works for the good of those who love him' (Rom. 8:28).

God, I know that You want me to trust You when I cannot trace You. Help me, dear Father, to do just that – to believe in Your goodness even when seemingly bad things happen in my life. In the name of Your precious Son Jesus I pray. Amen.

The one safe place

For reading & meditation – Psalm 106:1–12

'Give thanks to the LORD, for he is good; his love endures
for ever.' (v1)

How do we go about building confidence in a God who allows bad things to happen to good people, and to do it in a way that is in complete accord with Scripture? I know of only one way – to gaze upon the cross. Theologians throughout the ages have asserted that the cross is the one fixed point in the universe where God's character is made clear. In my own life I have experienced a number of tragedies, and I have stood by the side of countless others as they have gone through personal afflictions. Always the cross has held us steady.

FURTHER STUDY

Rom. 5:1–11;
Col. 2:13–15

1. What is the
ultimate proof
of God's love
and goodness?

2. How can the
tragedy of the
cross be a place
of triumph?

A number of years ago I stood in St James' Church in Cape Town, shortly after the congregation had been subjected to an attack from terrorists who sprayed the worshippers with bullets and threw hand grenades into their midst. A number were killed and some seriously maimed. My heart was sick as I saw volunteers in the church trying to remove the blood stains from the floor, and I remember wondering how God could let this happen. The clergyman in charge of the church, Bishop Frank Retief, invited my colleagues and myself to pray and, as we prayed, my thoughts went to the cross. Once again I reminded myself, as I had done so many times before, that a God who gave His Son to die for me on Calvary just has to be good. That is where I stand whenever I am tempted to question God's goodness – I stand at the cross. There the matter of God's goodness has been validated for all time, and in the light that comes from the cross I am able to make my way in the darkness.

**My Father and my God, whenever I am tempted to doubt Your
goodness help me to take my stand at the foot of the cross for there,
in its light, I see light. In Jesus' name. Amen.**

Give thanks

For reading & meditation – Matthew 15:29–39

'Then he took the seven loaves and the fish, and when he had given thanks, he broke them and gave them' (v36)

Another characteristic of those who possess a deep inner spiritual strength is a thankful heart. 'So far as thanksgiving is concerned,' said Dr W.E. Sangster, 'the mass of people can be divided into two classes: those who take things for granted, and those who take things with gratitude.' I wonder to which group you belong?

In the book Ten Golden Rules for Financial Success, Gary Moore gives this as the first rule: count your blessings. In that chapter he talks about Sir John Templeton, a financier and a philanthropist, who gave millions of pounds away each year to people all over the world. Sir John, he says, followed this principle in his life: every morning when he woke he lay still on his bed and thought of five things for which he could be thankful. He believed that until you can recognise the good things that are going on around you, you do not have a proper basis for handling life. At this point you might say: 'It was all right for Sir John Templeton with all that wealth, but what about me? I have to struggle to make ends meet.' If that is your reaction, it is my hope that over these next few days you will begin to focus not so much on what you don't have but on what you do have.

FURTHER STUDY

Deut. 8:6-18;
Luke 17:11-19

1. How may we
be deceived
into not being
thankful?

2. Why can
thankfulness
and gratitude
be forgotten?

Before Jesus took the loaves and fish and handed them to the disciples He gave thanks. Jesus made it a practice to thank God for His goodness in all things. He was constantly giving thanks. And so can we.

My Father and my God, I want to join the ranks of those who take things with gratitude. Help me cultivate a thankful and praising heart; teach me how to count my blessings. In Jesus' name. Amen.

Count your blessings

For reading & meditation – Psalm 147:1–20

'Sing to the LORD with thanksgiving; make music
to our God on the harp.' (v7)

Many people begin their day by turning on the radio and listening to announcers telling them what is wrong with the world. Sir John Templeton believed that for every problem we face we will find ten blessings if we look for them. But such is our crass human nature that we are more often drawn to bad, rather than good, news.

Newspapers generally bring to our attention the worst in life. An editor told me: 'There is something in human nature that makes people buy a newspaper that has the most horrible or sensational headlines. Bad news sells newspapers much better than good news.' How sad that so many are not sufficiently independent to realise that for every problem in the world there are, as Sir John Templeton said, ten blessings.

FURTHER STUDY

Psa. 136:1-26

1. Consider how God is praised for each detail of provision.

2. What is the constant memorable refrain? Take time to meditate on it.

Some time ago I talked to a Christian man who was obviously blessed with an inner spiritual strength, and I put to him the idea that one of the characteristics of spiritually secure people is that they have a thankful and praising heart. 'I have never thought of it before,' he said, 'but hardly an hour goes by without my heart rising in praise and gratitude to God for something or other.' 'What things?' I asked. After pausing briefly he said: 'Things like the fertile earth, my five senses, a measure of health, an unimpaired reason, the love of my family, the song of the birds, the laughter of children...' On and on he went. Do you thank God for the common blessings that can so easily be overlooked? Don't wait until you lose them to be grateful.

God, forgive me if I go through the day overlooking the common blessings of life. Help me develop keen sight so that I do not miss one of the multiplicity of Your benefits to me. Give me a thankful heart, dear Lord. In Jesus' name. Amen.

Don't miss the mercies

For reading & meditation – Colossians 3:1–17

'Let the peace of Christ rule in your hearts...
And be thankful.' (v15)

We ended yesterday with the thought that we ought not to wait until we lose the blessings of life to be grateful. Most of us enjoy the blessing of unimpaired reason. Do we thank God for that? Look around you today. Think of such things as the wonder of the universe, the fact that the sun rises and sets with mathematical precision, that the stars stay on their courses and so on. Yes, there are storms and famines and natural disasters (we cannot deny them), but when all things are considered, there is more to be thankful for than to mourn over.

FURTHER STUDY

Eph. 2:1-10;
Heb. 4:14-16

1. What is the greatest mercy of God we can be thankful for?

2. How do we obtain mercy?

A thankful and praising heart is one of the biggest barriers against reactive depression. Those who are quick to note the good things that happen (not just the bad) and focus on them seem to better withstand melancholy and despondency. This isn't to say that feelings of depression or low mood never overtake them, but they seem to know how to deal with them better by focusing and thinking more about the good than the bad.

It is not always easy, of course, to give thanks. How can you thank God for cancer, for example? As one who has experienced a battle with this disease, I can say that though one cannot thank God for cancer, there are many mercies surrounding it for which one can be thankful: the fact that God does not desert us at times of illness, the tenderness and concern of those who give medical attention, the love and encouragement of others and so on. There are mercies to be found at the heart of tragedies. Look for the mercies and be thankful for them.

Father, forgive me that so often I look for the tragedies and miss the mercies. I cannot ignore the bad things that happen, but help me not to dwell on them. I will start today to count not the bad things but the blessings. Amen.

'When did I ever fail thee?'

For reading & meditation – Psalm 103:1–22

'Praise the LORD, O my soul, and forget not all his benefits' (v2)

St Teresa of Avila was depressed one day. It seems she had forgotten the many deliverances and blessings that God had given her. In the midst of her darkness God came to her and said: 'When did I ever fail thee? I am today what I have always been.' Her depression quickly lifted and her heart was filled with praise.

Recently I read about a diligent man who used to note carefully in a book the blessings he received from God – the special blessings. On the last day of the year he would count them all. Often they

FURTHER STUDY

Deut. 32:15–18;
Psa. 105:1–15

1. When did
Israel abandon
and forget God?

2. How is God's
memory greater
than ours?

numbered thousands. If you too make a practice of noting the blessings of God that come either directly or indirectly from Him then I guarantee a new buoyancy will flow into your spirit. Perhaps you find it difficult to think of present blessings because you are engulfed in trouble. Then think of the blessings of the past. One great preacher said: 'God never gives a blessing just for the present, but for the future.' By that he meant a present blessing is a pledge of future

blessing. It is as though God says: 'I will do this for you now so that you will always know you are the object of my love.'

It's so sad that we forget the blessings of God so easily. That is why new dangers cause fear and uncertainty – we have forgotten past mercies. We would be calm and confident in present trouble if we remembered the deliverances that have already taken place. We would say to ourselves: 'The God who delivered me then will not desert me now.' John Newton, the slave trader who became a preacher and hymn writer, was assured of this: 'His love in time past forbids me to think He'll leave me at last in trouble to sink.'

Father, forgive me that I forget so soon past blessings and mercies. This is why I am fearful in the midst of trouble. I have a loving Father in heaven. Help me to remember that You are today what You have always been. In Jesus' name. Amen.

Watch the difference

For reading & meditation – James 1:1–18

'Every good and perfect gift is... from the Father of the heavenly lights, who does not change' (v17)

'**O**ne of the worst moments for an atheist,' said a preacher, 'is when he feels thankful for something that strikes him in creation – a beautiful sunset perhaps – and has no one to thank.' You are not in that position. As a Christian, you are able to give thanks for the blessings knowing, as James tells us in today's text, that they come 'from the Father of the heavenly lights'. To have a heart that traces 'every good and perfect gift' back to its source – a loving heavenly Father – is a great benefit.

The psalmist says: 'It is a good thing to give thanks unto the LORD (Psa. 92:1, KJV). Why is it? First, it keeps us oriented to the Highest, and cultivates an awareness that we maintain our existence on this earth not as a right but by the love of God. Second, it helps us conserve the concept of reverence without which every mortal mind is deficient. It reminds us who is in charge. Third, it preserves a sense of happiness and goodwill. Someone who has developed a spirit of thankfulness will face life buoyantly and confidently because they are conscious of the mercies that flow from heaven. The great preacher Charles Haddon Spurgeon said: 'It is a delightful and profitable occupation to mark the hand of God in the lives of His ancient saints and to observe His goodness in delivering them, but would it not be more interesting and profitable for us to notice the hand of God in our own lives?' Start every day by thinking of five things for which you can be thankful – and watch the difference in your days.

FURTHER STUDY

Psa. 92:1-8;
Phil. 4:4-7

1. Contrast the thankful and senseless man.

2. How can we experience God's peace?

Lord Jesus, how can it be that I have arrived at this stage of my life and have not cultivated a thankful heart? Now things must change. Help me start every day with thanksgiving. For Your own dear name's sake I pray.

Giving back to God

For reading & meditation – 2 Samuel 23:8–17

'But he refused to drink it; instead, he poured it out before the LORD.' (v16)

Today's passage records an incident that took place when David was repelling an attack by his old enemies the Philistines – a campaign described in 2 Samuel 5:17–25. Once the whole of Israel – the northern tribes as well as Judah – had accepted David as king, the Philistines attempted to isolate Judah. One day David looked out across the valley towards Bethlehem, the town where he grew up. No doubt feeling thirsty, he thought of the well at which he had often drunk. 'Oh, that someone would get me a drink of water from the well near the gate of Bethlehem!' he cried (v15). Quick as a flash three of his trusted men – 'mighty men' says Scripture – raced through the Philistine lines to the well, scooped up a flask of its clear water and returned safely to David's side. Stunned and amazed by their devotion and their costly gift, David accepted it, then poured it out on the ground in thanksgiving to God. How did the three mighty men react to this, I wonder? They would have understood, I think, that David's action was triggered not by a lack of appreciation but out of a deep desire to give something that was so precious to him back to God. It may also have been reminiscent for them of Jacob's drink offering (Gen. 35:14).

FURTHER STUDY

Gen. 22:3-14;
1 Chron.
29:10-20

1. What did Abraham offer God, and what was His response?

2. What did David acknowledge about his offering?

What gifts of love does God have in store for you today? The sudden smile of a friend you might meet unexpectedly, good news from someone far away, a gift of money perhaps. Will your heart rise in thanks to God for that?

Father, I echo that prayer in my own heart: what will You give me today that I might offer back to You in thanksgiving, in praise and adoration? Help me not to miss one single thing. In Jesus' name. Amen.

'No occasion to be thankful?'

For reading & meditation – Psalm 100:1–5
'Enter his gates with thanksgiving and his courts
with praise' (v4)

It was during the 1930s, when America was in a terrible economic depression, that the Association for the Advancement of Atheism raised a public protest against the President making the customary Thanksgiving Proclamation. Atheistic propagandists said: 'In a country where people are jobless, and farmers are marketless, and fields lie blistering without rain, there is no occasion to be thankful.' No occasion to be thankful? How short-sighted! These atheists obviously had no awareness of the air they breathed, or the light by which they saw, the love and laughter of children, the kiss of devotion from the lips of a mother or wife or the nobler qualities that suffering and loss seem to provoke.

FURTHER STUDY

Psa. 104:1–24,
32–34

1. What common things can we thank God for?

2. How can thankfulness affect us?

Even belief in the fall of man does not save one from amazement and shame at the myopic view many people have of the world around them. If we pause and reflect, we can find numerous causes for thankfulness – both small and large. I have come to the conclusion that one of the reasons why people can't thank God for the special blessings of life is because they fail to see Him in the common blessings of life – the gentle warmth of the sun, the first cry of a baby, the wonderful variety of food produced by the earth...

C.S. Lewis suggested that we 'shall not be able to adore God on the highest occasions if we have learned no habit of doing so on the lowest.' Miss out on the common things and you are likely to miss out on the bigger things. I hope you have already started to do this – to look out for things for which you can be thankful. And now that you have started the habit, keep your eyes and heart open.

Father God, there are some habits I would like to get rid of, but this is a habit I want to keep. Help me develop an eye that notices the good things of life, recognises them for what they are and gives thanks for them. Amen.

God's agents of blessing

For reading & meditation – 1 Timothy 2:1–11

'I urge, then, first of all, that... thanksgiving be made for everyone' (v1)

For one last day we meditate on the importance of cultivating a thankful heart. We should, however, make a practice not only of thanking God for His goodness but of thanking those also by whose hand His blessings come. When you say 'thank you' to someone who has been a channel of blessing to you it is amazing how much you will do for them as well as for yourself.

This story is one I have used before, but it so moving that it is worth repeating. It concerns a Methodist minister by the name of William Stidger of the School of Theology in Boston, Massachusetts. One day he began to think of the blessings God had given him throughout his life. As he did so, there came to mind the lady who had taught him in his first years at school. This lady had put a love of all things good in him, and so he wrote her a letter of thanks. This is the reply he received, written in a feeble script: 'My dear Willie, I cannot tell you how much your note meant to me. I am in my eighties, living alone in a small room, cooking my own meals, lonely, and, like the last leaf of autumn, lingering behind. You will be interested to know that I taught in school for forty years and yours is the first note of appreciation I ever received. It came on a cold blue morning and it cheered me as nothing has in many years.' Stidger was not sentimental, but he wept over that note.

Need I say more? God likes to be thanked, and He likes His people to be thanked also. Those with inner spiritual strength will have, among other things, a thankful heart. Ask God if there is someone that you could write to today to thank for being a blessing in your life.

FURTHER STUDY

Rom. 16:1-16;
1 Thess. 5:16-18

1. Who did Paul give thanks for and why?
2. What is God's will for us?

God, I feel sad when I think of the number of times I have failed to thank those through whom Your blessings have come into my life. From now on I must be more sensitive and alert. Help me dear Father. In Jesus' name. Amen.

Keep your balance

For reading & meditation – Mark 12:28–34

'Love your neighbour as yourself.' (v31)

We come now to another feature that is evident in those whose lives have 'something inside so strong': a loving and generous spirit. We are to love our neighbour as ourselves. The apostle Paul in Philippians gives a similar instruction: 'Each of you should look not only to your own interests, but also to the interests of others' (Phil. 2:4). Notice the word 'also'. Moffatt translates the verse like this: 'each with an eye to the interests of others as well as to his own.' As well as – here the two sets of interests are exactly balanced again.

The text before us today is one of the most misunderstood. Generally it is interpreted in this way: 'It is no good trying to love others until you love yourself. What you must do is to concentrate on loving yourself and then you will be able to love others better.' But what Jesus is saying here is that our concern for our own welfare is natural and should be matched by our concern for others. Don't we all like to have a good home, a happy home, a healthy home? Then seek that for others. Don't we all like to satisfy our hunger and thirst? Then be equally keen to feed those who are hungry but are unable to find food or feed themselves. In this verse Jesus is not commanding love, but presupposing it.

Everyone desires what they think is right and good for them, and this universal trait becomes the rule by which our attitude to others is to be measured. The challenge is not to love ourselves – we do that – but to have the same regard for others that we have for ourselves. Self-interest and other-interest are to balance.

FURTHER STUDY

Luke 10:25–37; 16:19–22

1. Why might we ignore the needs of others?

2. How was the rich man's life out of balance?

Father, enable me to get this straight because I so easily become unbalanced. May self-regard and other-regard be balanced as perfectly as possible. I need Your help in achieving this. Thank You, my Father, that I can count on Your help. Amen.

Self-love versus love of self

For reading & meditation – Romans 12:1–8

'Do not think of yourself more highly than you ought, but rather think of yourself with sober judgment.' (v3)

Yesterday's text, 'Love your neighbour as yourself' (Mark 12:31) is a pivotal one, and so we spend another day exploring it. The Old Testament contains close to 200 references that stress the need to have concern for one's neighbour, but it was Jesus who put the emphasis on loving your neighbour 'as yourself'. It is interesting that several New Testament writers pick up on this, two of them (Paul and James) quoting Jesus' words verbatim (Rom. 13:9; Gal. 5:14; James 2:8).

FURTHER STUDY

John 3:16–17;
1 Cor. 13:1–13

1. What motivates God?

2. How does Paul show true love to be other centred?

We should differentiate between two things, however: self-love and love of self. Self-love is positive, love of self is problematic. How often have you heard one person say of another: 'He/she loves him/herself too much'? What they are referring to are the characteristics of conceit, narcissism, arrogance or self-centredness that they observe in that individual. That is love of self – therefore unhealthy. Self-love is different; it regards the self as important and in need of proper attention, but not all-important – therefore healthy. But what about people who seem not to have a healthy regard for themselves? These people may have been wounded or scarred by various life events and could benefit from the help of a counsellor to gain a balanced sense of their worth.

It's all too easy for self-love to pass over into love of self. We need always to be on our guard, as Scripture warns us in today's text, so that we maintain the right balance. A question well worth considering as you go through the day is this: Is the love I have for myself a healthy self-love or an unhealthy love of self?

Help me, Lord, to evaluate myself and discover whether I am governed by self-love or love of self. I would be a healthy person – not thinking of myself too highly, nor too lowly either. Enable me to live like this. In Jesus' name. Amen.

You are what you think

For reading & meditation – Romans 12:9–21

'Love must be sincere.' (v9)

A lack of self-love may have roots in our childhood. Often it's the case that the way others regard us, especially in our developmental years, becomes the way in which we regard ourselves. If others have looked upon you as worthless, you may well have developed the same estimation of yourself. Importantly, however, often it is not people's actual estimation of us that has formed the building blocks for our self-concept, but what we consider to be their evaluation. Someone has summed it up like this: 'I am not what I think I am; I am not what you think I am; I am what I think you think I am.' Got it? The regard you have for yourself is the result of what you thought others thought about you.

People with a strong sense of spiritual assurance and the 'something inside so strong' we have been talking about are people with a clear sense of identity; they have a healthy sense of self-love and are comfortable with themselves. They have a strong base from which they can give love to others, and so they love in a non-manipulative way. They regard others in the same way that they regard themselves, and what they desire for themselves they desire for others also; they give as much time and attention to the needs of others as they give to their own wants and desires.

If you don't have a healthy sense of self-love then you will give out love in order to get love back. Your love will have strings attached to it. But how do we come to a balanced view of self-love if it has been blocked? Find out tomorrow.

FURTHER STUDY

Titus 3:3-7;
Luke 5:1-11

1. What does God think of you, even at your worst?

2. How did Simon view himself?

**Father, I sense I am on the verge of a breakthrough. Hold me close as I face the challenge of being the person You want me to be. I long for it with all my heart. Lead on dear Father. I will follow.
In Jesus' name. Amen.**

Crazy for you

For reading & meditation – 1 John 4:7–21

'This is love: not that we loved God, but that he loved us and sent his Son as an atoning sacrifice for our sins.' (v10)

I f you do not have a healthy sense of self-love, how do you go about developing it? A lack of self-love is often found to have its roots in relational difficulties. If you think or believe no one loves you, you may well conclude that you are not worth loving. Yet just as lack of self-love lies in relationships, so also does the restoration and resolution. It begins with coming to terms with the reality that no matter how deprived of love you may have felt before, Jesus has a love for you that is unconditional, perfect and will never be taken away.

FURTHER STUDY

2 Sam. 9:1-13;
Luke 7:36-50

1. What did Mephibosheth think of himself?

2. How does Jesus think of us differently?

For some, the fact that God loves them frequently needs reinforcing. When people struggle with this, it's often due to misunderstanding the true nature and character of God. A caricatured image and misinterpretation of the compassionate Father heart of God is somehow developed, and consequently people shy away from the vulnerability of opening their wounded hearts and lives to God for fear of being further hurt. We know that 'We love because he first loved us.' (v19) As we open our hearts to receive from God, His love flows in and turns the machinery of our souls and fans the flames of love and we, in response to His love, love Him in return. We love in response to His good and perfect unconditional love. What do you think God thinks about you? Let me tell you. He's crazy about you! Inscribe our text for today on your heart. Meditate on it. You are loved. This is where it begins: a progressive journey that will grow in confidence and trust. Just like any other relationship, it needs investment and nurture to grow strong and healthy.

Father God, give me the courage and trust to be open to receive Your love. Make today an unforgettable day. Help me to walk not just in my head's knowledge but in my heart, in a new and fresh revelation of Your love for me today. Amen.

Generosity that generates

For reading & meditation – Matthew 6:19–24

'The eye is the lamp of the body. If your eyes are good,
your whole body will be full of light.' (v22)

For two more days we reflect on the thought that those with 'something inside so strong' are people with a loving, generous spirit. It is interesting that some Bible translators substitute the word 'generosity' for 'goodness' in the list of fruits of the Spirit given in Galatians 5:22–23, J.B. Phillips being one of them. I find it interesting, too, that Moffatt translates our text for today in this way: 'The eye is the lamp of the body: so, if your Eye is generous, the whole of your body will be illumined.'

To think of the word 'good' or 'goodness' in terms of generosity gives us a new perspective. The eye is our outlook on life, our whole way of looking at things, and when our eye is generous then our whole personality is illumined – lit up. 'The generous eye and the generous attitude,' said one preacher, 'are at the basis of all sound relationships, for no relationship can develop unless there is generosity on both sides.'

FURTHER STUDY
John 1:35–39;
Acts 3:1–10

1. How did Jesus display generous hospitality?

2. How did Jesus generate a generous attitude in His disciples?

Jesus was generous towards everyone and because of His generosity His whole personality was full of light. When He is allowed to generate His generosity within us – when we begin to see everything through His generous eyes – then similarly our whole being is flooded with light. I shared this thought with a friend some time ago and, after pausing for a moment, he said: 'His generous eye saw in me what I couldn't see, and it has generated generosity in me towards others.' This comment, I think, is one of the most beautiful I have ever heard. Always remember that the generous eye fills the whole body with light.

**Heavenly Father, help me make generosity the basis of all my
dealings with everyone I meet today. And not just today but every
day. Help me be the channel, not the stopping place, of Your
generosity. In Jesus' name I ask it. Amen.**

The most famous colt

For reading & meditation – Luke 19:28–44

'its owners asked them, 'Why are you untying the colt?'
They replied, "The Lord needs it."' (vv33–34)

After the disciples had told the owners of the colt that features in the story we have read today, 'The Lord needs it,' suppose they had replied: 'No, He can't have it. We need it too.' For the rest of their life they would have most certainly regretted it. Later, I imagine, they realised that they had provided a service for the Master, and that their colt was the most famous colt in history.

Suppose, also, that the little boy who figures so prominently in the story of the feeding of the 5,000 had hidden his loaves and fish from the disciples. He and the crowd would have missed out on one of the most sensational miracles Jesus initiated (see John 6:1–13). And imagine how different the story would have been if the disciples, when they realised the loaves and fish that Jesus had blessed were being multiplied, had told the crowd: 'This is not a free lunch; you have to pay for it.' The miracle of multiplication would have come to an end.

FURTHER STUDY
Acts 4:32–37;
2 Cor. 8:1–15

1. How were the members of the Early Church generous to one another?

2. What tests the sincerity of our love and faith?

From what we have been saying, I hope it is quite clear that when we are generous with others, we ourselves are blessed. We guard against being generous in order that we might gain a blessing – that would be putting self ahead of others. We are generous because it is the right thing to do. Meanness ought not to characterise the children of a God whose magnanimity and large-heartedness is so wonderfully displayed both in Scripture and in creation. Be a generous person and, as night follows day, your inner strength will increase and you will be naturalised in generosity.

Father, I am making the decision right now that my approach will be one of generosity. Help me find the good, further the good and do good in everything. I want to become naturalised in generosity. In Jesus' name. Amen.

Life holds no shipwreck

For reading & meditation – Acts 28:1–10

'When this had happened, the rest of the sick on the island came and were cured.' (v9)

We have now reached the last day on the theme 'standing strong'. At the beginning we asked: can we realise God within us in such a way that no matter what happens on the outside we will remain strong and secure on the inside?

Jesus had a core inner strength, and He passed it on to His early disciples. Take Paul, for example. When testifying before King Agrippa, he said: 'I pray God that… all who are listening to me today may become what I am, except for these chains' (Acts 26:29). Not one word of self-pity – pity only for those who did not share his inner composure. Paul's inner strength was also very evident when the ship on which he was sailing was about to be wrecked in a severe storm. 'Keep up your courage, men,' he instructed, 'for I have faith in God that it will happen just as he told me' (Acts 27:25). Soon after he had spoken these words Paul the prisoner took charge, gave the sailors orders and saved himself and the whole company. Later, after they had been shipwrecked on Malta, he healed all those on the island who were ill.

FURTHER STUDY

Psa. 56:1-13;
1 Tim. 1:12-19

1. What was the cause of the psalmist's hope and inner strength?

2. What were the reasons for Paul's transformation?

The inner strength that Jesus displayed was shared not only by Paul but also by all Jesus' disciples. The Early Church was filled with men and women who had 'something inside so strong'. But can we share it in this age too? Is it for some and not for others? With all my heart I say there are divine reinforcements available for all who give their lives to God. Life holds no shipwreck that need leave us a wreck. Together with God we can stand strong in the storm.

Father, I am about to move on to other themes and other spiritual lessons. But help me not to forget what I have learned. Stay close to me and help me build into my life every one of the principles I have been considering. Amen.

Bringing Down Giants

David - the giant-killer

For reading & meditation – 1 Samuel 17:1–58

'The LORD... will deliver me from the hand of this Philistine.'
(v37)

Over the next couple of months we will look closely at some of the things that may be standing in our way as we seek to move on with God and enter into all the fullness of Christ. I have chosen to refer to issues that hamper our spiritual growth and discipleship as 'giants', because of the way in which they loom over us and intimidate us. Giants often appear intimidating and threatening and can strike fear into the hearts of those who have to confront them. Take, for instance, the well-known story of David's encounter with the giant Goliath, which we have read today.

FURTHER STUDY

1 Sam. 5:1-4;
Heb. 11:32-34

1. What happened when the Philistine god met the ark?

2. How did David overcome the giant?

Day after day Goliath paraded along the slopes of the Valley of Elah, bellowing out challenges to the Israelites. Over 9 feet tall and clad in armour that weighed about 125 pounds, he must have presented a fearsome figure. His war cries boomed across the valley with alarming regularity – every morning and evening for 40 days – but no one in the camp of Israel felt able or equipped to accept his challenge. However, on to the scene came a young shepherd boy by the name of David. He could not believe the way his fellow Israelites – God's chosen people – allowed themselves to be intimidated by Goliath. You know the outcome. With a sling, a small stone and a mighty confidence in God, the young shepherd boy ended the giant's reign of fear and intimidation once and for all.

Are there any 'giants' looming large on the horizon right now? The chances are some are intimidating you at this very moment. Together let's set out to quieten them once and for all.

**My Father and my God, with the sling of faith, the stone of truth
and the strength that lies in Your mighty name, I set out today to do
battle with all the 'giants' that loom large in my life. May I end the
year in glorious victory. Amen.**

The Spirit's expertise

For reading & meditation – 2 Corinthians 10:1–18
'The weapons we fight with are not the weapons of the world.' (v4)

O ne thing must be clear before we set out to identify some of the 'giants' that stand on the horizon of our lives and eclipse the Son. And that one thing is this: we overcome not through any special formulas or techniques but by trusting in the name of the living God.

We live in a day when people seem to be turning more and more to literature on self-help and psychology for methods of dealing with the problems that invade their lives. King Saul, you

FURTHER STUDY
1 Sam. 16:1–13;
Eph. 6:10–17
1. What was different about David?
2. What are the weapons of our warfare?

remember from the passage we read yesterday, set out to dress David in his armour. The young shepherd boy must have looked somewhat comical in Saul's coat of mail and helmet. He wasn't used to moving around dressed like that. It just didn't feel right. He was far more comfortable with a sling, a stone and a steadfast trust in God. David's greatest defence was his inner shield of faith. It kept him cool and composed in the midst of the greatest danger.

But don't run away with the idea that because David slew Goliath with just one stone set in a sling, slaying a giant is a simple matter. It requires trust, dedication, discipline and skill. The weapons of our warfare, as Scripture says, may not be carnal, but they are weapons nevertheless and are effective only in the hands of dedicated disciples. Using the sling of faith and the stone of truth is less cumbersome than wielding a sword, a club or a spear, but it requires just as much practice. The resulting expertise, however, is born not of the flesh but of the Spirit.

Almighty God, help me to understand this truth that the weapons of the Spirit must be handled with precision and expertise. Give me that expertise. In Jesus' name. Amen.

'The Spectre on the Brocken'

Today I want to pull out the files and look at the 'mug shot' of the first 'giant' that intimidates so many of us – fear. Is this giant looming large on the horizon of your life at the moment? Is its frightening appearance making your life a misery? Hold fast. Don't run. And don't dress up in Saul's armour either. Instead, let's together learn some of the spiritual principles that must be put into operation if the giant of fear is to be slain.

Before we look at these principles, however, consider this: some fears have no basis in reality. They are as unsubstantial as the 'The Spectre on the Brocken'. The Brocken is the highest peak of the Hartz mountains in Germany. For centuries it was rumoured by people who lived in the valley below that a giant lived on the summit. Credible witnesses swore they had seen him. But with the advance of learning, people grew sceptical and began a careful investigation. They found that the 'giant' was seen only at sunrise or sunset (when the sun's rays are almost horizontal), and when the Brocken itself was free of cloud but the neighbouring peaks were covered with mist. Before long they realised what was happening. The ghostly and terrifying spectre that people saw on the peak was nothing but a magnified and distorted image of themselves. They were trembling at their own reflection.

Some of our fears are like that. They are not real – simply the result of an unhealthy imagination. So take time to look over your fears. You will find that most fears – yes most fears – exist only in the imagination.

FURTHER STUDY

Matt. 14:25–36;
17:1–8

1. Why was the disciples' fear false?

2. Why might we be afraid of God?

Father, I am so grateful that I need not live in intimidation. I can be free from fear. Help me sweep all litter from my mind that it may be Your dwelling place. And Yours alone. In Jesus' name I pray. Amen.

No false remedies

For reading & meditation – Isaiah 31:1–9

'Woe to those who go down to Egypt for help... but do not look to the Holy One of Israel' (v1)

Fear has many faces: fear of failure, fear of rejection, fear of meeting new people, fear of heights, fear of enclosed spaces, fear of thunder and lightning, fear of unemployment, fear of financial reversal, fear of the future, fear of dying – and even fear of fear itself! Fear, we must understand, is different from anxiety. Often we equate the two but strictly speaking they are different emotions. Anxiety is a vague and unspecified apprehension; fear usually has a specific object.

FURTHER STUDY

Psa. 20:1–9;
Eph. 5:15–20

1. Contrast how people try to overcome fear.

2. What was Paul's advice?

We saw yesterday that the first step in dealing with fear is to look over your fears and separate the real from the imaginary. Next, we decide to resist all unbiblical routes taken to get rid of fear. No dressing up in Saul's armour. What are some of the less helpful routes people go down in an attempt to rid themselves of their fears? One is alcohol. They get drunk to forget or run away from their fears. But the following morning, when the effects of the alcohol have worn off, the fears are all back. Another route taken to escape fear is overeating. Food can be exceedingly comforting and induces pleasant physical sensations that can mask the effects of fear.

However, every diversion, whether it is drink, overeating, illicit sex, gambling or entertainment, are cul-de-sacs – dead ends. They lead only to deeper difficulty. So make up your mind not to take any quick-fix routes to escape fear. No subterfuge can ever be a refuge. We need to close unhealthy doors so that the right one is more obvious. When we see the right door – towards Jesus – we can then walk boldly through it into release.

Father, help me not to take a road with a dead end when trying to deal with my fears. May I decide to trust You with my life knowing that I need no false remedies. I need You, Father. And only You. Amen.

Open-eyed honesty

For reading & meditation – 1 Peter 4:1–11

'be clear minded and self-controlled so that you can pray.'
(v7)

Having begun to separate our real fears from the imaginary ones, and having decided to avoid all quick-fix solutions to ridding oneself of fear, the next step is this: look the real fears straight in the face. This is the way of God: complete honesty. There must be no attempt to deceive the mind, to entice it into entering a fool's paradise. 'No one can play tricks on the universe and get away with it,' says one Christian writer, 'least of all the universe of the mind.' The verse that most clearly expresses the need to face things rather than evade them is Matthew 24:6: 'You will hear of wars... but see to it that you are not alarmed.' In other words, confront fears and don't be scared. Jesus is the One who is speaking here. His way is the way of open-eyed honesty.

A further step we take in dealing with fear is this: learn the art of prayer, for fears dissolve in God's powerful presence. Samuel Chadwick, one-time principal of Cliff College in Derbyshire, England, said: 'The one concern of the devil is to keep the saints from praying. He fears nothing from prayerless study, prayerless work, prayerless religion... but he trembles when we pray.' One woman I knew was troubled by fear concerning the future. Whenever it loomed before her she would get down on her knees, pray and repeat the Lord's Prayer. She told me that after doing that a number of times the fear went away.

In fact, one of the greatest fears that prayer destroys is the fear of the future. And it dissolves it by assuring us that though we do not know what the future holds, we are held by the One who knows the future.

FURTHER STUDY

Mark 14:32–42;
Eph. 6:18–20

1. How did Jesus overcome fear?

2. Why did Paul request prayer?

Father, I see that in the place of prayer my fears are not so much solved as dissolved. Forgive me that often I make prayer the last instead of the first resort. Help me become a more prayerful person. In Jesus' name I ask it. Amen.

'The three omnis'

For reading & meditation – Psalm 91:1–16

'I will say of the LORD, "He is my refuge and my fortress, my God, in whom I trust."' (v2)

The 'smooth stone' for overcoming fear is one that I have struggled to define so I am going to call it 'attachment to God'. Attachment to God suggests a relationship with God in which one does not use prayer merely as a defence, but moves on to the kind of prayer that welds us to Him. Henri Nouwen says that all of our lives may be freed from fear if we are content to glory in His presence. I think this means living in the knowledge that we are always in God's presence, that we are all attached to a God who is omnipotent, omniscient and omnipresent. The three 'omnis', as they are sometimes referred to by theologians, capture such wonderful truths that I want to spend a little time exploring them with you today.

FURTHER STUDY

Num. 13:26–14:10

1. How did the spies' view of God affect their own views?

2. Why were Joshua and Caleb different?

Consider with me the first of these 'omnis' – omnipotence. This declares that God is all-powerful. And He makes His strength available for our needs. We only have to attach ourselves to God (as our text for today highlights) for Him to become our fortress. Take next His omniscience, meaning He is all-knowing. As we gain strength to face our fears by leaning on the all-powerful God so we also gain strength from His wisdom. James counsels us: 'If any of you lacks wisdom, he should ask God, who gives generously to all without finding fault' (James 1:5). Then third, omnipresence. This means God is present everywhere. I cannot go where He is not. Because I am in Christ nothing about my life can be Christ-less. He is with me both in the present and in the future.

When we see God as He is and as our attachment to Him deepens then fears are reduced to their proper size.

Gracious and loving God, I see that life is attachment – attachment to You. Help me use prayer not merely as a defence against fear but to develop my knowledge and experience of Your omnipotence, omniscience and omnipresence. In Jesus' name. Amen.

Fear - not from God

For reading & meditation – 2 Timothy 1:1-12

'For God did not give us a spirit of timidity, but a spirit of
power, of love and of self-discipline.' (v7)

Before we leave the subject of fear it is important to understand
that some fears are healthy and work positively in our lives.
Fear of getting hurt or killed, for example, is one of the best
policemen on our traffic-infested streets. The fears I have been
talking about are those that are harmful and debilitating. This kind
of fear, we must bear in mind, is prompted by Satan.

Now let me make myself clear: I do not believe that every fear is
a demon but I do believe that all crippling and debilitating fear has
the deceiver behind it. The devil wears many masks
while attempting to divert our Christian lives, and
fear is one of his most convincing. For anyone who
lives in the Valley of Elah and daily has to contend
with Satan stomping into their life shouting, 'I defy
you,' take a stand like David and reply: 'You come
against me with sword and spear and javelin, but I
come against you in the name of the LORD Almighty'
(1 Sam. 17:45). So now, without going overboard on
this matter of rebuking the devil (as some Christians appear to do),
be aware that the Holy Spirit dwells in you and you can calmly and
confidently stand up to fear in the authority that is yours in Jesus.

Remember your resistance comes from an inward trust based
on your personal relationship with Jesus. It wasn't just the sling
and the stone that caused Goliath to fall. It was the sling, the stone
and the mighty name of Jehovah. Take your stand now against
every crippling fear in your life, and resist the work of Satan in
Jesus' mighty and powerful name.

FURTHER STUDY

Gen. 3:1-10;
1 Pet. 5:6-11

1. What was
behind Adam's
fear?

2. How can we
resist the devil?

**Loving Father, may Your Spirit reinforce my spirit this very hour so
that I will rise up as David did and in Your mighty name see every
crippling fear crash to the ground. May my rebuke be Your rebuke.
Amen.**

'Fear not!'

For reading & meditation – 1 John 4:7–21

'There is no fear in love. But perfect love drives out fear'
(v18)

No one lived a life so completely free of every fear as did Jesus Christ. When we look at His life we see Him demonstrating the truth of today's text: perfect love casts out all fear. We should never forget that Jesus lived in our world, and one of the reasons God became flesh was that we could learn what God is like and how to live the life of God here on earth. It was a world then (as it is now) of accident, earthquake, famine, treachery, corruption, lust and war. Disease was common in the world where Jesus lived and death was frequently brutal. Crucifixion was a regular occurrence in those days, and Jesus would have seen people dying in slow agony on Roman crosses.

FURTHER STUDY

Psa. 5:7;
19:7–11;
Rom. 8:31–39

1. What type of fear is good?
2. Why can we 'fear not'?

Jesus taught His disciples that fear (properly understood) has only one object – God. 'I will show you whom you should fear,' He said to His disciples on one occasion. 'Fear him who... has power to throw you into hell' (Luke 12:5). The fear that Jesus spoke about is not a fear 'that has punishment'. Rather, it is what someone has described as 'the awed and fitting fear of a mortal for his God'. It is filial and trusting. When we fear God – fear Him in the most constructive sense of that word – then we will fear nothing else.

One of Jesus' favourite phrases was 'Fear not'. Again and again it rang out: 'Fear not'. How was it that He was so free of fear? Because of His complete confidence in His Father who was on the throne, and knowledge that all His purposes were wise and good. Assured of this His mind had no dark places in which fear could hide. May our minds become more like His.

Lord Jesus Christ, give me Your mind I pray – a mind in which there are no dark places where fear can hide. Drive this truth deep within me – that God sits on the throne so all is well.
For Your own dear name's sake. Amen.

'It is good for Me!'

For reading & meditation – Matthew 26:36–46

'My soul is overwhelmed with sorrow to the point of death.'
(v38)

We spend another day meditating on why Jesus, when He was here on earth, lived a life that was never paralysed by fear. 'But what about Gethsemane?' someone might say. 'Didn't He demonstrate there a certain degree of fear?' The incident in the Garden of Gethsemane needs special exploration to discover the true meaning of what went on in Jesus' heart, but I do not believe the emotion He exhibited was fear. Whether dealing with an angry mob, a madman, or a storm at sea our Lord seemed never to be afraid.

We found one reason for that in yesterday's meditation – His complete confidence in His Father in heaven and belief that all His purposes are wise and good. Here is another: His faith in His Father's ability to bring good out of all that happened. Jesus accepted everything with the assurance that whatever God allowed, He did so because it could be used to advance His eternal purposes. In the face of the most crushing thing He had to face Jesus probably told Himself something like this: 'If my Father allows this then it is good for me!' We see that most clearly in Gethsemane. 'Shall I not drink the cup the Father has given me?' Jesus asked (John 18:11). Note the words 'the Father has given me'. Men were about to lift Him up on a cross but He saw that His Father had a purpose even in that.

Jesus knew that His Father who was great in creation was mighty in transformation also. These two facts alone were enough to keep Jesus free from fear even in the face of crucifixion. They are enough for us too.

FURTHER STUDY

Gen. 50:15-21;
Rom. 8:28-30

1. Why was Joseph's suffering good for him and others?

2. How did Paul share Jesus' attitude?

Father, just as Your Son was free of all intimidating fear so may my life be also. Help me inwardly digest the two truths I have looked at over these past couple of days until they are absorbed into my whole being. In Jesus' name. Amen.

Two kinds of jealousy

For reading & meditation – Proverbs 27:1–11

'Anger is cruel and fury overwhelming, but who can stand before jealousy?' (v4)

We continue pulling out the 'mug shots' of some of the giants that threaten our lives, and look now at one of the most formidable of them all – jealousy. If there was ever a time to plunge your hand into the stream, grab a few stones, load up your sling and in the name of Jesus take aim, it is when this Titan is around. Perhaps you are under threat from this very giant at the moment. Let's explore this together.

The word 'jealousy' is used in the Bible in two senses: constructive jealousy and destructive jealousy. The teaching of the Bible concerning jealousy cannot be properly understood unless this is kept in mind. An instance of good jealousy is found in the words: 'I, the LORD your God, am a jealous God' (Exod. 20:5). Because God loved His people with an abounding and pure love He was jealous for them. He was not jealous for Himself but jealous for them – for their highest good. His interest was not primarily in Himself but in the good of His people. But this is not the way in which the word 'jealousy' is usually used. The more common form of jealousy is as pernicious as the other is praiseworthy.

FURTHER STUDY

Exod. 34:5-14;
2 Cor. 11:1-3

1. List some characteristics of God.

2. How did Paul show godly jealousy?

'Jealousy is envy born of some deep love of self,' says one writer. This is how it works. You love something or someone very much and desire to possess it or them completely. But the thing or person you love slips out of your hands into the possession of another. You then begin to experience the burning acidity of jealousy. And in some cases love quickly turns to rage – deep, dark, abiding rage. 'Who can stand before jealousy?' asks our text for today. Who indeed!

Lord God, help me bring down the giant of jealousy once and for all so that it might never again plague my life. Remove the shadows cast by jealousy from my face and also from my heart. In the name of Christ my Saviour and Deliverer I pray. Amen.

Jealousy's peculiarity

For reading & meditation – Proverbs 6:20–35

'for jealousy arouses a husband's fury, and he will show no
mercy when he takes revenge.' (v34)

Yesterday we noted that jealousy has been defined as 'envy born of some deep love of self'. It is the feeling of coldness and resentment that rises up when something or someone you wanted is about to be, or is being, possessed by another. Jealousy can also occur when a person hears somebody else being praised, somebody with whom they had compared themselves to and thought themselves superior. Jealousy is also the dislike that turns to bitterness when someone attracts more attention than you, or experienced success more than you have.
The peculiarity of this vice is that it is not usually directed against those who might seem most likely to provoke it – the people who far outstrip us in attainment. Often it is focused on those who are similar to us. 'Doctors are rarely jealous of people who come from another group,' says one psychologist, 'such as schoolteachers, businessmen, and so on. They are jealous of their peers – the people who are most like them, someone with whom they match themselves in thought.'

FURTHER STUDY

1 Sam. 18:5-16;
20:30-33;
Joel 2:18-27

1. How did Saul's jealousy affect his relationships?

2. How did God's jealousy affect His relationships?

Some distinguish between envy and jealousy and point out that though the words are frequently used interchangeably, there is a difference. Charles Swindoll puts it like this: 'Envy begins with empty hands mourning for what it doesn't have. Jealousy begins with full hands but is threatened by the loss. It is the pain of losing what I have to someone else, in spite of all my efforts to keep it.' One thing is sure – the giant of jealousy is a killer. We must make up our minds in God's name to halt it.

**Father God, I come to You for freedom. I do not want to be in
bondage to a giant. If jealousy is threatening the peace of God in my
life then together let us bring it down. I know You will do Your part.
Help me to do mine. Amen.**

'A mental cancer'

For reading & meditation – Genesis 4:1–16

'on Cain and his offering he did not look with favour. So Cain was very angry, and his face was downcast.' (v5)

We have all seen logs caught on rocks in midstream and prevented from being carried any further by the current. Likewise many Christians are hung up on the rocks of jealousy so life flows past them. Jealousy was Cain's sin. I realise Scripture mentions Cain's anger rather than his jealousy, but the anger was doubtless the consequence of his jealousy. Interestingly the Hebrew word for jealousy is qua-nah, which means literally 'to be intensely red'. The term is descriptive of someone whose face is flushed as a sudden rush of blood indicates the surge of strong emotions. Cain was jealous of Abel because Abel's offering had been accepted while his own was rejected. No doubt his face was red with emotion as he saw God smile on Abel's sacrifice, and not until Abel's blood had been poured out into the earth did his jealousy and anger subside.

FURTHER STUDY

Luke 15:11–32

1. How did jealousy distort the elder brother?

2. Did he have a genuine grievance?

This account brings to mind the story of another two brothers, as told by Jesus in the parable we call 'The Prodigal Son'. The younger brother squandered the money given to him by his father in selfish and indulgent living. His was a sin of the flesh. The elder brother had a different kind of problem; jealousy – a sin of the spirit. And when the curtain comes down on that immortal story we see the man who sinned in the flesh being forgiven and inside the father's house, while the man who sinned in the spirit is holding on to his jealousy and remains outside. Jealousy distorts and throws everything out of focus. A woman who was delivered from jealousy said: 'I've been healed of a mental cancer.' She called it by its right name.

Father, I want no cancer eating at the heart of my relationships. Show me the steps I need to take in order to be freed from its paralysing grip. I ask this in Jesus' name. Amen.

Jealous? Me?

For reading & meditation – 2 Corinthians 12:11-21

'I fear that there may be quarrelling, jealousy, outbursts of anger' (v20)

Jealousy can decimate friendships, dissolve a romance, destroy a marriage and disrupt family unity. I have even seen it ruin a whole church and separate leaders from one another.

There is a fable that tells how one day the devil came across some minor fiends trying to tempt a holy hermit. They experimented with the seductions of the flesh but it got them nowhere. 'Your methods are too crude,' said the devil. 'Watch this.' Going up to the hermit he asked: 'Have you heard the news? Your brother has been made bishop of Alexandria.' A scowl of malignant jealousy clouded the face of the holy man.

How can the giant of jealousy be slain? First we have to admit that it exists. This might seem to be stating the obvious but I have known many who were loath to admit that their souls were plagued with jealousy. If they suspected it, they shrank from it. Of course it can be humiliating to admit to things in our lives that we wish were not there. And pride can play its part in this too. Pride rebels at the idea that we can be jealous of another person, especially when we perceive them as being unworthy of comparison with ourselves. Jealous? Me? Of her? Of him? So we brush aside the fact that we may be jealous and go on for a few more years denying the deadly emotion that is ruining our lives.

For 40 days Goliath intimidated the camp of Israel. But then came the 41st day, which heralded the end for the giant from Gath. I hope that this day marks the end for jealousy in your life.

FURTHER STUDY

Gen. 37:1-11, 16-24,28

1. Why were the brothers jealous?

2. How did this affect them?

God my Father, indeed let this day mark the end for any jealous attitudes that may be overshadowing my life. Give me the faith of David to believe that as I do the possible, You will do the impossible. In Jesus' name. Amen.

Serving one another

For reading & meditation – 1 Corinthians 12:12–31

'Now you are the body of Christ, and each one of you is a part of it.' (v27)

Once we have recognised that jealousy is a problem in our lives what should we do? We must go to the root. Look on jealousy, I suggest, as self-centredness. Jealousy, we saw earlier, is 'envy born of some deep love of self'. Jealousy strives to put self forward – wanting what others have for itself. Go to the root of the problem by self-surrender and jealousy will drop away – rootless.

What a different climate there would be in the Church if everyone could see and accept this. The Church is a community where we belong to, and serve, one another. For example, a good worship leader helps me worship. A good singer aids my song. I can rejoice in the good administrative ability of a church secretary. There is no need for jealousy because that other person is part of the Body of Christ, just as I am.

FURTHER STUDY

Gal. 5:13-26;
Phil. 2:1-8

1. What is the origin of jealousy?

2. What is an antidote?

I am convinced that most of our problems have their roots in an unsurrendered ego. We can be saved but not yet fully surrendered. It took me years after I had committed my life to Christ to enter into a full surrender. In the book Masks of Mercy by Robert Frost one of the characters, Jonah, brings the subject around to the life of another character, Jessie. She counters: 'Let's change the subject. It makes me nervous.' And Jonah replies: 'That's all the great questions ever make you.' It makes us nervous, too, to get close to the root of our problems – self-centredness. But deal with it we must.

I say again: jealousy is often rooted in self-centredness. If jealousy is a problem in your life, repent of holding on to self-centredness, and make a complete surrender to God.

Loving heavenly Father, help me see that when I let go of my resistance to self-surrender then I am able to be free of jealousy too. I repent of my self-centredness and surrender my whole being into Your hands today. In Jesus' name. Amen.

Right comparisons

For reading & meditation – John 21:15–25

'When Peter saw him, he asked, "Lord, what about him?"'
(v21)

We continue considering what steps we can take, with the help of Jesus, to bring down the giant of jealousy. Another thing we can do is this: stop looking around to see what is happening to this, that and the other person. Your acceptance and approval comes from God alone. In the passage before us today we find Peter saying to Jesus: 'Lord, what about him?' Did Peter have a little lingering jealousy of John? We can't tell for sure. Some commentators seem to think so. One says: 'Peter was jealous of John as Pentecost had not yet burned it out.' Whether or not he was jealous, it seems pretty clear that his gaze at that moment was John-ward instead of Jesus-ward.

FURTHER STUDY

2 Cor. 10:12–18;
Heb. 12:1–4

1. Why is comparison foolish?

2. How does looking to Jesus affect us?

The tendency to compare ourselves with others is strong in us all. Constantly comparing ourselves with others can do us a great deal of harm emotionally and spiritually. If we conclude we are better than those with whom we compare ourselves we can be trapped into pride. If we conclude we are inferior to them we can be lured into envy. Jesus draws near to us and says: 'Don't compare yourself with others. Compare yourself with me. Accept me as your standard. Accept my help and work to this end.' That comparison becomes spiritually fruitful and the stumbling block is made a stepping stone.

To compare and align ourselves with Jesus is a healthy spiritual discipline, and one that has been practised throughout the centuries by those who have known God intimately. So keep your eyes fixed on Jesus and refuse to compare yourself with anyone else.

Merciful God, help me I pray to adjust this tendency I have to make comparisons so that those I make are directed towards You, not others. Forgive me that so often I have compared myself with others instead of You. Now, by Your grace, let it be different. Amen.

'Gaze on Him alone'

For reading & meditation – John 3:22–36

'that man who was with you... is baptising, and everyone is going to him.' (v26)

We spend one more day reflecting on how to bring down the giant of jealousy. When we are rightly related to God and fully surrendered to Him we become conscious that each one of us has a place in the plan of God – and that His plan is best. Being convinced of that we need not envy anyone. We see from the passage before us today that when the disciples of John discovered Jesus was attracting large numbers of followers they said: 'Rabbi... everyone is going to him' (v26). John replied that he was a 'friend of the bridegroom', and added: 'He must become greater; I must become less' (v30). In other words: 'I know my place and I'm happy in it.'

FURTHER STUDY

John 12:42–43;
Heb. 2:9–3:6

1. What was the problem of the leaders?

2. How can the power of jealousy be destroyed?

Once we are rightly related to God, and we are caught up in His infinite love and wisdom, knowing they are guiding our course, why wouldn't we be happy with our place? In His will is our peace. When we have established a right relationship with God (the key to it all) then He takes from us the eagerness for human praise that is the cause of so much jealousy. It is the intense longing for admiration that leads many people into difficulties. They want the applause, the flattery – this is how they come to envy the people who get it. Jesus would have us live independent of human praise. He would have us fix our gaze on Him and Him alone, only caring what He thinks of us – not what others do.

So now, take out your sling. Put in it the stone of truth (the thoughts we have been reflecting on over the past few days) and tell Jesus how much you want Him to overcome in your life.

Loving heavenly Father, I have lost many battles in my life because I wanted to experience the feelings of praise more than the joy of bringing glory to You. Now it's different. I shall aim the stone but the glory will be Yours. Amen.

Run-away desires

For reading & meditation – Mark 7:14–23

'out of a person's heart... sexual immorality... eagerness
for lustful pleasure' (vv21-22, NLT)

Another giant that overshadows the life of many a Christian
is lust and unhealthy desire. Those who struggle in this area
say that all other giants are as nothing in comparison. By lust
and desire I mean unrestrained and unhealthy desires. Many will
admit to having an occasional lustful or unhealthy desire, but the
situation I am describing here is when life is not merely visited
by occasional desires but is dominated by them. One man whose
life was governed by unhealthy desire put it like this: 'My mind
is a merry-go-round of lustful images.' This problem
seems to afflict men more than women; however
many women have spoken in counselling sessions
about burning with lust towards others.

Desire, as such, is one of the God-given aspects
of the personality. Without it life would be dull and
monochrome. But when desire becomes our master
rather than our servant then something has to be
done about it. Buddha tried to help people overcome
desire by cutting the root of desire itself. But I believe you cannot
cure the ills of life by eliminating an integral part of life. You can get
rid of a headache by cutting off your head, but it is a drastic remedy!

There is a way of living that is exemplified by the horse that lies
down in harness and won't move. There is another way, which
may be likened to the horse that runs away, breaks the harness
and smashes everything. What is necessary is to find the balance
between lying down and running away. We can't stop lustful
thoughts arising in our minds but we can stop them residing there.

FURTHER STUDY

2 Sam. 13:1-15;
1 Cor. 7:8–9

1. How did
Amnon's
desires smash
everything?

2. What did Paul
acknowledge?

**Dear God, help me to face my own God-given nature – help me to
understand how not to be driven and dominated; apart from by You.
Be the master of my desires. I give the reign into Your hands.
Control them for me. In Jesus' name. Amen.**

Celebrated, not shamed

For reading & meditation – Ephesians 6:10–20

'Therefore put on the full armour of God, so that... you
may be able to stand your ground' (vv13-14)

Sadly more families have been decimated, marriages
shipwrecked and relationships sown with the threads
of distrust by this issue than any other. Because of its close
collaborator and co-conspirator, shame, it's not often addressed
openly. How sad. As we have briefly already touched upon, sexual
desire is a God-given aspect of our personalities, not to be ashamed
of but celebrated. Like much in this world, when left to humankind
and taken out of the context of God's original design, things get
bent out of shape and misunderstood. It's perhaps
compounded today by the inappropriate use of sex
in advertising and sales. We live in an age where we
are constantly bombarded with sexualised images in
our papers, magazines and now the internet. There
has been much written in the press about the harm
caused not just to adult relationships, but to children
also, by easy access to internet pornography.

FURTHER STUDY

Prov. 2:1-19;
Psa. 101:1-3

1. What can help
us stand firm?

2. How can
we reduce our
exposure to
sexual imagery?

As followers of Jesus we can, and should, take the
lead on helping people find a way sensitively though this confusing,
and at times overwhelming, maze, so that we can emerge free
from shame and able to build whole, healthy relationships that
encourage trust, love and faithfulness. There is no doubt that many
of you today reading these notes will be struggling with unhelpful
and unhealthy thoughts. As we explore this issue over the next
few days, gaining some biblical insights, understanding how we
are wonderfully and fearfully made, we will all walk in a greater
freedom of who we are and how we can live without guilt and
shame – enjoying His good gifts from above.

**Lord Jesus, as You draw near to me now help me to draw near to
You. Give me the courage to trust You with this area of my life, so
that I might walk in true freedom and light. In Your name Amen.**

A judge's downfall

For reading & meditation – Judges 14:1–20

'His father and mother replied, "... Must you go to the uncircumcised Philistines to get a wife?"' (v3)

One preacher I heard described Samson as a 'he-man with a she-weakness'. It is interesting that the very first words we hear him utter in the Scriptures are these: 'I have seen a Philistine woman... now get her for me as my wife' (v2). Samson was born of godly parents and set apart from his birth to be a Nazarite (see Numbers 6), but as soon as he was a man he became set on taking an attractive Philistine woman to be his wife. Was this natural desire or lust? Though natural desire was obviously present, I think it was about to cross the line and become lust.

Several things said about Samson in Judges suggest that though he was appointed to be one of Israel's judges he was unable to conquer the giant of lust. In chapter 14 we find that his desire for the Philistine woman was so great that he married her – even though the Philistines were the longstanding enemy of Israel and worshippers of idols. And God had decreed that no Israelite should take an idol-worshipper as his wife (Deut. 7:3–4). In chapter 16 we discover Samson spending a night with a prostitute, and later setting up home with another Philistine woman – Delilah. He became so preoccupied and obsessed by his lustful desires that the time came when he didn't even know the Lord had departed from him (16:20). The result of Samson's affairs is known to us all. The strong man was taken captive, had his eyes gouged out, his hair shaved and finished up as a grinder in a Philistine prison. His eyes would never wander again. What can we conclude from all this? Lust is a flame no one dare fan. You'll get burned if you do.

FURTHER STUDY

2 Sam. 11:2-27

1. How did David's desires lead to greater sins?

2. Contrast the integrity of Uriah with David's behaviour.

Father, since sexual desire is a part of me – a creative part of me – show me how to prevent it becoming chaotic. Because of Your Son you can bring peace and order where chaos reigns. Establish Your peace and order in my life. Amen.

'No respecter of persons'

For reading & meditation – 1 Thessalonians 4:1–12

'For God did not call us to be impure, but to live a holy life.'
(v7)

Yesterday we looked at the downfall of a judge who was brought low through lust. Sadly it's not uncommon to read or hear of people from all walks of life, whether it's celebrities, politicians and even church leaders, who have derailed not only their own lives but also those around them because of unhealthy and unrestrained sexual desire. I mention this not to be judgmental but to show that no one is immune from sexual temptation. Lust is no respecter of persons. Its alluring voice can persuade the most intelligent minds to believe a lie.

FURTHER STUDY

2 Sam. 12:1-14;
15:13,30

1. How were David's eyes opened?

2. How would his sin grind him?

I once spent hours counselling an academic who was brought to court for a sexual offence. He could see the destructive nature of his act but said: 'My feelings overwhelm my intelligence.' It made me think of the silver-tongued orator of Rome, Mark Anthony. Of him it was said that in his youth he was so consumed with lust that his tutor once shouted in disgust: 'O Marcus! O colossal child... able to conquer the world but unable to resist a temptation!'

Some years ago, in Bexhill-on-Sea – a town on the south coast of England – people discovered that the trees in a lovely leafy avenue were dying. They investigated and found that a gas main running underneath them was leaking. Everything above the ground appeared fine but the trees were being poisoned from beneath. There will be people reading these lines today who are in a similar position. Their lives are being poisoned from beneath – by lust. Who can save them from this condition? Let them hear the good news – Jesus can.

My Creator and my God, take me by the hand lest I be lost in unhealthy desire. For if I get off the track here I find myself in a maze that grows more and more dense every moment. Master me so that I shall not be mastered by anything else. Amen.

Master or slave?

For reading & meditation – 2 Peter 2:4–22

'a man is a slave to whatever has mastered him.' (v19)

We ended yesterday by asking: When life is being poisoned from beneath, driven by lust, who can help us? And we said that Jesus is able and willing to come to our aid in every struggle, no matter how much of a stranglehold it has upon us. But just how does a person go about being set free from lust and unhealthy desires?

I suggest that first we recognise healthy sexual desire for what it is – a God-given desire. It is neither moral nor immoral in itself but according to its use. There is no shame in healthy sexual desire. It's when it becomes unrestrained and demanding – or directed to the wrong person – that difficulties develop. Sexual desire is divine in origin and comes to us as a natural part of personality. If it ceased then the human race would vanish from the earth. God did few things more wonderful when He made us than to share with us the pleasure of creation. But though He gave us life pervaded by great instincts, God never said that every instinct has to be satisfied, that to want a thing is reason enough for taking it. Some argue that sexual desire is not an appetite on the same level as the desire for food or water. We can live without sex but we cannot live without food or water.

FURTHER STUDY

Matt. 6:24–34;
1 Cor. 7:1–7

1. What key principle applies to sexual desire?

2. How should people regard sexual desire?

So bring the fact of sex into the open in your thinking, and at the same time invite Jesus to guide your thoughts on this issue. Settle it once and for all that sex is not your master – Jesus is. If you put sex first it is likely to corrupt your whole life. If you put Jesus first He will co-ordinate your whole life. Sex will then be a part of life rather than your master.

God, I see that if sexual desires take Your place and rule me then I shall become their servant. Once again I confess You are my Lord. May no other be my master. In Jesus' name. Amen.

Our reply to unhealthy desires

For reading & meditation – Romans 6:1–14

'sin shall not be your master, because you are not under law, but under grace.' (v14)

There are those who claim that unhealthy sexual desire and lust relates to the body and is thus a physical problem. Their remedies therefore run along this line: eat the right foods, have plenty of physical exercise and keep your body under control. Now it would be untrue to say that lust has no physical aspects, but it is more a problem in our thinking than a physical one. No sharp distinction can be drawn between mind and body. The mind does not live within the body as a kernel exists within the shell of a nut. Mind and body interrelate in a mysterious way. What affects the mind can affect the body, and what affects the body can affect the mind. But I repeat: lust is more a problem of the mind than the body.

FURTHER STUDY

Gen. 39:4-12;
2 Tim. 2:20-22

1. How could we respond to lust?

2. What should we pursue?

In fact I can go further and indicate which part of the mind is involved. It is the imagination. This is the battleground where much of the fighting that unhealthy desires provoke takes place. A picture, a word, a story, an advertisement, a glance, an odour – almost anything can trigger a thought in the mind, and the whole being then becomes hot with desire.

Lay hold of this: to overcome and be free depends on the skill and speed with which an unhealthy desire is managed in the mind. If a man or woman turns their thoughts to Jesus, thinks about Him, talks to Him and makes this a firm routine whenever tempted, it will save their wandering thoughts from escalating into lust. One writer puts it like this: 'When Lust suggests a rendezvous, send Jesus Christ as your representative.' Remind yourself that you are united with Christ so are no longer a slave to this 'giant'.

Lord, help me establish the firm routine of disciplined thinking so that when unhealthy ideas invade my mind I turn my thoughts immediately to You. I supply the willingness; please supply the power. Help me Lord Jesus. Amen.

Loving Him above all else

For reading & meditation – Mark 12:28–34

'Love the Lord your God with all your heart and with all
your soul and with all your mind' (v30)

The point we made yesterday – of gaining freedom in your thinking – is an important one so I want to say a little more about it before we move on. Emerson stated: 'The ancestor of every action is a thought.' This being so, then we can stop the action at the place of the thought. Don't dally with the thought saying: 'I won't dismiss the thought, but I'll stop before I do anything about it.' You won't, for in any battle between the imagination and the will the imagination always wins. All action begins with a thought; the thought becomes the action; the action becomes the habit and the habit a lifestyle.

But there is more to this problem than simple mind control or the exercise of the will, and if I were to leave the matter there I would be failing you both as a Bible teacher and a counsellor. The ideas I have suggested are only the fences along the sides of an open road – the open road that leads to being passionately taken up with Jesus. I believe you can expel one desire only by a higher desire, one passion by a stronger passion. Let the love of Christ, therefore, be the love that consumes all other loves. All the safeguards and accountability will not ultimately save you unless the love of Christ is at the centre.

G.K. Chesterton said: 'When a man knocks at the door of a brothel he is looking for God.' I believe he is making the point that God has placed a thirst for Himself deep in every person's heart. Unless that thirst is quenched by Him we will begin to look for other ways to satisfy it – sensual satisfaction being one of them.

FURTHER STUDY

Gen. 29:13-21;
Rom. 8:5-17

1. How did Jacob's love for Rachel consume his thinking?

2. How can we gain freedom in our thinking?

Lord Jesus Christ, I would so fall in love with You that all lesser loves become unnecessary. Help me to lose myself in You so that I can find myself. Blessed Saviour, I love You. Amen.

Creative desires

For reading & meditation – 1 Corinthians 6:12–20

'Do you not know that your body is a temple of the Holy Spirit, who is in you?' (v19)

We spend one more day looking at the various ways by which we can overcome the giant of lust and distracting unhealthy sexual desires. It is more (we said) than a matter of mind control or the exercise of the will. The heart of the issue is the matter of the heart. Is our heart taken up with Christ and fully occupied with Him? If so, then His love brings all other love under His control.

But what about those who are not married, and are denied by Scripture the ordinary outlets of sexual expression? Are they doomed to a life of repression? This extraordinary passionate nature of sexual desire, as you know, I believe is part of our creativity. However this is not limited to physical creativity alone.

FURTHER STUDY

Exod. 19:10-19;
Acts 9:36-39

1. How did the people prepare to meet God?

2. How did Dorcas express her creativity?

Restricted in one area, creativity can express itself in another. It can find expression in ways such as the creation of new systems of thought and new methods of helping and ministering to others. Its passion and energy can be expressed in other areas of life also. History is replete with people who have committed to a life of celibacy and achieved tremendous works of service living active, full, satisfying lives – their desires have not so much been repressed but expressed in a different sphere. Those who are single or bereft of a spouse need not despair because of their sexual desires. Let God lead you into new areas of creative activity that will benefit His kingdom.

Remember, the God who delivered Goliath into the hands of David is just the same today. Take aim in His strength and even this giant will fall.

Lord Jesus, because You were human, sexual desire must have been in You as it is in me – yet You were without sin. Teach me the art of creativity so that what is blocked on one level can be released on another. For Your own dear name's sake. Amen.

Memories of the past

For reading & meditation – Isaiah 43:14–28

'Forget the former things; do not dwell on the past.' (v18)

We continue dipping into God's files of 'most wanted' villains in order to identify some of the intimidating and devastating 'giants' that threaten us. The one I select now may not be easily recognisable, but believe me, is active in the lives of countless Christians.

It is difficult to put a name to this intimidator but it is best described as the giant of shame. Part of its work is to revive memories of things that are best forgotten. Shame picks on us, reminding us of an action, thought or omission in our past – a sin that has been brought to the cross and forgiven – and works to make sure we will not forget it. Whenever we feel we have left the failure of the past far behind, shame's voice booms across the valley of our souls to remind us that even though God has forgotten our sin it will make sure we will never forget it. Shame jeers: 'How could you have done such a thing? Call yourself a Christian? What if people knew the kind of person you really are?'

FURTHER STUDY

Isa. 65:16–25;
2 Cor. 5:16–21

1. What will be remembered?

2. What has happened to the past?

I have been amazed at the number of people I have met who have told me that even though they knew God had forgiven them for some ugly moment of the past, memories and feelings of sorrow and remorse remained to such a degree that a dark shadow was cast over their life. The giant who keeps alive memories that ought to be forgotten makes sure of that. Those tormented by shame are filled with feelings of self-contempt that hinder them from moving on in the work of God. Turn the giant over to Jehovah. He's the best giant killer there is.

Father, I want to be rid of this taunting giant undermining my life with reminders of my past that You have forgiven. You defeated Satan once and for all on Calvary. Now apply that victory to my life here in the present. In Jesus' name. Amen.

Just holding the coats

For reading & meditation – Acts 7:54–60

'Meanwhile, the witnesses laid their clothes at the feet of a young man named Saul.' (v58)

We continue looking at the issue for those who have received the forgiveness of God for something in their past, but whose memories continue to be lacerated by shame. Paul the apostle had a 'past'. The first time his name is mentioned in the New Testament is in connection with a judicial murder.

Paul is without doubt the greatest figure in the Church next to Jesus, but when we first meet him he is implicated in a dreadful crime. Stephen had defended himself with great skill before the

FURTHER STUDY
Gal. 1:13–24;
1 Tim. 1:12–17

1. How did Paul acknowledge his past?

2. Why did Paul's past not define his future?

Sanhedrin, but no sooner had his speech finished than they set upon him and dragged him out of the city to stone him to death. Historians say that it was a form of execution that came very close in brutality to crucifixion. Flung against a wall, the victim was pounded with stones until all life had gone out of him. Despite this barbaric act, Stephen died with dignity. He followed the Saviour's example by praying in his last moments: 'Lord, do not hold this sin against them' (v60). And Paul (then Saul) was

there. No wound on the martyr's body could be attributed to him. He had simply been looking after the coats of those who murdered him. But he was an accessory before and after the fact. Though he might have left the scene saying to himself, 'I had nothing to do with it', the blood of the first martyr was on his hands

Yet Paul found forgiveness. And years later, he said: 'Forgetting what is behind and straining towards what is ahead, I press on towards the goal' (Phil. 3:13–14). He was not glad about what he had done but he did not allow the past to determine his future.

Gracious God, help me forget the bad things of the past. May I be like Paul who, having been forgiven, did not allow his 'past' to intimidate him. In Jesus' name. Amen.

What it means to forget

For reading & meditation – 2 Peter 1:1–11

'he is short-sighted and blind, and has forgotten that he
has been cleansed from his past sins.' (v9)

The question facing us now is this: How do we go about
annihilating this giant that seeks to paralyse us by reviving
memories of our past, which has been forgiven? Let's first be clear
about what we are saying, as a wrong understanding can lead to
unrealistic expectations and dampening disappointment.

Some psychologists tell us that it is impossible to forget anything.
All our thoughts (they claim) are stored up inside us, and though
they may be beyond the reach of recollection they are not outside
our cognitive make-up. We may not be able to recall
them at will, but they are not forgotten. Sometimes,
of course, an accident or a trauma will produce what
is known as amnesia (loss of memory), but with this
condition memories are not so much lost as unable to
be recalled. I do not believe it is part of God's purpose
to erase unpleasant memories from our memory
banks. He does, however, take the sharp edge off
them and helps us avoid an emotional overload.

FURTHER STUDY

Gen. 41:44–52;
Acts 26:9–18

1. How was
Joseph always
reminded to
forget?

2. What did Paul
remember?

On the top of one of my thumbs is an ugly scar. And I remember,
albeit dimly, what caused it. Once, when I was using a sharp blade
to cut some paper, it slipped and the blade penetrated my thumb.
A few unpleasant hours followed, but now the memory of the
accident is all but forgotten. The pain has gone and the memory
is faint. There are things in our past that can be remembered as
dimly as that. Give God the chance and He will help you forget
anything that it would be harmful to remember. Not the event,
but the acute recollection of it.

My Father and my God, I see that forgetting does not mean all my
memories are wiped, but that by Your grace the sharp edge is taken
off them. If I am in need of this special ministry let grace flow into
my open wounds. In Jesus' name. Amen.

Repenting of 'repentance'

For reading & meditation – 2 Corinthians 7:1–16

'Godly sorrow brings repentance that leads to salvation and leaves no regret' (v10)

How then do we work with God to annihilate the giant who seeks to paralyse our lives by replaying memories of things that are best forgotten? First, we need to be sure that we have brought it to God in repentance. I am aware that I am continually drawing attention to this subject of repentance in my writings, but I do so because I believe it is seriously misunderstood in some church circles. The path to God (as you know) is the path of repentance. Yet so often our repentance is not what it should be. Wasn't it

FURTHER STUDY
Matt. 3: 4-10;
John 8:3-11

1. What was John's attitude to repentance?

2. What was Jesus' attitude to the woman?

George Whitefield who said, 'Our repentance needs to be repented of, and our tears washed in the blood of Christ'? Why should he say that? Because often our repentance is not really repentance at all. It is only remorse or fear. We can be sad, even tearful, not because of what we have done but because we have been found out or may yet be found out.

When I was a pastor, more than once I went to court with a young man who had got himself into trouble and who appeared to be repentant. I would speak on his behalf and then, when he was let off, all the distress would instantly disappear. He wasn't sorry at all. He was only sorry about the price he feared he would have to pay. What I thought was repentance was nothing more than apprehension and passing remorse – a shabby counterfeit.

Many have no sense of forgiveness because they have not called out to God in repentance. Repentance is not only being sorry for sin, but being sorry for the self-centredness that prompted the sin. Sin is self in the place God ought to be.

Lord, forgive me that so often I am not sorry for sin but sorry for the trouble that my sin causes me. My repentance needs to be repented of. Help me to truly understand this vital issue of repentance. In Jesus' name I ask it. Amen.

Remembering to forget

For reading & meditation – Jeremiah 31:31–37

'For I will forgive their wickedness and will remember their sins no more.' (v34)

We continue examining the nature of true repentance. On more than one occasion while I was a pastor I stood by, counselled and prayed with an unmarried young girl who was in anguish because she thought she was pregnant. I would help her find forgiveness and do all I could to assist her to plan for her future. And then she would discover she was not pregnant after all. So often the distress would depart and the girl would appear happy again. That was not wrong, but the real tragedy lay in the fact that her behaviour was now seen in a new light – not as sin at all, just an unfortunate mistake. Her repentance was not real repentance – just remorse and passing fear.

Now let every one of us be on our guard against feeling superior about this. Hasn't our repentance been less than authentic at times? Haven't we been sorry, not because we have offended God and broken His holy laws, but because we have lost our inner peace? Haven't we been cast down, not by genuine sorrow over sin, but because we have suffered some personal deprivation? What does God say to a truly repentant people? He gives the message of our text today: 'I will... remember their sins no more.' Note the phrase 'I will remember no more.' Whether or not God can forget is a moot point. I am not sure myself that God forgets in the sense that His memory of events is erased. The reality, I think, is that He remembers to forget. This might seem to be playing with words but the truth we all ought to be glad of today is this: when we repent of our sin – truly repent – then the forgiveness that God gives is absolute and eternal.

FURTHER STUDY
Matt. 18:23-35;
1 John 1:5-10

1. How was the servant's distress not heartfelt?

2. What is God's promise?

Dear God, may the sense of forgiveness permeate my soul. I know that when I truly repent You truly forgive. Help me move forward with the light and steady step of someone who has been forgiven by God. In Jesus' name. Amen.

On forgiving yourself

For reading & meditation – Romans 8:28–39

'Who will bring any charge against those whom God has chosen? It is God who justifies.' (v33)

Probably right now someone reading my words is being taunted by the giant of shame. An issue for which God has forgiven you is being drawn to your attention by the terrible Titan. I know that *Every Day with Jesus* is read by a number of men and women who are in prison as a consequence of some crime they have committed. To such I want to say today: if you have genuinely repented of what you did then although the law and consequences still have to take their course, God has eternally and absolutely forgiven you.

FURTHER STUDY

Jer. 50:18–20;
Micah 7:18–20

1. What happens if we search for a record of past sins?

2. What does God delight in?

Others reading these lines may not be in a physical prison but in a psychological one. The giant of shame threatens to bring some forgiven sin out from your past and ruin your reputation. Before you surrender your case as hopeless and abandon the fight, go over the things I have said during these past few days. Understand what it means to genuinely repent. Consider restitution. But talk that matter over with a minister or counsellor before doing anything about it as sometimes restitution can be a very complex issue requiring great thought and care. Then ask yourself this: God has forgiven me; have I forgiven myself?

When a sense of shame remains after having been forgiven by God, one might begin to suspect the presence of pride. What you may be saying to yourself at some deep level of your emotional life is this: 'How could I have ever done that? Me, of all people?' Hear the pride? Self-hate and self-contempt is rooted in pride, so recognise what is going on and repent even of that. Now, just as you forgive others, forgive yourself. God has forgiven you.

Father, forgive me if by my pride I make the job of the giant of shame so much easier. May I put in my sling the smooth stone of truth that I have learned these past days and bring down this Titan once and for all. In Jesus' name. Amen.

Under the broom tree

For reading & meditation – 1 Kings 19:1–21

'[Elijah] came to a broom tree, sat down under it and prayed that he might die.' (v4)

The next face we come across in the files of God's 'most wanted' villains is that of the giant of despair. Fortunate are those who have never been intimidated by this Titan, bellowing out threats with a basso profundo voice that sounds like a dozen out-of-tune tubas.

Elijah, the great prophet of Israel, knew what it was to have an encounter with the giant of despair. Let's consider how this devout man of God falls prey to the deepest form of depression. The prophet has just experienced a tremendous victory over Ahab and the Baal-worshippers but then the giant of despair is ushered in by Ahab's wife Jezebel. She predicts that Elijah's life will be over within 24 hours. Though this mighty man of God has overcome all previous threats, and contributed to the public humiliation of false prophets and priests, somehow Jezebel's statement finds its mark. Elijah runs for his life. Finally he sinks in utter despair beneath the broom tree and says: 'I've had enough, LORD Take my life' (v4). Did God rebuke him? Or tell him how disappointed He was with him? No, He loved him and ministered to him by allowing him to take a long rest – He even provided him with a meal. Later He gave him a close friend by the name of Elisha to encourage him. Gently He reminded him of all they had done together and this helped the prophet to get a new perspective.

Elijah came back from despair and depression. And so can you. The good news is that this giant too can be defeated. I know, for at one time I had an encounter with it myself.

FURTHER STUDY

Exod. 32:30-32;
Jonah 4:1-11

1. Identify Moses' emotions.

2. Why was Jonah's perspective wrong?

My Father and my God, help me in the hour of pressure and crisis to remember what You did for Elijah. The last word is always with You. And that last word is deliverance. I am so grateful. Thank You, my Father. Amen.

Spiritual highs and lows

For reading & meditation – 2 Corinthians 1:1–11
'We were under great pressure...
so that we despaired even of life.' (v8)

It's strange how periods of depression can follow times of great spiritual elation and victory. We saw Elijah affected in this way yesterday. Fresh from a stunning victory on Mount Carmel the prophet became vulnerable and frightened. He cried out to God beneath the broom tree, not words of praise, but a plea that his life might end. Surely no despair can be greater than that.

Baffling as it may be, it is not unusual to find oneself at a low ebb following a period of great vision or renewal. Some time ago

FURTHER STUDY
1 Sam. 30:1-8;
Psa. 42:1-11

1. How did David overcome despair?

2. How did the psalmist express his confusion?

I ministered at a conference in Adelaide, Australia, along with the Bible teacher Bob Mumford. Bob warned the congregation about what he called 'post-convention depression', which he described as the low feelings we get following a spiritual high. This dejection is not clinical depression, which needs medical treatment, but it must be guarded against nevertheless for the giant of despair will step in and take advantage of our vulnerability.

The apostle Paul appears to have become despondent during his great missionary journey into Asia. They were under such great pressure, he says, that they despaired even of life. Paul's despair and Elijah's despair took quite different forms, of course. The prophet's despair was of such a nature that he wanted his life to end. The apostle's despair was because his life might end. But they were both affected by despair nevertheless. Why did God allow such a thing to happen to the great apostle? This is how Paul understood it: 'that we might not rely on ourselves but on God' (v9). God can use even despair to advance His purposes for us.

Father, give me the confidence that no matter what happens in my life You are standing by ready, willing and able to turn everything to my spiritual profit. I may sink into despair but I need not stay in it. Amen.

It can be done

For reading & meditation – Job 1:1–22

'The LORD gave and the LORD has taken away;
may the name of the LORD be praised.' (v21)

If we are to overcome despair when it hits our lives we need to understand something of its dynamics. By 'dynamics' I mean the elements that go to make it the debilitating power it is. Top of the list is a sense of loss. Whenever I talk to a person who is in the grip of despair the first thing I try to understand is their perceived sense of loss. Loss comes in two general categories: the loss of those we love, and the loss of things we love.

I once heard about a man whose wife had just died. As soon as he saw the spark of life fade from her eyes he picked up a knife and attempted to kill himself. Fortunately another family member was able to intervene before he did himself great harm. Despair can set in very quickly and sometimes have serious consequences when a loved one dies. The other kind of loss is the loss of things we love – the loss of one's job, the loss of an object desired, the loss of a goal, the loss of wealth and so on.

FURTHER STUDY

Job 2:1-10;
Psa. 43:1-5

1. Contrast Job and his wife.

2. How did the psalmist speak to himself?

Job was a man who experienced both the loss of those he loved and the things he loved. Three times in the chapter we have read today we find the phrase 'while he was still speaking'. Did you sense as you read those words the rapid succession of events described? One after another the calamities struck. Job lost those he loved – his ten sons and daughters – and the things he loved – the herds that made him wealthy. How did he respond? He was devastated but not in despair. He didn't blame God; he worshipped. Imagine that! It's difficult not to fall victim to the giant of despair in such circumstances, but with God's help we can respond like Job.

Father, forgive me if, when tragedy strikes, my tendency is not to worship but to whine. How I long to have the deep inward trust that Your servant Job so wonderfully demonstrated. Draw closer to me, Lord, as I draw closer to You. In Christ's name. Amen.

Three cardinal virtues

For reading & meditation – 1 Corinthians 13:1–13

'And now these three remain: faith, hope and love.' (v13)

We saw yesterday that one element underlying despair is a sense of loss. And loss, we said, comes in two general categories: loss of those we love and loss of things we love. But as we delve deeper into the dynamics of despair we find that the greatest loss is the loss of hope. I turned to my dictionary a few moments ago to see how it defined despair. This is what it said: 'a complete loss or absence of hope; thing that causes this whether by badness or unapproachable excellence'.

FURTHER STUDY
2 Cor. 5:1-5;
Heb. 6:13-20
1. What is our guarantee of hope?
2. What is an anchor for the soul?

Throughout time writers and artists have been divided on the subject of hope. You may have seen a print of the famous picture by G.F. Watts called *Hope*, which shows a blindfolded woman sitting with bowed head on a sphere and holding in her hand a lyre. Only one string of the instrument remains unbroken, only one star shines in the dark sky. There is a story that when it was first shown in London, two homeless men who had crept into the building to get out of the cold were overheard discussing it. 'Hope,' said one, 'why is it called *Hope*?' To which the other replied, gazing at the figure perched precariously on the sphere: 'I suppose because she hopes she won't fall off.' Many think of hope like that – as being precarious, an illusion, a vanity, a dream. 'Hope is the most hopeless thing of all,' said one cynic.

How different is Scripture's view of hope. Paul tells us in today's passage that it is one of the three cardinal virtues of the Christian faith. But for hope to be real hope it needs to be linked to Christ. All other hopes are illusions.

Gracious Father, I see that all is not lost while I have hope. And in You hope is more than an illusion, more than a mere pipe-dream. I may lose things and I may lose loved ones but I will never lose You. So I can go on – no matter what happens. Thank You. Amen.

God's ends

For reading & meditation – Lamentations 3:19–33

'Yet this I call to mind and therefore I have hope' (v21)

Y ou do not have to be widely read to notice how the world's view of hope is quite different from that of Scripture. Schopenhauer, the distinguished German philosopher, looked upon hope as the bait by which nature makes us serve her interests rather than our own. Indeed, many writers seem to regard hope as vain, poor and deceptive.

But hope, as we saw yesterday, is something quite different in the Scriptures. Hope is intimately interwoven with Jesus. Paul speaks of the patience or endurance of hope (1 Thess. 1:3), and hope that does not disappoint us (Rom. 5:5). The author of the epistle to the Hebrews makes what seems a paradoxical statement when he likens hope to an anchor for the soul that is firm and secure (Heb. 6:19). Why this contrast between the view of the world and the view of Scripture? The answer is not difficult. They are talking about different things. There is genuine hope and there is the counterfeit – a shadow of hope. There is gold and there is gilt. What the world often means by hope (with a few exceptions) is optimism. Of course optimism is much better than pessimism. Every health professional knows that. But optimism is not enough to hold us when our expectations are not realised. 'It's alright,' an optimist told me when I visited his wife in hospital because she was seriously ill. 'She's going to get better.' But I conducted her funeral before the week was out. Optimism alone is not enough to save us from despair. We need Christian hope: hope that is tied to good ends – God's ends.

FURTHER STUDY

1 Thess. 4:13–18;
1 Pet. 1:3–9

1. How can there be hope even in death?

2. How can living hope produce something more valuable than gold?

Father, I see that my hope is only as good as that to which it is tied. How thankful I am that my hope is in You. Help me always to see past earthly issues to heavenly ones. And remind me that nothing will ever cause You to vacate Your throne. Amen.

'The larger story'

For reading & meditation – Daniel 3:1–30

'the God we serve is able to save us...
But even if he does not' (vv17-18)

How different Christian hope is to the optimism displayed by the world. The Christian faith and community experiences hope that is not inflated and unrealistic optimism, but rather a quiet and unquenchable hope drawn directly from Jesus. And the language that comes easily to optimists is avoided by us.

Rather, we take the attitude of the three young men whose story is recorded in the passage before us today. They were confident that God could deliver them from the burning fiery furnace, but if not, they said, they would still take their stand on His principles. Triumphal boasting of a victory or wishful anticipation that things will go the way we think they should is not what the Christian life is all about. It is based not on what we think is best but what God thinks is best.

The ground of our hope is that God is writing what Dr Larry Crabb calls a 'larger story'. By 'larger story' he means the purposes of God for our lives, which often are quite different from our purposes. So deceptive is our human nature (even though we may have been Christians for decades) that we prefer not only to write our own story but to direct it, produce it and star in it also. The three young men in today's passage sensed that God was writing a bigger story than they could compose and wanted to be part of it. They were ready for their own plans to be crossed in order to be part of a much larger story. That is the hope that holds us and helps us rise from the depths of despair. At times things don't go our way because they are going His way.

FURTHER STUDY

Phil. 1:12-21;
1 Pet. 3:13-18

1. What larger story did Paul explain?

2. What is our reason for hope?

My Father and my God, forgive me that I so easily forget my life is part of a larger story. And forgive me also that often I am more concerned about how You can fit into my story than how I can fit into Yours. Cleanse me and help me, dear Father. Amen.

Beating a hasty retreat

For reading & meditation – 2 Corinthians 4:1–18

'We are hard pressed on every side, but not crushed;
perplexed, but not in despair' (v8)

Having looked over the past few days at the dynamics of despair, today we ask ourselves: how do we go about actually defeating this fearsome giant? Like David we have a stone to put in our sling that, coupled with confidence in God, will bring down the giant of despair. What is that stone? It is the stone of truth. But what particular truth? This: that despite all appearances to the contrary God is at work and He is good.

It has been said that these twin truths are the most difficult to believe, especially for the victims of some great loss. I can vouch for that, both from my own experience and my experience with others. So how can we hold on to these truths when we are in the midst of dark and difficult circumstances that bring us to the brink of despair? We retreat to the cross. The cross symbolises for us God's ultimate wisdom and love. From one perspective Calvary appears to have all the elements that spell out despair. But from another it spells out hope – hope that no matter how dark things look, a divine purpose sweeps through everything. Everything!

FURTHER STUDY

Rom. 8:28–30;
2 Tim. 1:8–12

1. What did Paul know?

2. How did he regard suffering?

When life falls to pieces all around you it is not easy to believe that God is active. And it is certainly difficult to believe that God is good. But as we have just said, the cross bears truth to that. Though circumstances may appear desperate, in reality that can never be so. Take your stand at the cross and hold on to that. Hope, remember, is more than optimism. When the shallow hopes of the world are dead, hope on in God. Then, like the apostle Paul, you will be able to say: 'We are perplexed, but not in despair.'

Father, how thankful I am for the cross – the one high point in a dark and mysterious universe. May the truth it symbolises be the 'stone' in my sling that brings down the giant of despair. In Jesus' name. Amen.

The tallest Titan

For reading & meditation – Proverbs 16:9–20

'Pride goes before destruction, a haughty spirit before a fall.' (v18)

Giants are tall, tough and terrifying. Of that there can be little doubt. We now meet the tallest of the Titans, and one that almost everyone has to do battle with at some time or another – pride. This (in my opinion) is the most dangerous of the giants we have considered so far. For pride, theologians conclude, is the most deadly sin of all.

When I have made this point publicly – that pride is the most destructive of all giants – someone has usually come up to me

FURTHER STUDY
Isa. 14:12–15;
Ezek. 28:12–17
1. How did the morning star regard himself?
2. Why did the king of Tyre become proud?

afterwards and said something like this: 'I can think of sins that are worse than pride. Murder, for example. Or lust. Or envy. All these are more deadly than the sin of pride.' Notwithstanding this argument, I believe the theologians are right. St Augustine, one of the greatest Christian thinkers, held that view. So did Thomas Aquinas. Dante did too. And, if it were necessary, I could add a hundred more famous names. In the Bible pride is revealed as

the original sin. This is what turned an angel into a devil and, in turn, emptied heaven of a host of angels (see Jude v6).

But how can pride be defined? Pride is the ego in the place God created for Himself. This is the essence of this awful soul disease. It puts self in the centre. It struts and shouts and brags. It has the attitude 'I... I... I'. It dethrones God in the human heart and instates the puffed-up ego. Can you see now why it is the ugliest and deadliest of all sins? It gives self, not God, the supreme position. Such is its ruinous nature that William Law said of it: 'Pride must die in you or Christ will not be able to live in you.'

Lord Jesus, I see that You and pride are incompatible. May the giant of pride be dealt a death blow in my life over these next few days so that it will never be able to intimidate me again.
For Your own dear name's sake. Amen.

The devil's handiwork

For reading & meditation – Psalm 8:1–9

'When I consider your heavens... what is man that you are mindful of him?' (vv3-4)

Before we begin to do battle with pride we must be clear as to the perniciousness of its nature and see it for the enemy that it is. Pride, we said yesterday, is self in the place of God. Spiritually minded people echo the words of the psalmist: 'the LORD is God. It is he who made us, and we are his; we are his people, the sheep of his pasture' (Psa. 100:3). But pride both rejects and resists any dependency. William Henley, in his poem 'Invictus', spoke for the rebellious when he declared blatantly: 'I am the master of my fate, I am the captain of my soul.'

FURTHER STUDY

Dan. 4:25-37;
Ezek. 31:2-12

1. What did Nebuchadnezzar learn?

2. Why was the king of Egypt destroyed?

When men and women claim to be the measure of all things, to be able to run their own world (although I do often wonder how and when did it first become theirs?), to solve their own problems, secure their own salvation and manage their own destinies, they push God aside and take over His role in the universe. Indeed, as one person has put it: 'The principle of pride, when taken to its nth degree, is capable, in intention at least, of pushing God out of the very universe He made.'

Dr A.C. Craig, a twentieth-century theologian, illustrated this well by changing the words of the psalm before us today so that it reads: 'O Man, how excellent is thy name in all the earth! Who has set thy glory above the heavens? When I consider thy inventions, the work of thy fingers, the aeroplanes and atomic bombs which thou hast made, what is God that I should be mindful of Him, or the Son of God that I should reverence him?' Pride originates in the devil's lies and deception and could be described as the devil's finished handiwork.

Gracious Father, the more I see the evil nature of pride and what it has done to Your universe, the more I want to be rid of it. Out of all the deliverances You have given me, this could be the greatest. I wait with eager anticipation. Amen.

Deceitful thinking

For reading & meditation – Proverbs 11:1-11

'When pride comes, then comes disgrace, but with humility comes wisdom.' (v2)

The word 'pride', like 'jealousy', can be used in two different ways. There is a healthy form of pride as well as a negative and destructive one. It is good for men and women to have pride in their work, their appearance, their achievements, their families and so on. A person without pride, in this sense, you might argue would lack self-respect. Please remember that when I speak of pride I mean its destructive and unhealthy aspect.

Pride not only denies that God is the Creator and Upholder of the universe, but relegates every other person to a minor role in it. The proud man or woman never sees other persons as equal but as inferior, as minor actors in a play in which he or she is the leading character. One writer tells of a valet who spoke of his master in these terms: 'He had to be the central figure in everything. If he went to a christening he wanted to be the baby. If he went to a wedding he wanted to be the bridegroom. If he went to a funeral he wanted to be the corpse.' You may have heard of the nurse who was so conceited that when she took the pulse of one of the men in her ward she always knocked off a few degrees to allow for the impact of her personality on the patient!

FURTHER STUDY

Acts 12:21-23;
14:8-18

1. Why did Herod die?

2. Contrast his attitude with that of the apostles.

However, before we laugh for too long we ought to take a look inside our own hearts to see if pride lingers there. When we really understand what pride is we realise it is the greatest sin of all. One commentator says of it: 'It can even make virtues vicious and the other vices more vicious than they were.' It is deceitful thinking that dismisses pride as harmless.

Loving God, give me clear insight to see pride for what it really is and the courage to face the fact that it may have a deeper hold on me than I have realised. Gently expose any deceitful thinking in my soul. Help me my Father. In Jesus' name. Amen.

One great snare left

For reading & meditation – Luke 18:9–14

'For everyone who exalts himself will be humbled, and he
who humbles himself will be exalted.' (v14)

Yesterday we made reference to the quotation '[Pride] can even
make virtue vicious and the other vices more vicious than
they were.' How can this be so? The other vices grow in the soil of
vice: stealing out of covetousness, fornication and adultery out of
unrestrained sexual desire, murder out of hate and the desire for
revenge, lying out of a heart filled with deceit. But pride is more
subtle. It propagates itself in the soil of virtue also.

How easy it is, for example, for good people to convince
themselves that they are the author of their own
goodness. Readers who have been Christians for
some time and have developed a strong devotional
life, have regular prayer times, put aside their tithes
in an orderly way and spend time studying the
Scriptures, can still be trapped by one great snare
– the temptation to believe that they have done it all
by themselves and are better than others.

FURTHER STUDY

Ezek. 16:1-22

1. What did
the woman
(Jerusalem)
trust in?

2. What did
she forget?

The Pharisee stood in the Temple, looked up to
heaven and said: 'God, I thank you that I am not like other men –
robbers, evildoers, adulterers – or even like this tax collector. I fast
twice a week and give a tenth of all I get' (vv11–12). And it was all
true. He was not lying. So why did Jesus tell this story? Because of
his pride. He did not recognise the grace of God in the maturity in
his spiritual life. He thought he had achieved it. The tax collector
was different. He cried out, 'God, have mercy on me, a sinner' (v13),
and went back to his home justified. One individual had God at the
centre of his life; the other had... himself.

**Father, I accept that it is easy to attribute my growth in spiritual
matters to my own efforts. Forgive me if I have done this. I am what
I am by the grace of God. Help me never to forget that.
In Jesus' name I ask it. Amen.**

One hell... one heaven

For reading & meditation – Proverbs 21:20–31

'The proud and arrogant man - "Mocker" is his name; he behaves with overweening pride.' (v24)

Yesterday we looked at the Pharisee who appeared to be within hailing distance of the summit of sanctity but tobogganed to the bottom because of pride. Nothing is more concerning to God than self-righteousness because it treats the blood of Christ with arrogance and presumption, regarding Calvary as unnecessary. Pride can even trap us by causing us to feel superior to those it has ensnared. Like the old lady who, after listening approvingly to the story of the Pharisee and the tax collector, commented to her friends on the way out of church: 'Well, thank God I'm not like them Pharisees!'

FURTHER STUDY

Mark 10:13-16;
John 6:12-15

1. Why was Jesus indignant?

2. How did Jesus respond to public acclaim?

I hope you can now see why I am convinced that pride is the deadliest sin and the most formidable of all the giants on God's 'most wanted' list. But how do we combat pride? Once again, by taking the stone of truth and aiming it at the giant with the assurance that the battle is God's. And the truth that helps overcome pride is the truth about Christ, recorded in the four Gospels. Read through them with this question in mind: How did Jesus walk through this world? See how He embodies that great quality humility, which, of course, is the very opposite of pride.

Pride takes various forms and often is not easily noticed. But in Jesus' light evidences of pride that are hidden in the soul's dark places are revealed. William Law who, as we noted earlier, stated, 'Pride must die in you or Christ will not be able to live in you,' also said: 'Look not on pride only as an unbecoming temper, nor at humility only as a decent virtue... One is all hell and the other all heaven!'

Lord, only when I look into Your Word can I see how deeply pride has poisoned my spirit. Help me spend more time looking at that source of light. In Jesus' name. Amen.

The marks of pride

For reading & meditation – Philippians 2:1–11

'Who, being in very nature God... made himself nothing'
(vv6–7)

We are saying that the best way in which to fell the giant of pride is to consider Jesus and look at ourselves in the light of His life. It is so unhelpful and unproductive to compare ourselves with others; it is good to compare ourselves with Him. What are some of the other evidences of this thing called pride? One is remembering insults long after you have forgotten sorrows. Another is staying upset when someone has treated you with contempt. Yet another is being oversensitive about your background. To these we can add being unduly concerned about such matters as your present status, abilities, power to get your own way and perceived lack of education. There are, of course, many more.

Bring your life now to Jesus and measure yourself against Him. And don't forget, I am using the word 'pride' or 'proud' in its unhealthy sense. Is status all-important to you? Is that what you are proud of? He who was God of very God laid it all aside and confined Himself to humanity. Are you proud of your birth and your family? He grew up in a poor home in Nazareth. Are you proud of your profession? He was a carpenter. Are you proud of the social circle in which you move? He moved mainly among tax collectors and sinners. Are you proud of your abilities? He said: 'By myself I can do nothing' (John 5:30). Are you proud because you can intimidate people and get your own way? He said: 'I seek not to please myself but him who sent me' (John 5:30). Are you proud of your position? He said: 'I am among you as one who serves' (Luke 22:27).

FURTHER STUDY

Mark 10:35–45;
Phil. 3:3–9

1. Contrast the attitudes of Jesus and the disciples.

2. How did Paul view his special background?

Gracious God, the more I compare myself with Your Son, the more clearly I see how deeply pride has become entrenched in my soul. My hope now is in You. I know You will not fail. Amen.

What an amazing sight!

For reading & meditation – John 13:1-17

'I have set you an example that you should do as I have done for you.' (v15)

Look with me, finally, at Jesus on the last night of His incarnate life. As it is time for the Feast of the Passover Jesus has borrowed a room to celebrate the feast, and now all is ready – not just the meal, but the water jugs and basins and towels. During the meal Jesus gets up from the table and proceeds to wash the disciples' feet. This task would normally be considered menial and performed by a servant, but Jesus undertakes the task Himself.

Imagine what this must have looked like to the first-century disciples! What would it have looked like today?! He who is God of very God stoops to wash the disciples' feet. This was His answer to their pride. It was an act done deliberately to emphasise the point that greatness lies not in being served but in serving. In dramatic terms it sets forth the need for selfless service, which would later be exemplified by Jesus' death upon the cross. One Gospel tells of the disciples arguing among themselves during this meal (Luke 22:24-27), and by washing their feet Jesus, in one stroke, sweeps from their minds the idea that the great are those who lord it over others and remain 'uncontaminated' by menial tasks.

FURTHER STUDY

Matt. 3:13-17;
Luke 14:7-11

1. How did Jesus humble himself and what was the result?

2. What prompted Jesus' teaching?

We must learn to understand our pride for what it really is. But as you hurl your stone of truth at this giant and see it fall, remember not to have pride in your efforts. The victory is God's, not yours. We cannot claim to be the architect of any virtue or victory. If we do, the giant may fall but will not be beheaded so will be free to rise again.

Father, let me live so closely to Your Son and know Him so intimately that His humility replaces all my pride. And help me see that every virtue and every victory is down to my weakness being made strong in You. Amen.

The invasion of revenge

For reading & meditation – Leviticus 19:1–19

'Do not seek revenge or bear a grudge against one of your people' (v18)

Another giant we have to confront and bring down if we are to experience the freedom and joy that characterises those who are moving on with God, is the giant of revenge. The passion for revenge is grounded deep in our fallen human nature. Some psychologists describe it as a compound of self-regard and anger. Through the long history of the human race the desire to 'get even' has disrupted families, provoked wars and is one of the major reasons for the institution of systems of public justice.

Everyone who comes into the world receives at some time a 'hard knock'. But hard knocks are of different kinds. Some arise from accidental circumstances, for which no one is to blame. Others arise from situations where, because of a person's foolhardiness rather than intent, we find ourselves on the receiving end of some trauma or tragedy. But there is a great dissimilarity between those knocks where no ill will was intended, and those

FURTHER STUDY

Psa. 38:5–15;
1 Pet. 3:8–9

1. How should we respond to insults?

2. What should characterise our inner self?

caused because someone deliberately set out to hurt. Counsellors know that the most difficult wounds to heal are those inflicted intentionally. The stab that was meant to injure; the hurt that was cruelly and consciously planned. These are the wounds that fester, and in some people generate a passion for vengeance that can remain in their heart until the day they die. I have known people who have gone to their graves well before their time consumed by anger and bitterness. If you are having a battle with the giant of revenge then make up your mind that the struggle must come to an end. The Titan must be slain – and without delay.

Gracious Father, I see that from the beginning You have encouraged Your people to get rid of the desire for revenge. Forgive us that we allow our lives to be controlled by unhelpful passions rather than by healthy ones. Help us be free of all corrupting passion. In Jesus' name. Amen.

A virus in the mind

For reading & meditation – Romans 12:9–21

'Do not take revenge, my friends, but leave room
for God's wrath' (v19)

The passion for revenge is like a virus in the mind. It breeds bitterness, depression and disease. Sometimes (though certainly not always) it is a contributing factor to mental health issues. The longing to 'get even' can do more harm to a person harbouring that desire than the one or ones who caused the desire for revenge in the first place.

Once, in a church I pastored, I watched a man become consumed with bitterness because a careless motorist killed one of his children. Everyone in the church stood with him, shared his sorrow, loved and cared for him and even when he referred to the careless motorist as a 'murderer' no one disagreed. However, when the initial shock had passed he showed such a desire for revenge that people became concerned, and I felt it necessary to speak to him about it. 'My anger and bitterness is justified,' he argued. 'That "murderer" took away one of my beautiful children, and I will never let go of my bitterness until I know he too is lying in his grave.' We talked together how eventually this attitude would ruin not only him but also his relationship with his family. But sadly he continued to burn with rage. I stood by helplessly as his family grew afraid of him and the atmosphere in the home became darker and darker. Eventually he lost not only a child, but his whole family too – alienated, not by the accident, but by his own resentment. To cultivate the virus of resentment is as harmful as cultivating a virus in the body.

FURTHER STUDY

Gen. 27:41–45;
Luke 9:51-55

1. How did
Esau console
his grudge?

2. Contrast
the attitudes
of Jesus and
the disciples.

Father, You are always encouraging us to be rid of our desire for revenge, for You see the harm that resentment wreaks upon the whole person. Help us see it too – and be rid of it. In Jesus' name. Amen.

Sand in the machinery

For reading & meditation – Hebrews 12:14–29

'See to it that... no bitter root grows up to cause trouble and defile many.' (v15)

There can be little doubt that cultivating the desire for revenge fills hearts with bitterness and resentment and injures both body and soul. If the desire for revenge is not dealt with, it will soon turn a vengeful person into a desolate, embittered individual. One doctor says: 'Resentments and the passion for revenge put the whole physical and mental system on a war footing all the time and then the person concerned becomes a drained personality.' He added: 'I once saw a man kill himself inch by inch simply by thinking of nothing but hatred of a relative who had sued him. Within a year or two he was dead.'

Once I observed an experiment in which a strong person was asked to think about someone he liked and have good thoughts about that person, at the same time holding one arm outstretched. As he did, the individual conducting the experiment tried to pull down the outstretched arm, but failed. Then the person was asked to think of someone he disliked and have bad thoughts about them, still holding out his arm. The other individual was then able to pull down the outstretched arm with ease. Why? I was told our whole being – body, soul and spirit – will not function at its best when we harbour bitterness and resentment.

FURTHER STUDY

Lev. 19:15–18; James 3:9–18

1. How can frank rebuke prevent hate in the heart?

2. What is the source and result of bitterness?

We are not created for anger and rage; we are created for love. When we hate we violate the design that God built into us. When we say of another, 'He burns me up,' that's true. Though you want to burn him or her up all you succeed in doing is burning yourself up.

Loving heavenly Father, we see that You have made us for love. Forgive us for having introduced into the delicate fabric of our being the havoc of anger and rage. We are made for You and Your way is love. Help us live that way. In Jesus' name. Amen.

The havoc of hate

For reading & meditation – Ephesians 4:17–32

'Get rid of all bitterness, rage and anger, brawling and slander, along with every form of malice.' (v31)

By now I hope you are convinced that to cultivate a passion for revenge is to nurture ill health. Hate plays strange tricks with the memory. It exaggerates injuries and militates against time's healing touch. To use Shakespeare's phrase, it curdles 'the milk of human kindness' and stunts the development of the soul.

I heard of a farmer whose crops were threatened by a flock of crows. He caught one of them and tied a small stick of dynamite to it, lit the fuse, then turned it loose, expecting it to blow itself up in mid-air and thus frighten the other birds. Instead the crow flew into his barn and the explosion wrecked the barn. Our hates and resentments are always more destructive to us than they are to the objects of our hate.

FURTHER STUDY

Gen. 4:1-12;
1 John 3:11-18

1. How did Cain's wrong feelings produce wrong actions?

2. What happens if we do not love?

How can we be rescued and restored from this consuming passion? Who can help us bring down the giant of revenge? Jesus can! When He was here on earth He said: 'Love your enemies, do good to those who hate you, bless those who curse you, pray for those who mistreat you' (Luke 6:27-28).

He is our living example. There are some who claim that normally people cannot be free of the desire for revenge. They are probably right so far as those who do not know the grace of God are concerned. But they are quite wrong when it comes to those who do. Throughout time Jesus has entered the lives of men and women who have been consumed with hatred and has wiped clean the slate and removed their desire for revenge, replacing it with love. He can do it now for you.

Father, how patient and persistent is Your love. You love me as I am but too much to let me stay as I am. Help me overcome the hurts I harbour for I see that when I cherish them they hurt me even further. In Jesus' name I ask it. Amen.

The spirit of the cross

For reading & meditation – Luke 23:32–43

'Jesus said, "Father, forgive them, for they do not know what they are doing."' (v34)

So how do we overcome the desire to 'get even'? How do we fell the great giant of revenge? Our weapon is the smooth stone of forgiveness. 'Ah, easier said than done,' I hear you say. 'Jesus may have been able to do that but I am not Jesus.' My gentle response is this: if Jesus lives in you then He can also love in you.

The first person ever to die for Jesus (as we saw earlier) was Stephen. He was unjustly murdered. But Jesus lived in him and loved in him. As the stones pounded the life out of his body his last words were a prayer. A prayer, you remember, that was similar to that spoken by Jesus after they hammered him to a cross: 'Lord, do not hold this sin against them' (Acts 7:60).

So let me say again, if Christ lives in you then He can also love in you. The crucial factor is how much you are prepared to relinquish control of your life. Some give the Lord little space in their lives and wonder why they cannot put into operation the more challenging biblical truths, such as forgiveness of others, reconciliation and so on. Here, then, is the simple principle that I have found that explains much of the mystery as to why some Christians are able to achieve much more than others: the more territory Christ occupies in our heart the more effective will be His influence on what we say or do. The spirit of forgiveness expressed in the first words Christ spoke from the cross – 'Father, forgive them' – can be found in your heart if you allow Jesus to have full sway in your life. In His strength you too can forgive injuries, pray for your enemies and love them to the end.

FURTHER STUDY

Matt. 5:38-48;
Gal. 2:19-21

1. How does Christ transform our natural instincts?

2. How did Christ have full sway in Paul's life?

Wise and loving God, is this really possible? Can I respond to those who hurt me in the same way that Jesus did? If Your Son lives in me it must be so. Occupy the whole of my heart, dear Lord, so that there is room for nothing but You. Amen.

The right thing to do

For reading & meditation – Colossians 3:1-17
'Forgive as the Lord forgave you.' (v13)

The only way to slay the giant of revenge, we are saying, is by the smooth stone of forgiveness. But is forgiveness always effective? I have heard it argued (where a criminal act is concerned) that to forgive the perpetrator of a crime is to ignore the consequences of crime and thus encourage criminals to act with impunity. Punishment, they say, is necessary, if society is not to be undermined, and simple forgiveness is counter-productive if it does not deter people from doing wrong.

FURTHER STUDY

Matt. 6:9-15;
Mark 11:20-25

1. How does forgiving others benefit us?

2. How does not forgiving others harm us?

But justice is different to revenge; the two are not synonymous. In the case of revenge a person insists on being the judge in their own quarrel. Where justice is concerned the injured party hands the matter over to society for someone else to be the judge. I have known many people forgive a criminal for the offence he or she committed against them, but society has decreed: 'You may have forgiven them, but in order that justice be done we will now take over and ensure that they face the consequences of their actions.'

We must accept the fact also that sometimes forgiveness seems not to beget a moral response in the one forgiven. But that is no reason not to forgive. Jesus' prayer of forgiveness after the soldiers had hammered Him to the cross – 'Father, forgive them' – does not appear to have broken the stony hearts of these men. Was it then a useless prayer? No, it was the Godlike response to evil. They could hammer the life out of Him but they could not hammer the love out of Him. Forgiveness, whether received or not, is always the right response.

Father, help me not to see forgiveness as a means of changing people but as the right response at all times. In my own strength I cannot forgive. But I am ready to be made willing. Take my willingness and then empower me. In Jesus' name. Amen.

Free!

For reading & meditation – 1 Peter 2:13–25

'When they hurled their insults at him, he did not retaliate'
(v23)

I once heard Dr W.E. Sangster preach a sermon in which he outlined the three basic elements of forgiveness as demonstrated by Christ on the cross. First (he said), Christ forgave them. He cried to God not for vengeance but for forgiveness. He handed the responsibility for justice over to His Father. Second, He prayed for them. There is nothing like prayer to cleanse hate out of the heart. Of course I hasten to add there was no hate in Jesus' heart. But that does not make His example less helpful. Praying for someone who has hurt you will dissolve any seeds of resentment there may be in your heart. Third, He served them. Their unrighteousness and hostility could not deter Him from loving. He was as free to escape from the cross as He was to walk away from the cliff-top at Nazareth when the people wanted to hurl Him off. He accepted death on the cross because He knew there was no other way that sin's power could be broken and reconciliation brought about between God and humankind. He knew this was all part of God's larger story. Those for whom Jesus prayed did not know He was dying for them but that made no difference. He served them.

FURTHER STUDY

Mark 15:22–32;
Matt. 26:47–56

1. How was
Jesus treated?

2. How could He
have responded?

To those who feel they cannot follow these principles my reply is this: it's hard, but not impossible. Put your hand in the stream of God's provisions and you will find the stone you need to defeat the giant of revenge once and for all. It is the stone of forgiveness. Forgiveness is not guaranteed to rid you of your enemies but it will rid you of your enmity. You are free.

Lord Jesus, You who prayed for Your enemies on the cross, help me whenever I am wronged to forgive my enemies too. And also to pray for them. In Your peerless and precious name I ask it. Amen.

The 'poor me' syndrome

For reading & meditation – Luke 22:39–46

'Pray that you will not fall into temptation.' (v40)

We have one final giant to encounter before we bring these meditations to a close – the giant of self-pity. We looked at self-pity in October's issue but let me now expose the strategy of this cunning colossus.

Like all the giants we have looked at previously self-pity relies upon threats and intimidations to make its conquests. It is particularly successful with those who feel life has never given them a chance, those who have been hampered from the start by some difficult circumstances. Self-pity urges: 'Give up. You never had a chance. How can you expect to get on when so much is against you? You poor thing – quit now and take refuge in me.' Self-pity, you see, acts as an anodyne (a painkiller) to the soul. It is sometimes referred to as a victim mentality as it causes people to focus on themselves and their own feelings rather than facing the issues of life with courage.

FURTHER STUDY

1 Kings 19:1–21

1. Why did Elijah feel isolated?

2. How did God reassure Elijah that he was not on his own?

While I was in New Zealand a woman came up to me during a break in the seminar I was conducting and told me that something I had said had made her realise she was wallowing in self-pity. She had sought forgiveness for it and came to tell me of her release. 'What caused the self-pity?' I asked. 'I got caught on the rebound,' she said, 'and then lapsed into self-pity. In that mood I became involved in a series of events that has since blighted my life. Tonight, however, I have found forgiveness and I'm free.' Her life had been marred by sin to which she became susceptible in a mood of self-pity. When our misfortunes dominate our thoughts then temptation has even greater power.

My Father and my God, I wonder how many sins have gained access into my life when I have lapsed into a mood of self-pity. I am dealing here with a force that is bigger than I. But You are my Deliverer. Free me from the power of this giant. For Jesus' sake. Amen.

No bed of roses

For reading & meditation – 1 Peter 5:1–11

'Your enemy the devil prowls around like a roaring lion looking for someone to devour.' (v8)

It would be hard to exaggerate the dangers of self-pity. It robs a person's courage and steals the will to win. It disregards the fact that 'life is more tragic than orderly', as Oswald Chambers put it. Nothing can be more dangerous than thinking that because we are Christians we should spend our days on a bed of roses. We live in a fallen world and should never forget that.

Self-pity is a solvent that dissolves faith and pushes a person deep into doubt, where they find constant reasons for thinking that God does not keep His promises and that He forgets, at times, to be gracious. Self-pity also makes one entirely self-centred (as opposed to other-centred) so that one's own problems become of greater concern than the tragedies affecting the lives of others. But perhaps the worst thing about self-pity is that it exposes a person to temptation and causes them to focus on things other than God. When faith ebbs it is easy to become careless, and I know of many who, having lapsed into self-pity, made shipwreck of their lives.

FURTHER STUDY

Num. 11:4–17;
1 Tim. 1:18–19

1. How did self-pity breed more self-pity?

2. What may happen if we do not fight self-pity?

It is true that many people find themselves in circumstances that easily give rise to complaint. Some bemoan their inherited problems, for some it means it is hard for them to get on in the world. Or perhaps they were orphaned at an early age and brought up in a children's home without much love. Maybe the trouble is quite different. It may be something purely physical – that makes life difficult. But remember, no matter how hard life might seem, self-pity is not the answer. Though it may bring temporary relief it is not a permanent solution.

Father, prevent me from settling for temporary relief when I can find a permanent solution. Help me go to the roots of my problems and find release there. Save me from lapsing into self-pity. In Jesus' name I ask it. Amen.

'Be happy'

For reading & meditation – Isaiah 53:1–12

'Surely he took up our infirmities and carried our sorrows'
(v4)

Ironically, many people relate to the experience of feeling more depressed at certain occasions or times of the year when one is expected to be happy. Birthdays can be difficult, and some people feel worse at Christmastime, for example, than at any other time of the year. Statistics reveal that more people suffer from depression at Christmas, and self-harm rates often rise during that period also.

What is the reason for this? It is because of the added pressure and expectation to be joyful. 'Why have you got such a long face?' people say. 'Be happy.' Such pressure is more than some people can take so they lapse into self-pity and depression. Every faithful minister will know something of the dismal thoughts people carry in their hearts, which seem even darker when set against the bright lights and festivities of celebrations happening in the background. The thought that one was an unwanted child, the recollection that there is some mental instability in the family, the depressing feeling that one's intelligence is below the average, the sense of loneliness or loss and so on.

FURTHER STUDY

Mark 14:32-36;
Heb. 4:14-5:10

1. How did Jesus rise above self-pity?

2. Why can we be confident Jesus will not condemn our self-pity?

If these or similar dark thoughts fill your mind today, let me remind you that God in Jesus took upon Himself the heaped-up sorrows of the whole human race and, however unfriendly the world may seem to you today, I want to reassure you that Jesus knows and cares. Do you need courage to face the next few days? He can give it to you. All He asks is that you acknowledge your need of Him and He will be there to help you and sustain you. Come to Him in prayer now and ask for His help.

My Father and my God, as I face the demands and expectations of life, I come to You to find the grace and power that I need. I know You will not let me down. I draw from Your resources in Jesus' name. Amen.

Some unfamiliar aspects

For reading & meditation – Luke 2:1–20
'Mary... was pledged to be married to him and was expecting a child.' (v5)

The circumstances of Jesus' birth were unusual in many ways. It was obvious to all who knew Mary that she had conceived before she was married, and the tongue of scandal would soon have been busy. It's always striking how there are people who seem to enjoy pointing at and accusing good people who appear to have stumbled.

Does it require a vivid imagination to picture Jesus' life in Nazareth in the years He was growing up? At times he was probably aware of gossip, the pointing and staring of others retelling and refuelling the lie and perception of his parenthood. Consider also Jesus' family tree. He had a tainted lineage. It was certainly nothing to boast about. Included in his family tree are some famous names, but there are some infamous ones as well. David is there, but so is Bathsheba. Ruth is there, but so is Rahab. Does your family tree give you concern? Then no one understands you better than Jesus. Perhaps you feel you have always been at a disadvantage because you lost a parent early in life. There is a tradition in the Church that Joseph died while Jesus was still young. The years in Nazareth would not have been easy for Him. He busied himself at the bench as a carpenter and was 30 before His ministry began.

FURTHER STUDY

Mark 6:1–6;
John 1:1–14

1. How did people respond to Jesus in His home town?

2. How can our darkness cease?

Jesus knows all our difficulties and problems. Draw close to Him now and let Him dissolve all inclination to feel sorry for yourself. In the presence of One who had so much against Him accept His love today.

Jesus, thank You for reminding me of these aspects of Your life here on earth that are often overlooked. You have worn my flesh, measured its frailty and know just how I feel. All honour and glory be unto Your peerless and precious name. Amen.

Truly worth remembering

For reading & meditation – 2 Corinthians 12:1-10

'for Christ's sake, I delight in weaknesses, in insults, in hardships, in persecutions, in difficulties.' (v10)

It occurs to me that you may be saying to yourself at this stage of our meditations: 'Jesus had reserves of strength to draw upon that are not available to me. I cannot be expected to live as He did.' Well, let's consider how one of His most famous followers – the apostle Paul – was able to make it through life without feeling sorry for himself.

More than once in his letters Paul talks about some great difficulty he was facing. Some think the trouble was ophthalmia. Others believe it was recurring malaria. And some consider it was epilepsy. No one knows for sure. What we do know is that he sought God at least three times for it to be taken away. Yet we never read of Paul feeling sorry for himself as a result of his problem. He prayed about it and accepted it knowing that God's 'power is made perfect in weakness' (v9).

FURTHER STUDY

Heb. 2:10-18;
James 5:17-18

1. How are we just like Jesus?

2. How are we just like Elijah?

You might say: 'But Paul was an exceptional man. I am just an ordinary person with no great advantages.' Then listen to the testimony of Dr Robert C. Barnes, professor of counselling at Hardin–Simmons University in the USA. When he was 13 he was struck down with polio – just two years before the polio vaccine became available. Drawing strength and courage from God, he still pursued God and His purposes for his life. I listened to him make what I consider to be one of the most significant statements I have heard with the exception of those recorded in the Bible: 'I knew that no disease, no accident, could take anything away from me that I needed in order to fulfil the purposes the Creator had for my life.' If that's not worth remembering then I don't know what is.

My God and Father, I belong to You in the same way that Paul did – and Robert Barnes does. Let that same courageous and creative spirit that supported them also support me. Instead of sighing, help me to sing! Amen.

Wanted at a wedding

For reading & meditation – John 2:1–11
'Jesus and his disciples had also been invited to the wedding.' (v2)

Comb the Gospel records and not once will you ever find a trace of self-pity in Jesus Christ. He is described as 'a man of sorrows' (Isa. 53:3) but He was never sorry for Himself. Nobody with self-pity in his heart could have inspired strong men to give up all to follow Him. Who would follow a whiner? Nobody wants a whiner at a wedding either. But they wanted Jesus at the wedding in Cana. And later, when He told a would-be disciple that He Himself had no place to lay His head (Matt. 8:20), it was not to evoke his sympathy, but a frank intimation of what the young man would be taking on. I have heard some argue that Jesus revealed self-pity when He cried out on the cross 'I am thirsty' (John 19:28). None but the unbelievably callous would find signs of self-pity in that statement. Surely the dying can ask for a drink without being accused of complaining.

Jesus' freedom from self-pity is all the more wonderful when we delve into the details of His life. We do not know at what point the awareness came to Him that He was the Son of God and had a mission to save the world, but it is clear that once He was aware of it He knew what it would entail: alienation from loved ones, the implacable hate of His enemies, the need to travel throughout the length and breadth of Israel and finally an ignominious death upon a cross. The temptation to indulge in self-pity would have been enormous. But He moved forward resolutely and courageously. His courage came from knowledge of the fact that nothing could happen to Him without God permitting it, and that everything God permitted He would use.

FURTHER STUDY

Matt. 16:21-28;
John 12:23-33

1. Contrast the thinking of Jesus and Peter.

2. How did Jesus respond to His own troubled heart?

Dear God, You permit only that which You can use; help me to fully understand this. Help me not merely to consider this truth but lay hold on it. In Jesus' name. Amen.

A great teacher

For reading & meditation – Philippians 4:10–20

'I can do everything through him who gives me strength.'

(v13)

Do you feel you have a lot to complain about? Maybe you have a physical or psychological issue that you feel holds you back or gives others an advantage in life over you. Perhaps you are not as young as you were and you struggle with health issues or feel inwardly ashamed of your social or family circumstances, your cultural situation and standing or maybe even your education or your youth.

Alfred Adler, the man who coined the term 'inferiority complex',

FURTHER STUDY

2 Sam. 9:1-13;
1 Cor. 1:26-30

1. How did
Mephibosheth
regard himself?

2. What kind of
people does God
choose and use?

said that because of a physical weakness in his life he was plagued by a sense of insignificance and inferiority. But even adverse physical factors can be used by the Holy Spirit to bring glory to God. Think of Helen Keller for example – deprived of hearing and sight she still remained radiant in spirit.

No physical or psychological difficulty can prevent God using us – as long as we give ourselves to Him and His purposes. With God difficulties can be made to yield a spiritual profit. Adversity is one of our greatest teachers. And God uses it to polish His jewels. If Psalm 139 is true, and I believe it is, God is never far from you and is with you in any constriction/restriction that you feel may be in your life at the moment. Others may not see all that God has placed in your life right now – but God does. As you bring your hopes and desires to Him, together you will be able to achieve the most amazing things for the kingdom of God. God has confidence in you and has committed Himself to you, so today you can have confidence in Him.

Gracious God, keep watch over my spirit and keep me sound there. Save me from all self-pity, and let me be outgoing and positive, taking on myself the problems of others. In Jesus' name. Amen.

All is not lost

For reading & meditation – 2 Corinthians 9:6–15
'And God is able to make all grace abound to you' (v8)

Are you ready now to slay the giant of self-pity that may be towering over you? You have already been given the stone that you need to put in your sling. Feel its smoothness once again: no disease, no sickness, no infirmity can take from you whatever you need to fulfil the purposes of God for your life. So when this cunning giant stands over you and demoralises you with words such as, 'You never had a chance... give up... console yourself with self-pity,' put your trust in God and hurl this stone at it with all the force you can muster.

The ablest man I have ever known was struck down with a disease that could have put him out of action for the rest of his life. But he didn't moan or complain about this major setback. He slew the giant of self-pity and went on to make a contribution to life that was quite astonishing. Don't be so unwise as to envy those who seemingly have every advantage in life; the absence of advantage is sometimes the greatest advantage of all. Many will never get anywhere because they have not been provoked by awkward circumstances. Dr G. Campbell Morgan said of a certain young preacher: 'He is a good preacher, but when he has struggled a bit and overcome, he will be a great preacher.'

Let everything spur you on towards God and His grace. Go forward in hope. God is above you, Jesus and the Holy Spirit are within you, the angels of God are around you – what more could you need? Life may not have given you much of a chance, but in God you have every chance.

FURTHER STUDY

2 Tim. 2:1-7;
1 Pet. 4:7-11

1. How can we be strong Christians?

2. What should we do with the grace we receive?

Lord Jesus Christ, You who overcome every difficulty in life, live Your life so fully and powerfully in me that I too will be able to overcome every difficulty in my life. For Your own dear name's sake I ask it. Amen.

The sword of Goliath

For reading & meditation – 1 Samuel 21:1–9

'David said, "There is none like it; give it to me."' (v9)

In the passage before us today we come across an intriguing though somewhat sad incident in David's life. Having incurred the wrath of King Saul, and parted from his friend Jonathan, he makes his way to Nob. There he deceives Ahimelech the priest by telling him he is on a mission for the king that demanded the utmost secrecy. Why David should lie we cannot say, but clearly he is a long way from being the David of the psalms now!

When David asks for food the priest tells him that only the bread

FURTHER STUDY

1 Sam. 17:45-51;
Luke 4:1-14

1. How did David use Goliath's own sword against him?

2. Contrast how Jesus went in and came out of the wilderness.

that has been consecrated to God is available and, according to the law of Moses, could be eaten only by those who were ritually clean. However, men who were engaged in active military service and were not in contact with their wives were regarded as 'clean'. So Ahimelech, believing this to be true of David, offers him the consecrated bread. Having been given the bread David then asks Ahimelech if there is a sword he can have and is told that lying behind the ephod is the sword of Goliath. 'There is none like it,' says David, 'give it to me'. The sword that was once used against him in an attempt to secure his destruction is now about to be used by him in his own defence.

This incident suggests a thought, namely that the very weapons that the enemy intends to bring about our defeat can, through divine ingenuity, be put to our use. That same truth can be put this way: in every obstacle there is an opportunity, in every difficulty a door, and in every stumbling block a stepping stone. In God's service everything can be used – everything.

My Father and my God, many years ago through the prophet Isaiah You said: 'no weapon forged against you will prevail' (Isa. 54:17). But now I see there is more – the weapons forged against me can be used by me. Thank You. Amen.

Never too late

For reading & meditation – Joshua 14:6–15
'the Anakites were there… but, the LORD helping me,
I will drive them out' (v12)

My final word to you is this: you are never too young or too old to slay a giant. Some of you may be thinking: 'Well I'm a bit set in my ways now that I've past 30 (or 40 or 50) so I'll just have to stay the way I am.' Not true. Look at Caleb. He was 85 and eager to drive out the giants that were in the hill country of Hebron. (The Anakites, as we see from Deuteronomy 9:1–2, were a giant-like people.) At a time when it would have been easy for Caleb to have pulled out and settled back in his chair, he fearlessly set out to finally banish them from the Promised Land. A quiet retirement was not for Caleb.

An American sociologist said recently that by their mid-thirties most people have ceased to acquire new skills and attitudes. Stop and think, those of you who are over 30. Are you in danger of settling down spiritually and mentally? Are you losing your passion for life naturally and spiritually? Don't settle for the status quo. If there are giants threatening you that need to be brought down, go do it!

FURTHER STUDY

Num. 13:26-33,
14:20-24;
Luke 2:36-38

1. What was different about Caleb?

2. Who did God choose to speak about Jesus to?

Let me remind you of the principles once again. First, don't run. Stand your ground. The Lord of hosts is with you. Second, don't dress up in Saul's armour. Natural defences and resources are not much help in times of spiritual battle. Third, dip your hand in the cool, clear stream of God's Word and pick up one of the smooth stones of truth. Fourth, put it in your sling to signify your willingness to do battle. Then fifth, with a strong confidence in God take aim and shoot at your giants! Remember that the battle is the Lord's – He will help you bring down any giants for good.

> **Gracious and loving God, help me not to limit You by protesting:**
> **'I'm too set in my ways to change now.' I commit myself afresh to**
> **being all You want me to be. I hear Your call to battle.**
> **Here I am Lord. Send me. Amen.**

More one year devotionals by Selwyn Hughes

Each compact devotional contains a whole year's worth of daily readings, covering six specially selected themes from *Every Day with Jesus*.

Walking in His Ways
Includes these issues:
Changing Times – Unchanging Truths, God's Last Word, The Surprises of God, Bringing the Bible to Life, The Peak of the Epistles and The Grand Design.

ISBN: 978-1-85345-314-4

Price **£7.99**

A Fresh Vision of God
Includes these issues:
The Vision of God, From Confusion to Confidence, The Beatitudes, The Power of a New Perspective, The Corn of Wheat Afraid to Die and Heaven-Sent Revival.

ISBN: 978-1-85345-121-8

Price **£7.99**

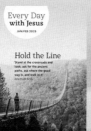